METADATA

Marcia Lei Zeng and Jian Qin

Neal-Schuman Publishers, Inc.
New York London

Don't miss the companion Web site that accompanies this book available at:

www.neal-schuman.com/metadata/

Published by Neal-Schuman Publishers, Inc.
100 William St., Suite 2004
New York, NY 10038

Printed and bound in the United States of America.

The paper used in this publication meets the minimum requirements of American National Standard for Information Sciences-Permanence of Paper for Printed Library Materials, ANSI Z39.48-1992.

Library of Congress Cataloging-in-Publication Data

Zeng, Marcia Lei, 1956–
Metadata / Marcia Lei Zeng and Jian Qin.
p. cm.
Includes bibliographical references and index.
ISBN 978-1-55570-635-7 (alk. paper)
1. Metadata. I. Qin, Jian, 1956– II. Title.

Z666.7Z46 2008
025.3—dc22

2008015176

Contents

Part II. Metadata Building Blocks

Part III. Metadata Services

List of Illustrations

Figures

Exhibits

Tables

Preface

Although rooted in library and information science (the first metadata scheme targeted for Internet resources—the Dublin Core Metadata Element Set—was proposed in 1995), metadata has expanded its territory beyond traditional libraries and is now a widely adopted vital solution for describing the explosively growing, complex world of digital information.

As many organizations turn to metadata applications for managing massive quantities of digital information, demand increases for information professionals who are prepared for the immediate tasks at hand. During the past decade, this book's authors have engaged in teaching metadata and information organization courses as well as conducting research in this area. The authors have also had opportunities to provide training for professionals and to act as consultants for digital library projects. The experience we accumulated through teaching, research, and consulting motivated us to write a textbook that systematically introduces metadata concepts and principles through the incorporation of practical examples and learning assessment materials.

Metadata is both a textbook and an instructional guide for practitioners. As a textbook, its primary purpose is to provide educators with a convenient and reliable source for teaching metadata-related courses in universities or in continuing education programs for information professionals. Among the unique features of this book are instructional materials such as sample problems and solutions and hands-on tutorials. These instructional features also make *Metadata* an ideal resource for practitioners who wish to use the book for self-study or on-the-job training.

While focusing on metadata concepts, principles, and applications, the book also covers trends, innovative ideas, and advanced technologies in metadata research and practice that will have significant implications in the years to come. The wide application of metadata in different domains has created different communities of practice, each of which defines a metadata structure based on its own norms and needs. We will therefore cover the conceptual and practical knowledge that is fundamental to all application domains. This is not an overview of all existing metadata standards, nor is it an interpretation of individual metadata schemas. Although many of those will be mentioned or discussed and their features will be referenced as examples, the text is not a step-by-step manual for creating metadata records. Rather, it identifies commonalities among metadata schemas and focuses on the design and profiling processes as they relate to the needs of application domains and environments. The inclusion or exclusion of a schema in this book should not be interpreted as a sign of favoritism or preference for one schema over another.

Focus and Organization

The topics covered in this book are selected and organized based on an outcome-oriented learning philosophy which holds that regardless of learners' locations or backgrounds, we can expect them to be able to learn the how-tos of metadata application design, implementation, and evaluation, in addition to understanding the underpinning theory. This approach allows learners of all kinds and skill levels to adapt the knowledge and practices they obtain from this book to the domains in which they work. Therefore, we concentrate on the tasks typical to successful implementation of metadata application projects. Such tasks include applying an existing standard to a project, establishing localized element sets or application profiles by drawing elements from multiple metadata schemes, and performing advanced tasks related to services, integration, and assessment.

Metadata is divided into four parts: "Fundamentals of Metadata," "Metadata Building Blocks," "Metadata Services," and "Metadata Outlook in Research."

The first part includes Chapters 1 and 2. Starting with metadata application scenarios, Chapter 1 introduces the definitions, types and functions, principles, and anatomy of metadata. It provides a bridge for readers from abstract scenarios to real-world applications of metadata functions and structures in digital environments. Chapter 2 introduces metadata standards within major application domains. We emphasize semantics of the element sets, the needs of domain-specific information objects, and the functions these standards aim to fulfill. Standards covered in Chapter 2 include those for general purposes, cultural objects and visual resources, learning objects, archives and preservation, rights management, scientific data, media, and agents.

The second part of the book moves from general fundamentals to metadata building blocks. Chapter 3 is devoted to the development of the structure and semantics of a metadata schema. It discusses perspectives and techniques for assessing needs in different project environments: identifying desired elements and refinements for an element set, controlling the values in value spaces, creating application profiles, and establishing crosswalks between or among element sets. The last section explains what should be included in best practice guidelines and how guidelines should be presented.

While Chapter 3 discusses how semantics in metadata elements and their structures are defined, Chapter 4 details how the schema will be encoded and how the semantics are controlled by using namespaces. XML Schemas from a flat structure element set, a hierarchical structure set, and an application profile provide useful examples. The goal and outcome is to provide a basic understanding of the issues that may arise in applications regarding schema encoding.

Chapter 5 is a major component of the text, dedicated to the issues and techniques related to creating metadata records. It can be considered as consisting of two major topics: the issues related to metadata records and the issues regarding encoding. Conceptual models are first presented to provide a better understanding about metadata statements that form the descriptions of the resources. The discussion then turns to the granularity of records, i.e., levels of description at which a metadata record may be created. We emphasize creating sharable records because interoperability is an important concept in metadata applications. Discussion of metadata resources and tools presents the options that records may be created by human catalogers fully or partially, generated by computer programs, or converted and harvested from other sources. Chapter 5 gives these issues a closer examination. Encoding metadata is a long and comprehensive section, in which metadata storage methods are introduced first, followed by details and examples of expressing metadata records in HTML/XHTML, XML, and RDF. The last section covers other methods related to metadata records, such as linkage, wrapper, display, and parallel metadata.

The third part of the book brings together metadata services that have appeared in recent years. Chapter 6 introduces the types of infrastructures for these services. Standards in XML, RDF, data communication, policies, and procedures promise an exciting yet challenging future for metadata services. Detailed explanations are applied to metadata registries and repositories (including the metadata harvesting protocol). For each of these services, we look at the functionalities of the service, basic components, and types of models so that learners gain a basic understanding of these advanced topics. Chapter 6 summarizes the emerging approaches to ensure optimal metadata discovery through discussions involving metadata retrieval technologies and methods of exposing metadata and maximizing its usage. Chapter 7 offers a systematic view of the issues and methodologies of measuring metadata quality. Evaluation criteria, measurement processes, and methods of evaluation are discussed in detail. Chapter 8 summarizes the methods of ensuring and achieving interoperability based on research of this all-important issue. Interoperability approaches are analyzed at the schema, record, and service levels. Examples are selected from projects throughout the world.

The final section draws attention to the research landscape. Chapter 9 reviews major research areas in metadata architecture, modeling, and metadata semantics that are not discussed in detail in the rest of the text.

As professional educators, we understand the importance of exercises and practical examples in a textbook. Each chapter in this book provides a recommended reading list, some with a series of practice and assessment instruments. In addition to general exercises at the end of major chapters, the digital library prepared for instructors contains detailed exercises and hints for some assignments. All exercises have been created as an interactive component, available either on an instructor's CD-ROM from the publisher or via this book's accompanying Web site. We hope that our experience in metadata research, teaching, and consulting will offer our readers a unique, enlightening, and holistic approach to the topic.

Part I
Fundamentals of Metadata

1

Introduction

Digital information exists in every area of modern life: in the office, at home, and on the road. Every organization and individual faces the challenge of organizing digital information of all types and formats, while also being able to find the correct or desired information in a timely manner (and with acceptable precision of sufficient depth). For a long time, libraries and information database producers were the primary agents organizing and providing both information and efficient search tools. The techniques and technologies they used are often proprietary and idiosyncratic. Along with the rise of the Internet, Web-based technologies enabled the creation of mass information and publication through a low-barrier platform—anyone who can use a text or image editor can now create digital documents or objects and publish them directly on the Web. Such technology greatly democratized the publication and dissemination of information and resulted in an exponentially faster increase in the volume and complexities of digital resources. Individuals, organizations, communities, and governments now face the tasks of organizing the massive amounts of digital information in their systems before they can effectively discover, locate, and use it when needed.

At present, the Internet and the World Wide Web (WWW) have become the new library catalogs, indexing databases, dictionaries, encyclopedias, newspapers, schools, entertainment centers, and many other sources and places that we used to *physically* access. How do we find the sources we need and the places we want to go on the Web or within an internal Web site? We use search engines, of course. However, how do they take us where we need to go in the world of digital resources? What makes search engines work? Moreover, what makes them work effectively? The "invisible hand" of efficient organization is embodied in *metadata*. When one types a keyword into a major search engine or, better yet, into a digital library's search field, the chances are good that the keyword is one of thousands in an index. The index may be compiled from a metadata repository or extracted from full-text documents. The document information displayed in the search results pages is a typical instantiation of metadata: it describes what a document is, what it is about, and where one may locate it. Let us examine the following two examples of metadata application.

A Maths Dictionary for Kids (www.amathsdictionaryforkids.com/maths/dictionary.html, accessed 2007) is an interactive tool designed for K–6 grade-schoolers to learn mathematical concepts by allowing children to follow the instructions and practice math problem solving. Teachers preparing lessons may incorporate the interactive exercise for math games into instructional materials; they can then search learning objects by topic, e.g., "math," or by form, e.g., "interactive games," and combine different criteria to filter out irrelevant information. In this case, *grade level, subject, form,* and other metadata fields enhance the precision of a query in a system already designed to produce more relevant results.

Today, a search in a digital library produces hundreds of displayed results. The user then must wade through a morass in order to select relevant information and may eventually give up in frustration. Here, the "tolerance for ambiguity" (the patience, perseverance, and equanimity necessary when an answer, a resource, or the results of one's work are not immediately forthcoming)—which is the hallmark of the researcher—is not commonly found with everyday users. The use of metadata, however, allows the system to perform post-search processing and present the results in categorized groups. As Figure 1-0-1 shows, the search system in the Gateway to Educational Materials (GEM: www.thegateway.org) provides a categorized list of clustered results (at the lower right-hand corner) by using the subject terms assigned to metadata records. Among the 85 items matching the search query *math lesson plan,* four are in *arts,* two are in *educational technology,* 24 are in *mathematics,* and so forth.

The previous examples demonstrate that metadata is capable of performing the following tasks:

- Describing what resources are and what they are about, and organizing those resources according to controllable criteria.
- Allowing resources to be found by relevant criteria, aggregating similar resources, and providing pathways to the location of the desired information.
- Facilitating metadata exchange and enabling interoperability.
- Providing digital identification and description for archiving and the preservation of resources (NISO, 2004).

1.1 A Brief History

The organization of objects and phenomena into either classes or sets of relationships is one way in which humans communicate. Before the Internet, organizing information in libraries, archives, museums, and other types of institutions was governed by highly structured rules and standards such as the *Anglo-American Cataloguing Rules Revised,* Second Edition (AACR2) and MARC (*MAchine-Readable Cataloging*). The content representation was guided by semantically rich classification schemes and lists of subject headings, e.g., the *Dewey Decimal Classification* (DDC) and the *Library of Congress Subject Headings* (LCSH). The information objects being organized were primarily physical, i.e., information was packaged in some sort of container or packaged as books,

Figure 1-0-1. Categorized search result display in GEM.

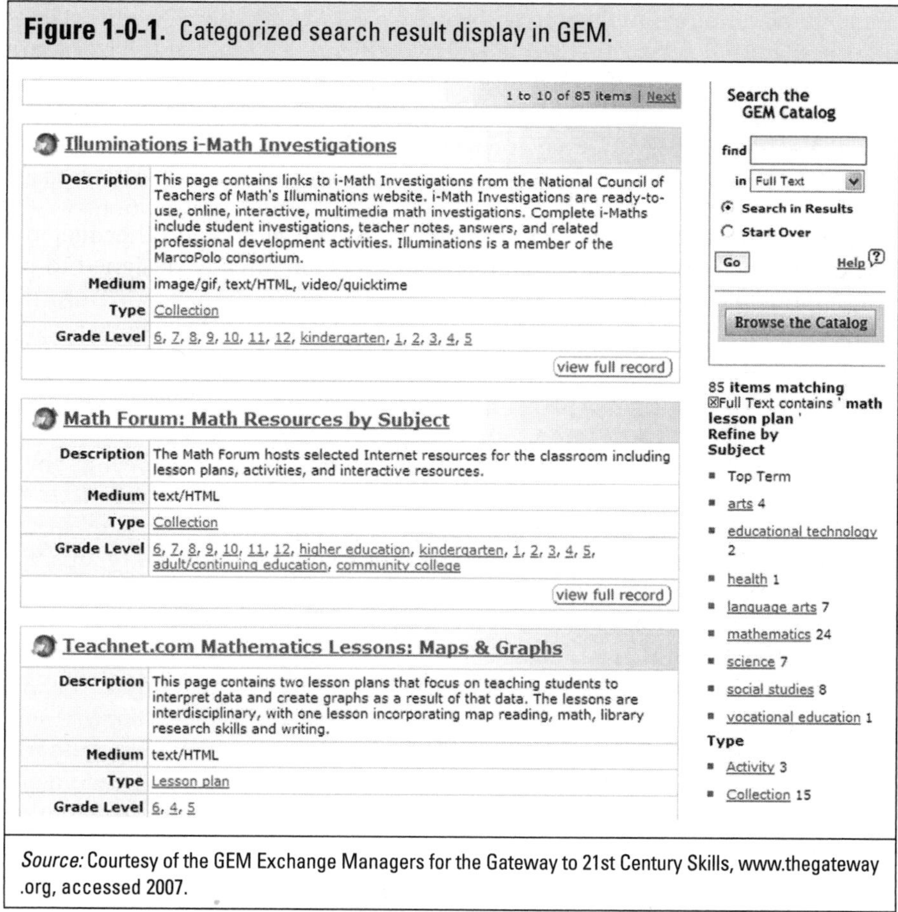

Source: Courtesy of the GEM Exchange Managers for the Gateway to 21st Century Skills, www.thegateway.org, accessed 2007.

journals, CD-ROMs, audio/video cassettes, film reels, and more. A large amount of human catalog work and intervention was involved in the process, not only because of the physical nature of information objects but also because complex rules and standards governed the relationships among these objects. All of these factors made it very difficult, if not impossible, for computer programs to take over metadata creation tasks from human catalogers. However, the level of sophistication and maturity of information technology also played an important role in pre-WWW cataloging as evidenced by the production of MARC-compliant AACR catalog cards then mass-produced in Dublin, Ohio, by the Online Library Computer Center (OCLC). OCLC remains the central authority for all descriptive and technical cataloging that provides bibliographic and other formatted packages that Online Public Access Catalogs (OPACs) allow users to access in all libraries.

Pre-Internet cataloging (e.g., typewritten cards) played a significant role in assisting users to find what they needed *and* to know whether an item was located in the stacks, and whether collocated items of the same subject area made the adventure into the musty rows of books worthwhile. The purposes of pre-Internet cataloging were twofold: (1) to provide rich bibliographic descriptions and relationships between and among data of heterogeneous items and (2) to facilitate sharing these bibliographic data across library boundaries. While AACR2 and MARC have done a meritorious job in accomplishing those purposes, they have fallen short on several important fronts in Internet-based resource descriptions, e.g., management of digital rights, preservation of digital objects, and evaluation of resources based on authenticity, user profile, and grade level.

Metadata development in the Internet era took off in the first half of the 1990s when the Internet was becoming a "household" word for libraries and institutions that manage and use large amounts of digital information on a daily basis. During that period, distributed information repositories over the Internet grew at an exponential rate. The chaotic Internet-based information called for mechanisms of description, authentication, and management, which prompted the development of new guidelines and architectures by different communities. Several parallel development areas in metadata existed in the early 1990s. The scientific community started looking for solutions to organize the rapidly increasing scientific data, which prompted the debut of the *Content Standards for Digital Geospatial Metadata* (CSDGM) in 1992 by the Federal Geographic Data Committee (FGDC). In the humanities community, the Text Encoding Initiative (TEI), an international organization founded in 1987, released the first version of *Guidelines for Electronic Text Encoding and Interchange* (TEI Guidelines) in 1994. As an international and interdisciplinary standard, TEI Guidelines "focus (though not exclusively) on the encoding of documents in the humanities and social sciences, and in particular on the representation of primary source materials for research and analysis" (TEI: www.tei-c.org/Guidelines/index.xml, accessed 2007).

The library community also took action to develop metadata standards as a solution to resource description and discovery problems. OCLC initiated a project in 1994 to experiment with cataloging Web resources by using the AACR2 and MARC format. Over 200 volunteer librarians created more than 2,500 records for Internet resources (1995), which became the precursor of the invitational Metadata Workshop held in 1995 at OCLC in Dublin, Ohio. The *Dublin Core* was born and emerged from this historically significant workshop. Following the first Dublin Core workshop, a metadata movement soon spread rapidly to other continents and across research, educational, and governmental institutions, as well as businesses, and many organizations. The following represent some of the many metadata standards developed since the 1990s:

- Categories for the Description of Works of Art (CDWA)
- Visual Resources Association (VRA) Core Categories
- Learning Object Metadata (LOM), Institute of Electrical and Electronics Engineers (IEEE)
- Encoded Archival Description (EAD)
- Metadata Object Description Schema (MODS)

- PREMIS: PREservation Metadata Implementation Strategies
- ONline Information Exchange (ONIX)
- Digital Object Identifier (DOI)
- The Friend of a Friend (FOAF)
- MPEG-7 (the standard for description and search of audio and visual content)
- Public Broadcasting Metadata Dictionary (PBCore)

Metadata projects increased greatly during the late 1990s. The DCMI (Dublin Core Metadata Initiative) home page formerly maintained a list of metadata projects and the number quickly increased into the hundreds, gathered from all across the world. Publications about metadata dominated Internet forums, professional journals, and conferences. The main reason for this proliferation is because no limit exists for the type or amount of resources that metadata can describe, nor are there any limits to the number of overlapping standards for any type of resource or subject domain. The past decade witnessed a continual expansion and evolution of metadata research and practices at almost all levels and areas where human activities and digital information converge.

1.2 Definitions

The term *metadata* was used before the advent of the Internet, primarily in computer science to specify information about database objects and/or program objects. Broadly speaking, metadata encapsulates the information that describes any document or object in both digital and traditional formats. Metadata is often simply defined as "data about data" or "information about information." As research and applications have evolved, metadata has been refined to "structured information that describes, explains, locates, or otherwise makes it easier to retrieve, use, or manage an information resource" (NISO, 2004: 1). The DCMI defines metadata as "data associated with either an information system or an information object for purposes of description, administration, legal requirements, technical functionality, use and usage, and preservation" (DCMI Glossary, 2005). *Metadata*, like *data*, is expressed as singular or plural. It is usually singular in the sense of a kind of data, but when referring to values in metadata statements, the term designates things one can count (Turner, 2003; NJ-BGIS, 2007). It is also referred to in the literature as "meta data" and "meta-data." In this text we use more precise phrases for the many related concepts that are sometimes mistakenly used, typically a *metadata statement* (e.g., <title = "ABC">) or a *metadata record* (i.e., a particular instance that a set of metadata elements is applied to for describing an object) is abbreviated as "metadata." Several of these concepts are discussed in Chapter 5, together with the abstract models that have been developed by the metadata community.

A great number of metadata standards have been developed or proposed by different communities and subject domains. A key component in these standards is the *element set* (more appropriately, the *scheme*) that defines the structure and semantics of elements. For example, the international standard *Dublin*

Core Metadata Element Set (DCMES) defines 15 core elements that should be used to describe distributed information resources on the Internet for discovery purposes. The metadata community has used a number of terms in different contexts to refer to metadata *element sets*, in addition to the ways that they are represented in machine-processable formats. The terms "metadata schemes," "metadata standards," "element sets," and "metadata schemas" have subtle differences but are used interchangeably in the literature. These phrases are explained and differentiated in the text where necessary.

Components of metadata have also been addressed differently by various communities. For example, a database designer may call metadata elements "data fields" instead of "elements," while a metadata developer may see metadata as an abstract model that can be implemented through a schema and a set of guidelines. In this case, the abstract model would explain the concepts and relationships between classes of concepts and properties in the domain for which the schema is to be designed, whereas the schema itself would define a set of elements, attributes, and rules for value spaces.

1.3 Types and Functions

Metadata applications use metadata records to describe a resource by recording *title, creator, keywords,* and other information, which is analogous to the technical cataloging of a library. However, several important characteristics make it distinctive from the traditional catalog. First, the administrative function of metadata is facilitated by knowing when and how a record was created (by whom and from where), what technical details it contains, and who has access privileges. Rights management and preservation are the most important types of *administrative metadata*. Digital resources can often be easily accessed, copied, modified, or deleted, which in turn can trigger violations of copyright, access permissions, and licensing rules. In addition, serious difficulties may develop in preserving digital resources for use by future generations of software. Administrative metadata will record information on rights and the technical characteristics of a resource, which will be used for organized administrative tasks and management. In addition to describing the resource's characteristics, the metadata may also be used to describe how this resource should be or has been used, e.g., what platform and software is required to run a digital object, and what are the targeted ages or grade levels of a learning object.

Metadata is different from library cataloging because resources that it works with extend beyond traditional format. Contemporary metadata, increasingly concerned with digital resources, brings two major benefits: (1) users can navigate directly from a metadata record (i.e., a surrogate of a resource) to the resource on the Internet or point to where its physical location might be; and (2) "automatic processability," which allows a metadata creation agency to process certain types of resources directly through computer programs so that the metadata records (or a portion of those records) may be generated by automatic (computer program) processes. Automatic metadata generation indicates a minimal amount of (or none) human intervention, and so is cost-efficient for metadata records creation. Library materials, on the other hand, are dependent upon human catalogers to record the data manually into a rigid format, typically the MARC format.

Defining types of metadata is both contextual and dependent upon application domains. The Getty Information Institute (1983–1999), now the Getty Research Institute, of the J. Paul Getty Trust published a well-known book *Introduction to Metadata: Pathways to Digital Information* in 1998 (Gill et al., 1998) and made its online versions (Baca, 2000–2008). It identifies five types of metadata and their functions: *administrative, descriptive, preservation, technical,* and *use* metadata (Gilliland, 2000). In a booklet published by the National Information Standards Organization (NISO), metadata types are given three summative groupings that have been widely accepted by the metadata community:

- Descriptive metadata describes a resource for purposes such as discovery and identification;
- Structural metadata indicates how compound objects are put together;
- Administrative metadata provides information to help manage a resource, and includes technical, rights management, and preservation metadata. (NISO, 2004: 1)

Organizing digital resources and providing services for retrieving and using them is a complex process that requires various metadata used for different purposes and functions. The most essential display and describe the digital resource. The metadata community typically calls this the *description* of resources. The validity of classic data elements used in cataloging and indexing will be found here: *title, author, abstract, keywords, publisher,* and *date.*

If a digital resource consists of multiple objects or parts, the data elements should be able to capture such information, especially when the sequence and levels of the objects are the most important. A typical example is the digitization of manuscripts, in which each page is often scanned as an image. The *structural* metadata is critical for keeping the content as represented in scanned images in the correct sequence. *Technical* metadata describes when and how the digitized manuscript was created, as well as its file type and other related information. *Rights management* metadata is concerned with intellectual property rights of the manuscript both in its original form and in the digitized form, and *preservation* metadata contains information needed to archive and preserve the manuscript images. All of these types of metadata will offer functions necessary for resource discovery, organizing electronic resources, facilitating interoperability, digital identification, and archiving and preservation (NISO, 2004).

1.4 Principles

The Dublin Core Metadata Initiative was motivated by the guiding principle of producing a metadata element set simple enough for creating and maintaining metadata records, and thus the elements would also conform to existing and emerging standards at the international scope, and also be interoperable among collections and indexing systems (Weibel and Hakala, 1998). These requirements translate into three primary principles for the construction of ideal metadata: *simplicity*, *extensibility*, and *interoperability*. By simply taking only those data elements necessary and so maintaining a minimum set of elements for easy deployment, it must be equally important for the metadata to be flexible enough to accommodate specialized needs. This suggests that metadata schemas should allow applications to introduce new elements and constraints for localized description needs. Extensibility is generally understood in two ways: (1) the ability of a metadata schema to offer a core set of elements that will unify different models of resource description; and (2) the ability to link a simple metadata record to a richer, more complex description of resources (Dempsey and Weibel, 1996). Extensibility requires metadata systems to allow for the addition of new elements and/or subelements to existing ones in a schema, while the new elements are selected from existing metadata standards or can be established at the local level. Interoperability is defined as "the ability of multiple systems with different hardware and software platforms, data structures, and interfaces to exchange data with minimal loss of content and functionality" (NISO, 2004: 2).

As metadata development evolved, the early requirements for metadata were eventually extended and elucidated to be a more inclusive and refined set of principles. Duval et al. (2002) pointed out, "*Principles* are those concepts judged to be common to all domains of metadata and which might inform the design of any metadata schema or application. *Practicalities* are the rules of thumb, constraints, and infrastructure issues that emerge from bringing theory into practice in the form of useful and sustainable systems" (Duval et al., 2002: www.dlib.org/dlib/april02/weibel/04weibel.html, accessed 2007). In their paper, metadata principles were extended to also include modularity, refinement, and multilingualism. *Modularity* refers to building metadata into *blocks*, so that data elements, vocabularies, and other building blocks in different metadata schemas may be assembled into new schemas in a syntactically and semantically interoperable way. Different metadata modules, e.g., for discovery, rights management, preservation, or instructional management, expressed in a common syntactic idiom such as Extensible Markup Language (XML), should be able to be combined in compound schemas as needed, which would embody the functionality of each constituent. *Refinement* aims at precise detail that determines how much description a schema should require. *Multilingualism* focuses on aspects of language and culture, and when adopting metadata architecture, the designer needs to take into account linguistic and cultural diversity (Duval et al., 2002). These principles address the issues one may encounter in one form or another in both metadata schema design and record generation processes. As principles, they represent a set of basics that all metadata designers should consider when creating each project. These principles also have a direct effect on how to implement metadata projects and simultaneously make them sustainable for long-term utilization, preservation, and interoperable for sharing and reuse.

1.5 Anatomy of a Metadata Standard

Metadata standards provide guidelines regarding structure, values, and content. These are also the basis for developing software programs and tools that can lead to good descriptive cataloging, consistent documentation, shared records, and increased end-user access (Baca et al., 2006). Section 1.1 provided a list of well-known metadata standards. What are these components and what roles do they play in formulating a schema and structuring a metadata record? Let us take a closer look at the inside of a metadata standard.

The backbone of a metadata standard consists of a set of elements. Each element is given an explanatory name, label, and definition. Sometimes a note (annotation) is provided to document the change history of the element and the mapping between this and similar elements in other standards. The Dublin Core Metadata Element Set provides *name*, *URI* (Uniform Resource Indicator), *label*, *definition*, *comment*, and *references*, for example, for the element *date* (see Figure 1-5-1).

Elements in a metadata standard may be structured in different ways and presented in an *element set* scheme. For example, a standard may simply put all elements into a linear list, i.e., a flat structure, while others may use a hierarchical structure to indicate a parent-child relationship between elements. Labeling elements often follows some naming conventions, i.e., whether elements need to be capitalized, how compound-word elements should be used, and when abbreviations are appropriate.

The next component of a standard is a set of constraints and guidelines for how data values should be recorded when generating metadata records. The standard specifications usually provide, in addition to element definitions, format rules for the types of values (e.g., number, text, date, and so on) that should be consistently applied to all elements. Taking the *date* element defined in DCMES (see Figure 1-5-1) requires an indication of how a date, e.g., date="050603", should be formulated as "yymmdd" or "mmddyy." In a

Figure 1-5-1. An entry for DC element *date*.

Term Name: date	
URI:	http://purl.org/dc/elements/1.1/date
Label:	Date
Definition:	A point or period of time associated with an event in the lifecycle of the resource.
Comment:	Date may be used to express temporal information at any level of granularity. Recommended best practice is to use an encoding scheme, such as the W3CDTF profile of ISO 8601 [W3CDTF].
References:	[W3CDTF] http://www.w3.org/TR/NOTE-datetime

Source: DC 1.1: http://dublincore.org/documents/dces/, accessed 2007.

metadata instance embedded in a Web page, the <meta name="DC.date" scheme="iso8601" content="2006-05-03" /> tag indicates that the value of *date* element follows ISO 8601 (Data elements and interchange formats—Information interchange—Representation of dates and times) and should be read as 2006 May 3 rather than 2006 March 5. Another example is the *subject* element, which in many standards requires a controlled vocabulary or classification scheme to constrain the number and source of values. If the record has assigned terms from the LCSH, the subject element may use the scheme attribute to tell users that the subject headings come from LCSH. These rules and vocabularies are designated *value encoding schemes.*

The guidance provided in metadata standards assists with the correct implementation of principles, and offers best practices guidelines for localizing the usage in both the implementation and creation of metadata records. This assists metadata creators in making the right choices about which data values as well as what order, syntax, and form that the data values should be entered into any record. It also reflects the best practices that have been culled from particular user communities. Best practices may vary greatly in scope and level of detail. Some standards provide guidance in a user manual or recommendations, while others offer well-established subject vocabularies, name authorities, or term lists developed by an authoritative source. A higher level of guidance would be to provide rules, recommendations, and examples for selecting, ordering, and formatting data used to key selected elements. Data contents guidelines may be found in the documentation of element sets in most metadata specifications, and sometimes monographic publications, e.g., *Cataloging Cultural Objects* (CCO).

Defined element sets are often represented in XML and the resultant structures are known as *metadata schemas.* These representations define what an element means and how it will be encoded in a machine-processable format.

Figure 1-5-2 provides an illustration of metadata components. A metadata schema provides a framework for structuring data in records, while the labels of elements indicate function or define the data. User manuals or best practices guidelines ensure a sound technical (and consistent) metadata element set, as well as the correct application of a set when creating records. The metadata record example in Figure 1-5-2 presents four of the DC metadata elements (*title, creator, publisher,* and *date*). Chapters 3 and 4 provide further explanation.

Certain standards may maintain both a simple version that contains only basics and a full version with additional element *refinements* (see DC examples, Chapter 2). Standards that employ attributes to modify and refine elements also need to maintain these sets of attributes and their allowable values (see MODS examples, Chapter 2). With an increase in XML applications, metadata standards developers now often provide a version of the element sets expressed in an XML schema, e.g., CDWA's offspring: CDWA Lite. Many developers have also created crosswalks to map their own elements with the elements of other related standards.

In the next chapter selected metadata standards are introduced, with the focus on their *semantics* rather than syntax or how metadata records should be

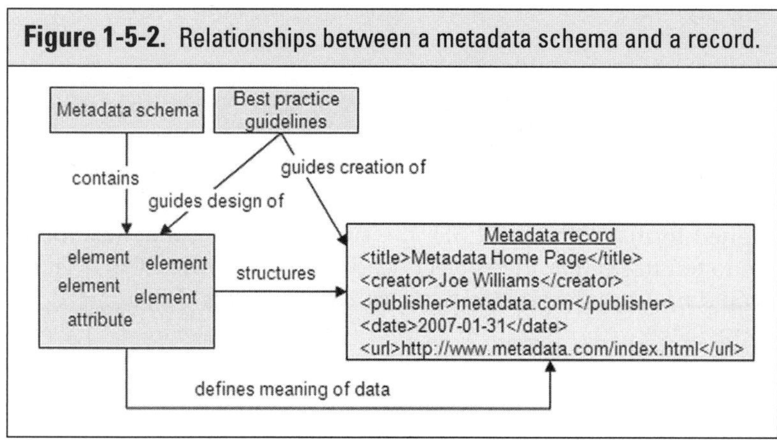

Figure 1-5-2. Relationships between a metadata schema and a record.

created using these standards. Those topics are detailed in Chapters 3, 4, and 5, which cover the structure and semantics of metadata schemas, the syntax of schema encoding, and the issues and practices in generating metadata records, respectively. Chapters 2 through 5 serve as building blocks to design metadata schemas and create metadata records. Chapters 6 through 8 cover more advanced topics concerning metadata services, interoperability, and evaluation. Chapter 9 discusses research developments of the past thirteen years, and touches on trends of the near future.

Suggested Readings

Caplan, Priscilla. 2003. "Metadata Basics." In *Metadata Fundamentals for All Librarians*. Chicago: American Library Association: 1–11.

Gilliland, Anne J. 2000. "Setting the Stage." In *Introduction to Metadata: Pathways to Digital Information*, edited by Murtha Baca. Online Edition (Version 2.1). Los Angeles, CA: Getty Information Institute. Online Edition Version 2.1. Available: www.getty.edu/research/conducting_research/standards/intrometadata/setting.html.

Jul, Erik. 1995. OCLC Internet Cataloging Project. *D-Lib Magazine* [Online], December 1995. Available: www.dlib.org/dlib/december95/briefings/12oclc.html.

NISO. 2004. *Understanding Metadata*. Bethesda, MD: NISO Press. Available: www.niso.org/publications/press/UnderstandingMetadata.pdf.

Weibel, Stuart, Jean Godby, Eric Miller, and Ron Daniel. 1995. *OCLC/NCSA Metadata Workshop Report*. Available: http://dublincore.org/workshops/dc1/report.shtml.

2

Current Standards

Metadata-related standards have been created by different communities for specific purposes—to guide the design, creation, and implementation of data structure, values, content, and exchange in an efficient and consistent manner. They include:

- Standards for *data structures*—Metadata *element sets* (usually referred to as *schemes*) are standards for data structures and semantics. The most well-known and widely used one is the Dublin Core Metadata Element Set (DCMES).
- Standards for *data content*—Data content standards are created to guide the practices of metadata generation or cataloging. The *Anglo-American Cataloguing Rules*, Second Edition (AACR2) has been used for cataloging in the bibliographic universe for many years. Newly published guidelines or rules include *Cataloging Cultural Objects* (CCO): *A Guide to Describing Cultural Works and Their Images* and *Describing Archives: A Content Standard* (DACS), both of which are content standards for describing cultural objects and archival materials that extend the boundaries of traditional cataloging.
- Standards for *data values* (referred to as *value encoding schemes* in a metadata standard)—These include controlled term lists, classification schemes, thesauri, authority files, and lists of subject headings. Some of these controlled vocabularies include thousands of terms and their semantic relationships (e.g., the *Library of Congress Subject Headings* [LCSH] and the *Art and Architecture Thesaurus* [AAT]), but there are many that only contain a small number of terms or codes.
- Standards for *data exchange*—Standards for data exchange may be separately designed *or* bound together with the element sets. They are referred to as different "formats" when discussed in the context of data exchange and communication, e.g., the *MARC 21 Format for Bibliographic Data* (MARC 21). MARC 21 is an instance of an international standard, ISO 2709, *Information and documentation—Format for information exchange,* for bibliographic description in computer-readable format. Most metadata standards now use a generalized markup language, Extensible Markup Language (XML), to express their element sets and create their metadata schemas.

The term-phrase *metadata schema* is often used interchangeably with the term-phrase *metadata standard*. In the literature, the word "schema" usually refers to an entire element set as well as the encoding of the elements and structure with a markup language.

This chapter introduces selected metadata standards for *data structures*. The focus is on their element sets, and *not* on their expression formats, value encoding schemes, or implementations in practice. Chapters 3 and 4 explore the basic building blocks of a metadata schema. Chapter 5 discusses applying metadata standards to create metadata instances (records). This text will not cover content standards; that subject needs to be studied in other texts or courses that concentrate on content standards and how they are applied in libraries, archives, museums, data centers, and other institutions.

"In today's digital libraries environment, in which individual collections of massive heterogeneous objects need to be unified and linked in a single resource, we are witnessing both the growth of different metadata and the attempts to reconcile the common attributes in the existing overlapping standards" (Ercegovac, 1999: 1165). The list of metadata standards in subject domains and communities, which in many cases do overlap, is very long and is still growing. Here we intend to introduce representative standards that have been widely used, discussed, and studied in various communities. They are selected also because they are emblematic of the different aspects of metadata functions in terms of the broad areas that encompass the descriptive, structural, technical, administrative, preservation, and rights management interests. What is mentioned in passing or discussed in detail is never meant to be an exhaustive list of standards. The inclusion or exclusion of a standard in this chapter (or the entire text) should not be interpreted as our favoring one schema more than another.

2.1 Metadata for General Purposes

The past 15 years witnessed the impact of *metadata* not only in the descriptive bibliographic universe but also in efforts to describe and access information on the entire Web. When the word *metadata* is mentioned, a natural association that immediately comes to mind is the Dublin Core, probably the term that occurs most often in metadata literature. The Dublin Core has the most mapped element sets among and across domain-specific and community-oriented metadata standards. However, this term and the element set that the term represents did not drop from the sky. The origin and development of this general-purpose metadata element set finds its foundation in the library and information sciences field(s) that explored and pioneered computerized cataloging and indexing of information resources for many years. The well-known MARC standards are the most comprehensive and exhaustive cataloging standards created prior to the advent of the digital age. The MARC family has undergone a transformation during the past 15 years to meet the requirements of the digital age. MARC 21 is the foundation for the *Metadata Object Description Schema* (MODS), which is currently the most comprehensive descriptive metadata standard. DC and MODS will be introduced in this section because they come from two separate (yet interrelated) paths. Both aim at enhancing the function of *discovery* of global information resources.

2.1.1 Dublin Core (DC)

As a general purpose metadata standard, the compatibility aspect emphasized by the Dublin Core Metadata Initiative (DCMI) can be found in the following three major ways that have been implemented in the overall DCMI movement up until the present:

1. Dublin Core semantics: Dublin Core metadata elements, extensions and refinements, and controlled vocabularies
2. The shared data model (DCMI Abstract Model): Sets an underlying grammar
3. The implementation agreements: Application profiles.

This section is solely dedicated to the DC Core semantics. Components that support and exemplify DC semantics are found in Chapter 3 in addition to the discussion that follows.

2.1.1.1 The Basic Description Mechanism

An invitational Metadata Workshop sponsored by the OCLC Online Computer Library Center and the National Center for Supercomputing Applications (NCSA) was held in **Dublin, Ohio**, in March 1995, and has since earned its reputation as the birthplace of contemporary metadata. From this workshop the term and definition *metadata = data about data* started to be cited everywhere in the literature, and the name *Dublin Core* began to be recognized beyond the library and information communities.

> Fifty-two librarians, archivists, humanities scholars and geographers, as well as standards makers in the Internet, Z39.50 and Standard Generalized Markup Language (SGML) communities, met to identify the scope of the problem, to achieve consensus on a list of metadata elements that would yield simple descriptions of data in a wide range of subject areas, and to lay the groundwork for achieving further progress in the definition of metadata elements that describe electronic information. (Weibel et al., 1995: http://dublincore.org/workshops/dc1/report.shtml)

This simple core metadata element set was developed to respond to the call for improving the description required for the exponential growth of distributed information objects and repositories on the Internet.

At the time the Dublin workshop was held, primarily two types of resource descriptions existed for networked electronic documents: (1) automatically generated indexes used by search engines (e.g., Lycos), which often contained too little information to be of use, and (2) the cataloging records created by professional information providers who followed the MARC and TEI (Text Encoding Initiative) header formats. Both were costly and difficult to implement, and were virtually impossible to adopt within the mainstream for description of the vast quantity of electronic documents available on the Internet. The Dublin Metadata Workshop endeavored to transcend the weaknesses posed by both of these two extremes for description. It was believed that in order to provide a simple and manageable structure for describing networked electronic resources, only those elements necessary for the *discovery* of the resource should be considered. This template for describing Web pages or a library catalog card for Web objects should be simple enough for nonexperts to understand.

> If only a small amount of human effort were required to create the record, more objects could be described, especially if the author of the resource could be encouraged to create the description. And if the description followed an established standard, only the creation of the record would require human intervention; automated tools could discover the descriptions and collect them into searchable databases. (Weibel et al., 1995: http://dublincore.org/workshops/dc1/report.shtml)

This basic description mechanism was designed to be simple and powerful, able to be used in all domains, applicable to any type of resource, and extensible enough to work for specific solutions (Baker, 2005). The design of the DC element set, from its origin, confirmed the basic principles of simplicity, compatibility, and extensibility (as discussed in Chapter 1). After a few years of testing and discussions, the DCMI officially confirmed its 15 core elements. The *Dublin Core Metadata Element Set* (DCMES) version 1.1 was then approved as an American and international standard (NISO Z39.85-2001 and ISO 15836: 2003). In 2007, DCMES version 1.1 was further revised and then passed as NISO Z39.85-2007 (presently its most current version).

2.1.1.2 Dublin Core Semantics

The Dublin Core semantics are documented in three types of specifications developed by the DCMI community: the metadata elements (the 15 elements), extensions and refinements (other elements and element refinements), and controlled vocabularies (encoding schemes).

1. Metadata elements

The 15 core elements in DCMES represent an interdisciplinary consensus on basic element sets for resource discovery. They are designed as a flat structure, i.e., no hierarchical relationships occur among the DC elements. All elements are optional, repeatable, and can occur in any order. In order to understand them better, we can subdivide the elements into three main categories: (1) content of any information-bearing object typically has attributes such as title, subject, type, description, and source; (2) content also has an intellectual property relationship with the creator and contributor of the content, the publisher of the object, and the rightful owner; and (3) *manifestations* of the content have attributes such as date, format, language, and identifier. As an example: the same technical report may be released as a Hypertext Markup Language (HTML) document, a Portable Document Format (PDF) file, or a Microsoft Word file at different times (i.e., date). They would have a different date, format, and URIs on the Web, but their content would remain the same. An international organization (e.g., the United Nations) Web site may manifest in multiple languages, and although the instantiation attributes of it might be different, the content remains the same. On the other hand, some versions may also have different publishers with varying access and usage permissions, and contributors may vary when the same content is expressed in different formats and languages. It should be obvious that some metadata statements (e.g., *title, description*) can be reused when the instantiation (e.g., *date, format*, or *identifier*) is different. Therefore it is possible to avoid mixing contrasting manifestations within one record (Figure 2-1-1).

By understanding the elements as subdivided into the three previously mentioned categories, they can be better applied in practice to ensure the consistency of DC's *One-to-One principle.* As Hillmann's *Using Dublin Core* (2005) explains, Dublin Core metadata generally describes one manifestation or version of a resource, rather than assuming that manifestations stand in for one another. A digital image of the Mona Lisa, for instance, has much in common with the original painting, but it cannot be considered the same as the painting. As such, the digital image should be described as a resource unto itself, and most likely the creator of the digital image needs to be included as a *creator* or *contributor* (rather than Leonardo Da Vinci). Of course the metadata description for the original Mona Lisa will have the necessary elements that describe the original creator, type, format, etc. The relationship between the reproduction and original work can be established with attributes such as *subject,*

Figure 2-1-1. Dublin Core 15 elements seen from three categories.

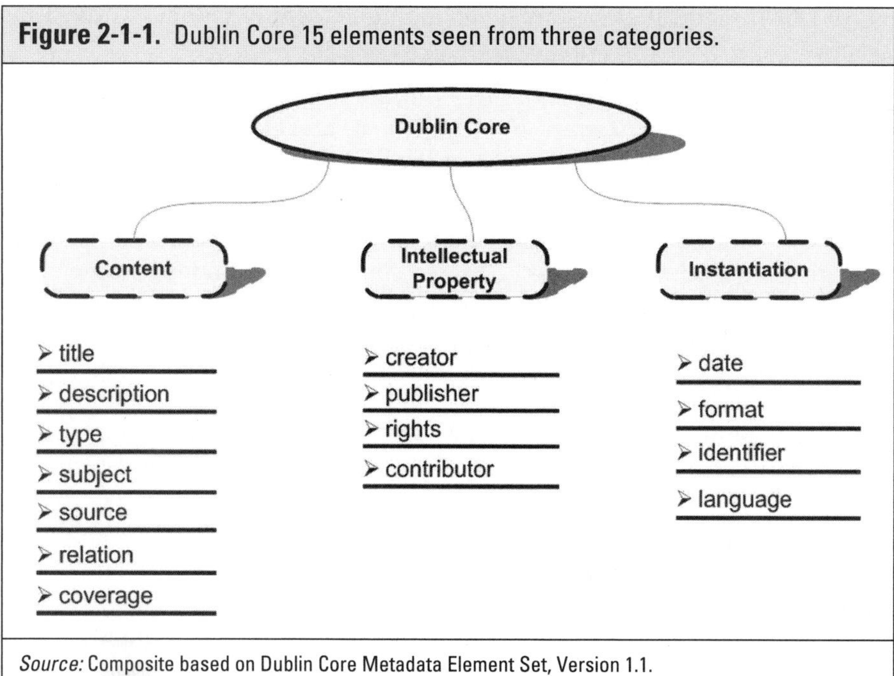

Source: Composite based on Dublin Core Metadata Element Set, Version 1.1.

description, part of the *title*, and *relation*. This assists users in determining whether they need to go to the Louvre to view the original, or whether their needs can be met by viewing a reproduction (Hillmann, 2005).

2. Extensions and refinements

In order to improve the semantic precision of the DC elements, a set of *qualifiers* was first introduced in an official document *Dublin Core Qualifiers* (http://dublincore.org/documents/2000/07/11/dcmes-qualifiers/, accessed 2007), and issued by the Dublin Core Usage Committee in 2000. Examples include "tableOfContents" which narrows the "description" element, or "issued" which narrows the "date" element. These qualifiers, together with the 15 core elements, resulted in a version that has been referred to as the "*Qualified Dublin Core*." In turn, the original 15 version has been referred to as the "*Simple Dublin Core*." At present, the term *qualifiers* has been replaced by *refinements*. Table 2-1-2 presents all of the *refinements* together with the value *encoding schemes* (which is integral to the third part of the DC semantics discussed in the following text).

Previously qualifiers had to be used together with the elements that they refine, for example: <title.alternative>ABC</title>. Since 2003, all refinements were declared as *terms* and are maintained in the *DCMI Metadata Terms* documentation, and the refinements are considered *properties* as well, although they refine other properties (i.e., elements). This confirmation enables refinements to stand alone in metadata descriptions, e.g., <alternative>ABC</alternative>. In the practices of digital collections, particularly metadata digital repositories, both usages may co-exist.

All DCMI metadata *terms* are given a unique identity within DCMI namespaces:

- http://purl.org/dc/elements/1.1/ (for the legacy DC-15 elements)
- http://purl.org/dc/terms/ (for all elements and element refinements)
- http://purl.org/dc/dcmitype/ (for the DCMI Type vocabulary)

The element *title*, for example, is identified by its Uniform Resource Identifier (URI), i.e., "http://purl.org/dc/elements/1.1/title" in legacy dc: or "http://purl.org/dc/terms/title" in dcterms:. Chapter 4 broadens the understanding of the namespaces that DC uses. At this point, however, we need to remain focused on the semantics of Dublin Core.

A number of additional elements and element refinements beyond the core—e.g., *audience*—reflect the needs of the different discourses and practices of diverse communities; however, these elements must be approved by the DC Usage Board. *Audience* (including two refinements: *Mediator* and *Education Level*), *Provenance, Rights Holder, Instructional Method, Accrual Method, Accrual Periodicity,* and *Accrual Policy* are additional elements registered in the DC Terms namespace.

3. Controlled vocabularies

Controlled vocabularies are another essential part of the DC semantics. The DCMI community identified and registered a number of *encoding schemes*

Table 2-1-1. DC 1.1 elements, refinements, and encoding schemes.

Element	Refinement	Encoding Scheme
Title	alternative	
creator		
subject		DDC NLM LCC UDC LCSH MESH
description	tableOfContents abstract	
publisher		
contributor		
date	created dateCopyrighted valid dateSubmitted issued available modified dateAccepted	W3CDTF
type		DCMIType
format	extent medium	IMT
identifier	bibliographicCitation	URI
source		URI
language		RFC 4646 RFC1766 ISO639-2 RFC3066 ISO639-3
relation	isVersionOf hasVersion isReplacedBy replaces isRequiredBy requires isPartOf hasPart isReferencedBy references isFormatOf hasFormat conformsTo	
coverage	spatial temporal	Box ISO3166 Point TGN Period W3CDTF
rights	• accessRights • license	

Source: Compiled according to *DCMI Metadata Terms*, 2008-01-14: http://dublincore.org/documents/demi-terms/.

(see right-side column of Table 2-1-1). The encoding schemes are employed to control the values that are entered in a metadata statement, e.g., the correct way to enter a value about the written *language* used in this document: "English," "en," "eng," or "en-US." The governing controlled vocabulary in this case is the international standard, ISO639-2, *Codes for the Representation of Names of Languages*, in which "English" is assigned the code "eng." These are called *vocabulary encoding schemes* because they provide the authoritative *vocabularies* to be used. They include widely used subject headings (LCSH, *Medical Subject Headings* [MeSH]), classification schemes (*Dewey Decimal Classification* [DDC], *Universal Decimal Classification* [UDC], *Library of Congress Classification* [LCC]), the vocabulary that the DCMI created (*DCMI Type Vocabulary*), and other specialized schemes. Other types of schemes are the *syntax encoding schemes*, which set rules about formatting a string in a standardized way. For example, "2007-11-08" follows the W3CDTF, *W3C Encoding Rules for Dates and Times* (a profile based on ISO 8601), which ensures that the meaning of this string is interpreted as 2007 November 08. Chapter 3 includes more detailed discussion about value encoding schemes.

2.1.1.3 More About DC

The Dublin Core Metadata Element Set (DCMES) has been used for describing resources for discovery purposes all over the world. The individual elements have also been incorporated into many other domain-specific and community-oriented metadata standards (see following sections) and *application profiles*, which combine elements from more than one standard. The DC is essential to understanding all metadata standards because of its pivotal role in standards development historically, as well as in its role as *the* standard of integration for divergent metadata standards. Almost all metadata standards and application profiles have also created *crosswalks* in order to map their elements to DC elements.

The newest contributions from the DCMI community were made in two other major areas that facilitate interoperability among all metadata activities and products: the *DCMI Abstract Model* (2007), and the use of application profiles. The *DCMI Abstract Model* provides a shared data model that enables interoperability at a higher level. It is similar to a lingua franca that everyone will be able to use as a common grammar. The abstract model is primarily targeted to the developers of software applications that support DC metadata, researchers involved in developing new syntax encoding guidelines for DC metadata, and designers developing related metadata application profiles. The abstract models of DC and other standards are covered in Chapter 5. With the incorporation of application profiles, DCMES, a general purpose metadata element set, is able to be utilized or integrated into multiple communities and domains. Application profiles ensure that metadata projects will concur with Dublin Core standards and practices. Application profiles are discussed in Chapters 3 and 8. Precise details of creating metadata records are elaborated in Chapter 5.

2.1.2 MODS and the MARC Family

Metadata in its broadest sense also includes traditional cataloging data stored in computer systems. The large amount of cataloging data (which is still growing) in the legacy MARC formats is a vast and valuable repository of information, but needs to be read, processed, retrieved, and used by the new technologies and tools. We turn here to an overview of the developments to transform MARC into new interoperable formats. It is noteworthy that the new formats are not simply a matter of mechanically converting MARC data fields into XML tags, but that more semantics are also being added to meet new needs for old data. Metadata Object Description Schema (MODS) was designed for this reason.

2.1.2.1 The Reasons for MARC Transformation

Most readers studying metadata are likely to have already taken other coursework introducing the MARC formats and the AACR2. *Understanding MARC Bibliographic: Machine-Readable Cataloging* (Furrie, 2003, www.loc.gov/marc/umb/) provides an excellent introduction to MARC in order to gain a more fundamental and detailed explanation and understanding.

MARC 21 is an instance of an international standard, ISO 2709, *Information and documentation—Format for information exchange*. Often referred to as one unified format (i.e., MARC format), MARC standards have several formats for different types of data. Although they all commonly use *numbers* to designate data *fields* (elements), each is used for different purposes. Among them, *MARC 21 Format for Bibliographic Data* is used to describe and define the material; *MARC 21 Format for Authority Data* is used to control the authoritative forms of names for persons, titles, organizations, or meetings. MARC was developed at the Library of Congress in the late 1960s and has evolved in a series of changes during the past 40 years. The MARC 21 formats are the current versions being used, and are maintained by the Library of Congress (www.loc.gov/marc/, accessed 2007).

In terms of specificity, structure, and maturity, MARC is a highly structured and semantically rich metadata. Its purposes are to represent rich bibliographic descriptions and relationships between and among data of heterogeneous library objects, and to facilitate the sharing of these bibliographic data across local library boundaries. The concerns of MARC becoming a potential metadata standard (along with AACR2) are as follows. First, AACR2, MARC 21 formats, the *Library of Congress Rule Interpretations* (LCRI), and updates and changes to cataloging rules and MARC format applications require dedication, study, practice, and continual updating by professionals whose responsibilities are the cataloging conventions associated with libraries' technical services. As Weibel et al. (1995) pointed out, richer records, created by content experts, are necessary to improve search and retrieval. Formal standards (such as the TEI Header and MARC cataloging) will provide the necessary richness, but such records are time-consuming to create and maintain, and hence may be created for only the most important resources. Second, although MARC formats are very comprehensive and are capable of describing any kind of resource, they do not fare well with regard to management needs, e.g., intellectual property and preservation, or evaluative needs, e.g., authenticity, user profiles, and grade levels. Third, the new needs created by modern technology require the use of a generalized data exchange mechanism for the legacy MARC data and other non-MARC format data (mostly expressed in XML) to communicate. This last issue continues to exist and becomes more serious because libraries receive metadata data from publishers in ONIX (Online Information Exchange) or TEI formats, or from digital libraries in the Dublin Core format. The descriptive metadata may also come as part of digital objects in the format of any XML schema.

2.1.2.2 MARCXML

Although many ways exist to make MARC records compatible with other metadata records, developing a standard for converting MARC records into XML records will benefit data conversion for the library community as well as for all metadata creators. Let us first examine a MARC 21 (2709) record machine view in Exhibit 2-1-1 (emphasis added).

Everyone agrees that it is difficult to decipher the meanings of these long numerical strings. From the emphasized data string, perhaps one can discern that the value in the **100** field should be counted from the number 357 ASCII character, then continue for 30 characters longer, and again begin at the 245 field. The **245** field is 74 characters long, beginning from the number 387 character (357+30=387). This informs a machine that from 357 to 386, the value is for Field 100, that is, "author = Slavinski, Nadine, 1968-." This communication format was designed when database storage space was still an issue, especially for those variable-length (not fixed) fields. It is still efficient and accurate today,

Exhibit 2-1-1. A MARC21 (2709) record viewing by machine.


```
00967cam 2200277 a 4500
001000800000005001700008008004100025020005300229
040001800282050002400312082002100336100003000357
245007400387260004400461300003500505440001200540
500002000552650004200572651002500614
   3471394  19990429094819. 1 931129z1994   wauab
001 0 eng         a    93047676        a0898863872
(acid-free, recycled paper) : c$14.95
 aDLC cDLC cDLC   00  aGV1046. G3 bG47
1994 0 a796. 6/40943 220 1  aSlavinski,
Nadine, d1968- 10 aGermany by bike: b20 tours
geared for discovery / cNadine Slavinski.
 aSeattle, Wash. : bMountaineers, cc 1994.
 a238 p. : bill., maps ; c22 cm.  0 aBy bike
 aIncludes index.  0 aBicycle
touring zGermany xGudebooks.
```


Source: Reproduced from Guenther 2004: slide 9, with permission.

and appropriate for the communication of data (as long as one has the system program to interpret it correctly). Other issues concern when to merge and integrate other non-MARC format data. For example, to integrate DC records into a MARC-based database, it is necessary to convert DC records into MARC records, and they must then be stored, indexed, and exchanged with this format. Another limitation of MARC is its inflexible output process. In contrast, XML-based processing can easily produce different output forms.

MARCXML is a framework for working with MARC data in an XML environment, and was developed by the Library of Congress's Network Development and MARC Standards Office in the early 2000s (MARC XML Design Considerations, 2004). A MARCXML record would be an exact equivalent of the MARC (2709) record in terms of the content. The conversion to and from MARC 21 (2709) records to MARCXML records is lossless. For example, in the following "transliteration" of the previous record, the same metadata description about the author can now be easily found in the record (note emphasis in Exhibit 2-1-2).

Exhibit 2-1-2. A MARCXML record based on the MARC 21 (2709) record shown in Exhibit 2-1-1.

```
<record xmlns="http://www.loc.gov/MARC21/slim">
  <leader>00967cam  2200277 a 4500</leader>
  <controlfield tag="001">3471394</controlfield>
  <controlfield tag="005">19990429094819.1</controlfield>
  <controlfield tag="008">931129s1994    wauab    001 0 eng  </controlfield>
  <datafield tag="020" ind1=" " ind2=" ">
      <subfield code="a">0898863872 (acid-free, recycled paper) :</subfield>
      <subfield code="c">$14.95</subfield>
  </datafield>
  <datafield tag="040" ind1=" " ind2=" ">
      <subfield code="a">DLC</subfield>
      <subfield code="c">DLC</subfield>
      <subfield code="d">DLC</subfield>
  </datafield>
  <datafield tag="050" ind1="0" ind2="0">
      <subfield code="a">GV1046.G3</subfield>
      <subfield code="b">G47 1994</subfield>
  </datafield>
  <datafield tag="082" ind1="0" ind2="0">
      <subfield code="a">796.6/4/0943</subfield>
      <subfield code="2">20</subfield>
  </datafield>
  <datafield tag="100" ind1="1" ind2=" ">
      <subfield code="a">Slavinski, Nadine,</subfield>
      <subfield code="d">1968-</subfield>
  </datafield>
  <datafield tag="245" ind1="1" ind2="0">
      <subfield code="a">Germany by bike :</subfield>
      <subfield code="b">20 tours geared for discovery /</subfield>
      <subfield code="c">Nadine Slavinski.</subfield>
```

(Cont'd.)

Exhibit 2-1-2. A MARCXML record based on the MARC 21 (2709) record shown in Exhibit 2-1-1 *(Continued).*

```
    </datafield>
  <datafield tag="260" indl=" " ind2=" ">
      <subfield code="a">Seattle, Wash. :</subfield>
      <subfield code="b">Mountaineers,</subfield>
      <subfield code="c">c1994.</subfield>
  </datafield>
  <datafield tag="300" indl=" " ind2=" ">
      <subfield code="a">238 p. :</subfield>
      <subfield code="b">ill., maps ;</subfield>
      <subfield code="c">22 cm.</subfield>
  </datafield>
  <datafield tag="440" indl=" " ind2="0">
      <subfield code="a">By bike</subfield>
  </datafield>
  <datafield tag="500" indl=" " ind2=" ">
      <subfield code="a">Includes index.</subfield>
  </datafield>
  <datafield tag="650" indl=" " ind2="0">
      <subfield code="a">Bicycle touring</subfield>
      <subfield code="z">Germany</subfield>
      <subfield code="x">Guidebooks.</subfield>
  </datafield>
</record>
```

Source: Reproduced from Guenther 2004: slide 11-12, with permission.

With the MARCXML format, conversion to, and exchange with, any record expressed in XML becomes relatively easy and simple. The same MARC record can be converted into a DC record (see Exhibit 2-1-3). Behind this transformation is a converting table that maps the MARC field codes to the DC element names, e.g., the MARC *100* field is mapped to the DC *creator* element. Another benefit of using MARCXML is to use Extensible Stylesheet Language (XSL), which allows description of how files encoded in XML are to be correctly

Exhibit 2-1-3. A DC record converted from the MARCXML record shown in Exhibit 2-1-2.

```
<rdf:Description xmlns:rdf="http://www.w3.org/1999/02/22-rdf-syntax-ns#"
xmlns:dc="http://purl.org/dc/elements/1.1/">
  <dc:title>Germany by bike : 20 tours geared for discovery </dc:title>
  <dc:creator>Slavinski, Nadine, 1968-</dc:creator>
  <dc:type>text</dc:type>
  <dc:publisher>Seattle, Wash. : Mountaineers, </dc:publisher>
  <dc:date>c1994.</dc:date>
  <dc:language>eng</dc:language>
< dc:subject>Bicycle touring</dc:subject>
</rdf:Description>
```

formatted or transformed. Using different stylesheets, the same content can be displayed in different styles that users can select.

2.1.2.3 Metadata Object Description Schema (MODS)

MARCXML is, from the encoding format point of view, a transformation of MARC. Nevertheless, it only enhances the communication of machines. Still, the method of expressing fields in numbers and using subfields and indicators is quite unique in comparison with the majority of metadata formats. Conversely (as discussed previously), the comprehensive and overwhelming number of MARC fields remain barriers to its use for describing resources on the Internet by noncatalogers. This prevents MARC records from being easily connected to, and integrated with, other metadata records (or digital repositories). At the same time, there still exists the demand for rich hierarchical descriptive metadata in XML, especially for describing complex digital library objects. One of the main concerns about DC is its simple element set. Libraries have created rich cataloging records for many decades and are also hesitant to give up their practices and products.

In 2002–2003, the Network Development and MARC Standards Office at the Library of Congress collaborated with metadata experts and developed the *Metadata Object Description Schema* (MODS). Its current status is Version 3, released in 2006. MODS is intended to be able to carry selected data from existing MARC 21 records as well as to enable the creation of original resource description records. The top elements are shown in Figure 2-1-2.

MODS' features and its relationship with MARC can be seen as follows:

- MODS' semantics originate with MARC. The element set includes a subset of MARC fields. The elements generally inherit the semantics (i.e., meanings of fields) of MARC.
- MODS uses language-based tags rather than numeric ones, e.g., <name type="personal"> instead of "100."
- In some cases MODS regroups elements from the MARC 21 bibliographic format, e.g., <name type="xxx"> for both "1xx" and "7xx" fields.
- MODS uses attributes to refine elements. In the previous example, *type* is an attribute that defines the type of *name* in a statement. The use of attributes resembles the functions of MARC's subfields, e.g., <namePart *type="date"*> 1968-</namePart> corresponding to subfield $d in the 100 field, in the record below (emphasis added).
- MODS does not assume the use of any specific cataloging code such as AACR2.

In the record shown in Exhibit 2-1-4, the same data that appeared in previous exhibits is converted into a MODS record. The top level elements of MODS, as illustrated in Figure 2-1-2, all have subelements. Both the elements and subelements may have their own attributes, which is why attributes are used in the *name* element. The *name* information is specified by the attribute, *type="personal."* The subelement <namePart> is repeated three times and the content is differentiated with a *type* attribute to indicate

Figure 2-1-2. MODS top level elements.

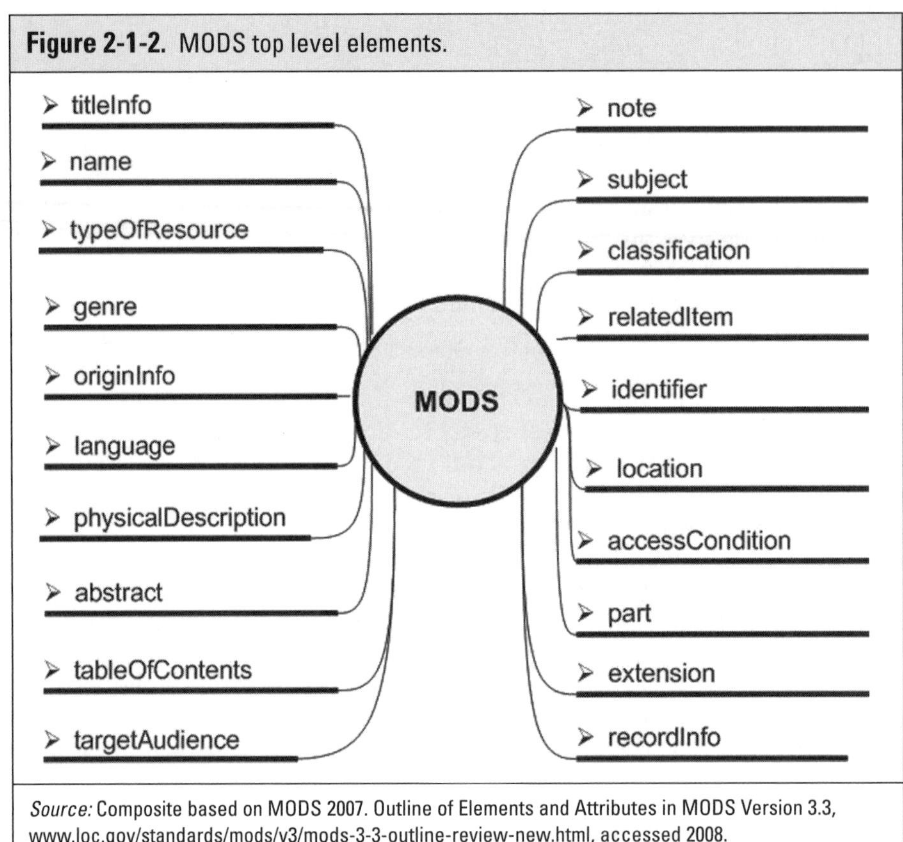

Source: Composite based on MODS 2007. Outline of Elements and Attributes in MODS Version 3.3, www.loc.gov/standards/mods/v3/mods-3-3-outline-review-new.html, accessed 2008.

whether the value is a "given" name, "family" name, or birth "date" of the person.

Taking another example from the record, the *subject* information is also differentiated by subelements of subject: *topic* and *geographic*. The attribute and value, *authority="lcsh"* indicate where the subject headings are selected from (LCSH). This is a basic approach to ensure that the value (a subject term) recorded here will retain its correct meaning when converted (or merged) into other databases. The allowable values of an attribute are often predefined. The same attribute used with a different element will have different values. Figure 2-1-4 provides a graphic interpretation of the element *subject*, its subelements such as *topic*, *geographic*, and *hierarchicalGeographic*, and the sub-subelements of *hierarchicalGeographic*, including *continent*, *country*, *province*, and so on. A general attribute for all of them is *authority*. A name of the controlled vocabulary (e.g., "lcsh") must be provided as the value for this attribute. The legends used in Figure 2-1-4 and other figures are explained in Figure 2-1-3.

More standards have this form of hierarchical structure and remain to be discussed in this chapter. They employ a *hierarchical structure* (with elements and subelements) that presents the relationships of the *elements*, as well as

Exhibit 2-1-4. A MODS record converted from the MARCXML record shown in Exhibit 2-1-2.


```
<mods xmlns="http://www.loc.gov/mods/">
<titleInfo>
  <title>Germany by bike : 20 tours geared for discovery /</title>
</titleInfo>
    <name type="personal">
        <namePart type="given">Nadine</namePart>
        <namePart type="family">Slavinski</namePart>
        <namePart type="date">1968-</namePart>
        <role><roleTerm type="text">creator</roleTerm></role>
    </name>
    <typeOfResource>text</typeOfResource>
    <originInfo>
      <place><placeTerm type="code" authority="marc">wau</ placeTerm>
              <placeTerm type="text"> Seattle, Wash. :</placeTerm>
    </place>
        <publisher>Mountaineers,</publisher>
        <dateIssued>c1994</dateIssued>
        <issuance>monographic</issuance>
    </originInfo>
    <language>
      <languageTerm type="code" authority="iso639-2b">eng</languageTerm>
    </language>
    <physicalDescription>
      <extent>238 p. : ill., maps ; 22 cm.</extent>
    </physicalDescription>
    <note type="statement of responsibility">Nadine Slavinski.</note>
    <note>Includes index.</note>
    <subject authority="lcsh">
        <topic>Bicycle touring</topic>
        <geographic>Germany</geographic>
        <topic>Guidebooks.</topic>
    </subject>
    <classification authority="lcc">GV1046.G3 G47 1994</ classification>
    <classification authority="ddc" edition="20">796.6/4/ 0943</classification>
    <relatedItem type="series">
        <titleInfo><title>By bike</title></titleInfo>
    </relatedItem>
    <identifier type="isbn">0898863872 (acid-free, recycled paper) :</identifier>
    <identifier type="lccn">93047676</identifier>
    <recordInfo>
        <recordContentSource>DLC</recordContentSource>
        <recordCreationDate encoding="marc">931129</ recordCreationDate>
        <recordChangeDate encoding="iso8601">19990429094819.1
        </recordChangeDate>
        <recordIdentifier>3471394</recordIdentifier>
    </recordInfo>
```


Source: Reproduced from Guenther 2004: slide 18-19, with permission.

Figure 2-1-3. Legend used in graphics generated from XML schemas.

Content model symbols		Components in content model	
Sequence		Mandatory single element	title
Choice		Single optional element	start
All		Mandatory multiple element containing child elements	copyInformation 1..∞
		Element referencing global element	mods 1..∞
		Model group	modsGroup 1..∞
		Attribute	attributes authority

using *attributes* to modify or define elements. The underlying reason for using this kind of form is to adhere to the XML encoding syntax rules.

Definitions of MODS elements are available as an online resource (www.loc.gov/standards/mods/, accessed 2007). A list of MODS to MARC mapping (www.loc.gov/standards/mods/mods-mapping.html, accessed 2007) presents all MODS elements and the corresponding MARC fields, subfields, and indicators. A simplified version of MODS, *MODS "Lite,"* uses only those elements that correspond to the 15 Dublin Core elements in DCMES version 1.1.

MODS is a standard for creating rich descriptive metadata, and is used for large-scale endeavors such as the Library of Congress Web archiving projects. However, its potential is far greater than a single metadata standard. Considering the huge number of already existing (and still increasing) MARC records, MODS serves as an interoperable core for the convergence between MARC and non-MARC XML descriptions.

Both DC and MODS are general purpose metadata standards. DC is extremely simple and therefore easy to implement; MODS has sufficient specificity but is more complicated in application, especially for nonlibrary professionals. DC has a flat structure and loose control of values; MODS is hierarchical and requires high consensus and agreement about syntax and value control. DC has been adopted by the Open Archives Initiative—Protocol for Metadata Harvesting (OAI-PMH), see Chapter 6); MODS is the major descriptive format of the Metadata Encoding and Transmission Standard (METS). Nevertheless, they share the common goal of the *discovery* of information resources in the digital age. The rest of the chapter will introduce domain-specific or community-oriented standards and attention will be drawn to other aspects of

Figure 2-1-4. Subelements, attributes, and predefined list of attribute values for the *subject* element (extracted from MODS XML Schema, generated with ALTOVA®'s XMLSpy®).

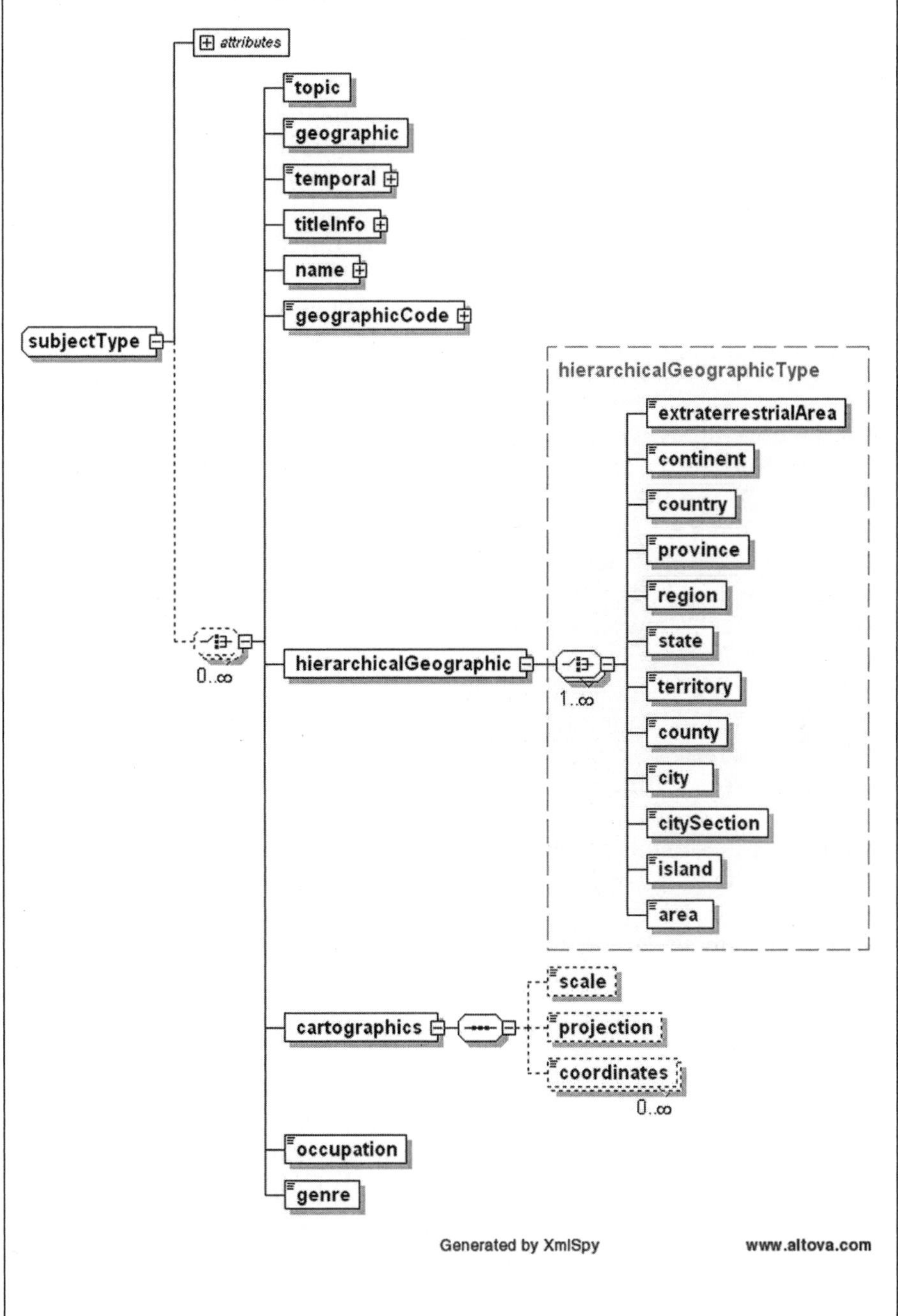

resources, e.g., the metadata of use, administrative, structural, technical, and rights management.

2.2 Metadata for Cultural Objects and Visual Resources

Digital collections and digital library projects for cultural objects and visual resources have been a focus of many cultural heritage institutions of the world. These collections have made access available to thousands of cultural treasures and include works of art, architecture, other material culture, groups and collections of works, and their related image representations. Two influential names need to be acknowledged when introducing metadata standards for cultural objects and visual resources: the Getty Information Institute, and the Visual Resources Association (VRA). The former Getty Information Institute (1983–1999) of the J. Paul Getty Trust in Los Angeles, California, published a number of important standards in the 1990s. They are available online, and continued with ongoing updates by the Institute's successor, the Vocabulary Program and Digital Resource Management of the Getty Research Institute. These include highly recognized and widely used *data value* standards consisting of the *Art and Architecture Thesaurus* (AAT), the *Getty Thesaurus of Geographic Names* (TGN), and the *Union List of Artist Names* (ULAN). Together with the members of the VRA Data Standards Committee, a *date content* standard, the *Cataloging of Cultural Objects* (CCO): *A Guide to Describing Cultural Works and Their Images* was edited by Baca et al. and published at the behest of the VRA in 2006. In addition, standards for *data structures and semantics*, most notably the *Categories for the Description of Works of Art* (CDWA) and the *Visual Resources Association Core Categories* (VRA Core), have formed the foundation of metadata practices in the communities of museums, visual resource collections, as well as the libraries, special collections, and archives whose personnel also continually work with cultural objects and visual resources. CDWA may be likened to the root of a tree whose concepts, model, and semantics of the metadata standards for cultural objects and visual resources have multiplied into resources in the midst of prolific new growth. It is both necessary and important to introduce CDWA in some detail here. All discussion in this section is based on documents made freely available by the standards considered, with minimal interpretation or commentary.

2.2.1 Introduction to CDWA

Categories for the Description of Works of Art (CDWA) issues "[g]uidelines for the description of art objects and images, including a discussion of issues involved in building art information systems" (CDWA, 2006 www.getty.edu/research/conducting_research/standards/cdwa/). The CDWA, initiated in the early 1990s, is a product of the Art Information Task Force (AITF), funded by the J. Paul Getty Trust, with a two-year matching grant from the National Endowment for the Humanities (NEH) to the College Art Association (CAA). The task force included representatives from the communities that provide and use art information: art historians, museum curators and registrars, visual resource professionals, art librarians, information managers, and technical specialists. The current edition edited by Baca and Harpring was revised in 2006.

The functional impact of CDWA is more of a framework than a set of elements designed for implementation. CDWA has 31 broad categories and more than 380 subcategories. Its purpose is to provide a framework for mapping existing art information systems and for developing new systems. CDWA also identifies vocabulary resources and descriptive practices that make information located in diverse systems more compatible and accessible (CDWA, 2006). Therefore, links to files of personal and corporate name authority, place and location authority, general concept authority, and subject authority are extensively indicated along with the CDWA categories in the specification. The standard aims to present the content of databases by describing and accessing information about cultural objects and related visual resources. This need for comprehensive coverage resulted in the creation of 31 broad categories (see Figure 2-2-1). A small subset of categories are considered *core* (marked with a star in Figure 2-2-1)

Figure 2-2-1. CDWA broad categories.

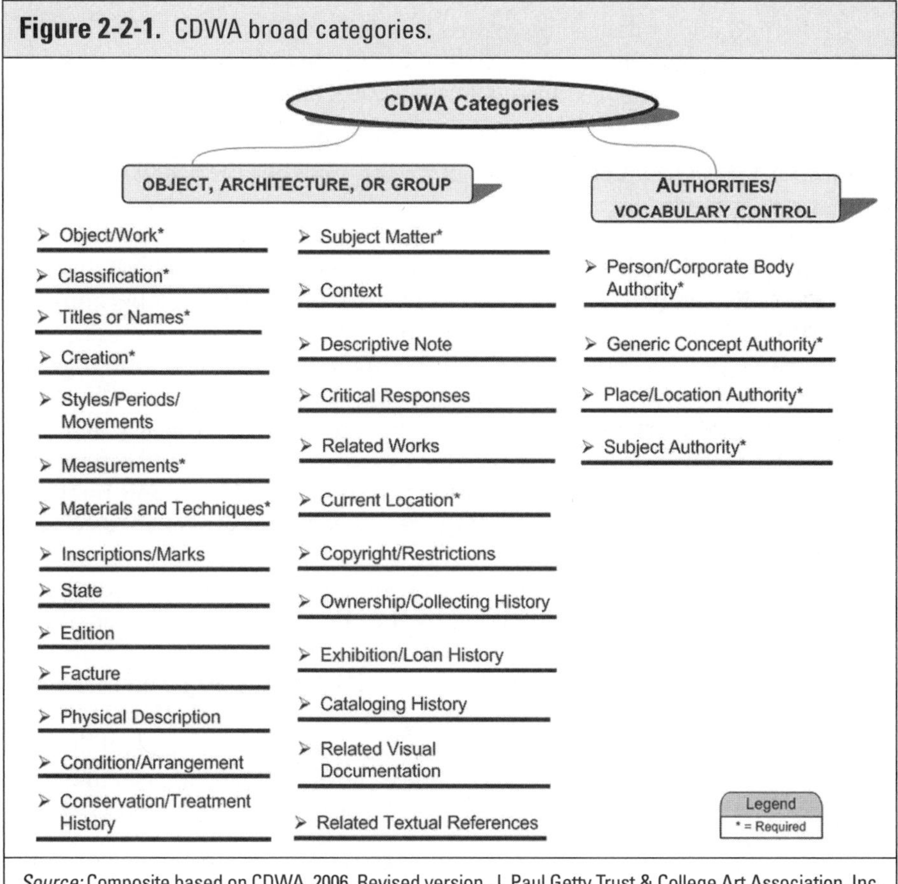

Source: Composite based on CDWA, 2006. Revised version. J. Paul Getty Trust & College Art Association, Inc.

and they represent the minimum information necessary to identify and describe a work. A full list of categories is available from the CDWA (www.getty.edu/research/conducting_research/standards/cdwa/categories.html#list, accessed 2007).

CDWA has provided detailed mapping to important metadata standards' elements: MARC, DC, EAD (Encoded Archival Description), METS (Metadata Encoding and Transmission Standard), Describing Archives: A Content Standard (DACS), and more. CDWA has become the basis for a number of derived metadata standards and content standards: VRA Core 3.0 and 4.0, Object ID (an international standard for describing art, antiques and antiquities), CDWA Lite (CDWA simplified version encoded as XML), CCO, and *A Guide to the Description of Architectural Drawings* of the Architectural Drawings Advisory Group (ADAG) and the Foundation for Documents of Architecture (FDA).

2.2.2 Important Concepts

In addition to being a conceptual model, CDWA also defines numerous important concepts in the "discussions" sections presented under each category that were inherited and enhanced by related standards CDWA Lite, VRA Core, and CCO. The first concerns *catalog levels*, which helps the metadata creator to determine *what* is being described (CDWA, 2006: Object/Work—Catalog Level; CCO, 2006).

- *Item:* An individual object or work, which may be composed of multiple parts or components.
- *Group* (an archival group or record group): An aggregate of items that share a common provenance, and often contains many different objects. Groups are usually defined by repositories and may have several subgroups that are established by archival principles of provenance.
- *Volume:* Paper, vellum, papyrus, or other materials that are bound together. Examples include printed books, manuscripts, sketchbooks, or albums.
- *Collection:* Multiple items that are conceptually or physically arranged together for the purpose of cataloging or retrieval. A collection differs from an archival group in that the items in a collection are bound informally for convenience and do not necessarily share a common provenance or otherwise meet the criteria for an archival group.
- *Series:* A number of works that were created in temporal succession by the same artist or studio and intended by the creator(s) to be seen together or in succession as a cycle of works.
- *Set:* An assembly of items that the creator intended to be taken as a whole (e.g., a tea set, a desk set, a pair of terrestrial and celestial globes).
- *Component:* A part of a larger item. Unlike an item that can stand alone as an independent work, the component typically cannot or does not stand alone.

Understanding the levels of cataloging is important because of the different practices that exist in professional communities.

The second set of important concepts is about *work* and *image* (VRA Core 4.0, 2007; Baca et al., 2006). A work is a distinct intellectual or artistic creation limited primarily to objects and structures made by humans. An image is a visual representation of a work, typically existing in photomechanical, photographic, or digital format. The relationship between works and images is many-to-many. This means that a work may have one or more visual representations, and the opposite is also true. VRA 3.0 provides a set of sample records in which it demonstrates this many-to-many scenario: a *chair* is documented by a *photograph*, and the photograph is later copied to a *slide* format, and then it is scanned to create a *digital image* (VRA Core 3.0: Example 3, www.vraweb.org/resources/datastandards/vracore3/examples.html, accessed 2007). In these records each should have a different creator, physical measurement, material, technique, date, current location, etc., despite all being related to the same work. This is especially important because in practice, metadata creators may not be exactly clear about what they are describing. For example, a black-and-white photograph depicts the dining room furnishings of the Frederic C. Robie House, which were designed by Frank Lloyd Wright. Should the record describe the photograph or the dining room? If treating this photograph as a work by the photographer Henry Fuermann, then all the metadata statements in this record are about the photograph; e.g., the creator would be Fuermann (and not Frank Lloyd Wright), *gelatin silver print* (rather than *furniture*) would be the value for the *type* element, the measurement would be for the photograph, and the creator's role would be *photographer* rather than *designer*. This distinction helps to avoid mistakes often found in digital collections; e.g., a person who scanned an image or designed a related Web page designates herself as the *creator* of a photograph from her grandmother's high school graduation, or enters the photographer as the creator of the original furniture in the example just outlined. CDWA, CDWA Lite, and VRA Core all require distinguishing the type of resource to be described either as a *work* or an *image* (at the very beginning of any record). Once determined, the whole record will describe the work or image, without any ambiguity. During implementation a digital collection creator may decide if it is necessary (and affordable) to create records for *both* the original work and images, and also determine the primary focus of the metadata in a given project. A "*collection*" type is also added in VRA Core 4.0, so it is also now required to distinguish among "*work*," "*image*," and "*collection*."

The third set of concepts is about *intrinsic* and *extrinsic relationships* of related works. An intrinsic relationship is a direct relationship between two works, existing in the following circumstances of whole-part, group and collection, series, and component. An intrinsic relationship is essential and *must* be recorded to enable effective searches. An extrinsic relationship is defined as two or more works having an informative (but not essential) relationship, so the cataloger does not need to identify the extrinsic relationship during the cataloging process. Extrinsic relationships are generally temporal, conceptual, or spatial in this context.

The fourth important set of concepts is about *display* and *indexing* issues, and tags. Display indicates how the data looks to the end user in the database, on a

Web site, on a wall or slide label, or in a publication. Indexing refers to how data is indexed (that is, which indexing terms are assigned to it), sorted, and retrieved. For a long time, metadata creation has been heavily slanted toward indexing. CDWA Lite and VRA Core 4.0 both include display tags in their schemas. (For display and indexing issues, see Chapter 5.)

CDWA also developed an important entity-relationship model that has been adopted by CCO. The model presents the relationships of metadata instances (records) between and among *work*, *image*, *source*, and entities controlled by authorities such as *person or corporate body*, *subject*, *geographic place*, and *concept*. For CCO a work and various entities can be linked "verbally" through records in a relational database (see model discussion in Chapter 5).

These standards have provided extensive examples of metadata records. Coverage of the objects by these standards is comprehensive and represents typical situations that may be encountered while creating metadata. Sample records with (or without) XML coding, full records, and records for display purposes are more useful. In the specifications of CDWA Lite and VRA Core 4.0, XML tagging examples are provided throughout, element-by-element.

2.2.3 The Element Sets of CCO, CDWA Lite, and VRA Core

One should clearly be able to see the interrelated view and concepts defined by these metadata standards for cultural objects and visual resources; however, differences occur between the respective element sets. The following discussion focuses on the elements included in these standards, but does not detail their application in metadata instances.

2.2.3.1 CCO (Cataloging of Cultural Objects)

Although CCO is a content standard that provides guidelines for selecting, ordering, and formatting data used to populate elements in a catalog record, it specifies a set of core elements (see Table 2-2-1) that comprise the most important descriptive information necessary to create a record for a work and an image. Its 116 elements and subelements are derived from the 385 CDWA metadata elements (called "*categories*" in CDWA).

CCO recommends that a minimal record should include most (if not all) core metadata elements; a minimal record should contain data values for all of the required core elements whenever possible. The minimal description refers to a case in which one includes all that is necessary; CCO provides a large number of examples that accompany the detailed instructions.

2.2.3.2 CDWA Lite

CDWA Lite, as the name suggests, represents a "lighter version" of CDWA, and contains the core elements used to describe cultural objects. It is based on the required categories, structure, and the guidelines issued by CDWA (discussed previously). CDWA Lite is also informed by the cataloging rules of CCO. Briefly then, the description of each element, the attributes used for an element, whether an element is repeatable or required, and how the value is

Table 2-2-1. CCO chapters and elements.

CCO Chapter	Element	Required?	Controlled? How?	Link to Authority
1. Object Naming	**Work Type** Title Title Type Language **Resource**	y y n n n	y n Controlled list Controlled list y	Concept authority Source Authority
2. Creator Information	**Creator display** **Controlled Creator** **Role** Creator Extent Attribution Qualifier	y y y n n	n y y Controlled list Controlled list	 Name authority Concept authority
3. Physical Characteristics	**Measurements display** **Materials and Techniques display** Edition display State display Inscriptions Facture Physical Description Condition and Examination—history Conservation and Treatment—history	y y n n n n n n n	[Sub-elements of some elements are controlled by controlled list]	[Some sub-elements are linked to authorities]
4. Stylistic, Cultural and Chronological Information	Style Culture **Display Date**	n n y	y y n	Concept authority Concept authority
5. Location and Geography	**Current Location display** Creation Location display Discovery Location display Former Location display	y n n n	[Some sub-elements are controlled by controlled list]	[Some sub-elements are linked to authorities]
6. Subject	Subject display **Controlled Subject** Extent Subject Type	n y n n	n y Controlled list Controlled list	 Name, place, concept, subject authorities
7. Class	Class Display Controlled Class	n n	n Controlled list	
8. Description	Description (Descriptive Note) Other Descriptive Notes	n n	n n	[Some sub-elements are linked to authorities]
9. View Information	**View Description** **View Type** View Subject display View Display Date	y y n n	n Controlled list n n	[Some sub-elements are linked to authorities]

Source: Composite based on CCO, 2006: 44–45. *Note:* Required elements are boldfaced.

to be controlled are all based on CDWA and CCO. Semantically CDWA Lite corresponds to CCO, particularly the key concepts discussed in section 2.2.2, and also the entity-relationship model that guides the management of the many types of relationships among all the entities. Technically, however, CDWA Lite may be understood as the CDWA/CCO required categories mapped to an XML schema, which provides rules for both structure and semantics for information exchange that allows information to be encoded in a way that computers can understand and humans can read. To be able to contribute to a union catalog and other types of digital repositories, CDWA Lite is designed for preparing metadata records that can be harvested using the OAI Protocol for Metadata Harvesting. The overall structure of CDWA Lite is illustrated in Figure 2-2-2.

It is important to pay attention to the *administrative metadata* in addition to the *descriptive metadata* in CDWA Lite. This is the significant difference of metadata for cultural objects from other types of resources. Information about rights, reference resources, images, as well as other meta-metadata about the records themselves are all considered very important. For the descriptive meta-

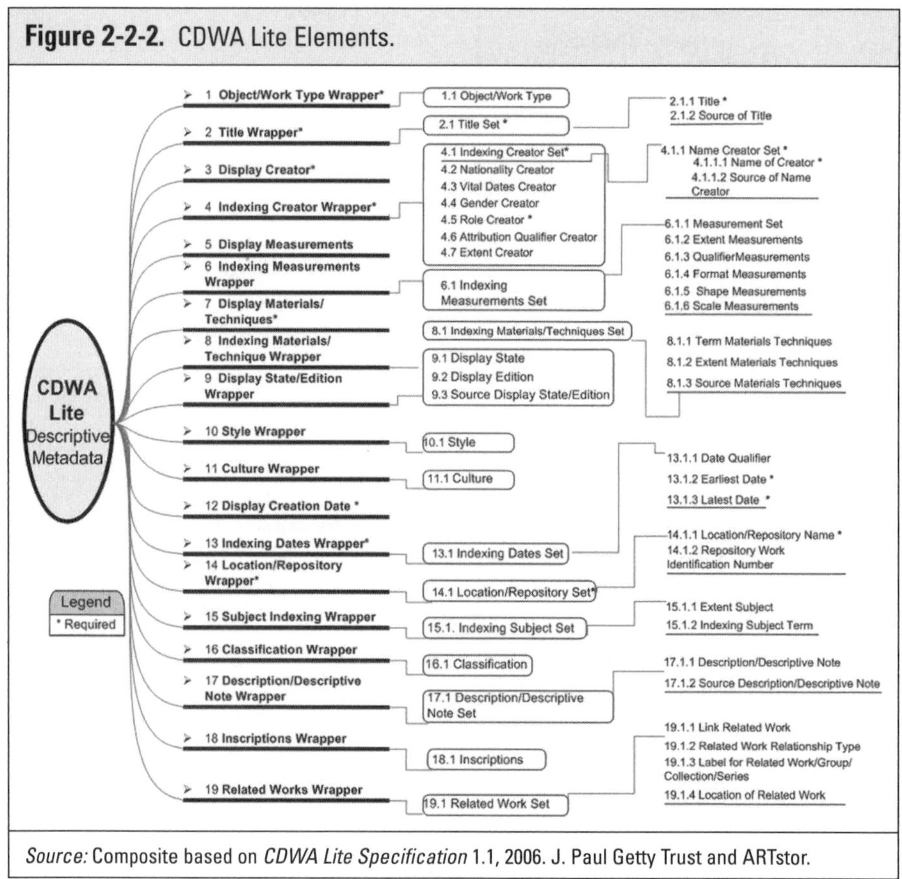

Figure 2-2-2. CDWA Lite Elements.

Source: Composite based on *CDWA Lite Specification* 1.1, 2006. J. Paul Getty Trust and ARTstor.

data, *works* are the emphasis, although metadata about images is also included. In CDWA Lite, elements for wrapping purposes (wrappers and sets) are used to group the related elements for display and indexing together (see Chapter 5 on *linkages* and *wrappers*).

2.2.3.3 The VRA Core Categories

VRA Core Categories were developed in response to the needs of the visual resource collections. The greatest difference between an "average" visual resource description and a description in the bibliographic universe "is probably that the source of the description is something other than the item itself which is a basic tenet of AACR2. This is not to be contrary but merely that most works of art do not include the title, creator, imprint, and series information usually found in library materials. Furthermore, the tradition of art historical scholarship is to leave the determination of such information to the repository responsible for a work of art or to art historians. Many images of art works are received with some description from the vendor or other source and that may be the only information available on which to base the cataloging or metadata" (CC: DA Task Force on VRA Core Categories, 2001: 5).

VRA Core enables a database to contain and associate both *work* records describing an actual art object and *image* records describing representations of views of that object (slides, digital images, or others) held by an institution. Version 3.0, the most widely used version thus far, consists of a single element set that combines two separated elements for *works* and *images* from the 2.0 version released in 1997. The categories/elements of VRA 3.0 find their origin in the CDWA standard. The difference between version 3.0 from CDWA is not only the size of the elements (17 total form a single Core), but also the structure. VRA Core 3.0 is similar to Dublin Core's earlier structure that is characterized by its flat structure plus "qualifiers." All 17 elements in VRA Core 3.0 are optional, repeatable, with no certain order of precedence. Unlike CDWA, VRA Core 3.0 elements do not have subelements; instead, the element is modified by a qualifier. Half of the elements reflect specialized needs for describing the visual resources (as emphasized in Table 2-2-2). Also, the exclusion of administrative elements (emphasized in CDWA Lite), mirrors the characteristics of a visual resource collection, e.g., a slides collection center (very different from a library or a museum). Qualifiers are even more specialized in comparison with those previously used as Dublin Core qualifiers.

VRA Core 4.0 (www.vraweb.org/projects/vracore4/index.html) was released in 2007. The changes to this new version have been made in order to make the VRA Core XML-compliant. The changes of the elements are not significant, but the structural change is dramatic. For example, element qualifiers in 3.0 have been converted to subelements and attributes (see Figure 2-2-3) following the rules of XML encoding syntax. Note that the text in brackets in the figure indicates attributes for the particular element. All attributes have predefined values and are available from the VRA Core specification.

The entire VRA Core 4.0 structure has departed from DC and moved toward consistency with CDWA Lite, similar to MODS, LOM, and EAD 2002 (see

Table 2-2-2. VRA Core 3.0 elements and qualifiers.

Record Type Type Title • Title.Variant • Title.Translation • Title.Series • Title.Larger Entity **Measurements** • Measurements.Dimensions • Measurements.Format • Measurements.Resolution **Material** • Material.Medium • Material.Support **Technique** Creator • Creator.Role • Creator.Attribution • Creator.Personal name • Creator.Corporate name	Date • Date.Creation • Date.Design • Date.Beginning • Date.Completion • Date.Alteration • Date.Restoration **Location** • Location.Current Site • Location.Former Site • Location.Creation Site • Location.Discovery Site • Location.Current Repository • Location.Former Repository ID Number • ID Number.Current Repository • ID Number.Former Repository • ID Number.Current Accession • ID Number.Former Accession	**Style/ Period** • Style/Period.Style • Style/Period.Period • Style/Period.Group • Style/Period.School • Style/Period.Dynasty • Style/Period.Movement **Culture** Subject Relation • Relation.Identity • Relation.Type Description Source Rights

Source: Composite based on VRA Core 3.0: www.vraweb.org/resources/datastandards/vracore3/index.html, accessed 2007. Emphases reflect elements for describing the visual resources when compared with DCMES.

section 2.4). In principle, VRA Core 4.0 continues to follow the 1:1 principle developed by the Dublin Core community, i.e., only one object or resource may be described within a single metadata description set. How the description sets are linked to form a single record is a local database implementation issue. The "one-to-many" relationships are also well-supported by linkages established in the *relation* element, e.g. parts and whole for complex works, and between multiple images and a single work.

In version 4.0, a third *record type* has been added for collections: *collection*. Again, a record will be created for any one of the three types:

- *Work:* A unique entity such as an object or event.
- *Image:* A visual representation of a work in either whole or part.
- *Collection:* An aggregate of work or image records.

A significant change was made to the *creator* element. It has been renamed *agent* and has subelements of *name, role, culture, dates,* and *attribution. Culture,* which existed as a single, free-standing element in 3.0, is now recorded in two different places: as a subelement under *agent,* and as a free-standing element *cultural context* in which the work was created. Another noticeable change from Core 3.0 is the restructuring of the *ID number* element. An ID associated with a repository is now recorded as a subelement (i.e., *refid*) of *location.*

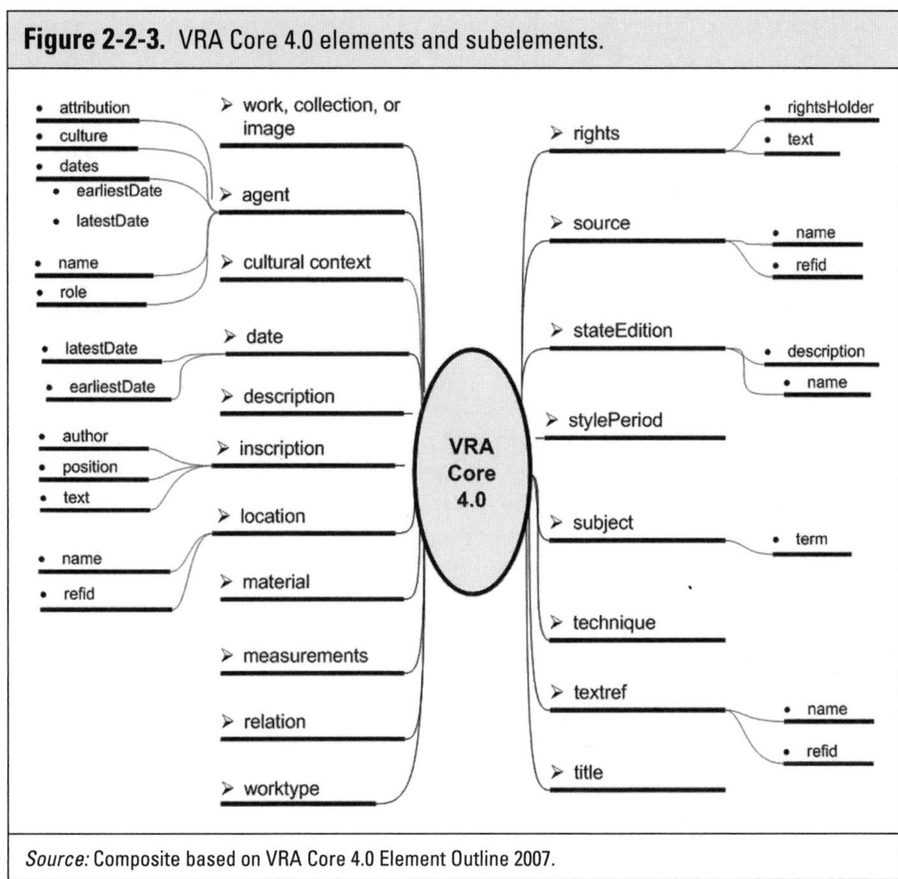

Figure 2-2-3. VRA Core 4.0 elements and subelements.

Source: Composite based on VRA Core 4.0 Element Outline 2007.

VRA Core 3.0 provided the groundwork upon which the CCO editors developed data content guidelines. VRA Core 4.0 has reflected practices elaborated upon in CCO which have influenced the methodology behind Core 4.0, specifically in the differentiation of data values for display and indexing.

2.2.3.4 Object ID

Object ID (www.object-id.com/, accessed 2007) is an international standard for describing art, antiques, and antiquities, used particularly to combat art theft. It is the result of collaboration between the museum community, police and customs agencies, art dealers, the insurance industry, and devotees of art and antiques. The Object ID Checklist (www.object-id.com/checklist/check_eng.html, accessed 2007) is a select set of elements from CDWA, and includes only ten elements to answer key questions about a recovered stolen object. In order, they are *Type of Object, Materials & Techniques, Measurements, Inscriptions & Markings, Distinguishing Features, Title, Subject, Date or Period, Maker*, and *Description*. Additional recommended categories are *Inventory Number, Related Written Material, Place of Origin/Discovery, Cross Reference to Related Objects*, and

Date Documented (Thornes, Dorrell, and Lie, 1999). With an attached photograph of the object, these records assist registering and communicating the object information necessary to identify stolen or missing objects throughout the world. This example shows how useful a metadata standard can be (in the sense that both CDWA-as-framework and Object ID combine to form a very simple element set).

As indicated at the beginning of this section, metadata for cultural objects and visual recourses have received increasing attention and the community has developed standards for data structures, data values (controlled vocabularies and authorities), and data contents (e.g., CCO, DACS). To comprehend and ensure the process of creating good metadata records, one needs to study those standards also. Other controlled vocabularies that are widely used by this community include *Thesaurus for Graphic Materials, I: Subject Terms* (TGM I) and *II: Genre and Physical Characteristic Terms* (TGM II) developed by the Library of Congress, as well as *Iconclass*—a subject-specific classification system. Iconclass is a hierarchically ordered collection of definitions for objects, persons, events, and abstract ideas that can be the subject(s) of an image, and is maintained at the Netherlands Institute for Art History (Rijksbureau voor Kunsthistorische Documentatie, or RKD).

The metadata standards introduced in this section are clearly different from those introduced in other sections (which have very different foci and user communities). These standards do reflect the characteristics of resources typically found in museums and visual resource collections. However, this should not prevent the sharing and accessing of resources created, regardless of standard. In fact, all of these standards are interconnected and interoperable through the careful design of the element sets and the common exchange format that has been adopted. Technical metadata standards for images have also been designed by developers that extend beyond the cultural heritage resource community, some of which will be introduced in other sections of this chapter.

2.3 Metadata for Educational Resources

Educational resources are also called learning objects, which are defined as "any entity, digital or non-digital, which can be used, re-used or referenced during technology supported learning" (IEEE-LTSC WG-12, 2005: http://ltsc.ieee.org/wg12/, accessed 2007). Educational materials encompass a broad spectrum of information object types and contents. There are *structural, functional,* and *production views* of educational resources depending on which field they are studied from (Qin and Hernández, 2006). The *structural view* reflects the way that educational institutions organize their academic programs, i.e., a curriculum consists of courses, a course contains lessons, a lesson includes sections, and so forth. It serves the needs of academic programs to deliver systematic knowledge and training in disciplines or subject domains. The *functional view* is closely related to instructional design and technology. Each unit of study assumes the role of a framework and encapsulates various objects such as learning objective, prerequisite, role (learner and staff), activity, and environment (Koper, 2001). The *production view* covers the form or format aspects of educational resources; it considers how learning objects are physically produced, i.e., dynamically assembled from multiple smaller media objects or otherwise static objects (Wiley, 2000). The production view also includes those objects grouped by media type and format: simulation applet, interactive illustration, animation, streaming audio/video, and interactive map. Educational materials can also be classified by *product form*, e.g., lecture notes, tutorial, and bibliography. The views summarized here influence metadata representation in different ways, and not all views receive equal attention.

2.3.1 Metadata Needs for Educational Resources

Metadata has become necessary for educational resources because of the unique characteristics of the materials, coupled with an increasing emphasis on digital libraries as resource repositories.

First, resources used in teaching and learning need to be described with education-specific attributes (Dublin Core Education Community, 2007). The most common need for metadata is to create a description of attributes that an educational resource normally possesses. An example: the National Science Digital Library (NSDL) is the United States' online library for education and research in science, technology, engineering, and mathematics. Its metadata records are harvested from many digital collections that mainly described their collections using a general purpose metadata format within the bounds of the DC 15 elements (although perhaps with different labels). It would be very helpful if these records also used additional elements for educational attributes such as *audience* and *educational-level* that NSDL supports. At present only a small portion of the records created outside of the NSDL have done so.

Second, a need exists for *repurposing* a general resource as an educational resource (Dublin Core Education Community, 2007). With the advancement of shared digital repositories, this type of use is attracting greater attention. Preliminary steps to the full use of digital collections in an educational setting have been experimented with (and implemented) at many educational institutions. The Alexandria Digital Earth Project (ADEPT) of the University of California Santa Barbara designed and created services so that instructors may take advantage of digital libraries to construct and use learning materials, particularly for undergraduate classes. The three sets of collections include (1) a set of knowledge bases for more than 1,000 scientific concepts; (2) a learning object collection (approximately 2,000 objects that include images, maps, figures, videos, and simulation models), and (3) a collection of reusable presentation materials such as courseware for lectures. These are integrated and made usable with the ADEPT Digital Learning Environment model and architecture (ADEPT, 2003; Smith, Zeng, and the ADEPT Project Team, 2004). Elements to describe the education-specific attributes are of great interest to a learning-oriented organization or community that uses the resource.

The third need is provision of shortcuts to determine usage appropriateness of educational materials. Many of the educational materials are complex aggregations; they are large , consist of multiple resources with varying media types, and have intra- and interrelationships. They also require a particular technology to support running, loading, and manipulation. They demand minimum minutes/hours for completion and have various levels of interactions. Most of them also retain distinct use and access rights. More important, they are created with different audiences in mind. A Mars observation project designed for middle school students will be very different from the one designed for astronomy major undergraduates. Before instructors download or execute an action for educational materials they must first determine whether this material is appropriate for attaining their classroom goals (with affordable time and technology). For these educational materials, distinct metadata records are important surrogates. Information obtained from metadata records thus becomes a necessary component in decision making. As a result, metadata records for leaning materials must describe *the resources*, as well as *the use* of the resources.

2.3.2 IEEE-LOM

The activities led by the IEEE Learning Technology Standards Committee (LTSC) demonstrate the mainstream standards for learning object metadata, and cover areas of learning technology, digital rights, meta-metadata, and structured definitions related to instruction. LOM possesses a strong functional view, as evidenced by the purpose statement of the LTSC LOM Working Group:

- To enable learners or instructors to search, evaluate, acquire, and utilize Learning Objects.
- To enable the sharing and exchange of Learning Objects across any technology supported learning systems.
- To enable the development of Learning Objects in units that can be combined and decomposed in meaningful ways.
- To enable computer agents to automatically and dynamically compose personalized lessons for an individual learner.
- To compliment [*sic*] the direct work on standards that are focused on enabling multiple Learning Objects to work together within an open distributed learning environment. (LTSC, 2004b)

LOM has a more complicated structure than many other schemas, and integrates descriptive, administrative, and technical metadata. It prescribes the metadata elements by dividing them into nine *categories* (i.e., groups of elements) that represent a learning object.

1. *General:* Elements include *identifier, title, language, description, keyword, structure, coverage,* and *aggregation level.* This category closely matches the descriptive metadata elements contained in the Dublin Core.

2. *Life cycle:* Contains *version, status,* and *contribute* (including *role, entity,* and *date*).
3. *Meta-metadata:* This is a special category related to how a metadata record is, in and of itself, created and managed. The elements include *contribute, identifier,* and *language* of the record (not of the learning object), and the metadata *scheme* used. LOM recommends using vCard information for the value space of the *contribute-Entity* subelement. If a metadata creator already has an e-business card, an identifier can be linked to it and eliminate unnecessary repetition of personal information entry.
4. *Technical:* This category contains important properties of a learning object in terms of how it can be operated with supporting technologies, e.g., the *requirement* for platform and software version to run a particular learning object, *installation remarks, format, size,* and *duration* (see Figure 2-3-1).
5. *Educational:* Elements of this category such as for *interactivity type, interactivity level, typical age range,* and *typical learning time* are very special and have attracted attention among developers of metadata standards and application profiles (see Figure 2-3-2). Elements such as *semantic density* and *difficulty* are useful, but cannot be present in implementations themselves because of the subjective nature of the judgments. LOM provides seven controlled term lists for the value spaces of these elements, e.g., for the element *intended end user role* suggested terms are "teacher, author, learner, and manager," and for the element *context* suggested terms are "school, higher education, training, and other."
6. *Rights:* The *DC:rights* element corresponds to this category except that the LOM elements provide more detail, which include *cost, other restrictions,* and *description.*
7. *Relation:* only two elements (*type* and *source*) form this category. The *source* element has three subelements: *identifier, description,* and *catalog entry.* Because of this detailed specification, LOM makes it possible to link descriptions made with other markup languages. For example, a URI or local address of a particular mathematics formula that is marked up with MathML (Mathematical Markup Language) can be linked to or inserted here, while *source* indicates the markup language standard used (see also Shreve and Zeng, 2003).
8. *Annotation:* Including *person information, data,* and *description.* This category enables educators to exchange information as a community of practice. This is the place for instructors to share their assessments of learning objects and make suggestions for use in their educational activities. It is also a very useful social computing element. Again, LOM recommends using vCard information for the value space of the *person* element, so as to associate the comment with the information about when, and by whom, the comments were created.
9. *Classification:* Although mapped to *DC:subject,* this category contains more complicated data than simply subject terms or keywords, and is a category that has always caused confusion among metadata creators (especially nonlibrary catalogers). The structure of this category has several hierarchical levels, as shown in Figure 2-3-3.

Figure 2-3-1. Technical-related metadata elements in LOM (generated using ALTOVA®'s XMLSpy® software with LOM XML Schema).

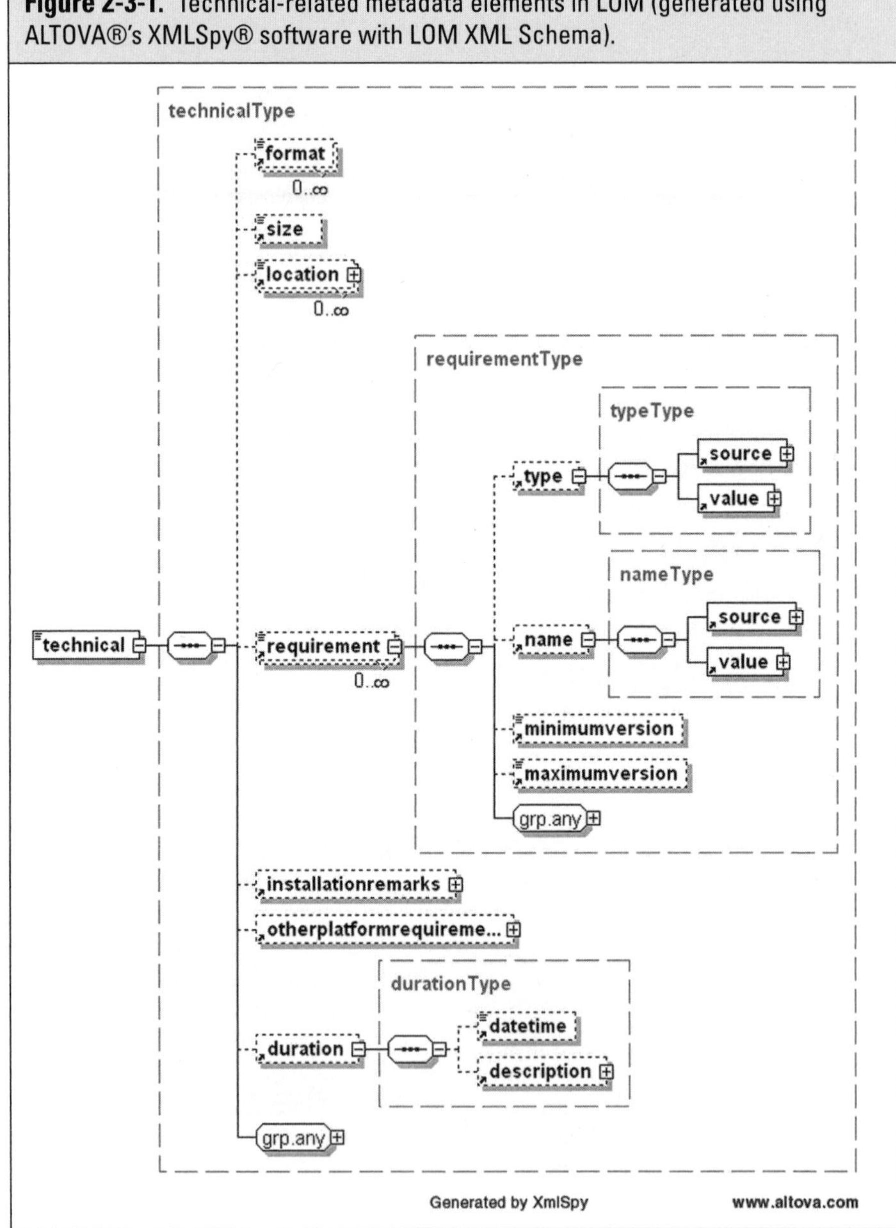

A list of suggested terms is provided for the first element of this classification category—*Purpose*—and includes "Discipline, Idea, Prerequisite, Educational Objective, Accessibility Restrictions, Educational Level, Skill Level, and Security Level." The second element is called *Taxon path*, which clearly intends to present a "taxonomic stairway" from a general level down to a specific entry in a

Figure 2-3-2. Educational-related metadata elements in LOM (generated using ALTOVA®'s XMLSpy® software with LOM XML Schema).

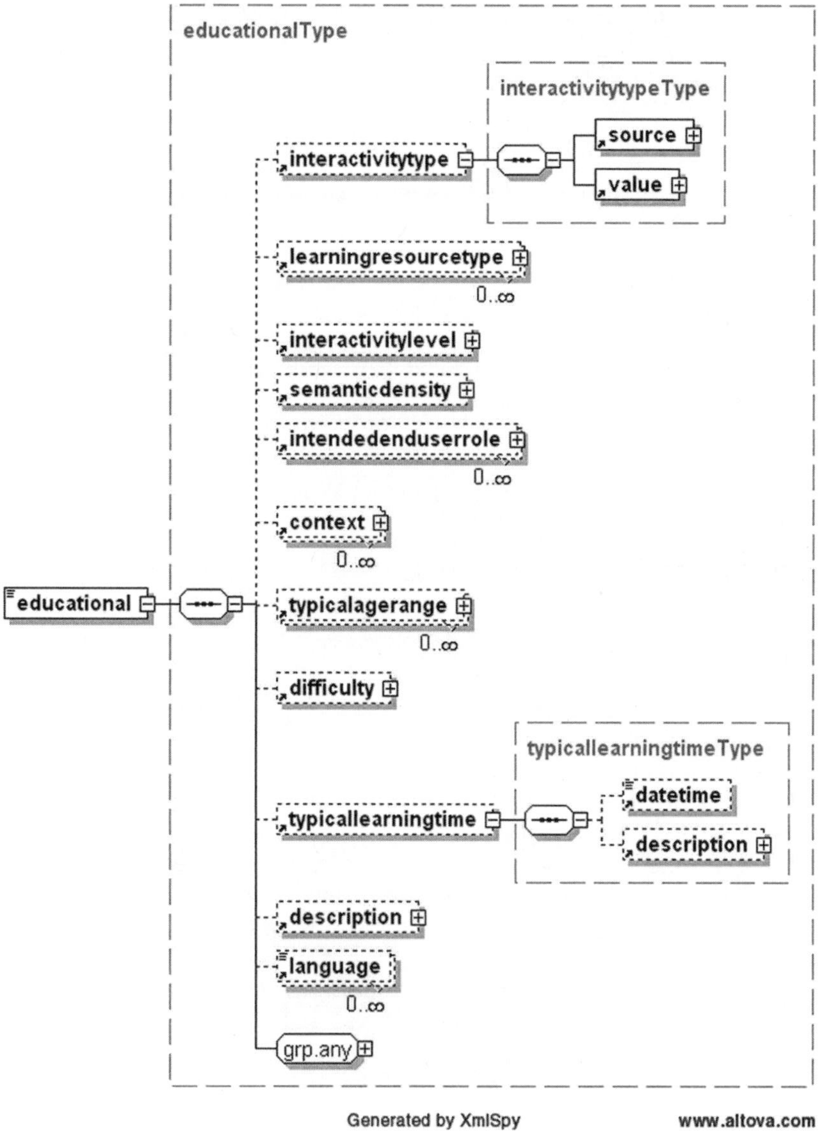

educationalType

interactivitytypeType

source

value

interactivitytype

learningresourcetype

0..∞

interactivitylevel

semanticdensity

intendedenduserrole

0..∞

context

0..∞

educational

typicalagerange

0..∞

difficulty

typicallearningtimeType

datetime

typicallearningtime

description

description

language

0..∞

grp.any

Generated by XmlSpy www.altova.com

classification. An example given by LOM demonstrates the taxonomical path, from physics to stethoscope: {["12" ("Physics")], → ["23" ("Acoustics")], → ["34" ("Instruments")], → ["45" ("Stethoscope")]} (LOM, 2002: 35). A taxon is a node that has a defined label or term. Here in ["12" ("Physics")], "12" is the identifier in the *ID* subelement, and the term "Physics" is the value associated

Figure 2-3-3. Subject-related metadata elements in LOM (generated using ALTOVA®'s XMLSpy® software with LOM XML Schema).

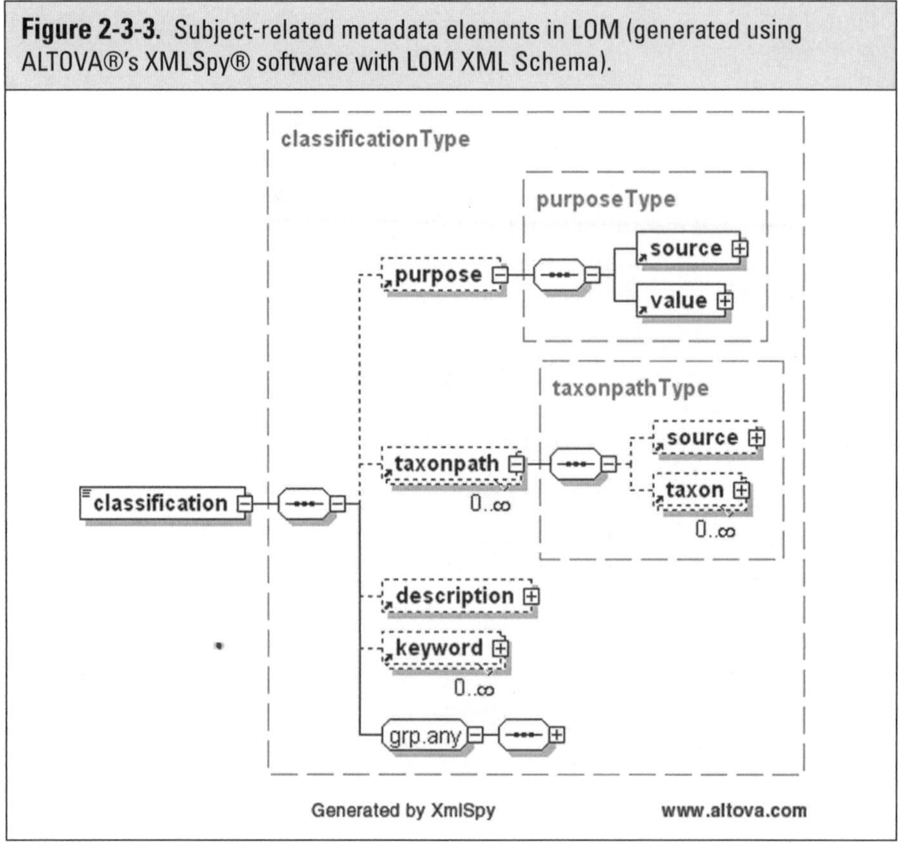

with the subelement *entry*. The *source* element gives the name of the classification system that these ID and terms elements were selected from. Additional elements, *description* and *keywords* are all used relative to the *purpose* element.

LOM demonstrates an important characteristic of learning object metadata: it not only *describes* an object but also describes *the use* of an object. The length specification of LOM categories, elements, and value spaces sometimes gives the impression that it is very difficult to implement, but in fact, the detailed notes, examples, and well-defined controlled vocabularies make LOM records creation easy to follow. The challenge lies in the decision of some subjective values, such as choosing a value to rank the difficulty of a leaning object as "very easy, easy, medium, difficult, and very difficult." CanCore, which is introduced in the next section, provides good guidelines on how to apply LOM.

2.3.3 CanCore

CanCore is a set of best practice recommendations. CanCore may also be considered an application profile that focuses on semantics and interpretation rather than on technical matters. CanCore and its guidelines emphasize refinement and explication rather than customization or modification, and have been intentionally developed to meet the needs of a broad range of communities (CanCore, 2004). In the *CanCore Guidelines for the Implementation of Learning Object Metadata* (Friesen, Fisher, and Roberts, 2002), for each category and the elements in a category, CanCore provides a table to present the usage of the elements in other application profiles, examples and explanations of applying the elements, and XML tagging examples.

Research related to IEEE-LOM and CanCore needs to be mentioned at this point. The education domain has been the most active in developing metadata application profiles. Friesen, Mason, and Ward (2002) studied The Le@rning Federation (TLF), (1) an application profile developed for Australian schools that is based on IEEE LOM, and (2) the LOM-based *CanCore Learning Object Metadata Application Profile* (CanCore) that was extracted from several federal and provincially sponsored e-learning projects. Their survey of the adoption of LOM elements in these two application profiles revealed two approaches to implementation. First, TLF uses a "unifying information models" approach to bring up the element definitions from both DC (a "flat" space) and LOM (a hierarchical space) to conform with ISO 11179 *Information Technology—Metadata Registries* (MDR) attributes (see also Chapter 6). Second, CanCore emphasizes data model explication and simplification through "combining best practices from existing data models, implementations and application profiles" and through "explicating its own normative decisions" (Friesen, Mason, and Ward, 2002).

Two more comprehensive surveys of LOM-based application profiles published in 2004 were studies about which elements in LOM were selected and how they were used (Friesen, 2004; Godby, 2004). Among other things, the educational elements were found to have been adopted by very few application profiles, which is ironic for a learning object metadata standard. Friesen states in his conclusions that "LOM structures make data portability difficult to realize using conventional and low cost technologies," and traditional authorship and publication elements are well utilized whereas elements specific for software development or instructional design teams are much less frequently used (Friesen, 2004). Godby's survey analyzed 35 LOM application profiles and examined the ratio between most and least commonly used recommended LOM elements. The study reveals that application profiles designed primarily for managing locally produced records include the most commonly recommended elements and support rich description while "meta-profiles" such as CanCore and UK LOM Core contain far fewer recommended elements because they are designed to promote interoperability among similar projects (Godby, 2004).

2.3.4 Gateway to Educational Materials (GEM) 2.0

Metadata researchers have been exploring ways of representing aspects of pedagogical functions and materials in metadata standards. The Gateway to Educational Materials (GEM) is an early metadata scheme that included the element *Pedagogy*, which has since been changed to *Instructional Methods* in

GEM 2.0 (GEM, 2004). The GEM Element Set v2.0 (http://64.119.44.149/schema/2002/08/15/gem#, accessed 2007) fully integrated the Dublin Core element set (DCMES) and qualifiers that are now included in DC Metadata TERMS. The DC 15 elements and other educational elements (*audience*, *instructionalMethod*, *provenance*, and *rightsHolder*) are parts of the GEM top elements. Four schemas (DC and GEM with both simple and qualified schemas) are combined into an application profile (www.thegateway.org/about/documentation/schemas/, accessed 2007). GEM 2.0 has a number of supplementary elements especially designed for handling educational materials:

- *Cataloging:* Information about the agency that created the GEM catalog record.
- *Essential Resources:* A brief, free-text listing of materials essential to the successful use of the entity by the teacher as stated in the entity being described.
- *Standards:* State and/or national academic standards mapped to the entity being described.
- *Pedagogy:* Denotes the student instructional groupings, teaching methods, assessment methods, and learning prerequisites of a resource. (Note: this element has been replaced by *dcterms:instructionalMethod* but still remains in the xml schema (http://64.119.44.149/schema/2002/08/15/gem#, accessed 2007).
- *Duration:* The recommended time or number of sessions needed to effectively use the entity being described.

Most of the GEM elements have qualifiers. The specification provides a detailed explanation of all elements, RDF and XML tagging examples, and a series of controlled vocabularies to be used for GEM value spaces.

2.3.5 Dublin Core Education Application Profile (DC-ED)

For the many projects that have already chosen to use DC instead of LOM, an extended DC application profile for educational resources would be beneficial. To respond to this need, a Joint DCMI/IEEE LTSC Taskforce has been working toward a combined DCMI/IEEE recommendation for using IEEE LOM Elements in Dublin Core metadata. A draft *Dublin Core Education Application Profile* (DC-ED AP, http://docs.google.com/View?docid=dn8z3gs_38cgwkvv) has gone through several revisions during the past few years. The DC-ED AP defines metadata elements used for describing properties of resources related to their use in teaching and learning. DC elements that are particularly important for describing educational resources, combined with selected LOM elements, form the element set of this application profile. Detailed annotations explain how and when the elements should be considered for use.

In compiling this application profile, the Taskforce noted the problems of conflicting terminology used to describe educational attributes of resources that may vary even within the same country using the same language. As a result, the DC-ED AP also suggests vocabularies for use and gives instructional notes on common situations when deciding on values in each element. The timeline of the Taskforce's working schedule is to submit the AP to the Usage Board for formal review by the 2008 midyear meeting (Dublin Core Education Community, 2007).

2.3.6 SCORM

Sharable Content Object Reference Model (SCORM), a compilation of technical specifications for Web-based e-learning, is a product of the Advanced Distributed Learning (ADL) Initiative (www.adlnet.gov/, accessed 2008) of the Office of the United States Secretary of Defense. One of the primary purposes of the SCORM standards is to define interoperability between *learning content* and *learning management systems* (LMS), which are the two essential software systems required to facilitate e-learning. LMS are usually responsible for directing the learner to relevant training, tracking the learner's progress (e.g. data regarding score and current location) and maintaining the learner's transcript. SCORM makes it possible for any content that conforms to the SCORM specifications to work with any SCORM conformant LMS, and therefore achieve interoperability. In answering the question "What does SCORM allow e-learning to do for learners?", the ADL Web site responds "SCORM allows for scalable, reusable, sharable course content; discoverable learning content (enables interoperable repositories); the ability to find and move entire courses; vendor support for SCORM conformant COTS [(commercial off-the-shelf)] products; and, the development of adaptive learning systems that can assemble content to meet the learner's needs 'on the fly'" (SCORM® General Common Questions, 2007: www.adlnet.gov/help/CommonQuestions/SCORMGeneralQuestions.aspx#qWhatIn, accessed 2007). In December 2004, the U.S. Department of Defense mandated that all its e-learning purchases must conform to SCORM standards. A flow chart of ADL Certification for SCORM (www.academiccolab.org/certification/scorm/process.pdf, accessed 2008) is provided by the Wisconsin Testing Organization, a joint ADL Department of Defense (DOD)—University of Wisconsin co-laboratory.

Thus SCORM is a collection of specifications adapted from multiple sources to provide a comprehensive suite of e-learning capabilities that enable interoperability, accessibility, and reusability of Web-based learning content. The SCORM 2004 (version 1.3.3) standard consists of five books, and collectively totals more than 1,000 pages.

- *SCORM Overview:* Introduces SCORM and describes how the other books are related.
- *SCORM Content Aggregation Model* (CAM): Describes the components used in a learning experience, how to package those components for exchange from system to system, how to describe those components to enable search and discovery and how to define sequencing rules for the components. The Content Packaging is designed to support any number of levels (e.g., Course, Chapter, Unit, and Learning Step).

- *SCORM Run-Time Environment* (RTE): Describes the Learning Management System (LMS) requirements for managing the run-time environment, i.e., content launch process, standardized communication between content and LMS, and standardized data model elements used for passing information relevant to the learner's experience with the content.
- *SCORM Sequencing and Navigation* (SN): Describes how SCORM conformant content may be sequenced to the learner through a set of learner-initiated or system-initiated navigation events, e.g., how learners can issue navigation requests, and how those requests are interpreted by a SCORM run-time environment.
- *SCORM Conformance Requirements:* Details the conformance requirements that are verified by the ADL SCORM conformance test suite. (SCORM® General Common Questions, 2007; SCORM Overview, 2006)

These books are available for download as PDF files from the ADL Web site (www.adlnet.gov/scorm/index.aspx, accessed 2007). Extensions to *SCORM 2004* have been made by other institutions and industries. The SCORM Runtime Wrapper Extension for Dreamweaver MX, for example, gives instructional developers the ability to quickly create or update HTML content so that it complies with ADL standards for the runtime environment (Adobe Systems, 2007). Some vendors have also integrated metadata generation editors into their products because the ADL has discontinued developing and maintaining the tool. The SCORM Conformance Test Suite is available to anyone who wishes to use it for self-testing. ADL has Co-Labs and partnership labs in various countries to support ADL implementations and test products provided by vendors.

As indicated at the beginning of this section, educational materials encompass a broad spectrum of information object types and contents. Because they can be viewed, focused on, emphasized, and used from structural, functional, and production views, the metadata standards designed for them tend to be complicated. Two things need to be kept in mind about the metadata for educational purposes: the needs for having the metadata for discovery purpose cannot be met by simply describing the contents of the learning objects; the description must also assist with the appropriate use and reuse of those objects. This specialized mission requires that these standards strive to provide sufficient technical and educationally useful metadata elements.

2.4 Archival and Preservation Metadata

This section highlights archival and digital preservation metadata that have received increasing interest within the associated communities. Archival metadata mainly exists and functions as finding aids in the archival domain, and requires special and collection-level information being recorded for the multiform archival groups of materials. The Encoded Archival Description (EAD) introduced in this section describes a finding aid and its composition. At the same time, as digital archiving becomes a logical part of the entire cyberinfrastructure, an increasing awareness of the challenges posed by digital preservation—long-term retention of digital objects—has underscored metadata needs for digital objects beyond resource discovery. This section briefly introduces both the models *and* activities that guide the development of digital preservation metadata.

2.4.1 The Encoded Archival Description (EAD)

Finding aids have existed in the forms of card indexes, calendars of correspondence, published repository guides, inventories, shelf and container lists, registers, or electronic records. They are created by archival and manuscript repositories to provide information about specific collections. Although they may vary in style, their common purpose is to provide detailed description of the content and intellectual organization that archival collections maintain.

EAD is a standardized markup language employed for the encoding schema(s) of finding aids for use within and across repositories in a networked environment. EAD has been in use in the archival community for more than ten years, beginning with its origin as a research project at the University of California Berkeley (UC Berkeley) in the mid-1990s (EAD Working Group, 2006). In the discourse of the archival community, an archival group (or record group) is an aggregate of items that *share a common provenance*. An archival group may contain various numbers and types of items. An item is an individual object or work, which may be composed of multiple components (CDWA, 2006: Object/Work—Catalog Level). Physically, these items may be stored in folders and boxes and must be sorted by series (multiple boxes), by box, by folder, and by other criteria. Finding aids are fundamental tools to facilitate discovery of information within such collections. Archival metadata need to reflect these physical features of material organization. EAD developers at UC Berkeley pursued and developed the standard that remains valid today:

1. Ability to present extensive and interrelated descriptive information found in archival finding aids.
2. Ability to preserve the hierarchical relationships existing between levels of description.
3. Ability to represent descriptive information inherited by one hierarchical level from another.
4. Ability to move within a hierarchical informational structure.
5. Support element-specific indexing and retrieval. (EAD Working Group, 2006)

EAD is a pioneer implementation of a generalized markup language into a metadata encoding standard for the library and archival community (see section 5.5 on markup languages). Originally conceived of as an application of SGML (Standard Generalized Markup Language) Document Type Definition (DTD) (1996 Beta version), EAD was made compliant with XML immediately upon the emergence of XML (Version 1.0, 1998: EAD DTD). The current version is EAD 2002 in which "[t]he entire suite of DTD and entity reference files was reengineered to meet the needs of XML and related technologies that are currently in use" (EAD Working Group, 2006: Section EAD 2000—www.loc.gov/

ead/eaddev.html). The standard is maintained in the Network Development and MARC Standards Office of the Library of Congress (LC), in partnership with the Society of American Archivists. Before further discussion of EAD elements and structures, it is helpful to review several examples of finding aids.

Figure 2-4-1 is a screenshot of a finding aid's opening section (Printer-Friendly version) taken from the National Library of Medicine (NLM) History of Medicine Division Web site. The left side box presents the structure of a typical finding aid, consisting of data categories of descriptive summary, biographical note, collection summary, index terms, administrative information, restrictions, other descriptive information, and series descriptions. On the right side, the *Descriptive Summary* contains a collection number, creator of the archival materials, dates of the archive, quantity of the physical collection, and an abstract. All these pertain to the content of the entire group of archival materials: the *Cornelius Rea Agnew Papers, 1857–1888*. However, it should be noted that at the top of this screen is a statement of explanation about who is responsible for the finding aids and who encoded the finding aid content. This is the meta-metadata, data about this finding aid's creation, not about the content of the resource.

Archival materials are typically stored and managed in boxes containing folders that hold one or multiple items. *Series Descriptions* reflects such a

Figure 2-4-1. A screenshot of a finding aid's opening section.

United States National Library of Medicine
National Institutes of Health

Return to Web Version

History of Medicine

Finding Aid to the Cornelius Rea Agnew Papers, 1857-1888

TABLE OF CONTENTS

Archives and Modern Manuscripts Program, History of Medicine Division

Processed by HMD Staff

Machine-readable finding aid encoded by Dan Jenkins

Descriptive Summary

Collection Number:	MS C 272
Creator:	Agnew, Cornelius Rea (1830-1888)
Title:	Cornelius Rea Agnew Papers
Dates:	1857-1888
Quantity:	1 linear foot
Abstract:	In 1866 Agnew established the eye clinic in the College of Physicians and Surgeons of New York, and from 1869 until his death he was Clinical Professor of Ophthalmology and Otology in that institution. The collection consists of four manuscript boxes of correspondence covering the period from 1857 to his death in 1888.

Source: Courtesy of the National Library of Medicine, www.nlm.nih.gov/hmd/manuscripts/ead/agnew.html, accessed 2007.

physical arrangement. The materials in this archival group are listed according to the boxes and folders of the resource location (Figure 2-4-2).

Figures 2-4-1 and 2-4-2 indicate that a finding aid is a single document describing a group of archival materials about persons, organizations, or events for the purposes of control and access. As a result, creating finding aids is not just about describing the resource. The task also involves the following:

- consolidating information about the collection, such as acquisition and processing;
- recording provenance information, including administrative history or biographical note;
- describing the scope of the collection, including size, subjects, media;
- organizing and arranging; and
- functioning as an inventory of the series and the folders.

By examining the overall structure of an EAD record (illustrated in Figure 2-4-3), all data elements in the outermost wrapper element *<ead>* can be divided into three large groups of categories: *<eadheader>* (EAD Header), *<frontmatter>* (Front Matter), and *<archdesc>* (Archival Description). Both *<eadheader>* and *<archdesc>* are required elements.

Figure 2-4-2. Three screenshots of the archival content from the finding aid at the National Library of Medicine, displayed in Figure 2-4-1.

Series Descriptions

Correspondence

Box	Folder	
1	1	Ab - Agnew
2	2	Agnew
1	3	Agnew?
1	4	Al - Ber
1	5	Bi - Bu
1	6	
1	7	
1	8	
1	9	
2	1	
2	2	
2	3	
2	4	
2	5	
2	6	
2	7	
2	8	
2	9	

Other

Box	Folder	
4	1	Cornelius Rea Agnew, A Memorial Add… , 1890
4	2	Documents (Agnew)
4	3	Programs, Invitations, Announcement
4	4	Documents
4	5	Code of Ethics Legislation Material
4	6	Legislation Material (Printed Matter)
4	7	Printed Matter (of note)
4	8	"In Memoriam"
4	9	Programs, Invitations, Announcement
4	10	Programs, Invitations, Announcement
4	11	Programs, Invitations, Announcement
4	12	Cards - Invitations
4	13	Cards - Invitations

Other Descriptive Information

Index of Correspondents

Abbe, Robert
Abbott, F.E.
Adams, John G.
Alexander H.M.
Allen, Charles M.
Allen, Johnathan
Allen, R.
Altman, B.
Andrew, George L.
Arnold, B.G.
Ashhurst, John
Ayres, S.C.
Baldwin, J.G.
Ball, A.B.
Barker, Fordyce
Bass, Edgar C.

Source: Composite from www.nlm.nih.gov/hmd/manuscripts/ead/agnew.html, accessed 2007. Courtesy of the National Library of Medicine.

The *EAD Tag Library* (EAD Working Group. 2002–2007) explains the semantics of each of the elements in the current EAD specification. All of the following explanations regarding the EAD tags are based on the *EAD Tag Library* (EAD Working Group, 2002–2007: www.loc.gov/ead/tglib/index.html).

- *<eadheader>* (EAD Header) is a wrapper element for bibliographic and descriptive information about the finding aid document rather than the archival materials being described. Four subelements are available, and must occur in the following order: required element <eadid> (EAD Identifier), required element <filedesc> (File Description), optional element <profiledesc> (File Description), and optional element <revisiondesc> (Revision Description). These elements and their subelements provide: (1) a unique identification code for the finding aid; (2) bibliographic information, such as the author and title of the finding aid; (3) information about the encoding of the finding aid; and (4) statements about significant revisions.
- *<archdesc>* (Archival Description) is another wrapper element for the bulk of an EAD document instance, which describes the content, context, and extent of a body of archival materials, including administrative and supplemental information that facilitates their use.
- *<frontmatter>* (Front Matter) is an optional element (as indicated by a dotted-line enclosed rectangle in Figure 2-4-3). It is also a wrapper element that bundles prefatory text found antecedently to the beginning of the Archival Description. It centers on the creation, publication, or use of the finding aid rather than information about the materials being described. Examples include a title page, preface, dedication, and instructions for using a finding aid.

An important feature of EAD is its multileveled descriptions. The general description is targeted to the collection as a whole, e.g., scope and contents of the collection and administrative information. The second level is for an individual series of groups of materials (series and subseries). The last level describes the individual files or items.

We turn to an introduction of the EAD attributes associated with most of the elements, e.g., the type attribute of the date in the *<unitdate>* element, encoded as:

```
<unitdate type="inclusive">1943-1978</unitdate>,
```

In other words, the metadata statement has a pattern of:

```
<[tag] [attribute]="[value]">
```

These attributes provide values for named properties ([attribute]="[value]") of an element (see record encoding in Chapter 5). More than one attribute may be used for a single element, as in the metadata statement followed by the encoding:

```
<[tag] [attribute1] "[value1]" [attribute2]="[value2]">
   <unittitle encodinganalog="MARC 245" label="Title:">
   Cornelius Rea Agnew Papers</unittitle>
```

Figure 2-4-3. A graphical presentation of the EAD structure.

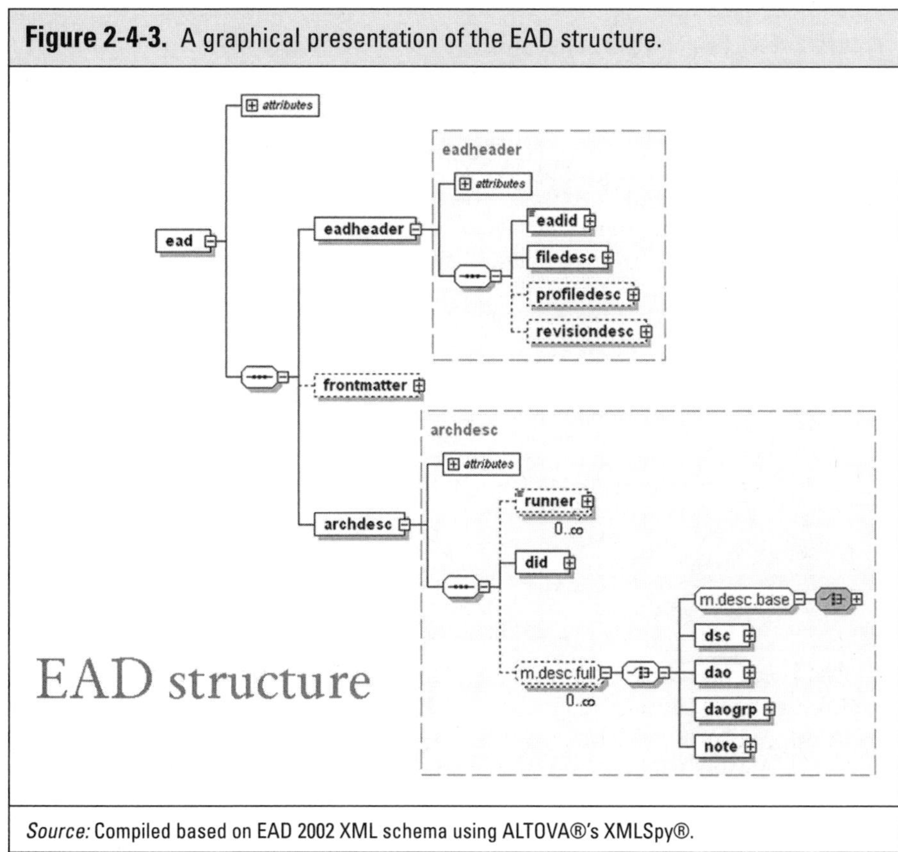

Source: Compiled based on EAD 2002 XML schema using ALTOVA®'s XMLSpy®.

It should be clear that the display on the screen in Figure 2-4-1 is based on the previous statement. This Title of the Unit (<unittitle>) has a label "Title," and so displays on the screen as:

Title: Cornelius Rea Agnew Papers

This example, in addition to other elements, such as <p> (paragraph), reveals that the EAD specification has mixed markups for both structure and display. These kinds of expressions have diminished, or the functions of tags have been clearly separated in recently developed XML schemas such as CDWA Lite and VRA Core 4.0.

An attribute can be associated with different elements. A list of allowed values may be predefined for different elements, e.g., for the *level* attribute used with <archdesc>, the allowed values are *class, collection, fonds, recordgrp, series, subfonds, subgrp, subseries,* or *otherlevel*. An attribute may be used with different elements. When the archival description element *<archdesc>* uses the *level* attribute, it identifies the character of the whole resource; when a <c> (Component) uses the *level* attribute, it identifies only the character of this component. In Figure 2-4-4, statements in each box indicate different values of *level*:

Figure 2-4-4. Examples of metadata statements under <archdesc> and <did> elements.

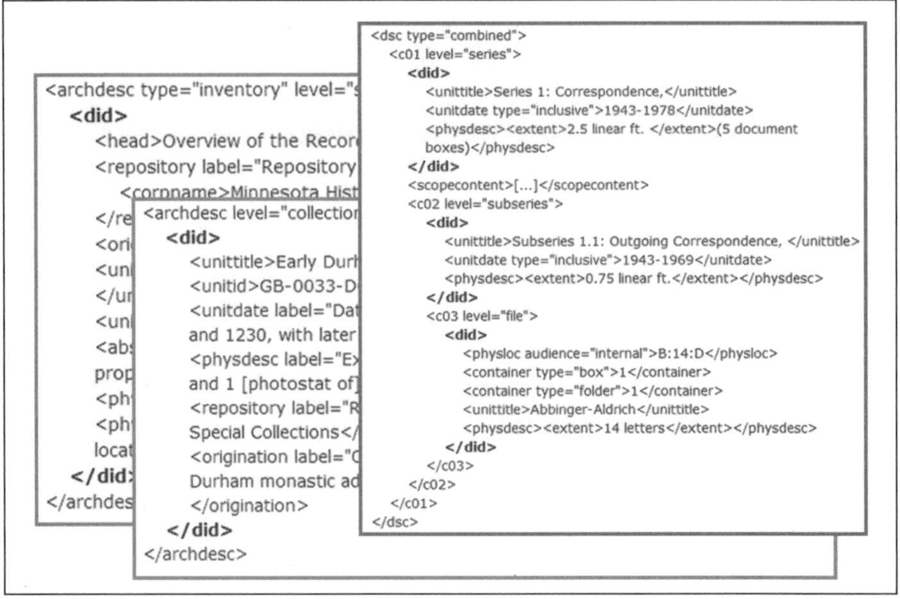

```
<archdesc type="inventory" level="s
   <did>
      <head>Overview of the Recor
      <repository label="Repository
         <corpname>Minnesota Hist
      </re
      <ori
      <un
      </ur
      <un
      <ab
      prop
      <ph
      <ph
      locat
   </did
</archdes
```

```
<archdesc level="collectio
   <did>
      <unittitle>Early Dur
      <unitid>GB-0033-D
      <unitdate label="Da
      and 1230, with later
      <physdesc label="E
      and 1 [photostat of]
      <repository label="R
      Special Collections</
      <origination label="C
      Durham monastic ac
      </origination>
   </did>
</archdesc>
```

```
<dsc type="combined">
  <c01 level="series">
    <did>
      <unittitle>Series 1: Correspondence,</unittitle>
      <unitdate type="inclusive">1943-1978</unitdate>
      <physdesc><extent>2.5 linear ft. </extent>(5 document
      boxes)</physdesc>
    </did>
    <scopecontent>[...]</scopecontent>
    <c02 level="subseries">
      <did>
        <unittitle>Subseries 1.1: Outgoing Correspondence, </unittitle>
        <unitdate type="inclusive">1943-1969</unitdate>
        <physdesc><extent>0.75 linear ft.</extent></physdesc>
      </did>
      <c03 level="file">
        <did>
          <physloc audience="internal">B:14:D</physloc>
          <container type="box">1</container>
          <container type="folder">1</container>
          <unittitle>Abbinger-Aldrich</unittitle>
          <physdesc><extent>14 letters</extent></physdesc>
        </did>
      </c03>
    </c02>
  </c01>
</dsc>
```

collection and *subgrp* for <archdesc>; *series* for <c01> (Component First Level), *subseries* for <c02> (Component Second Level), and *file* for <c03> (Component Third Level). Here *file* is a value that is not allowed for the *level* attribute in the <archdesc> element.

The example in the right side box of Figure 2-4-4 starts with a *<dsc>* (Description of Subordinate Components) element. This is a wrapper element that gathers the hierarchical groupings of the materials being described. The subordinate components can be presented in several different forms or levels of descriptive detail, which are identified by the element's required *type* attribute.

The *<did>* (Descriptive Identification) is a required wrapper element that groups elements that constitute a basic description of an archival unit. The various <did> subelements are intended as brief, clearly defined statements of information. This grouping ensures that the same data elements and structure are available at every level of description within the EAD hierarchy. It facilitates the retrieval or other output of a cohesive body of elements for resource discovery and visibility. The *type* attribute can be used to categorize the finding aid as an inventory, register, or other format.

A Component <c> provides information about the content, context, and extent of a subordinate body of materials. Components may be subdivided into smaller and smaller components and eventually reach the level of a single item, similar to the metadata statement in the <c03> section in the previous example. A component may be an unnumbered <c> or a numbered <c01>, <c02>, and so on. The *EAD Tag Library* lists up to a twelfth level of components (<c12>). The numbered components <c01> to <c12> assist a finding aid encoder to nest up to twelve component levels accurately. The <dao> (Digital Archival Object) and <daogrp> (Digital Archival Object Group) elements (not shown in the previous examples) allow linking to remote archival materials that are not part of the resource being described. These digital representations can be graphic images, audio or video clips, images of text pages, electronic transcriptions of text, and so on.

Creating finding aids is an intellectual-intensive process. The data encoding takes time, knowledge of archival materials, and extensive training to understand and apply EAD. To encode finding aids, one needs to first study how to describe archives. *Describing Archives: A Content Standard* (DACS) (Society of American Archivists, 2007) is a content standard that provides best practices guides and a set of rules mainly for describing archives, personal papers, and manuscript collections. Sometimes the use of EAD is a great burden for encoders. Working directly from an XML editor is always a challenge for finding aids content creators since they are not necessarily technologically savvy personnel. So selecting the right tool to do the encoding is imperative for creating more effective finding aids. The *EAD Cookbook 2002* (Society of American Archivists, 2004) provides practical, step-by-step assistance for the implementation of EAD. The Online Archive of California (OAC), a service of the California Digital Library (CDL) at the University of California, provides customized templates for generating collection through series/subseries-level finding aids that are compliant with EAD Version 2002. Therefore encoders do not then need to contend with XML tagging. Instead, they can input data directly into a form, or simply cut and paste segments of their non-EAD finding aids into the form. The form is then converted into a text file format and saved as an XML EAD file. The template program used to generate the encoding, which includes several sample templates, is available for downloading at the OAC Web site (www.cdlib.org/inside/projects/oac/toolkit/templates/, accessed 2007).

EAD header elements are Dublin Core and MARC compliant. The hierarchical structure of archival components also opens up opportunities for interoperability with the MODS or METS members of the MARC family. EAD is now the de facto international standard and has been adopted by archival communities around the world. The ability to integrate archival metadata with metadata from other domains is another reason that EAD is widely used.

2.4.2 Metadata for Digital Preservation

Information is now being produced in greater quantities and with greater frequency than at any time in history. The digital revolution has introduced new problems of obsolescence for software and hardware. In order to keep our documentary heritage available for future generations of users, large-scale programs need to be developed for its preservation. Technologically, digital preservation encompasses a broad range of activities designed to extend the usable life of machine-readable computer files and protect them from media failure, physical loss, and obsolescence. Digital preservation activities can be divided into three areas: (1) those that promote the long-term maintenance of a bitstream (zeros and ones); (2) those that provide ongoing accessibility of contents; and (3) those that ensure viability in terms of bitstream maintenance, indicating that information must remain intact (and readable) from the storage media, and this includes renderability (viewable by humans and processible by computers) and understandability (interpretable by humans). As these terms suggest, digital preservation deals with the issues of preserving a bitstream, but also aims to preserve the content, form, style, appearance, and functionality of an object. For the latter reason, metadata plays a critical role in the whole process of digital preservation.

Preservation metadata is the information infrastructure that supports all processes associated with digital preservation. More authoritatively, it is "the information necessary to maintain the viability, renderability, and understandability of digital resources over the long-term" (OCLC/RLG, 2004: 1). Preservation metadata addresses several key processes: an archived digital object's provenance (the custodial history of the object), authenticity, preservation activity, technical environment, and rights management. Metadata now functions beyond description of the resources. For scanned collections, metadata is necessary to record information about the digitization process; for born-digital resources and digitized resources, metadata is needed to document the preservation process, i.e., the actions taken to preserve the digital object, and any consequences of these actions that affect its look, feel, or functionality. Preservation metadata is used to document the attributes of digitized materials in a consistent way that makes it possible to identify the provenance of an item as well as the terms and conditions that govern its distribution and use (Rieger, 2007). Metadata will "help make an archived digital object self-documenting over time, even as the intellectual, economic, legal, and technical environments surrounding the object are in a constant state of change" (Lavoie and Gartner, 2005: 2).

Both the *Reference Model for an Open Archival Information System* (OAIS; ISO 14721) and *Preservation Metadata: Implementation Strategies* (PREMIS) are milestones for preservation metadata that are responding to the challenges of the digital age. PREMIS defines a "core" set of preservation metadata elements based on the OAIS information model. For that reason, OAIS needs to be introduced here.

The initiation of the OAIS Reference Framework was conceived to support the development of standards for the long-term preservation of digital information obtained from observations of terrestrial and extraterrestrial environments. NASA's Consultative Committee for Space Data Systems (CCSDS) Panel 2 coordinated the development of those standards. The OAIS Reference Model was approved as an ISO Standard in 2003 and also as a CCSDS Recommendation. "An OAIS is an archive, consisting of an organization of people and systems, that has accepted the responsibility to preserve information and make it available for a **Designated Community**" (CCSDS, 2002: 1 [emphasis in original]). This definition allows an OAIS archive to be distinguished from other domains associated with the term archive. In this reference model there is a particular emphasis on digital information, both as the primary forms of information held, and as the supportive information for both digitally and physically archived materials.

The achievements of OAIS include the establishment of a common framework of terms and concepts, the identification of the basic functions of an OAIS, and definitions of an information model. OAIS breaks "archiving" into a number of functional areas (e.g., *ingest, storage, access,* and *preservation planning*), defines a set of interfaces between the functional areas, and defines a set of data classes for use in archiving. Figure 2-4-5 provides an illustration of the functional entities that comprise the model (acronyms: Submission Information Packages [SIP]; Archival Information Package [AIP]; and Dissemination Information Packages [DIP]).

The OAIS model provides a conceptual foundation by including a taxonomy of information objects and packages for archived objects *and* the structure of their associated metadata (OCLC/RLG, 2005). OAIS has integrated terminology and views that are cross-disciplinary, particularly with traditional archivists, scientific data centers, and digital libraries. It takes into consideration preservation perspectives (media migration, compression, format conversions, and access service preservation) as well as archive interoperability. It addresses a full range of archival functions and is applicable to all long-term archival activities, organizations, and individuals working with information that may require long-term preservation. The OAIS categorizes information required for preservation as Content Information, Representation Information, Preservation Description Information (further divided into *Reference, Context,*

Figure 2-4-5. OAIS functional entities.

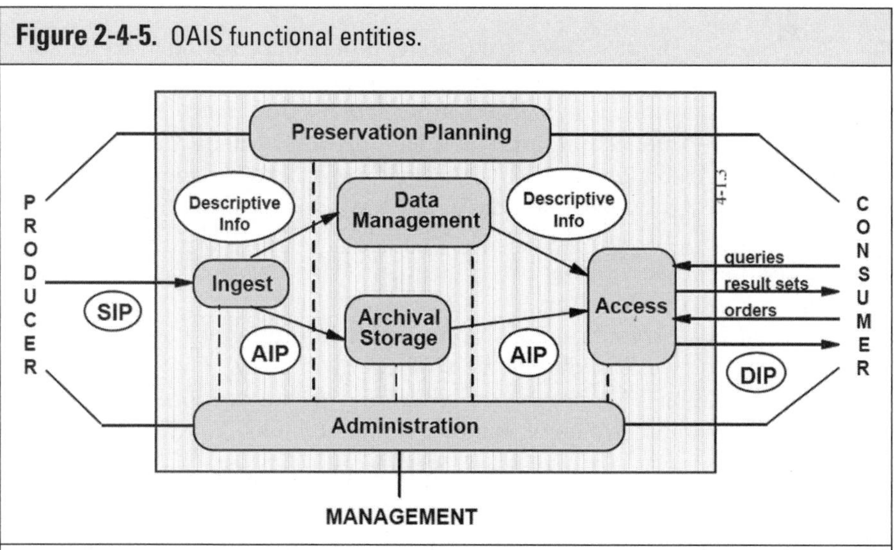

Source: Reprinted from CCSDS, 2002: 4-1, with permission from NASA Consultative Committee for Space Data Systems (CCSDS) Secretariat Office.

Provenance, and *Fixity Information*), and Packaging Information. However, although the OAIS Reference Framework has provided a high-level overview of the types of information needed to support digital preservation and established a basis for the development of additional related standards, it does *not* specify any implementation methods.

An implementation of the OAIS model is the *Preservation Metadata: Implementation Strategies* (PREMIS). PREMIS defines "preservation metadata" as the information a repository uses to support the digital preservation process (OCLC/RLG, 2005: ix). An international working group established by the OCLC and Research Libraries Group (RLG) first outlined the types of information that should be associated with an archived digital object in 2001–2002. Their report, *A Metadata Framework to Support the Preservation of Digital Objects* (OCLC/RLG, 2002) (simply referred to as the *Framework*), proposed a list of prototype metadata elements. Building on this, the PREMIS Working Group, convened by OCLC and RLG in 2003, conducted a worldwide survey of preservation repository implementations in the winter of 2003–2004 (OCLC/RLG, 2004). The *PREMIS Data Dictionary* version 1.0 and its supporting XML schemas were released in 2005. The *Framework* is regarded as an elaboration of the OAIS information model, explicated through the mapping of preservation metadata to that of the conceptual structure. The PREMIS work is viewed as a translation of the *Framework* into a set of implementable semantic units within the *Data Dictionary* (OCLC/RLG, 2005).

The PREMIS elements are to be used to record information that supports and documents the digital preservation process, and the information that supports the viability, renderability, understandability, identity, and authenticity of digital objects over time. Metadata elements are grouped and applied according to five entities defined in the *Data Dictionary* as:

1. "An *Object*, or Digital Object, is a discrete unit of information in digital form.
2. An *Intellectual Entity* is a coherent set of content that is reasonably described as a unit, for example, a particular book, map, photograph, or database. An Intellectual Entity can include other Intellectual Entities; for example, a Web site can include a Web page, a Web page can include a photograph. An Intellectual Entity may have one or more digital representations.
3. An *Event* is an action that involves at least one object or agent known to the preservation repository.
4. An *Agent* is a person, organization, or software program associated with preservation events in the life of an object.
5. *Rights*, or Rights Statements, are assertions of one or more rights or permissions pertaining to an object and/or agent." (OCLC/RLG, 2005: 1-1)

The dictionary provides comprehensive examples of metadata instances, including a Microsoft Word document complete in one file, an Electronic Thesis and Dissertation (ETD), a newspaper complex object, a Web site, a digital signature, and a photograph. The scope of this implementation-independent data dictionary needs to be given close attention and actively studied. PREMIS emphasizes recording digital provenance (the history of an object). Its features include the following characteristics:

- Descriptive metadata is out of scope.
- Metadata about Agents is limited.
- Technical metadata applies to all or most format types.
- Media or hardware details is limited.
- Business rules are essential for working repositories, but not covered.
- Includes information for preservation actions, not access.

The PREMIS XML schemas are maintained by the PREMIS Maintenance Activity, and hosted by the Library of Congress (www.loc.gov/standards/premis/, accessed 2007).

Preservation metadata incorporates a number of metadata categories, including *descriptive, administrative* (e.g., rights and permissions), *technical*, and *structural* metadata. Internationally, a number of large-scale digital preservation projects have attained significant achievements. Some of them also developed *technical metadata* data dictionaries. Related technical metadata standards for digital images include NISO's *Data Dictionary—Technical Metadata for Digital Still Images* (ANSI/NISO Z39.87-2006) and its further work with the LC Network Development and MARC Standards Office, *Metadata for Images in XML Standard* (MIX). Due to the complicated structures and elements, automatic metadata generation will be the key challenge for future preservation metadata work.

On the other hand, Rieger's report (2007) indicates that digitization processes of current large scale digitization initiatives (such as those being undertaken by Google, Microsoft, and the Open Content Alliance) often do not capture *structural metadata* tags, e.g., title page, table of contents, chapters, parts, errata, and index. The report suggests that it is important to include structural metadata in the definition and assessment of digital object quality. For example, checking the availability of structural metadata for complex materials such as multivolume books is critical in retaining the relationship information among multiple volumes.

In a network of heterogeneous digital archiving systems, throughout the digital information lifecycle, the sharing, reuse, and exchange of preservation metadata through standardized metadata creation (and internationally collaborated registries) can offer efficient, economical ways of acquiring and maintaining certain forms of preservation metadata (Lavoie and Gartner, 2005). PREMIS and other technical metadata standards also require technical support for implementation. The *Metadata Encoding and Transmission Standard* (METS), an XML schema designed specifically as an overall framework within which all the metadata associated with a digital object can be stored, will be a means to establish the essential link between archived content and the metadata that makes the content self-documenting through time. The METS Profiles that specify use of PREMIS have been developed by the LC and a number of university libraries (List available: www.loc.gov/standards/premis/premis-mets.html, accessed 2007). Most of the profiles have been approved by the METS Editorial

Board and registered with the Library of Congress, and include the contents covering Web site captures, recorded events, complex objects, and repository interoperability. METS is introduced in Chapter 5.

2.5 Rights Management Metadata

Rights management metadata is not a domain in itself. Although the recording of copyright-related information has often not been part of the cataloging tradition or metadata creation in libraries, museums, and archives (CDL Rights Management Group, 2006), it takes on a heightened importance in the digital age and Internet environment. Recording of copyright-related information has become essential to any digital collection and digital library project. This increased responsibility requires metadata creators to understand rights management metadata issues and best practices. Digital collections curators must meticulously review their rights to access, digitize, collect, and provide access to the selected works (i.e., distinct intellectual or artistic creations), and also properly inform users about their rights of use and reuse. Owners of digital collections and producers of works also need to protect their works' proprietary status and be able to convey and exchange rights information in a way that can be understood and processed by either human or machine. Rights metadata seen in this light plays a critical role in a process that occurs every minute all around the globe.

2.5.1 Rights Metadata Elements for User-oriented Rights Information

The first objective of rights management metadata in digital collections is to record user-oriented rights information in order to express factual information that allows users to make an informed copyright assessment of a given work. The second objective is to provide users with sources of further information about the copyright status, or indicate a person or institution that can be an authoritative agent for permissions (CDL Rights Management Group, 2006). Most of the metadata standards introduced in this chapter have included elements for such user-oriented rights information (as displayed in Table 2-5-1).

Additional core elements in these standards also function to register information about intellectual properties and assist the data provider and user to understand and comply with intellectual property laws or rights. Specific information suggested by Whalen (2008) include the name of the creator, including nationality, date of birth, and date of death (if applicable); title; date—the year the work was created; publication status; and, the date that rights research was conducted. Another objective of user-oriented rights management metadata is "to explicitly associate item-level copyright information with discrete digital objects, which enriches digital objects with copyright metadata at the point of creation, thereby preventing the creation of 'orphaned works' in the future" (CDL Rights Management Group, 2006: 1).

Table 2-5-1. Elements dedicated to rights information in selected metadata standards.

Standard	Category	Element	Subelements or refinements
DCMES		rights	accessRights license
DCTERMS		rightsHolder	
CDWA Lite		Rights for Work Rights for Resource	
LOM	6. Rights	6.1 Cost 6.2 Copyright & other restrictions 6.3 Description	
VRA Core 4.0		Rights	rightsHolder text
PBCore	18.00 pbcore-rightsSummary	18.01 rightsSummary	
MODS		accessCondition	

In practice, the *copyrightMD,* an XML schema for rights metadata (see www.cdlib.org/inside/projects/rights/schema/, accessed 2007) developed by the California Digital Library (CDL) Rights Management Group, sets a good example for presenting user-oriented rights information (Figure 2-5-1). The schema is designed for incorporation with other metadata standards for descriptive and structural metadata (e.g. CDWA Lite, MARC XML, METS, and MODS). These metadata are different from those intended for internal management purposes that instead serve as a recordkeeping mechanism for information such as donor agreement information and copyright permission request histories that are collected and gathered by institutions.

2.5.2 Rights-holder Communities' Metadata Activities

In the present digital age, traditional rights management of materials that have benefited from the materials' physicality faces serious new challenges because of the ease with which digital files can be accessed, copied, and transmitted. The activities of the Digital Rights Management (DRM) directly addresses the serious concerns of the content communities in a pragmatic series of project developments, and ". . . it is important to note that DRM is the 'digital management of rights' and not the 'management of digital rights.' That is, DRM manages *all* rights, not only the rights applicable to permissions over digital content" (Iannella, 2001 [emphasis in original]).

Figure 2-5-1. Subelements of <copyright> element defined by the *copyrightMD* schema.

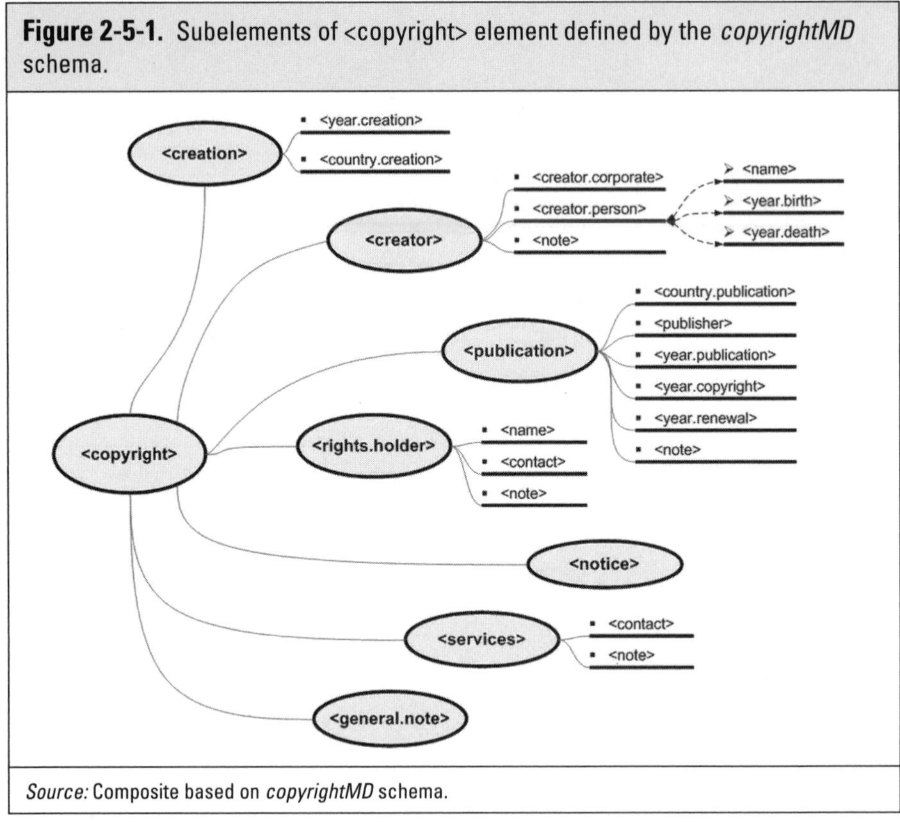

Source: Composite based on *copyrightMD* schema.

Rights-holder communities have initiated large-scale projects addressing metadata issues during the past decade. According to Iannella (2001), the first-generation of DRM focused on security and encryption as a means of resolving the issue of unauthorized copying. The second-generation of DRM expanded to cover the description, identification, trading, protection, monitoring, and tracking of *all forms* of rights usages over both tangible and intangible assets (including the management of rights holders' relationships). Among the many activities central to DRM, the <indecs> has developed as a conceptual model that guides the development of practical rights metadata schemes. Open standards such as Uniform Resource Identifiers (URI), Digital Object Identifiers (DOI), and the ISO International Standard Textual Work Code (ISTC) are typical schemes useful for rights identification. In the following, the <indecs> metadata framework and related standards DOI and ONIX (ONline Information Exchange) are introduced as examples of such initiatives.

2.5.2.1 The <indecs> Metadata Framework

The <indecs> is an acronym for ***in**teroperability of **d**ata in **e**-**c**ommerce **s**ystems* and is goal oriented toward finding practical solutions to interoperability issues affecting all types of rights-holders in a networked e-commerce environment

(<indecs>, 2000). The <indecs> metadata framework encompasses (1) a metadata model, (2) a high-level metadata dictionary, (3) principles for mappings to other schemas, and (4) a Directory of Parties. The most important influence exerted by the <indecs> is its four guiding principles, which the metadata framework is built upon. For the development of "well-formed" metadata to support effective e-commerce it must follow:

> **The principle of Unique Identification**
> Every entity should be uniquely identified within a unique namespace.
> **The principle of Functional Granularity**
> It should be possible to identify an entity whenever it needs to be distinguished.
> **The principle of Designated Authority**
> The author of an item of metadata should be securely identified.
> **The principle of Appropriate Access**
> Everyone requires access to the metadata on which they depend, and privacy and confidentiality for their own metadata from those who are not dependent on it. (<indecs>, 2000: 4)

The <indecs> takes into account three distinct but overlapping views of entities—a *general view*, and then within that a specific *commerce view* and *intellectual property view*. These three views enable the description of the principle metadata as it relates to e-commerce concerns (Rust and Bide, 2000). Nearly 400 data elements are listed in the tabular Framework Basic Metadata Dictionary, each one assigned a unique numeric <indecs> identifier, called iid (see Rust and Bide, 2000: 40-48).

The <indecs> project's main achievement is its conceptual model. Built upon and extending it, several <indecs> participants have developed specific <indecs>-based XML data interchange formats or schemas. EDItEUR, an international group for electronic commerce in the book and serials sectors, has produced the ONIX specification. The <indecs> 2RDD Consortium (http://xml.coverpages.org/indecs2rdd.html, accessed 2007) has developed a multimedia Rights Data Dictionary that has been adopted by MPEG-21 as the baseline technology for the new MPEG-21 rights data dictionary standard. The International DOI Foundation (IDF) developed the DOI.

2.5.2.2 DOI (Digital Object Identifier)

The DOI (Digital Object Identifier) is an umbrella term for a set of related initiatives centered on a persistent digital identifier (the DOI), a technology (managed by the Corporation for National Research Initiatives [CNRI]), and an organization (the International DOI Foundation [IDF]) (Rust, 1998; IDF, 2007). The *DOI* System is designed for the identification of content objects in the digital environment. Information about a digital object, including where to find it, may change over time—a journal article that was once available on the Web might be "moved" on a server; therefore the URL that previously worked would lead to a dead end. URLs generated by systems on demand, such as the URL of an article found in a bibliographic database, cannot precisely represent the article's location. In this situation, if the article had a persistent digital identifier it would not matter where or if it had been moved; it could be located. The DOI System is centered on the DOI—an identifier consisting of a *prefix* and a *suffix* that is separated by a *slash* (e.g., 10.1045/june2006-zeng). So with an assigned DOI name, any entity will have a persistent digital identifier and therefore can be found with its current information, including where it (or information about it) can be located on the Internet. To illustrate this in practice one may go to the DOI Web site (www.doi.org/, accessed 2007) and type or paste a DOI name (e.g., 10.1045/june2006-zeng) into the text box below "Resolve a DOI Name!" at the bottom of the page. The browser will immediately be redirected to the site of the resource associated with the DOI.

The full DOI element set for metadata is described by Paskin and Rust (1999), and is applicable for any creation. It contains 14 high-level elements (see Figure 2-5-2). These elements form a specific application of the <indecs> generic data model. Twelve elements are direct attributes of the creation, one is a related entity, *Event*, about the making or use of the creation, and the last is a *Creation link* to another creation (Paskin and Rust, 1999).

In this 1999 document, seven of the 14 form the *DOI Resource Metadata Kernel Declaration* (DOI Kernel) metadata set. The DOI® Kernel is the IDF's standard for a minimal public declaration of metadata to enable the simple discovery and

Figure 2-5-2. DOI elements.

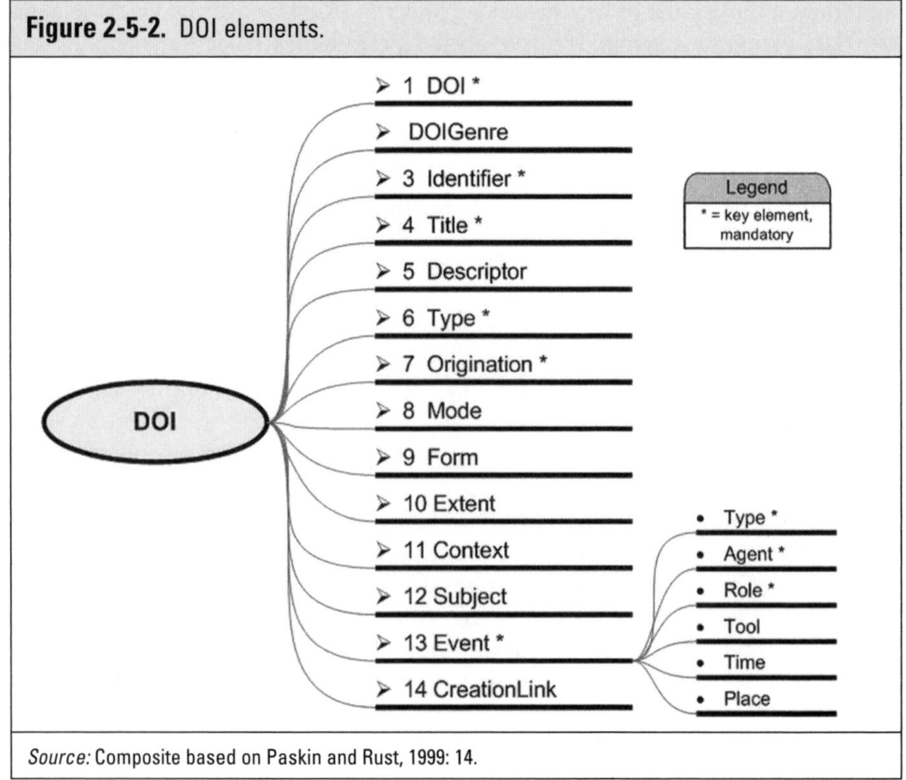

Source: Composite based on Paskin and Rust, 1999: 14.

disambiguation of created resources identified with a DOI name, formally specified in an XML schema (IDF, 2006a). The current version (9.0) *DOI Kernel Declaration* includes 11 elements: three administrative elements about the issuing of the DOI name and the Kernel itself: *registrationAgency, issueDate,* and *issueNumber*. Others include *resource, DOI name, resourceIdentifier, structuralType, mode, resourceType, resourceName,* and *principalAgent*. Among the elements, *structuralType* answers the question of whether a resource is a physical fixation, a digital fixation, a performance, or an abstract work; *mode* explains how it is perceived—audio, visual, audiovisual, or abstract. Some of the elements (e.g., *structuralType* and *mode*) have a prescribed set of allowed values that all Registration Agencies (RA) must recognize. Value sets created by RA for other elements and subelements must be registered in the data dictionary (iDD) for mapping purposes. The Kernel ensures that a basic set of interoperable, descriptive metadata exists so that DOI names can be discovered and disambiguated across multiple services and application profiles in a coherent way (IDF, 2006b).

2.5.2.3 ONIX (ONline Information Exchange)

EDItEUR (www.editeur.org/, accessed 2007) is an international group for electronic commerce in the book and serials sectors, and the developer of the *ONline Information EXchange* (ONIX), (www.editeur.org/onix.html, accessed 2007), a set of standards that publishers can use to distribute electronic information about their products to wholesale, e-tail and retail booksellers, other publishers, and anyone else involved in the buying and selling of books.

ONIX is a family of XML formats for communicating rich metadata about books, serials, and other published media, using common data elements, "composites," and code lists. The ONIX standard defines both a list of data fields about a publication and how to send that data in an "ONIX message." This ever-growing family already has a number of standards being released and used in the world, and additional activities such as embedding licensing terms within ONIX are also developing.

- *ONIX for Books* is the most widely used format and has already released its 3.0 version in 2006 and continues to add supplementary parts.
- *ONIX for Serials* has been developed in collaboration with the American standards organization NISO (the National Information Standards Organization). Three sets of application messages have been or are being defined and piloted:
  —SOH (serial online holdings) format
  —SPS (serial products & subscriptions) format
  —SRN (serial release notification) format
- *ONIX for DOI Registration* is a collection of DOI name registration formats that allows publishers and others to communicate the metadata required by a Registration Agency (RA) when recording the assignment of a DOI name.
- *ONIX for Licensing Terms* enables the expression of licensing terms in a standard XML format, links them to digital resources, and communicates them to users.

These formats have benefited libraries as well as publishers. Librarians have become able to automate the check-in and check-out phases of online (and paper) resources, assist in holdings management, and aid discovery and comparison of the range of offerings available. Cataloging and bibliographic agencies benefited from reduced loads of basic metadata harvesting and are able to speed up the process of assigning identifiers such as ISSN (International Standard Serial Number) and DOI.

2.5.3 Open Digital Rights Language (ODRL)

The Open Digital Rights Language (ODRL) is different from other digital rights management systems because the ODRL has no license requirements and is available as open source software. Intended to provide flexible and interoperable mechanisms to support transparent and innovative use of digital content in publishing, distributing, and consuming of digital media across all sectors and communities, the ODRL Version 1.1 was released as a W3C Note in 2002 (W3C, 2002, www.w3.org/TR/odrl/). Because of its open source status (free and non-proprietary), digital collections and digital libraries have been using it despite it not being a formal W3C Recommendation. Tools created for metadata generation, e.g., the *eduSource Repository-In-A-Box (eRIB) Suite of Tools* designed for generating LOM metadata records *Category 6 Rights* metadata (following CanCore guidelines), have plugged in this software to integrate rights metadata.

ODRL is based on an extensible model for rights expressions that involves a number of core entities (*assets, rights,* and *parties*) and their relationships. According to Version 1.1:

- The *Assets* include any physical or digital content.
- The *Rights* include *Permissions*, i.e., the actual usages or activities allowed over the Assets (e.g. allowed status of playing a video Asset), which can then contain *Constraints*, *Requirements*, and *Conditions*.
  —*Constraints* are limits to these *Permissions* (e.g. allowing play of a video for a maximum of five times).
  —*Requirements* are the obligations needed to exercise the *Permission* (e.g. required $5.00 payment each time a video is played).
  —*Conditions* specify exceptions that if true, immediate expiration of the *Permissions* occurs and renegotiation may be required (e.g. if a credit card expires then all Permissions are withdrawn to play a video).
- The *Parties* include end users and *Rights Holders*.
  —End users are usually the asset consumers.
  —*Rights Holders* are usually parties that have played some role in the creation, production, and distribution of the *Asset* and can therefore assert some form of ownership over the *Asset* and/or its *Permissions*.
- With these three core entities, the foundation model can then express *Offers* and *Agreements*.
- The model can also express the *revocation* of any Offers or Agreements (*Revoking Rights*).

- Most entities in the model can support a specific *Context*, which is relative to the entity, and can describe further information about that entity (or the relationship between entities).

Most recently, IEEE released its *IEEE Trial-Use Recommended Practice for Digital Rights Expression Languages (DRELs) Suitable for eLearning Technologies* (IEEE 1484.4-2007). This recommended practice facilitates the creation, management, and delivery of digital content for eLearning by technology that implements digital rights expression languages (IEEE, 2007).

ODRL, <indecs>, DOI, and other rights metadata initiatives share common characteristics that include international, multisector, multilingual, multimedia resources, and multiple communities. They usually are built on the many metadata standards developed and implemented by the diverse communities described throughout the text. A final notable characteristic is that instead of a flat or hierarchical structure (upon which most metadata schemas are modeled), rights metadata initiatives have more complex networked structures in which entities depend upon, are supported by, and interact with other entities.

2.6 Scientific Metadata

The purpose of this section is to briefly discuss the needs and activities related to scientific metadata standards. Due to their complexity and diversity, it is impossible to give an in-depth analysis to any one standard that might represent characteristics of standards designed for highly specific and different scientific domains. The following discussion demonstrates the needs for sufficient metadata, and not only for keeping all kinds of digital objects usable, but also for ensuring adequate (and legal) access and retrieval over the duration across all scientific data scales As digital curation is gaining more and more attention, the demand for metadata experts who have domain knowledge will dramatically increase. The discussion about research trends in Chapter 9 also confirms such a call in the current cyber-infrastructure development in the United States.

The past 30 years witnessed an exponential growth in the volume and complexity of scientific data. The terabyte (1 TB = 1024^4 bytes) and petabyte (1 PB = 1024^5 bytes) scales of scientific data create tremendous challenges for managing, storing, and accessing datasets. Scientific metadata in the context of this data is "all the information, additional to the raw data itself, which a potential user of the data would need to know to be able to make full and accurate use of the data in a subsequent scientific analysis. . . . [Scientific data are referred to as] the raw data that have been collected or generated in many ways, such as by measurement or observation of the environment, by carrying out an analytical experiment or by running a computer simulation" (Sufi and Mathews, 2004: 4). Part of such information is found within the origins and processing history (also called "lineage") of data objects and processes. These are critical for protecting potential data consumers from unintended consequences resulting from misinformation or mistaken assumptions about data collection methods, measurement precision, or scale (Bose and Frew, 2005).

User demand for information is expanding across the disciplines and is keeping pace with the growth of available scientific data. Geospatial data, for example, is generated by satellite imaging and may be utilized for land management and urban planning. Mercury emissions and contamination data may provide support for determining and implementing public health policies. Efforts to meet these demands raise complex questions and issues for cataloging, indexing, preserving, curating, and controlling access to scientific data and information; tremendous opportunity (and hard work) is created for those involved in metadata development and application. Since the size and scale of scientific data and information is often measured in gigabytes or terabytes, finding relevant data in massive distributed repositories (and using them properly) can become a daunting task for both expert and nonexpert users. Skillful creation of metadata therefore becomes extremely critical in order to facilitate data discovery, sharing, management, and preservation.

Scientific metadata standards began as early as 1993, when the first IEEE Meta-Data workshop was held at the Center for High Performance Computing in Austin, Texas. The workshop was inspired by clear-cut needs and still-pending broad, long-term solutions: (1) establishing selective/intelligent access to large amounts of data stored anywhere and in any form; (2) managing large amounts of data intelligently and easily; (3) exchanging data between heterogeneous organizations and systems; and (4) defining abstract data types and structures (Meta-Data Working Group, 1993). The group came to a consensus that metadata is information about the stored information entities that consists of semantic content, structural mapping to storage, type and encoding of elements, relationships among entities, format, structure, type, related data, and inferential/derived data. Metadata should also provide stored and accessible records for administration purposes as well as permissions, usage, and information history of the resource. The Meta-Data Workshop later turned into an annual Meta-Data Conference and has continued to convene almost every year since then.

An important goal of scientific metadata is to provide a complete description of datasets and services for discovery, preservation, and use. This seemingly simple goal, however, suggests manifold requirements for the kinds and types of scientific metadata (reflective of the differences between the disciplines). For data management, scientific metadata must support the preservation of data history, assessment of data age and character, and provide information about data liability and accountability. In data discovery, metadata describes themes and attributes, spatial and temporal coverage of data, and also data processing methods, data contributors, and data quality. These requirements determine the level of complexity of scientific metadata. One early standard used (and still used at present) by the *Global Change Master Directory* (GCMD) of the National Aeronautics and Space Administration (NASA) was the *Directory Interchange Format* (DIF) (Global Change Master Directory, 2007). DIF describes information about datasets and services and incorporates elements from the *Content Standard for Digital Geospatial Metadata* (FGDC, 1998). It contains three types of elements—required, recommended, and optional. The required elements include basic information necessary for identifying a dataset or data service whereas the recommended data fields cover the domain-specific description of the dataset or data service, such as instrument, platform, temporal coverage, spatial coverage, data resolution, quality, and revision history. The optional metadata elements in DIF serve more general functions for data and metadata management. Each of these 35 data fields expands into one or more elements in XML format.

The complexity of scientific metadata is reflected in the highly recognized *Content Standard for Digital Geospatial Metadata* (CSDGM), first released in 1994 and then revised in 1998. It has 334 different elements, of which 119 exist only to contain other elements (USGS, 2006). The standard divides the 300 plus elements into seven categories: *identification, data quality, spatial data organization, spatial reference, entity and attribute, distribution*, and *metadata reference* information (see Figure 2-6-1). These are top-level compound elements of the standard. A *compound element* is a group of *data elements* and other compound elements. All compound elements are described by data elements, either directly or through intermediate compound elements. "Compound elements represent higher-level concepts that cannot be represented by individual data elements" (FGDC, 1998: vii). CSDGM requires that *identification* and *metadata reference* information be mandatory, whereas others are mandatory-if-applicable. It is noteworthy that mandatory data elements may exist in a mandatory-if-applicable compound element or an optional data element may exist in a mandatory compound element. For example, *identification* information is a mandatory compound element in CSDGM, but in this category about half of the data elements are optional. Similarly, *data quality* is a mandatory-if-applicable compound element and has three data elements that are mandatory, two mandatory-if-applicable, and one optional.

In addition to those compound elements subsumed under the *Metadata* "parent" compound, there are three other special compound elements: *Citation Information, Time Period Information*, and *Contact Information*. These sections provide information used by other sections of the metadata standard (but otherwise never used in isolation). Adding to such complexity is the need for scientific metadata standards to be interoperable with other standards. CSDGM as a standard for geospatial data faces great challenges in representing interdisciplinary datasets in the forms of images and numerical data that might be coded by domain-specific formats. To address such challenges, CSDGM version 2 adopted extensions for remote sensing metadata that include elements for remote sensing platforms and sensors. It also endorsed two profiles, the *Biological Data Profile* (1999) and the *Shoreline Metadata Profile* (2001). The inclusion of these two profiles enhanced the description capabilities for "data that are not explicitly geographic (laboratory results, filed notes, specimen collection, research reports) but can be associated with a geographic location" (FGDC, 2007: www.fgdc.gov/metadata/geospatial-metadata-standards).

At the international level, ISO developed and approved an international geospatial metadata standard: ISO/TS 19115:2003 *Geographic information—Metadata*. Its element model applies broadly to scientific data in geospatial, biological, biodiversity, ecological, environmental, coastal management, and many other fields. The metadata elements in ISO19115 structure the elements through a core element set including seven mandatory (*dataset title, dataset*

Figure 2-6-1. CSDGM (Version 2 1998)'s top-level compound elements.

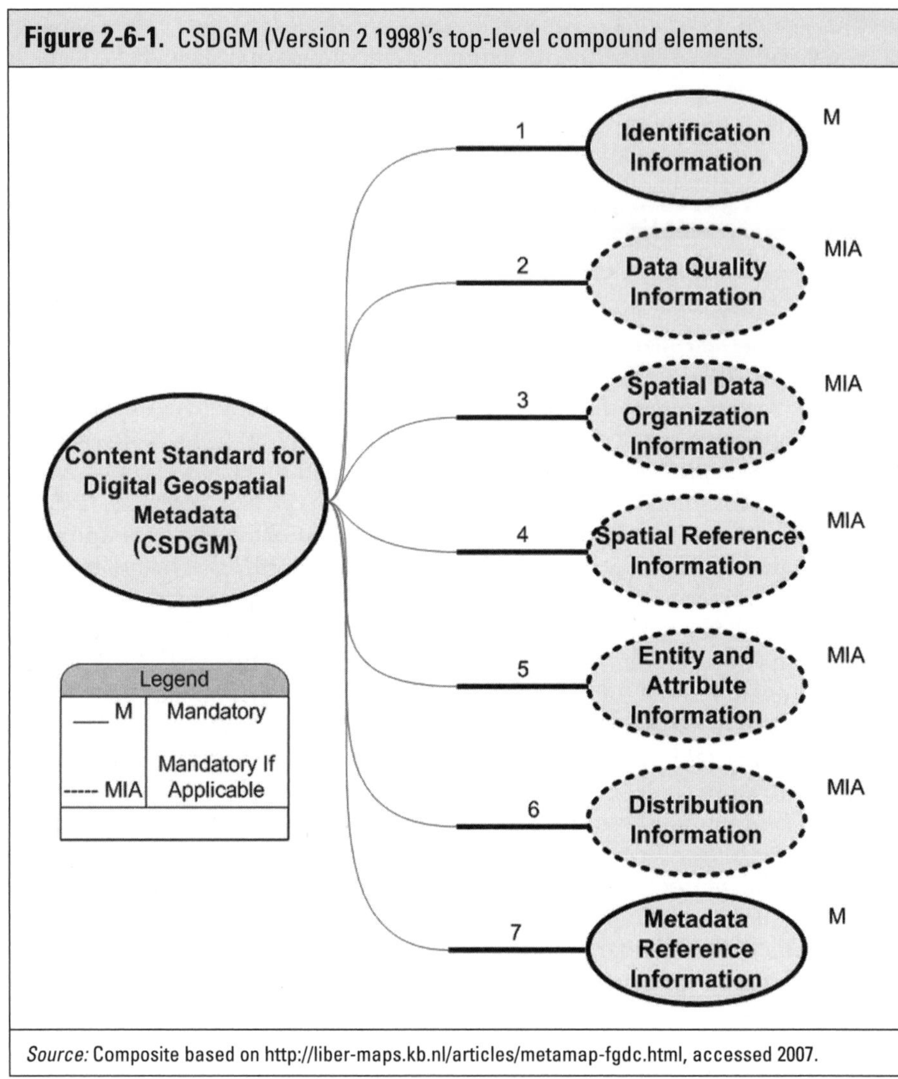

Source: Composite based on http://liber-maps.kb.nl/articles/metamap-fgdc.html, accessed 2007.

reference date, dataset language, dataset topic category, abstract, metadata point of contact, and *metadata date stamp*) and 14 conditional elements. The *dataset topic category,* one of the seven mandatory elements, contains 19 high-level subject categories that will quickly sort and access thematic information (FGDC, 2006). In light of these factors, the United States and Canada have agreed to revise their respective metadata standards to develop a common profile for ISO19115 to enhance interoperability of geographic information metadata in North America (NAP Metadata Working Group, 2007).

The landscape of scientific metadata appears to be heavily dominated by geospatial metadata standards. Hill (2006) has written an excellent book about georeferencing, and reviews the georeferencing elements included in metadata standards (in addition to those already outlined), which are: MARC, Dublin Core, Electronic Cultural Atlas Initiative (ECAI), Darwin Core, Digital Library for Earth System Education (DLESE) ADN Metadata Framework, and MODS. Hill points out, however, that the standards developed in the GIS community are highly complex and therefore inaccessible for general cataloging and indexing purposes, even at the level of the core element sets of the FGDC and ISO standards.

Other more specific metadata schemas or proposals dot the landscape within limited territories, e.g., the *NetCDF Climate and Forecast (CF) Metadata Convention* (Eaton et al., 2003). The CF conventions define metadata that provide a definitive description of data representation in each variable, and of the spatial and temporal properties of the data. CF is a standard for *use metadata.* It is different from *discovery metadata* in two major respects: (1) metadata is used at the time the data is processed and displayed; and (2) rather than identify datasets, the purpose of CF is to distinguish quantities (e.g., physical description, units, prior processing) and to locate the data in space-time and as a function of other independent variables (coordinates). As a result, CF provides only rudimentary discovery metadata, such as methods to record where and how a file is produced (Gregory, 2003).

Metadata as an important solution for scientific data management has been both widely accepted and actively explored. Metadata has been created for scientific data and information in many disciplines and cross-disciplines, including geographic data (Hill et al., 1999; Goodchild and Zhou, 2003), biodiversity data (Wiser et al., 2001), ecological data (Jones et al., 2001), and medical documents (Malet et al, 1999). Chervenak et al. (2000) propose a metadata service in which three categories of metadata will be needed to perform different functions: (1) *application metadata* that describes information content represented by data files, circumstances under which the data were obtained, and other information related to applications; (2) *replica metadata,* which maps data file instances to particular storage system locations; and (3) *system configuration metadata* that describes the fabric of the data grid itself such as network connectivity and details about storage system. The metadata service concept is also used in managing and accessing coastal data (Barde et al., 2005), data in Earth System Grid (ESG) and more. Semantic issues in data sharing and transferring prevail in many scientific metadata research conferences and publications. Workshops and conference panels on organizing the concepts of science and ontological research and applications in the biomedical domain have both debated the semantic issues and shared research information for creating scientific metadata that maximizes data discovery and retrieval.

Scientific metadata is perhaps the most complicated among all the subject and applications domains. The metadata development in these domains, however, seems to have taken two main directions. One focus is the *service-oriented* metadata development that maintains coarse metadata for collections of scientific data and information, such as the BioMed Central Catalog of Databases (http://databases.biomedcentral.com/, accessed 2007) and the science.gov portal (http://science. gov/) for federally (U.S.) sponsored research projects and related information. The goal of service-oriented metadata is to facilitate resource discovery through portals and catalogs. The other focus is *object-specific* metadata development that targets objects in a disciplinary or application domain. Although object-specific metadata also serves the purpose of resource discovery, it provides more important functions such as provenance, coverage, and data collection methods that are necessary for correct and appropriate scientific use.

2.7 Metadata for Multimedia Objects

Multimedia objects often contain both complicated technical and content data that require appropriate coding and description for delivery and consumption. "Metadata attached to multimedia resources can have many purposes and sources. They can be as simple as the time stamp attached to home video and digital still camera images, or as complex as storylines, interviews, and out-takes attached to movies prepared for digital video disc (DVD)" (Rising III and Jorgensen, 2007). Metadata tasks for describing multimedia present special challenges: (1) The range of objects is incredibly wide and complicated, including audio, speech, video, and 3-dimentional (3-D) models, to name a few. (2) These objects are used individually but may also be combined to form multimedia objects. (3) This domain cuts across many vertical disciplines and subject fields such as education, science, entertainment, and industries. Applications also consist of media on demand, media reuse, mobile applications, broadcast channel selection, multimedia editing, and multimedia directory services (Jorgensen, 2007: 4). There is a strong interconnection between different procedures of production, archiving, retrieval, preservation, and reuse of multimedia objects. These special challenges indicate the need for standardized multimedia descriptions that have drawn great attention from all interested sectors.

2.7.1 The MPEG Standards

The standards for coded representation of digital audio and video objects include those developed by the Moving Picture Experts Group (MPEG), a working group of the ISO/IEC (International Organization of Standards/International Electrotechnical Commission) established in 1988. The group has produced standards on which major products are based:

- MPEG-1: for Video CD and MP3
- MPEG-2: for Digital Television set top boxes and DVD
- MPEG-4: for multimedia of the fixed and mobile web
- MPEG-7: for the description and search for audio and visual content
- MPEG-21: for the Multimedia Framework

MPEG-4, formally known by its ISO/IEC designation "'ISO/IEC 14496'," has been a standard for multimedia of the fixed and mobile web since 1999.

MPEG-4 provides the standardized technological elements enabling integration of the production, distribution and content access paradigms of three fields: (1) digital television, (2) interactive graphics applications (synthetic content), and (3) interactive multimedia (World Wide Web distribution, and access to content).

MPEG-7 is a multimedia content description standard. Unlike other MPEG standards that deal with the actual encoding of multimedia, MPEG-7 targets the *content description* of multimedia objects. It specifies *tools* for the description of features related to both content and the information related to its management (Salembier and Benitez, 2007). This metadata standard for multimedia deserves further discussion.

2.7.2 MPEG-7

The MPEG-7 specification is formally known as ISO/IEC 15938 (*Information technology—Multimedia Content Description Interface*), and is organized into seven parts: Systems, Description Definition Language, Visual, Audio, Multimedia Description Schemes, Reference Software, and Conformance testing. MPEG-7 was designed to standardize four types of normative elements: (1) Descriptors (called Ds), (2) Description Schemes (called DSs), (3) a language to define the syntax of Ds and DSs, which is the Description Definition Language (DDL), and (4) coding schemes (see Figure 2-7-1).

The *Descriptors* (Ds) correspond to the *data features* such as visual (e.g. texture, camera motion) or audio (e.g. melody). The feature *Color* can be represented as a histogram or frequency spectrum. The *Color* feature has multiple Ds, including color quantization, dominant color(s), scalable color, color structure, and color layout. The *Motion* feature has four Ds: camera motion, object motion trajectory, parametric object motion, and motion activity.

The *description schemes* (DSs) refer to more abstract description entities. They are the specifications for the structure and semantics of *relationships* among components. The distinction between a DS and a D is that a D only contains basic data types and does not make reference to any other D. An example would be a movie that is temporally structured as scenes, with textual descriptions at scene level, and some audio descriptors of dialogues and background music (Martínez, 2005; W3C Multimedia Semantics Incubator Group, 2005; Chiariglione, 2005).

A set of *Description Tools* (DTs) dealing with generic as well as multimedia entities are defined in MPEG-7. DTs contain *Ds* for defining the syntax and the semantics of each feature (metadata element) and *DSs* for specifying the structure and semantics of the relationships between their components that may be both Ds and DSs. These DTs can be grouped into five classes according to their functionality: (1) content description tools, (2) content management tools, (3) content organization tools, (4) navigation and access tools, and (5) user interaction tools. In an example explained by Chiariglione (2005) and Martínez (2005), the *MPEG-7 Multimedia Description Schemes* (MDS) defines a set of DTs dealing with generic as well as multimedia entities. Generic entities

Figure 2-7-1. The main MPEG-7 elements.

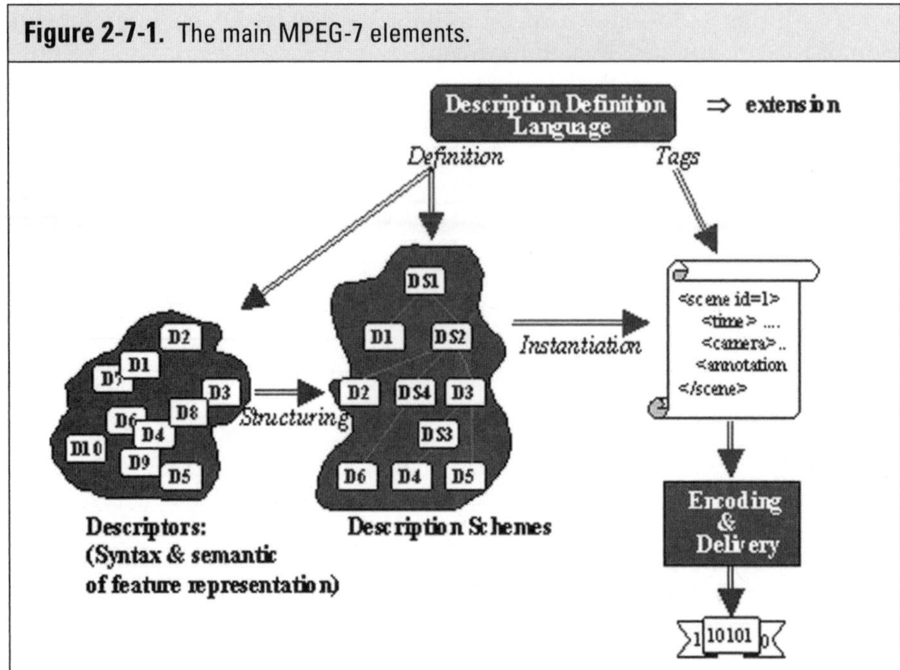

Source: Courtesy of Chiariglione, 2005: http://www.chiariglione.org/ride/inside_MPEG-7/inside_MPEG-7.htm, accessed February 23, 2008. *Note:* Ds (Descriptors) and DSs (Descriptor Schemes) are collectively called Description Tools (DTs).

(e.g., "vector," "time"), are features used in all media including audio, visual, and textual descriptions. More complex DTs are used when more than one medium needs to be described. MPEG-7 MDS DTs (either Ds or DSs) can be grouped in terms of functionality (Figure 2-7-2), although in practice they are used in a structured way to make use of the top-level elements and the selected profile.

The Description Definition Language (DDL) defines the syntax of the MPEG-7 DTs and allows the creation and extension of new DSs and Ds. System tools are employed to support binary coded representation for efficient storage and transmission, transmission mechanisms, multiplexing of descriptions, synchronization of description with content, and the management and protection of intellectual property in MPEG-7 descriptions (Martínez, 2005).

Although the specification is quite difficult to master, the impact of MPEG-7 is tremendous. It is equally important in industries and services such as radio and TV channels, art-galleries and museums, as well as e-business, education, and biomedical applications. Several initiatives would further improve the functionality and utility for a much broader range of user communities. One such initiative is the development and sharing of guides and best practices about the use of MPEG-7 for the noncommercial sector, thereby "reducing the

Figure 2-7-2. Functional groups of the *MPEG-7 Multimedia Description Schemes.*

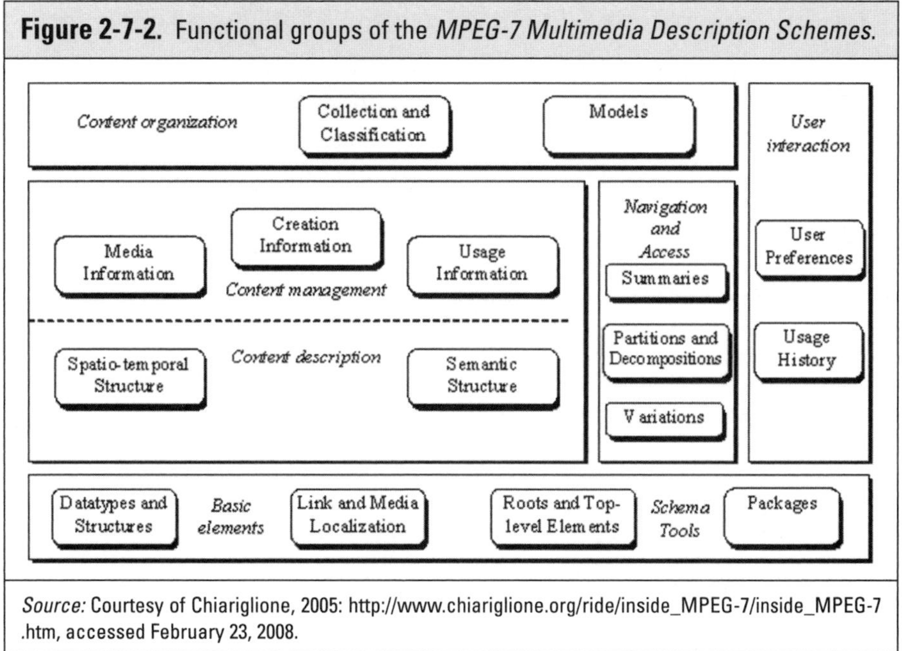

Source: Courtesy of Chiariglione, 2005: http://www.chiariglione.org/ride/inside_MPEG-7/inside_MPEG-7.htm, accessed February 23, 2008.

burden of interpreting the complex, and sometimes contradictory, documentation and ensuring consistent application" (Jorgensen, 2007: 1326).

2.7.3 ID3v2

ID3 is a metadata container most often used in conjunction with the MP3 audio file format and is actively used by software such as iTunes and Windows Media Player as well as hardware players such as the iPod and Sony Walkman. Each version of the ID3 data is quite different but commonly contains *Artist name, Song title, Year,* and *Genre* of each audio file (ID3v2Easy, 2006). ID3v2 is not entirely limited to musical audio; other types of audio files are also supported. The tags vary in size, and usually occur at the beginning of the file to better aid streaming media. The ID3v2 informal standard has defined a significant number of *frames* (i.e., elements). The two large groups are text information frames, including about 40 frames such as: title, composer, various dates, cover art, beats per minute (BPM), and copyright or license, and URL link frames including commercial information, copyright/legal information, and official Web pages. Approximately 30 additional frames cover comments, lyrics/text, and various identifiers and codes; although related, no hierarchical or group relationships are defined. Because there is no hierarchical structure, these frames require time to understand. Automatic extraction of metadata from these 80-plus frames requires numerous algorithms. Very few applications fully support all of the frame types enumerated in the ID3v2 specification thus far.

2.7.4 PBCore, the Public Broadcasting Metadata Dictionary

Metadata development in the digital arena has moved beyond descriptive and technical purposes, and more toward including administrative information (mainly regarding preservation and rights management). This shift can be seen from the newly developed PBCore, the *Public Broadcasting Metadata Dictionary* (www.utah.edu/cpbmetadata/). PBCore was created by the public broadcasting community in the United States for use by public broadcasters and related communities. Built on the foundation of the Dublin Core, at its top level PBCore contains four classes. A number of metadata elements are associated with those classes:

- *IntellectualContent* (20 elements describing the intellectual content of a media asset or resource)
- *IntellectualProperty* (nine elements related to creators, creation, usage, permissions, constraints, and use obligations associated with a media asset or resource)
- *Instantiation* (29 elements that identify the nature of the media asset as it exists in some form or format in the physical world or digitally)
- *Extensions* (two elements for additional descriptions)

In Figure 2-7-3, the containers are illustrated as *branches* that are thematically related metadata fields. An example of related elements bound together is *creator* and *creatorRole* within the Container *PBCoreCreator*. Elements are also called *leaves* where values such as a title, a date, keywords, rights information, mime types, media types, etc.) can be recorded. Overall, PBCore has four Content Classes, 15 Element Containers, three Sub-Containers, and 53 Elements.

2.7.5 Ongoing Research and Development

Multimedia content can be described either as *data-driven* or *knowledge-driven* approaches. The data-driven approaches "concentrate on acquiring fully automated numeric descriptors from objective visual content properties and perform semantic annotation and the subsequent retrieval based on criteria that somehow replicate human perception of visual similarity" (Dasiopoulou et al., 2007: 3). Such numeric descriptors are often low-level features that can be extracted directly from multimedia objects, and are subsequently used to derive high-level content representations. Extracting camera metadata for photo classification is an example of the data-driven approach. Boutell and Luo (2005) categorized camera metadata into four families: scene brightness, flash, subject distance, and focal length. Applying probabilistic methods of analysis and integration, low-level cues from the camera metadata allowed the integrated cues to be used to classify the photo collection in their experiment.

The knowledge-driven approaches "utilize high-level domain knowledge to extract appropriate content descriptors by guiding features extraction, analysis and elimination of the unimportant ones, descriptions derivation, and reasoning" (Dasipoulou et al., 2007: 4). Multimedia description ontologies are a typical

Figure 2-7-3. PBCore's *Content Classes* and *Containers.*

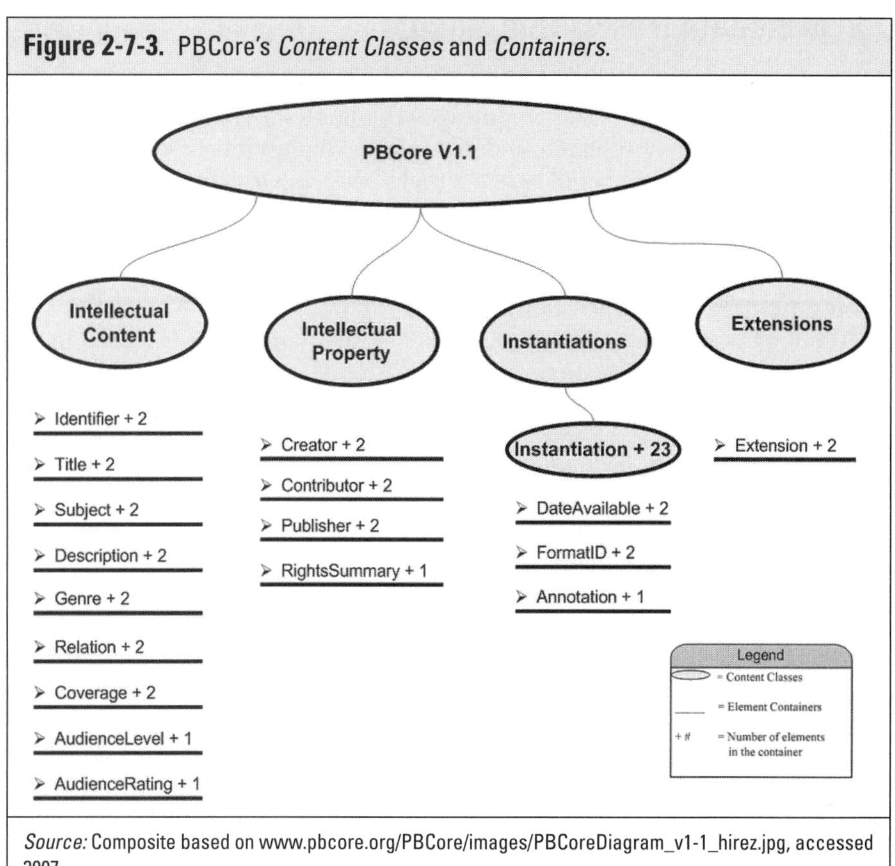

Source: Composite based on www.pbcore.org/PBCore/images/PBCoreDiagram_v1-1_hirez.jpg, accessed 2007.

knowledge-driven approach and have been used to categorize multimedia content metadata. Simou et al. (2005) developed the video descriptor ontology (VDO) for knowledge-assisted analysis of multimedia content. It consists of four principal descriptor concept classes: *region*, *feature*, *visual descriptor*, and *metaconcepts*, with each having more detailed visual descriptors subclasses. For example, the visual descriptor concept contains subdescriptors of color, texture, shape, motion, localization, and basic, all of which conform to the MPEG-7 descriptor scheme. The ontologies developed by the same group of researchers include the core ontology, visual descriptor ontology, multimedia structure ontology, and domain ontologies (Bloehdorn et al., 2005). Converting the MPEG-7 standard into an ontology, and encoding the MPEG-7 ontology in XML/RDF is intended to represent the semantics of MPEG-7 Description Schemes and Descriptors, although with certain limitations (Hunter, 2001). Despite MPEG-7 providing a framework for describing multimedia objects, its complexity and specific schemata can inhibit flexibility and syntactic interoperability due to the different characteristics of binary representation and textual representation.

2.8 Metadata Describing Agents

Social computing is a fresh, hot topic that has been discussed extensively at conferences in past years. Social computing is changing the way people use information for work, play, research, and everyday activities. It has been recognized and acknowledged that people are the things that link to other kinds of things we describe on the Web: they create documents, attend meetings, are depicted in photos, and so on. "Consequently, there are many things that we might want to say about people, not to mention these related objects (i.e., documents, photos, meetings etc.)" (Brickley and Miller, 2007).

Although not addressed as metadata per se, the standards introduced in this section focus on describing agents (people, groups, and organizations). When these agents create works and manifestations, they can be mapped to "name authority" files, i.e., the library community. In this scenario, however, it is a different matter. First, the agents described are not limited to being creators of works: the description is about being a part of society—their identification, characteristics, work and life, and friends. Second, the majority of these files are not created and maintained by an authority agent such as a library, yet the impact of such information that can be connected in many dimensions is unpredictable.

The *vCard* defines a format for an electronic business card (Internet Mail Consortium, 1996). The vCard was developed into a MIME Content-Type profile where attributes of *person object* are defined. A vCard is used to represent and exchange significant information about an individual (e.g., formatted and structured name(s), delivery address(es), email address(es), telephone number(s,) photograph(s), logo, audio clips, etc.). The vCard MIME Directory Profile also provides support for representing other important information about the person, e.g., date of birth, an audio clip describing the pronunciation of the name, longitude and latitude geopositioning information related to the person (annotations often written on a business card), Uniform Resource Locators (URLs) for a Web site, public key information, and more. (vCard MIME Directory Profile, 1998).

A W3C Note, *Representing vCard Objects in RDF/XML* (2002) specifies a Resource Description Framework (RDF) encoding of the vCard profile (see Chapter 5, Section 5.5 on RDF). The following is a simple vCard record:

```
<vCard:FN> John Doe </vCard:FN>
<vCard:BDAY> 1975-01-01 </vCard:BDAY>
<vCard:TITLE> Metadata Librarian II</vCard:TITLE>
<vCard:ROLE> Coordinator </vCard:ROLE>
```

More examples can be found at the W3C Web site (www.w3.org/TR/vcard-rdf#5, accessed 2007). The majority of the vCard property types have strings as their values (e.g., FN value John Doe in the above example) and are simply represented by their property type name and value as defined in the vCard specification. These include: FN, NICKNAME, BDAY, MAILER, GEO, TITLE, ROLE, CATEGORIES, NAME, SOURCE, NOTE, PRODID, and so on. Note NAME is a human-displayable text only about the vCard record itself (as surrogate of the person). Other property types are SOUND, PHOTO, LOGO, etc. The vCard has already been embraced and used by millions of people. By creating metadata records using other standards, e.g., LOM, vCard can be used in the categories that require information about people, e.g., the creator of a metadata record and the annotator.

FOAF (Friend of a Friend) has been evolving gradually since its creation in the mid-2000s and has been widely accepted by members of the Internet culture, especially in relation to the development of the Semantic Web. It is designed as a machine-readable and -understandable ontology describing persons, their activities, and relations to other people and objects. FOAF Vocabulary Specification 0.9 was released in 2007 (http://xmlns.com/foaf/spec/20070524.html). The *Classes* of FOAF are *Agent, Document, Group, Image, OnlineAccount, OnlineChatAccount, OnlineEcommerceAccount, OnlineGamingAccount, Organization, Person, PersonalProfileDocument,* and *Project*.

An agent could be a person, group, software, or physical artifact. *Person, Organization,* and *Group* are the subclasses of *Agent*. A *Person* could be alive, dead, real, or imaginary; *Organization* corresponds to social institutions such as companies, societies, and so on; the concept is intentionally quite broad. *Group* represents a collection of individual agents, informal and ad-hoc groups, long-established communities, organizational groups within a workplace, etc. Using FOAF, anyone can create a record for his or her personal information, work experience, and educational background, and (more important) the friends (or people) one knows. The latter is used most creatively to link people together in the networked society. Using a generator like *FOAF-a-Matic* (www.ldodds.com/foaf/foaf-a-matic.html), anyone can generate a FOAF record. FOAF has been extended or tailored by applications, e.g., FOAFCorp (Corporate Friends of Friends), for information tailored to connect people in the corporate world, e.g., board members who serve at different companies with their associates. The Web site (http://rdfweb.org/foafcorp/intro.html, accessed 2007) provides examples and graphic views of a network.

More recently, Internet social network services such as *Orkut, Facebook, Friendster,* and *MySpace* have been receiving more users who want to meet new friends and maintain existing relationships on the Web. They use specific markup languages and simple description templates to allow users to create their profiles, describe their social, professional, and personal details, and upload photos and videos, and set the option for which group (e.g., friends, friend's friends, everyone) of people would be allowed to view the particulars. These developments certainly deserve close attention for ongoing changes, improvements, and usage.

This chapter has described various metadata standards of data structure and semantics that are being developed for differing domain(s) purposes. The standards presented also reveal the distinct characteristics in terms of the types of metadata they focus on, e.g., descriptive, administrative, technical and structure, preservation, and rights management; and, the differently structured elements, whether a flat,, hierarchical, or networked structure. Regardless of what they are used for and by which community, they all have a common goal of ensuring interoperability. If we analyze their building blocks, we can find similar components, procedures, and methodologies that are used in common. The next three chapters blend different standards and describe these common building blocks.

Suggested Readings

For each section, read documents provided by the metadata standards (e.g., DC, MODS, CDWA Lite, VRA Core 4.0, LOM, EAD, PBCore, and so on); concentrate primarily on the specifications of the element sets and user guides. Exclude XML schemas prepared for machine processing.

Exercises

1. For each metadata standard you select to explore further, prepare one (or more) of the following documents. To obtain the full benefit of this exercise in study and application, it is not worthwhile to repeat what is already available on (or provided by) the standard's Web site:
   a. An outline of the schema's terms (e.g., DCMES' elements, qualifiers/refinements, and encoding schemes for value spaces. See example at: http://dublincore.org/documents/usageguide/qualifiers.shtml.
   b. A translated outline in a language in which you are fluent. You must be able to translate it on your own. The *name* (token) of an element should not be translated, but the *label* of an element should be translated.
   c. From either *a* or *b* create a graphic representation of one or both outlines (elements and subelements only, no encoding schemes). See example at: www.pbcore.org/PBCore/PBCore_by_Graphical.html.
2. Prepare a fact sheet (1–2 pages) about a selected standard. Use at least three references that are available on the Internet. Additionally, provide URL addresses to the major and authoritative sources provided for this standard. For an example, see the UMLS fact sheet. Note: its structure is intended to provide an example, and only that. It is not meant to be followed in a mechanical fashion. Available at: www.nlm.nih.gov/pubs/factsheets/umlsmeta.html.
3. Create metadata records (2–5) applying a selected metadata standard. You can either create them from any resource, or use the listed items included on the CD-ROM. The resulting records should concentrate on content rather than the encoding syntax.
4. Write a short essay (1–2 pages) about your observations of this standard based on your relative experience of creating metadata records using this schema. Compare with other schema(s) experience, where applicable.

Part II
Metadata Building Blocks

3

Schemas—Structure and Semantics

Metadata decisions may be made at different stages of a digital library project, and intelligent decisions are integral to successful implementation of the project. In the previous chapter we introduced some standards utilized by different communities; however, in most cases, the development of a digital collection does not start (or end) by adopting an existing standard without some adjustment or adaptation.

Questions that arise at the beginning stages of a digital collection project can be all-important and determine the quality and consistency of all subsequent phases of metadata creation, implementation, and interoperability. Some examples of the very real and practical questions to be asked would be: "Should we adopt a schema or create one?" "Which metadata standard should we follow?" "Do we need to modify the schema?" "Can we reuse existing catalog records in a new digital collection?"

Even though digital collections may have been built, metadata-related questions might remain: "We found that our metadata records are too simplistic and omitted important data. Should we go back to redo the records?" "We would like to merge our records with those from another collection, but they have used a different format. What should we do?" A well-established collection may also encounter new questions such as: "A large digital library project has requested that we provide our metadata for its repository. How can we convert our data to their format?" "We would like to join a union catalog, but all members employ different formats. How might we provide data for federated searching?"

In this chapter, we explore the decisions related to metadata schemas that a project might take: identifying desired elements, assembling a new element set or an application profile, creating crosswalks, selecting vocabularies for value spaces, and developing best practice guides.

3.1 Elements

Optimally, the design and planning of a digital collection should seek to embody the unique characteristics of a discipline and community and also fundamentally transform the way the data has been and will be presented, managed, accessed, used, and reused. The project therefore begins with an investigation of the specific discipline, community, and potential uses and/or users. The factors considered include the nature of collection objects; anticipated user needs; and constraints upon metadata creation, implementation, and quality control (staffing, funding, equipment, interoperability with institutional and community information systems/services).

3.1.1 Knowing the Difference

Textual vs. nontextual resources. A digitized collection for the same original resources can result in representation by differing formats. A digitized newspaper collection can exist as images, text, or a combination of the two. Nevertheless, accessing the information in the digitized newspaper may be very different depending on whether the results are textual or nontextual. Information retrieval technologies have made it possible to allow full-text searching or automatic extraction of keywords in text-based resources regardless of the documents being structured, semi-structured, or unstructured. With the rapid development and application of markup languages (e.g., general purpose markup languages such as XML, SGML and specialized markup languages such as Mathematical Markup Language [MathML]), semantically meaningful tags can be embedded within the text and provide a guide to precise, fielded indexing and searching. The power of retrieval algorithms has led some people to believe that there will be no need for human-generated metadata or catalog information in the future. However, it should be realized that many resources (e.g., a digital image or audio file) possess a more-or-less atomic information structure (or at least apparently so) to which internal content markup and full-text searching cannot easily be applied. For an image, only caption, file name, and text around the image are usually searched (not the image itself). In these cases the resource metadata record, i.e., the surrogate, bears the information burden. To provide more detailed metadata to describe the contents, increased semantically relevant understanding and interpreting are required of project creators and implementers.

Document-like vs. non-document-like objects. Metadata for document-like objects and non-document-like objects received extensive attention and discussion when thirteen elements were proposed to form the Dublin Metadata Core Element Set at the OCLC/NCSA Metadata Workshop (a.k.a. DC-1) in 1995 (Weibel et al., 1995). The 1997 CNI/OCLC Image Metadata Workshop (a.k.a. DC-3) explained that the defining characteristic of a document-like object is not its textual or graphical content; rather, it is whether the resource is bounded, or fixed (in that the resource looks the same, and has the same content, for all users). Therefore images, movies, musical performances, speeches, and other information objects characterized by being fixed are considered document-like objects as well (Weibel and Miller, 1997).

A more useful way to determine whether an object is document-like or non-document-like is to identify where and how the needed information for describing an object can be obtained. In a comparison between museum objects and bibliographical materials, Will (1997) found that museum objects often carry no descriptive statement whatsoever. Museum objects usually offer nothing comparable to the author or title of a published work. For museum objects and others alike, the metadata creator may be unable to transcribe anything offered directly by the source. Information about what an object is called, what it is for, and when and by whom it was made must all come from external sources: documentation that accompanies the object, separate reference works, and other experts (or the individual cataloger's specialized knowledge). If one uses a metadata schema that is for document-like objects to create a record for a museum object, the core or mandatory fields required (e.g., author, title, publisher, edition) become difficult to fill. Moreover, architecture, artworks, historical artifacts, and other three-dimensional objects bear rich content associated with history, culture, and society, as well as style, pattern, material, color, and technique. These are usually only addressed in the metadata schemas for non-document-like objects such as CDWA and VRA Core.

Original vs. digital surrogate of the work. Decisions about metadata also depend on the kinds of objects to be included in a digital library, to be described and managed: those created digitally (a.k.a. *born-digital*) or those converted into digital form from existing nondigital resources (a.k.a. *digital doubles*). From another perspective, the objects may be considered either original works or digital surrogates of original works. A majority of digital library projects for cultural, heritage, and educational resources display digitized images to represent original work. Although other surrogates such as photos or slides exist between an original work and its digital surrogate(s), major attention is often paid only to the work and associated digital images. CCO defines a *work* as a distinct intellectual or artistic creation limited primarily to objects and structures made by humans, which include built works, visual artworks, and cultural artifacts. An *image* is a visual representation of a work that typically exists in photomechanical, photographic, or digital format (CCO 2006: 4–5). A digital collection designer may decide to create metadata records for the original work only, or to generate records for the images as well. The decision will have a great impact on the information architecture that supports the management and linking of these records.

Collection level vs. item level. The question here is at what level will metadata records be created for all the objects in a collection? Other situations as to levels of granularity (concerning whether a record describes the entirety of a collection or individual items in the collection) and the information in a typical collection level record will be addressed in the next chapter (see also Chapter 5, Section 5.3, Levels of Granularity). As a preliminary decision, a project team must determine the appropriate level for both the objects to be described and the needs of an institution and community. CDWA has summarized the most common levels of cataloging in different disciplines as follows:

- Archives: group level—intellectual or physical groups.
- Museums: item level—assign accession numbers and other catalog information to every individual object in their collections.

- Libraries: volume level—typically do not catalog individual prints or illustrations in the pages of a volume.

CDWA defines an *item* as an individual object or work, which may be composed of multiple components. An archival *group* (or record group) is an aggregate of items that share a common provenance. A group may contain various numbers and types of items. A *collection* comprises multiple items that are conceptually or physically arranged together for the purpose of cataloging or retrieval. A collection differs from an archival group because the items in a collection are bound informally for convenience and do not necessarily share a common provenance or otherwise meet the criteria for an archival group (CDWA: Object/Work Catalog Level, 2000–, www.getty.edu/research/conducting_research/standards/cdwa/1object.html).

Digital collections that are established based on their physical counterparts in library special collections, archives, or historical societies often consider using collection-level metadata. Finding aids functioning as inventories, registers, indexes, and guides are created to provide detailed descriptions of both content and intellectual organization of the collections. These tools often provide contextual information about a collection's provenance and the conditions under which it may be accessed or copied, biographical or organizational histories related to the collection, notes describing the scope and content of the collection, and progressively detailed descriptions of portions or components of the collection combined with the corresponding accession numbers for identifying and requesting the physical entities (Hill et al., 1999). These features are quite different from those that describe items. EAD (introduced in Chapter 2) is a typical metadata standard for the purpose of creating collection-level metadata; it is clearly different from other standards that primarily focus only on the item level.

3.1.2 Communicating About the Functional Requirements

Communication about functional requirements is vitally important between users and the digital library, and between system and metadata teams. As part of the needs assessments of a digital library project, functional requirements for metadata can be assessed from an end-user viewpoint as well as from the standpoint of the data producer and all data/metadata service providers. Each user may have different needs, information-seeking goals, and searching techniques. These differences should influence and be reflected in the development of divergent metadata systems.

It cannot be emphasized strongly enough that a gap in communication about functional requirements might exist, yet easily be overlooked or ignored. An unfortunate truth today is that in many cases the very rich metadata created by catalogers or metadata librarians is never fully realized by users because of the limitations of searching and indexing systems and/or inadequate interfaces. On the other hand, a digital library's indexing and searching algorithm (as well as its interface) might have been designed according to a real or imagined "wish list," but the metadata records to be indexed might not provide the required data. In a given system for example, a search feature by school grade level is provided, but the metadata schema for this digital resource has not included any element for providing such information. Therefore nothing will be retrieved if a user used "grade level" to search this collection. This is just one problem found in the lessons learned from large digital collections (discussed extensively in Chapter 7). Communication about the functional requirements between both system designers and metadata creators is critical to the overall quality of a digital library.

Researchers for the EPrints UK project present their perspectives on both the internal (pertaining to the archive's Web user-interface) and external (pertaining to disclosed metadata) functional requirements and provide an example of a "Functional Requirements List" (see Figure 3-1-1). According to this list, the

Figure 3-1-1. A functional requirements list.

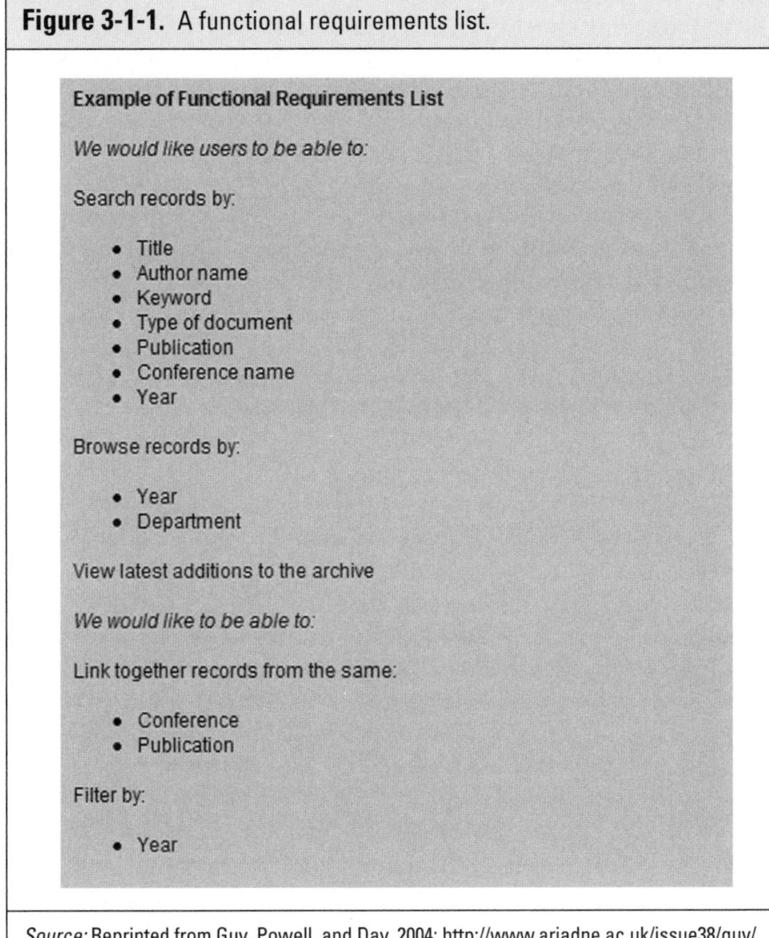

Example of Functional Requirements List

We would like users to be able to:

Search records by:

- Title
- Author name
- Keyword
- Type of document
- Publication
- Conference name
- Year

Browse records by:

- Year
- Department

View latest additions to the archive

We would like to be able to:

Link together records from the same:

- Conference
- Publication

Filter by:

- Year

Source: Reprinted from Guy, Powell, and Day, 2004: http://www.ariadne.ac.uk/issue38/guy/, with permission of *Ariadne*.

metadata must provide information for title, year, department, and so on to support each of the functions specified.

The DCMI definition of metadata covers the range of any system's functional demands very well: "data associated with either an information system or an information object for purposes of description, administration, legal requirements, technical functionality, use and usage, and preservation" (DCMI Glossary, 2005). This range shows that descriptive metadata alone does not adequately cover the information required by the information infrastructure. Some other metadata types employed for work applications include terms and conditions that describe rules for the use of an object, administrative data related to the management of an object in a particular server or repository, content ratings, provenance, linkage or relationship data of a content object to other objects, and structural data that defines the logical components of complex or compound objects and how to access those components (Lagoze, 1996). Mapping to these requirements is a chart of metadata typologies and functionalities summarized by Greenberg (2005) and presented in Figure 3-1-2.

To interpret this table, we can focus on Lagoze et al.'s interpretation regarding metadata that usually fulfills the function of *resource discovery* (see row two, column two in Figure 3-1-2). The *identification and/or descriptive metadata* type assists in the identification and retrieval of an object and includes elements that represent both the physical and topical attributes of an information object, e.g., *creator (author)*, *title*, and *subject*. Equally, *creator* is an important element of *provenance metadata* (see the sixth row of the table). This method of linking metadata type, function, and elements enables the functions that should be applied in defining desired elements. It is important to note that metadata acts

Figure 3-1-2. Metadata typologies and functionalities.

Lagoze et al. (1996):			Gilliland-Swetland (2000): Typology of 5 types of metadata	Greenberg (2001): Typology of 4 types of metadata (2 sub-types of Use metadata)	Caplan (2001): Typology of 4 types of metadata
Typology of 7 types of metadata	Metadata Functions "This type of metadata *facilitates*":	Element examples*			
Identification/ description metadata	*RESOURCE DISCOVERY/ INFORMATION RETRIEVAL*	Creator (Author), Title, Subject	Descriptive metadata	Discovery metadata	Descriptive metadata
Administrative metadata	*RESOURCE MANAGEMENT*	Price, Condition	Administrative and Preservation metadata	Administrative metadata	Administrative metadata
Terms and conditions metadata	*RESOURCE USAGE*	Rights, Reproduction restrictions	Administrative, Preservation, and Use metadata	Technical Use, Intellectual Use, and Administrative metadata	Administrative and linking metadata
Content ratings metadata	*RESOURCE USE BY APPROPRIATE AUDIENCES*	Audience	Use metadata	Technical Use and Intellectual Use metadata	Administrative and linking metadata
Provenance metadata	*RESOURCE AUTHENTICATION AND OTHER PROVENANCE-RELATED ACTIVITIES*	Creator, Source	Administrative and Use metadata	Authenticity and Administrative metadata	Administrative metadata
Linkage/ relationship metadata	*RESOURCE LINKING WITH RELATED RESOURCES*	Relation, Source	Administrative metadata	Authenticity and Administrative metadata	Linking metadata
Structural metadata	*RESOURCE HARDWARE AND SOFTWARE NEEDS*	Compression ratio	Technical and Use metadata	Technical Use metadata	Structural metadata

*Individual metadata elements can be multi-functional. For example, "source" metadata facilitates resource authentication and resource linking, and can be classed as both "Provenance metadata" and "Linkage/relationship metadata" following Lagoze et al.'s typology (for a discussion on metadata element multifunctionality see Greenberg, J. (2001)).

Source: Reprinted from Greenberg, 2005, with permission of *Cataloging & Classification Quarterly*.

both as inventory and user access tool, with additional provisions needed to avoid functional conflicts in concrete applications.

3.1.3 Identifying Desired Elements

Once the dimensions are established, one begins to gather the elements that will be used to compose the design. By understanding the options available to meet users' needs, collections' characteristics, and functional requirements, it becomes necessary to identify desired elements for a given project. In different projects and communities, the desired elements could be very diverse and divergent. The first step is to write down each element that constitutes a wish list:

- *Desired Element*
- *Explanation and Description of the Element*
- *Example*
- *Implementation* (M-Mandatory, O-Optional, R-Repeatable)

A collection of desired elements leads to the next step of a metadata project that will define the actual element set.

3.2 Element Set

An element set is a group of elements used to describe resources of a particular type or purpose. The next logical step after gathering a list of desired—or wish list of—elements is to make decisions on the actual element set. There are three main options: new design, adopting an existing set, or modifying an existing one. A testing procedure always remains in the loop of production no matter which option is chosen; therefore the process of development of an element set will involve revisions and iterations that continue even after the first edition is released. This section concentrates on the components, principles, and methodologies that must be considered in element set decision-making.

3.2.1 Basic Components

A metadata element set has two basic components: *Semantics* (definitions of the meanings of the elements and their relationships) and *Content* (declarations or instructions of what and how values should be assigned to the elements). In Chapter 2 we presented graphic illustrations that displayed the relationships between the elements of selected element sets. The question then is, for each element, what should be presented? Careful scrutiny of individual elements finds their common set of attributes such as label, name, and definition. An example from the DCMES is shown in Exhibit 3-2-1. For each element, there is usually a token (i.e., the term's name for use in machine-processing), a descriptive label (for human-understanding), and a definition, with additional comments or notes for the content.

Exhibit 3-2-1. An entry of DCMES version 1.1.

```
Term Name: creator
URI: http://purl.org/dc/elements/1.1/creator
Label: Creator
Definition: An entity primarily responsible for making the resource.
Comment: Examples of a Creator include a person, an organization, or a
service. Typically, the name of a Creator should be used to indicate the
entity.
```

Source: DCMES Web page: http://dublincore.org/documents/dces/.

Definition. A definition is a statement that represents the conceptual (and essential) nature of the term. The definition should be concise, clear, and whenever possible no longer than one sentence; it includes only the necessary information. The definition states what the concept is, rather than what it is not. Examples of definitions can be found in DCMES 1.1, particularly its 2006-12 revision (note the additional explanations in the comment line of the example in Box 2-3-1). Definitions can be revised as needed. The DCMES version 1.1 (also passed as NISO Z39.85-2007) has revised definitions of several elements used in both the NISO Z39.85-1001 and ISO 15836-2003 standards so that:

- *Format,* as defined in the DCMES 2006-12-18 document and NISO 39.85-2007 is: "The file format, physical medium, or dimensions of the resource."
- *Format,* as defined in the previous NISO Z39.85-2001 and ISO 15836-2003 is: "The physical or digital manifestation of the resource."

Because the elements themselves in these Dublin Core (DC) standards do not change, the element set is still referred to as version 1.1. Therefore, it is necessary for any implementers and application profile creators to pay careful attention to the updates and correctly cite the version and revision date of a document with eagle-eye precision.

Many element sets do not formally give definitions of the elements; rather, they use *explanation* or *description* to further specify the element to be used in their environments. Typically those are derived from a standard or extended into a new set of elements or application profile (e.g., *CDWA Lite* and *Electronic Theses and Dissertations Metadata Standard* [ETD-MS]).

Structure. The organization of elements. As illustrated by the metadata standards introduced in Chapter 2, elements are usually organized into two types of structures: flat or hierarchical (despite variations in the way they are presented).

- Flat structure has the following features:
  - All elements are equal, i.e., no subelements (e.g., DCMES 1.1 and VRA Core 3.0).
  - An element can be further refined. An element refinement (e.g., *available*) shares the meaning of a particular element (e.g., date) but with narrower semantics. In implementation they are usually used as

"qualifiers" (e.g., *date.available*). In DC standards, a refinement only alters one "parent" element (DCMI Grammatical Principles, 2003). The refinements can be used independently if they are additionally being treated as properties of a resource (e.g., *available* is defined as a "DC term" in the *DCMI Metadata Terms* specification; all DC terms are properties of a resource).

- Hierarchical structure has the following features:
  - Elements may have subelements that may also contain other subelements (e.g., MODS, VRA 4.0).
  - Both elements and subelements can have attributes. In the following example from VRA 4.0, the element *date* has two subelements (*earliestDate* and *latestDate*). Each of them also has an attribute (*type* for *date, circa* for the two subelements):

    date (type)
    —earliestDate (circa)
    —latestDate (circa)

    There are also global attributes (e.g., *source, href,* and *xml:lang*) that are optional and may be added to any element or subelement as needed.
  - These same subelements may be used repeatedly. In VRA Core 4.0 *earliestDate* and *latestDate* are also used as the sub-subelements of the subelement *dates* under element *agent*:

    agent
    —dates (type)
        earliestDate (circa)
        latestDate (circa)
  - A super-element set can contain several element sets. For example, LOM version 1.0 Base Schema is composed of nine *categories*, and each category contains a set of elements. The *6. Rights* category, for instance, states and aggregates the intellectual property rights and conditions of use with three elements: *6.1 Cost, 6.2 Copyright and Other Restrictions,* and *6.3 Description*. In PBCore, these categories are called *containers*. Similar to what LOM defines as *aggregators,* they do not directly have values as their leaf nodes (elements) do. In the following examples from PBCore, both 25.00 and 25.24 are containers, and 25.24.1-25.24.2 are elements that have values in working records.

    Content Class: Instantiation
      25.00 pbcoreInstantiation
        25.24 pbcoreDateAvailable
          25.24.1 dateAvailableStart
          25.24.2 dateAvailableEnd

This example also illustrates that hierarchical notations (expressed as numbers in this case) are used to reflect the conceptual levels of more comprehensive element sets, such as PBCore and LOM.

So far we have examined different structures for organizing elements. Although elements, refinements, and attributes are all considered properties of resources, these same properties may be modeled differently. For example, for the *date* of a *creator*, all of the following structures are valid. (Note that examples sometimes contain a "dates" element, which is a separate element that may be utilized for any resource, and is not bound to the "creator" element.) Each of these structures has pros and cons for implementation, especially for data conversion.

Content constraints. A standard may choose to separately release and register an element set that includes only the name, label, definition, and additional notes for each element. In a metadata standard's specification, however, more information for each element may be provided:

1. representation rules for content, e.g., capitalization rules or standards for representing time;
2. allowable content values, e.g., whether values must be taken from a specified controlled vocabulary or can be author-supplied, derived from text, or added by metadata creators working without a controlled term list;
3. links to corresponding elements in a related standard(s) (called crosswalks); and,
4. content rules for how content should be included, e.g., how to identify the main title.

Taking an example from VRA Core 4.0, an entry for an element may include all these constraints. Each element is crosswalked to the corresponding elements in its two previous versions (VRA Core 2.0 and 3.0), related standards (CDWA and DC), and a content standard (CCO). See Section 3.3 on value spaces, Section 3.5 on crosswalks, and Section 3.6 on best practice guides for detailed discussion.

Presentation. Presentation of the element set in a specification can vary according to whether it is bound with certain markup languages:

1. The most understandable format is obtained by presenting the basic element set without specific encoding, so that the structure, elements, definitions, and contents are coherent and clearly expressed (e.g., DCMES, CDWA, LOM). For example, in the DCMES, each element is expressed with a *term name* (the unique token assigned to the term); *URI* (the Uniform Resource Identifier used to uniquely identify a term); *label* (the human-readable label assigned to the term); *definition* (a statement that represents the concept and essential nature of the term); *comment* (including best practices); and *references* (a citation or URL of a resource referenced in the definition or comment) (see Figure 3-2-1). When refinements and encoding schemes are present in a specification, (e.g., *DCMI Metadata Terms*), other indicators include type of term (e.g., element, refinement, and encoding scheme); *status* (status assigned to term by an authority such as: recommended; conforming; obsolete; registered; and, endorsed); and *date issued* (date on which a term was first declared).

Table 3-2-1. Different structures for organizing the properties (using date of a creator as an example).

In an element set	**In a statement (expressed in XML, without specifying a prefix like "dc:")**
creator **date** ***earliest*** ***latest*** (Note: Italics indicate **refinements** of "date" **element**; they have to be used together with "date." There is **no** relationship between the elements "creator" and "date." Although this is theoretically correct, in practice this might only apply to a Name Authority file.)	<creator>John Doe</creator> **<date.earliest>1589</date>** **<date.latest>1670</date>** (Note: End tags apply only to elements, and not to refinements. If the record is converted to an unqualified format, values for <date.earliest> and <date.latest> will all be transferred into the <date> field; i.e.,"<date.earliest>1589</date>" will become "<date>1589</date>".)
creator ***role*** ***date-earliest*** ***date-latest*** dates (Note: Italics indicate **refinements** of "creator" **element**; they have to be used together with "creator." Again there is no relationship between element "creator" and the other element "dates"; "dates" is an element that may be utilized for any resource, and is not bound to "creator.")	**<creator>John Doe</creator>** **<creator.role>composer</creator>** **<creator.date-earliest>1589</creator>** **<creator.date-latest>1670</creator>** (Note: As with above, end tags apply only to elements, and not to refinements. All values will be transferred to the <creator> field if converting to an unqualified format; i.e., "<creator.date-earliest>1589</creator>" will become "<creator>1589</creator>".)
creator **name** **date** **earliestDate** **latestDate** dates (Note: Here all are elements: **element** "creator"; **subelements** "name" and "date"; and **sub-subelements** "earliestDate" and "latestDate." Again, "dates" is a separate element that may be utilized for any resource, and is not bound to "creator.")	**<creator>** **<name>John Doe</name>** **<date>** **<earliestDate>1589</earlestDate>** **<latestDate>1670</latestDate>** **</date>** **</creator>** (Note: Each element must have a closing tag no matter which level it is. Values only appear in the lowest level or leaf nodes, i.e., no value directly under <creator> or <date> because they are not the lowest level elements.)
creator **name** **date *(type)*** dates (Note: This is the model which uses all: elements, subelements, and attributes: **element** "creator"; **subelements** "name" and "date." Here "type" is an **attribute** of "date." As an attribute, its specific values might be predefined, e.g., "earliest" or "latest." See example in VRA Core 4.0. Again, "dates" is an element that may be utilized for any resource, and is not bound to "creator.")	**<creator>** **<name>John Doe</name>** **<date type="earliest">1589</date>** **<date type="latest">1670</date>** **</creator>** (Note: As with above: each element must have a closing tag; values only appear in the lowest level or leaf nodes. The attributes' names are not included in the closing tags; e.g., the closing tag is not </date type>, but just </date>.)

Figure 3-2-1. An entry for DC term (i.e., element) *date.*

Term Name: date	
URI:	http://purl.org/dc/elements/1.1/date
Label:	Date
Definition:	A point or period of time associated with an event in the lifecycle of the resource.
Comment:	Date may be used to express temporal information at any level of granularity. Recommended best practice is to use an encoding scheme, such as the W3CDTF profile of ISO 8601 [W3CDTF].
References:	[W3CDTF] http://www.w3.org/TR/NOTE-datetime

Source: DC 1.1. http://dublincore.org/documents/dces/, accessed 2007.

2. Some standards' basic element sets are already encoded with a markup language such as SGML or XML. EAD was first published as a SGML DTD and later an XML DTD (EAD Working Group, 2006). The EAD Web site provides an EAD Tag Library that contains descriptions of 146 elements, arranged alphabetically (www.loc.gov/ead/tglib/tlc.html). Because each element has both a tag and a name, the tag library also facilitates mapping through two indexes: for example, "*<c02>*" = "*Component (Second Level)*" and "*Description of Subordinate Components Group*" = "*<dscgrp>*".
3. More current standard specifications (e.g., CDWA Lite, VRA Core 4.0) provide both human-understandable entries and XML expressions for the elements. In CDWA Lite, the entries for elements include (1) a conventional set of information such as Element name, Element tag, Description, Repeatable or Non-repeatable, Required or Not-Required, and Data values; (2) Tagging examples (metadata statements expressed in XML); and (3) Display examples (see Figure 3-2-2).

Encoding/binding. When a metadata element set is encoded, the various results are called *schemas*-machine-processable specifications that define the structure and syntax of metadata in a formal schema language (DCMI glossary, 2005: http://dublincore.org/schemas/). The same element set can be encoded/bound with different encoding standards. For example, LOM has published its versions with three formats: ISO/IEC 11404:1996 Language Independent Datatypes, XML, and RDF formats (IEEE-LTSC WG-12, 2005: http://ltsc.ieee.org/wg12/). DCMI has used both XML Schemas and Resource Description Framework Schema (RDFS) to support the simple DC (without refinements) and qualified DC (with element refinements and encoding schemes). Encoding and binding of element sets is discussed in detail in Chapter 4.

Figure 3-2-2. An entry for element *Display Creation Date* from CDWA Lite

12. Element: Display Creation Date

Element tag: <cdwalite:displayCreationDate>

Description: A concise description of the date or range of dates associated with the creation, design, production, presentation, performance, construction, or alteration of the work or its components, presented in a syntax suitable for display to the end-user and including any necessary indications of uncertainty, ambiguity, and nuance.

Non-repeatable

Required

Data values: Formulated according to data content rules for display dates in CCO and CDWA. May be concatenated from controlled fields, if necessary.

Tagging examples:

<cdwalite:displayCreationDate>before 1480</cdwalite:displayCreationDate>

<cdwalite:displayCreationDate>illuminated in 2nd quarter of 11th century, binding from 12th century, with later additions</cdwalite:displayCreationDate>

<cdwalite:displayCreationDate>designed in 1913, cast in 1931 </cdwalite:displayCreationDate>

Display examples:

Creation Date: before 1480

Creation Date: designed in 1913, cast in 1931

Source: © J. Paul Getty Trust. *CDWA Lite: Specification for an XML Schema for Contributing Records via the OAI Harvesting Protocol*, 1.1, 17 July 2006: 17. Los Angeles: J. Paul Getty Trust, 2006. www.getty.edu/research/conducting_research/standards/cdwa/cdwalite.pdf, accessed January 28, 2008. Reprinted with permission.

As with the expression "the whole is greater than the sum of its parts" so too this applies to the principles of design. Although it is possible to use each available component independently, the power lies in the skillful coordination of all.

3.2.2 Principles for an Element Set to Follow

Good design structure is a result of the correct use of principles. In Chapter 1 primary principles for the construction of an ideal metadata element set were introduced, and among them three are indispensable for a good element set: simplicity, extensibility, and interoperability.

In creating an element set it is sometimes easy to fall prey to the idea that every attribute of a resource must be described. Unfortunately, this may lead to an overly comprehensive list of standards with excessive design of implicit elements, refinements, rules, and value constraints. *Simplicity* means to include only data elements required to maintain a minimum set of elements for ease of deployment. Metadata must also be flexible enough to accommodate specialized needs. *Extensibility* requires metadata systems to allow addition of new elements and/or subelements to the schema; the new elements are selected from existing metadata standards or are established at the local level. To ensure the principle of *interoperability*, data should be able to be integrated into a larger project and data structure should allow others to link to it. Metadata *reuse* (i.e., to make the records shareable and able to be used by other projects) should be retained at all times. Digital collection projects are not stand-alone. Only when a digital collection is integrated (physically or virtually) into a collaborative environment does it become more valuable and useful.

Collaborative opportunities have a direct influence on the metadata decisions in terms of interoperability and should be considered from the following standpoints:

1. *Organization-wide collaboration*. A project in an academic unit might consider digitization activities at university libraries, special collections, archives, museums, academic departments, administrative departments, and so on. Some of them may have already been data providers. Metadata reuse possibilities should be seriously examined and re-examined.
2. *Regional and statewide collaborative projects*. In Ohio, the "memory" collections, which have been built at the state, regional, county, and city levels (e.g., *Ohio Memory, Cleveland Memory*, and *Worthington Memory*) are publicly available and publish valuable collections of artifacts, photographs, documents, and other digitized materials. Other library consortia such as *OhioLINK* (The Ohio Library and Information Network) and *OPLIN* (The Ohio Public Library Information Network) have also launched digital collections and enforced implementation of particular metadata structures.
3. *National and international projects*. Major nationwide, large-scale digital library projects include *American Memory*, headed by the Library of Congress (LC), and the NSF-funded National Science Digital Library (NSDL); these projects have developed their own specific metadata policies and metadata application profiles. A new international project, the *World Digital Library*, which is commissioned by UNESCO, LC, IFLA (The International Federation of Library Associations and Institutions), and several national libraries with other libraries and cultural institutions from around the world, is also developing particular guidelines (including metadata) through an IFLA Working Group.
4. *Similar or related disciplines*. These include architecture projects, geography education projects, etc. For example, for earth science education, there are Alexandria Digital Earth Prototype (ADEPT), the Digital Library for Earth System Education (DLESE), NASA's Joined Digital Library.
5. *Similar or related media*. These include multimedia databases, image galleries, visual resources repositories, manuscript collections, company procedure documents, and so on.

If collections intend to be connected or integrated into any of these projects, their metadata policies, structures, best practice guides, and value constraints must receive rigorous and precise adherence.

3.2.3 Methods of Working from an Existing Element Set

Some existing standards will match one's desired element list better than others. It is possible, though, that no existing standard could meet the needs expressed through a desired list of elements. Decisions must be made regarding whether to adopt an existing element set, modify one, make an application profile, or even create a new set, and determine which is the most efficient approach for the project at hand.

The solution to those decisions rests upon semantics, which is the primary factor in the outcome. Consideration must be given to the meaning of an element (not simply considering a label) and its relationship with other elements. The suggestions in Table 3-2-2 should be interpreted by use of the "*If*. . . *then* form." For example, "*If* the desired elements defined by our project match the elements in the selected standard, and the relationships among elements also match, *then* our project should adopt the element set." If, after careful examination a particular standard satisfies the desired elements and/or ensures interoperability for the main collaborative project, then an element set can be defined for use by the project without modification.

A number of standards have already provided examples for modifying existing element sets, and their approaches can also be applied to localized sets. The results of the adjustment process can be claimed as a new standard or an application profile. The following list discusses various ways to modify element sets:

1. Deriving a new element set from an existing one is a common solution. This method allows different components to vary in depth and detail under a basic structure with common elements. In each case, the new element set is based on a "source" or "model" schema. TEI Lite is derived from the full TEI; CDWA Lite, VRA Core, and Object ID are all derived from CDWA; and, both MODS and MARC Lite are derived from the full MARC 21 standard. At the same time, changes may also occur in the encoding format (e.g., MARCXML), but the basic original semantics (element definitions and relationships) are retained.

Table 3-2-2. Matching situations and possible actions.

Desired Elements ← —— → Existing Element Set		
Desired Elements	**Element Relationships**	**Possible Actions**
matching	matching	adopt the element set
matching	not matching	modify the element set
not matching	n/a	create a new set or modify the existing element set
missing	n/a	create a new set or modify the existing element set

2. A related approach to derivation is to translate an existing schema into a different language. The semantics remain largely the same as the source schema. Examples include different language versions of the IPTC Core element set and DC element set.
3. Schema extension is a strategy employed to contend with specialized subjects, contents, or the needs of special communities of users. This derivation reflects the extensibility principle of metadata. Extensible metadata systems must allow for the extensions and expansions that meet the particular needs of a given application. Some of the results have their own namespace and become a different standard for a particular community:
   - The *Electronic Theses and Dissertations Metadata Standard* (ETD-MS) (www.ndltd.org/standards/metadata/current.html) uses 13 of the 15 DC elements and an additional element: *thesis.degree*. The standard (published in 2001) also revised the constraints and best practice guides based on the original DC element set.
   - The ADN (**A**DEPT (Alexandria Digital Earth Prototype), **D**LESE (Digital Library for Earth System Education), and **N**ASA's Joined Digital Library) item-level metadata schema (www.dlese.org/Metadata/adn-item/index.htm) extends the DLESE-IMS metadata framework, adding categories for geospatial and temporal characteristics.
   - The *National Library of Medicine (NLM) Metadata Schema* (www.nlm.nih.gov/tsd/cataloging/metafilenew.html) has been established based on the DC standard, including DC's elements, element refinements, encoding schemes, and vocabulary terms (see Figure 3-2-3). The Schema not only defines its own elements and element-refinements, but has also revised the constraints and obligations for each element. Its elements' indicators show three categories:
     (1) DC = Approved Dublin Core elements and qualifiers (e.g., *DC.Subject.MeSH*)
     (2) NLMDC = Approved Dublin Core elements with NLM-defined qualifiers (e.g., *NLMDC.Subject.NLMClass*)
     (3) NLM = NLM-defined elements (e.g., *NLM.Permanence.Level*)
4. Developing an application profile (AP) has become a dominant method during recent years. This method, overlapping with previously discussed text, can adopt, adjust, or extend elements from multiple element sets. (For a full discussion of application profiles, see Section 3.4.)

3.2.4 Testing the Element Set

Testing is crucial to specific decisions about a metadata element set to know which elements to include or exclude, which are necessary and core, and which add unnecessary clutter or dilute the power of the project design. Primary data providers should be given the opportunity to test the element set by creating metadata records for selected objects to be included in the digital collection. Sometimes it is also necessary to test more than one candidate element set, i.e., to compare different candidate element sets against the same testing sample (Zeng, 1999).

Figure 3-2-3. Selected elements defined by the National Library of Medicine Metadata Schema.

The key used for "Identifier" is:
DC = Approved Dublin Core elements and qualifiers
NLMDC = Approved Dublin Core elements with NLM-defined qualifiers
NLM = NLM-defined elements

Element: Permanence Level
Name: Permanence Level
Identifier: **NLM.Permanence.Level**
Definition: The extent to which a user can be assured that the resource will remain stable and available
Required: R
Repeatable: N
Comments: N/A

Element: Subject, MeSH
Name: Subject, MeSH
Identifier: **DC.Subject.MeSH**
Definition: Topic of the content of the resource, expressed in NLM Medical Subject Headings
Required: O
Repeatable: Y
Comments: N/A

Element: Subject, Class Number
Name: Subject, Class Number
Identifier: **NLMDC.Subject.NLMClass**
Definition: An NLM classification number which represents the topic of the content of the resource
Required: O
Repeatable: N
Comments: N/A

Source: Composite based on NLM Metadata Schema: www.nlm.nih.gov/tsd/cataloging/metafilenew.html.

3.3 Value Space

A value space is defined as the set of values for a given data type (ISO/IEC 11404:1996). In metadata standards, value spaces express the sets of values and/or rules specified for each element and stated in the element set. In the previous section, examples of data structures or metadata element sets were introduced. "Standards that govern the words (data values), and their selection, organization, and formatting (data content) are two other types of standards that must be used in conjunction with an agreed-upon data structure" (Baca et al., 2006: xi). This section provides resources related to data values, including examples from existing element sets. The titles of existing schemes are recommended by generally accepted metadata standards; the metadata community has referred to them as *value encoding schemes*, which include *syntax encoding schemes* and *vocabulary encoding schemes*. Closely related application issues are covered in Section 3.6 and a list of selected vocabularies is provided at the end of the book.

3.3.1 Value Spaces That Should Follow Standardized Syntax Encoding Rules

If "071210" represents a date in the twentieth century, which format does it represent: yy-mm-dd (1907, December 10), mm-dd-yy (July 12, 1910), mm-yy-dd

(July 1912, 10), or dd-mm-yy (07 December, 1910)? When such a string appears in a metadata record, it causes confusion; when searched by a system, it will significantly mismatch search queries. Therefore, *date* element consistency should be nearly universal. Dublin Core specifies the best practice when encoding values to the *date* element (for all examples—emphases added).

Example 1 (from DC):

> **Element Name:** date
> **Comment:** Date may be used to express temporal information at any level of granularity. Recommended best practice is to **use an encoding scheme**, such as the W3CDTF profile of ISO 8601.

Here ISO 8601 is the date and time representation standard. W3C-DTF (Date and Time Formats) is a profile of ISO 8601. The difference is that W3C-DTF is structured with hyphens when expressing date and time, The instruction provided by DC for *date* element ensures that all *date* values are presented as YYYY-MM-DD, using a "largest to smallest" unit pattern. This type of standard is also referred to as a *syntax encoding scheme* in the metadata community.

Use of an existing suggested standard or guideline ensures consistency with best practices, as with LOM's specification for the rights element. It points to a general rule, as shown in the next example.

Example 2 (from VRA 4.0):

> **RIGHTS**
> **Description:** Information about the copyright status and the rights holder for a work, collection, or image.
> **Data Values: MLA rules for bibliographic citation for print sources**.

Where there is no published standard to follow or when the standard is not specific or clear, it is still necessary to provide a common rule or further explanation for data values. The next example, taken from CDWA Lite, gives instructions on how to formulate a creator's name to display for end users (rather than for indexing purposes) under differing conditions.

Example 3 (from CDWA Lite):

> **Element:** Display Creator
> **Description:** The name, brief biographical information, and roles (if necessary) of the named creator or creators in the design and production of the work, presented in a syntax suitable for display to the end-user and including any necessary indications of uncertainty, ambiguity, and nuance. If there is no known creator, make a reference to the presumed culture or nationality of the unknown creator.
> **Data values: Formulated according to data content rules** for creator display in CCO and CDWA; may be concatenated from the Indexing Creator elements, if necessary. **The name should be** in natural order, if possible, although inverted order is acceptable. Include nationality and life dates. For unknown creators, **use one of the conventions** illustrated

in the following examples: "unknown," "unknown Chinese," "Chinese," or "unknown 15th-century Chinese."

3.3.2 Value Spaces That Require Standardized Vocabulary Encoding Schemes

Because of their roles in providing vocabularies to be used in an encoding process, standardized codes, controlled vocabularies, and authority files are all referred to as vocabulary encoding schemes in the metadata community.

3.3.2.1 Standardized Codes

A number of universal standardized schemes are available for certain types of data values such as codes for languages and countries. DC recommends using standardized codes for languages.

Example 4 (from DC):

Element Name: language
Definition: A language of the resource.
Comment: Recommended best practice is to use a controlled vocabulary such as RFC 4646.

A number of standards that define current codes representing languages used worldwide include RFC 4646, *Tags for Identifying Languages* and ISO 639.2, *Codes for the representation of names of languages—Part 2: alpha-3 code* (2006: http://www.loc.gov/standards/iso639-2/). These code standards provide lists and/or rules of using and registering a language code, e.g., two-letters (e.g., "en"), three-letters (e.g., "eng"), with subcodes (e.g., "en-US") as well as the names of the codes listed in different metadata standards as value encoding schemes. LOM, which suggests using ISO 639:1988 for the value space of Category *1.3 Language*, also states that "NOTE 5: . . . The language code should be given in lower case and the country code (if any) in upper case. However, the values are case insensitive" (IEEE 1484.12.1-2002, 2002: 11). Depending on the time a standard is issued, some obsolete code names might still exist in a current version of a metadata standard. For example, in combination with RFC 4647, RFC 4646 replaces RFC 3066, which replaced RFC 1766 (Phillips and Davis, 2006). Another widely used code list is ISO 3166-1 for country names. They contain all short country names and alpha-2 code elements officially published by ISO.

3.3.2.2 Controlled Vocabularies

The primary purpose of vocabulary control is to achieve consistency in the description of content objects and to facilitate retrieval. A controlled vocabulary can be a simple five-term list or a comprehensive thesaurus which shows not only hundreds of terms but also relationships among the terms. Basically, it is a list of terms that have been enumerated explicitly. This list is controlled by, and is available from, a controlled vocabulary registration authority. The ultimate goal is that all terms in a controlled vocabulary must have unambiguous, nonredundant definitions. At a minimal level, the following two rules must be enforced: (1) if the same term is commonly used to mean different concepts, then its name is explicitly qualified to resolve this ambiguity, and (2) if multiple terms are used to mean the same thing, one of the terms is identified as the preferred term in the controlled vocabulary and the other terms are listed as synonyms or aliases (ANSI/NISO Z39.19-2005: 5). Controlled vocabularies serve five purposes:

1. *Translation:* Provide a means for converting the natural language of authors, indexers, and users into a vocabulary that can be used for indexing and retrieval.
2. *Consistency:* Promote uniformity in term format and in the assignment of terms.
3. *Indication of relationships:* Indicate semantic relationships among terms.
4. *Label and browse:* Provide consistent and clear hierarchies in a navigation system to help users locate desired content objects.
5. *Retrieval:* Serve as a searching aid in locating content objects (ANSI/NISO Z39.19-2005: 11).

Almost all metadata standards require or recommend the use of controlled vocabularies for values associated with subject-related elements. DC recommends using controlled vocabulary for the data values associated with subject element. No specific scheme is listed in the following example.

Example 5 (from DC):

> **Element Name:** subject
> **Definition:** A topic of the resource.
> **Comment:** Typically, the topic will be represented using keywords, key phrases, or classification codes. **Recommended best practice is to use a controlled vocabulary**.

The DCMI Usage Board has included a number of controlled vocabularies and classification schemes that are used worldwide as the *encoding schemes* in the *DCMI Metadata Terms* document, including LCSH, *Medical Subject Headings* (MeSH), *Thesaurus for Geographic Names* (TGN), *Library of Congress Classification* (LCC), DDC, *Universal Decimal Classification* (UDC), and the *National Library of Medicine Classification*.

The DCMES provides an example of the vocabulary (i.e., *DCMI Type Vocabulary*) for the data values associated with the *type* element.

Example 6 (from DC):

> **Element Name:** type
> **Definition:** The nature or genre of the resource.
> **Comment: Recommended best practice is to use a controlled vocabulary such as the *DCMI Type Vocabulary*.**

The *DCMI Type Vocabulary* is a specialized controlled vocabulary that provides a general, cross-domain list of approved terms that may be used as values for the resource type element to identify the genre of a resource. The Vocabulary specifies the following terms: Collection, Dataset, Event, Image, InteractiveResource, MovingImage, PhysicalObject, Service, Software, Sound, StillImage, and Text.

VRA Core recommends a particular controlled vocabulary from the *Art and Architecture Thesaurus* (AAT), to be used for the data values associated with the *style period* element.

Example 7 (from VRA Core 4.0):

> **STYLE PERIOD**
> **Description:** A defined style, historical period, group, school, dynasty, movement, etc. whose characteristics are represented in the Work or Image. Cultural and regional terms may be combined with style and period terms for display purposes. **Data Values (controlled): Recommend AAT**.

VRA Core then provides more than one controlled vocabulary to be used for the data values associated with the *subject* element.

Example 8 (from VRA 4.0):

> **SUBJECT**
> **Description:** Terms or phrases that describe, identify, or interpret the Work or Image and what it depicts or expresses. These may include generic terms that describe the work and the elements that it comprises, terms that identify particular people, geographic places, narrative and iconographic themes, or terms that refer to broader concepts or interpretations. **Use of a Subject Authority, from which these data values may be derived, is recommended**.
> **Data Values: Recommend AAT, TGN, LCTGM, ICONCLASS, LCSH, LCNAF, Sears Subject Headings**.

Note: LCTGM = *Thesaurus for Graphic Materials* (by LC); LCNAF = *LC Name Authority File*, also known as *Anglo-American Authority File* (AAAF). ICONCLASS is a classification designed for art and iconography.

3.3.2.3 Name Authorities

Libraries and information services have a history of creating authority files to establish forms of names (for persons, places, meetings, and organizations), titles, and subjects used in bibliographic records. An authority record is the record of authority decisions, all or some of which may be used in a system display. It is basically the process of reaching a consensus on the name(s) of an entity, making cross-references from variant names, keeping track of those decisions, and displaying those decisions in information systems. A typical authority record using the MARC format is illustrated in Figure 3.3.1 where values in the 100 field define the preferred name, whereas values in the 400 fields are considered synonyms or aliases.

An authority file for geographical names (such as TGN [*The Getty Thesaurus of Geographical Names*]) helps to identify a particular place according to its

Figure 3-3-1. An authority record for "Clinton, Bill" in the FAST Authority File.

```
000      nz n
001      fst00088204
003      OCoLC
005      20040924145531.0
008      040924nneanz||babn n ana d
040      OCoLC   $b eng   $c OCoLC   $f fast
100 1    Clinton, Bill,   $d 1946-
400 1    Clinton, William J.   $q (William Jefferson),   $d 1946-
400 1    Blythe, William Jefferson,   $d 1946-
400 1    Klintūn, Bīl,   $d 1946-
400 1    Ḳlinṭon, Bil,   $d 1946-
400 1    Klinton, Bill,   $d 1946-
400 1    Klinton, Uil□i□a□m Dzhefferson,   $d 1946-
400 0    Kelindun,   $d 1946-
688      LC subject usage: 448 (2006)
688      WC subject usage: 2,104 (2006)
700 17   Clinton, Bill,   $d 1946-   $0 (DLC)n 82029644
```

Source: Reprinted from FAST—*Faceted Application of Subject Terminology*, http://fast.oclc.org/, with permission.

name, type, location, and historical context. For example, many places share the name *Columbus* in the United States, as shown in Figure 3-3-2.

An authority record will help to differentiate this particular *Columbus* located in Bartholomew County, Indiana, from other locations that also have the name *Columbus* (see Figure 3-3-3). This TGN authority record provides rich information including *Place types* ("inhabited place," "town," etc.), *Coordinates* (latitude and longitude), *Names* (current, historical, and vernacular), and *Hierarchical position*. TGN is recommended for data values for the *coverage* element in DCMES.

Example 9 (from DC):

> **Term Name:** coverage
> **Definition:** The spatial or temporal topic of the resource, the spatial applicability of the resource, or the jurisdiction under which the resource is relevant.
> **Comment:** Spatial topic may be a named place or a location specified by its geographic coordinates. Temporal period may be a named period, date, or date range. A jurisdiction may be a named administrative entity or a geographic place to which the resource applies. **Recommended best practice is to use a controlled vocabulary such as the *Thesaurus of Geographic Names*.** Where appropriate, named places or time periods can be used in preference to numeric identifiers such as sets of coordinates or date ranges.

CDWA Lite specifies that values for the element *name of creator* are controlled, and two authority files for names are recommended.

Figure 3-3-2. Display of place name entries that match the query "Columbus" in TGN.

5. ☐ **Columbus** .... (inhabited place)
(World, North and Central America, United States, Arkansas, Hempstead county) [2008001]

6. ☐ **Columbus** .... (inhabited place)
(World, North and Central America, United States, Colorado, La Plata county) [2251004]

7. ☐ **Columbus** .... (county)
(World, North and Central America, United States, Georgia) [2156155]
Columbus county

8. ☐ **Columbus** .... (inhabited place)
(World, North and Central America, United States, Georgia, Muscogee) [7013643]

9. ☐ **Columbus** .... (inhabited place)
(World, North and Central America, United States, Illinois, Adams county) [2027254]

10. ☐ **Columbus** .... (inhabited place)
(World, North and Central America, United States, Indiana, Bartholomew county) [7013644]

11. ☐ **Columbus** .... (inhabited place)
(World, North and Central America, United States, Kansas, Cherokee county) [2036215]

Source: © J. Paul Getty Trust. Getty Vocabulary Program. *Getty Thesaurus of Geographic Names* (TGN). Los Angeles: J. Paul Getty Trust, Vocabulary Program, 1988. www.getty.edu/research/conducting_research/vocabularies/tgn/, accessed January 10, 2008. Reprinted with permission.

Example 10 (from CDWA Lite):

> **4.1.1.1. Subelement:** Name of Creator
> **Description:** The names, appellations, or other identifiers assigned to an individual, group of people, firm or other corporate body, or other entity that has contributed to the design, creation, production, manufacture, or alteration of the work.
> **Comment: Use of a Personal and Corporate Name Authority,** from which the names, nationality, and dates may be derived, is recommended.
> **Data values: Controlled. For name, recommended: ULAN and AAAF**

Note: AAAF = *Anglo-American Authority File*, an international collaboration of *LC Name Authority File* and other major name authority files maintained in other countries. Several well-known authority files are recommended in many metadata standards and application profiles (listed in Appendix B of the book).

Figure 3-3-3. Display of a TGN authority record for "Columbus, Indiana, USA."

ID: 7013644 **Record Type: administrative**

Columbus (inhabited place)

Coordinates:
Lat: 39 12 00 N *degrees minutes* Lat: 39.2000 *decimal degrees*
Long: 085 55 00 W *degrees minutes* Long: -85.9167 *decimal degrees*

Note: Located on East Fork of White River; is a diversified industrial community surrounded by fertile prairie land; noted for modern architecture designed by distinguished architects, including I. M. Pei, the Saarinens, Harry Weese, and Robert Trent Jones.

Names:
Columbus (**preferred**, C ,V,N)
Tiptonia (H ,V,N) .... named for General John Tipton, who donated the land for the town
Tiptona (H ,V,N)

Hierarchical Position:
World (facet)
.... North and Central America (continent)
.... United States (nation)
.... Indiana (state)
.... Bartholomew (county)
.... Columbus (inhabited place)

Place Types:
inhabited place (**preferred**, C) .... founded in 1821, developed as a center on National Road
town (C)
county seat (C)
industrial center (C) .... base for Cummins Engine Company, which produces diesel engines; town also manufactures automobile accessories and electronics
agricultural center (C)
tourist center (C)

Source: © J. Paul Getty Trust. Getty Vocabulary Program. *Getty Thesaurus of Geographic Names* (TGN). Los Angeles: J. Paul Getty Trust, Vocabulary Program, 1988. www.getty.edu/research/conducting_research/vocabularies/tgn/, accessed January 10, 2008. Reprinted with permission.

3.3.3 Value Spaces That Should Have Predefined Lists of Terms

In many cases, a particular attribute of a resource, although necessary to have controlled values, may not be accurately described by existing controlled vocabularies (which either may be too large, comprehensive, or not specific enough). A list of terms can be predefined by metadata schema designers or implementers to describe aspects of content objects or entities that have a limited number of possibilities. Many metadata standards have provided small predefined lists of terms for particular elements' value spaces. For example, LOM specifies a pre-prepared list of terms for use in the value space of the *5.2 Learning Resource Type* element.

Example 11 (from LOM):

5.2 Learning Resource Type

Explanation: Specific kind of learning object. The most dominant kind shall be first.

NOTE: The vocabulary terms are defined as in the OED 1989 and as used by educational communities of practice.

Value Space: **ordered exercise; simulation; questionnaire; diagram; figure; graph; index; slide; table; narrative text; exam; experiment; problem statement; self assessment; lecture.**

Note: OED = *Oxford English Dictionary*. Sometimes an open-ended list is provided, with the most probable terms listed.

Example 12 (from CDWA):

> **6.1.5. Subelement: Shape Measurements**
> **Description:** The shape of a work, used for unusual shapes (e.g., an oval painting).
> **Data values: oval, round, square, rectangular, irregular, and others as recommended in CCO and CDWA.**

A predefined list does not need to become a formal controlled vocabulary, which also would require the arrangement of terms and their relationships. However, the conventions used to form a controlled vocabulary can still be applied. The defining characteristics of a list are that the terms:

- are all members of the same set or class of items (e.g., content type, language);
- are not overlapping in meaning; and
- are equal in terms of specificity or granularity (e.g., a geographic areas list does not mix continents with country or state names).

A predefined list can also be built based on an existing vocabulary. The NSDL Vocabulary-Subgroup developed a *Learning Resource Type Vocabulary*, which is an extension of the *DCMI Type Vocabulary*, with many more terms that are especially useful for educational materials. Another example is a list extracted from AAT for the work type element in VRA Core.

Example 13 (from VRA Core 4.0):

> **WORK TYPE**
> **Definition:** Identifies the specific type of WORK, COLLECTION, or IMAGE being described in the record.
> **Data Values** for WORK AND COLLECTION *type* (controlled vocabulary): recommend AAT.
> **Recommended data values** for IMAGE WORK *type* (**AAT terms**):
> **black-and-white transparency, color transparency** (for slides or positive transparencies), **black-and-white negative, color negative** (for negative transparencies), **photographic print** (for photographic prints), or **digital image**.

The requirement for consistent specificity can be explained with this example: in addition to paper, other materials such as wood, metal, and cotton cloth are used for making postcards. A short list can be made for the *materials* element in a postcard metadata element set. However, for postcards only made with wood, one may want to indicate that it is not a regular paper card (i.e., it is made of wood), but others may want to indicate that it is made of cedar, Hawaiian koa, or the inner bark of the mulberry tree. No matter which level of specificity is determined for a predefined list, the terms included should be equal in specificity or granularity.

Predefined lists should be registered in a metadata registry (e.g., DCMI Metadata Registry) either as a collection of all terms (an encoding scheme) or individual terms. This will help to eliminate redundant work by other projects and stimulate discovery and reuse of metadata so as to promote exchange and sharing of intellectual work. The CORES Registry (http://www.cores-eu.net/registry/; discussed in Chapter 6, Section 6.3), maintained by the UK Office for Library and Information Networking (UKOLN), is one public registry that contains dozens of encoding schemes.

Value spaces and best practice guides are inseparable for metadata standards. Best practice guides range from simple notes in an element set to large documents (see extended discussion in Section 3.6).

3.4 Application Profiles

Different user requirements and specialized local needs occur even within a particular community. The details (data structure, data values, and data contents) provided in some metadata schemas may not meet the needs of all user groups.

A typical approach to accommodating individual needs is to establish an *application profile* (AP), and it should be noted that the element sets following the extension approach described in Section 3.2 are sometimes regarded as application profiles as well. Whereas an existing element set is used as the basis for description in a particular digital library or repository, individual needs are met through specific guidelines or policies for application; this is called an application profile.

Application profiling is explained in the following definitions:

- A profile outlines the extent to which an existing schema would be applied and provides guidelines for its application in the environment in question. The concept is based on the idea that metadata standards are necessarily localized and optimized for specific contents (Johnston, 2003).
- An application profile is an assemblage of metadata elements selected from one or more metadata schemas and combined in a compound schema (Duval et al., 2002).
- Application profiles consist of data elements drawn from one or more namespaces, combined by implementers, and optimized for a particular local application (Heery and Patel, 2000).

Figure 3-4-1 illustrates an application profile that consists of properties (elements and element refinements) drawn from one or more namespaces (element sets). The application profile can then be used by one or more different applications in the process of creating metadata records. The use of application profiles ensures a similar basic structure with common elements, while allowing for varying degrees of depth and detail for different user communities.

3.4.1 APs Consisting of Elements Drawn from Other Schemas

Application profiles usually consist of metadata elements drawn from one or more metadata schemas, combined into a compound schema by implementers, and optimized for a particular local application (Heery and Patel 2000; Duval et

Figure 3-4-1. Illustration of an application profile consisting of metadata elements and refinements drawn from one or more namespaces.

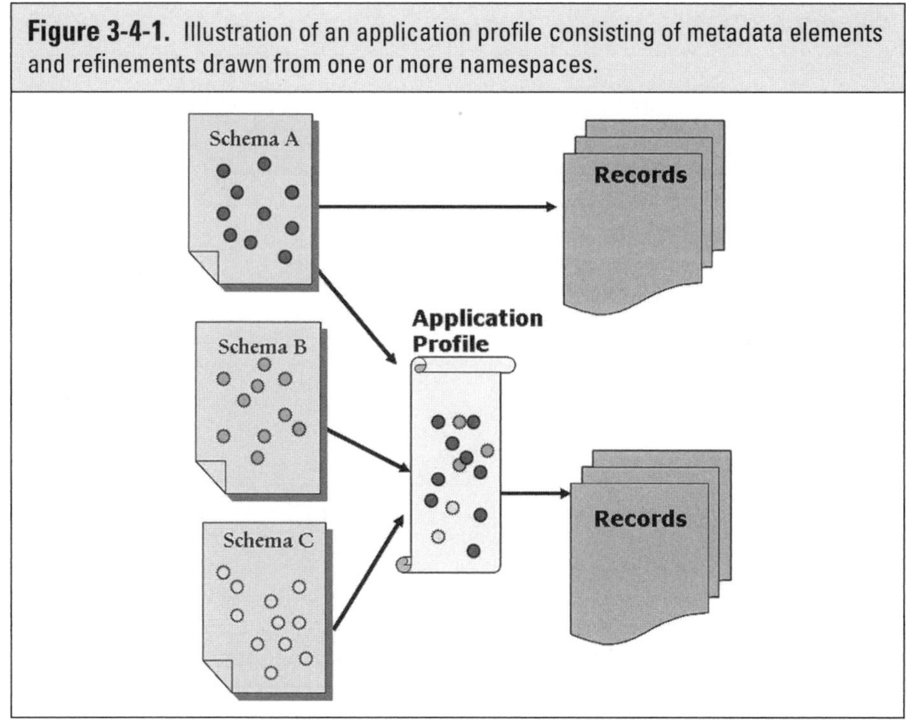

al., 2002). For example, the Australasian Virtual Engineering Library's *AVEL Metadata Set* consists of 19 elements (see Figure 3-4-2). In addition to supporting 14 DC elements (excluding the *dc.source* element), it also supports one AGLS (Australian Government Locator Service) metadata element: *AGLS.Availability*; one EDNA (Education Network Australia) element: *EdNA.Review*; and three Administrative elements: *AC.Creator*, *AC.DateCreated*, and *AVEL.Comments*.

From its inception, the NSDL has recommended that its collection projects use metadata elements from DC with three additional elements from IEEE LOM. Figure 3-4-3 illustrates a section from the NSDL_DC Metadata Guidelines for: (1) Element, (2) Recommended usage, (3) Simple definition/Notes, and (4) Sample XML tags. The elements from DC have a "dc:" prefix, refinements from DCMI Terms have a "dct:" prefix, and elements from IEEE LOM have an "ieee:" prefix. An AP may also provide additional documentation on how the terms used are constrained, encoded, or interpreted for particular purposes (Baker, 2003).

3.4.2 APs Based on One Schema but Tailored for Particular Application Communities

The creation of APs can also be initiated by groups who have created a standard, e.g., DCMI. Based on a single schema, APs are developed for different user communities. The DC-Library Application Profile (DC-Lib) clarifies the

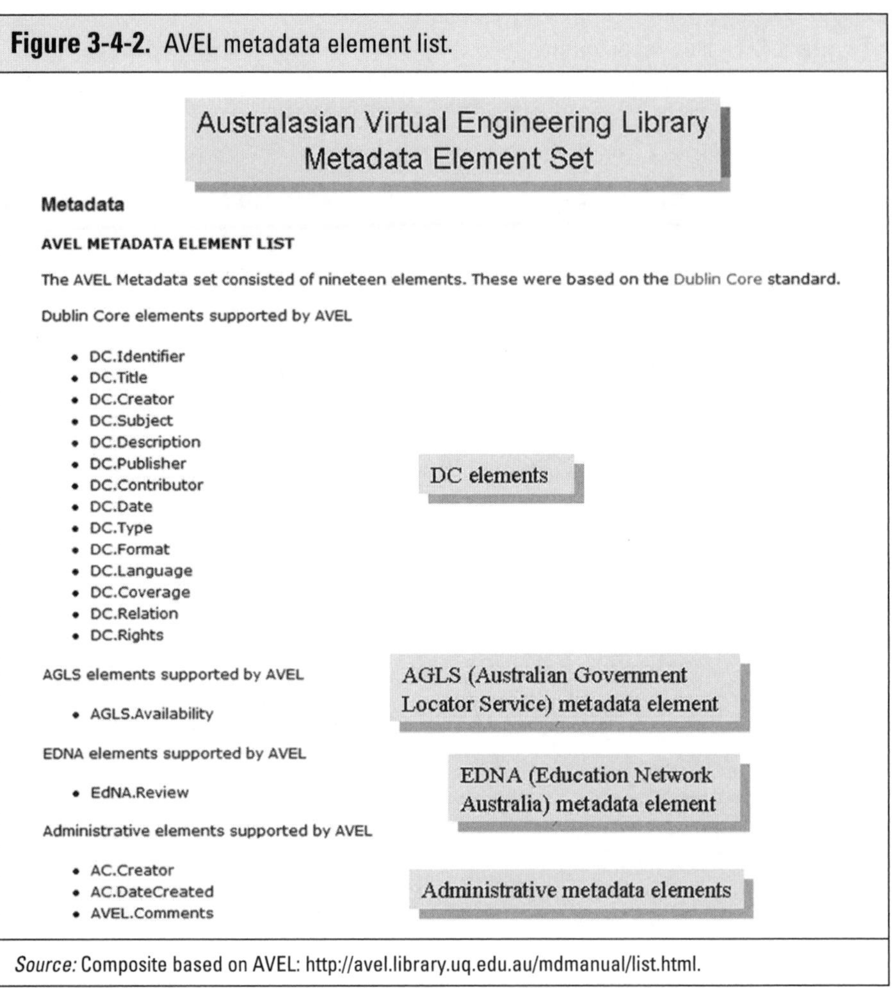

Australasian Virtual Engineering Library
Metadata Element Set
Metadata
AVEL METADATA ELEMENT LIST
The AVEL Metadata set consisted of nineteen elements. These were based on the Dublin Core standard.
Dublin Core elements supported by AVEL
DC.Identifier
DC.Title
DC.Creator
DC.Subject
DC.Description
DC.Publisher
DC.Contributor
DC.Date
DC.Type
DC.Format
DC.Language
DC.Coverage
DC.Relation
DC.Rights
DC elements
AGLS elements supported by AVEL
AGLS.Availability
AGLS (Australian Government Locator Service) metadata element
EDNA elements supported by AVEL
EdNA.Review
EDNA (Education Network Australia) metadata element
Administrative elements supported by AVEL
AC.Creator
AC.DateCreated
AVEL.Comments
Administrative metadata elements

Figure 3-4-2. AVEL metadata element list.

Source: Composite based on AVEL: http://avel.library.uq.edu.au/mdmanual/list.html.

use of the DC Metadata Element Set in libraries and library-related applications and projects. It defines the following:

- required elements;
- permitted Dublin Core elements;
- permitted Dublin Core qualifiers;
- permitted schemes and values (e.g. use of a specific controlled vocabulary or encoding scheme);
- library domain elements used from another namespace;
- additional elements/qualifiers from other application profiles that may be used (e.g., DC-Education: Audience); and
- refinement of standard definitions.

DC-Lib uses terms from two namespaces (see *Term URI* line in Figures 3-4-4 and 3-4-5): *DCMI Metadata Terms* (http://dublincore.org/documents/dcmi-terms/),

Figure 3-4-3. Sample metadata fields within the NSDL_DC metadata framework.

Date	Recommended	A point or period of time associated with an event in the lifecycle of the resource. Employ W3CDTF encoding scheme that looks like YYYY-MM-DD.	<dc:date>...</dc:date>
Created	Recommended	A refinement of the Date element	<dct:created>...</dct:created>
Available	Optional	A refinement of the Date element	<dct:available>...</dct:available>
dateAccepted	Optional	A refinement of the Date element	<dct:dateAccepted>...</dct:dateAccepted>
dateCopyrighted	Optional	A refinement of the Date element	<dct:dateCopyrighted>...</dct:dateCopyrighted>
dateSubmitted	Optional	A refinement of the Date element	<dct:dateSubmitted>...</dct:dateSubmitted>
Issued	Optional	A refinement of the Date element	<dct:issued>...</dct:issued>
Modified	Optional	A refinement of the Date element	<dct:modified>...</dct:modified>
Valid	Optional	A refinement of the Date element	<dct:valid>...</dct:valid>
Interactivity Type	Recommended if applicable	The type of interactions supported by a resource (active, expositive, mixed, undefined)	<ieee:interactivityType>...</ieee:interactivityType>
Interactivity Level	Recommended if applicable	The level of interaction between a resource and end user; that is the degree to which the learner can influence the behavior of the resource (very high, high, medium, low, very low)	<ieee:interactivityLevel>...</ieee:interactivityLevel>
Typical Learning Time	Optional	The typical amount of time for a particular education level to interact with the resource.	<ieee:typicalLearningTime>...</ieee:typicalLearningTime>
Format	Optional	Physical medium and/or file/MIME format	<dc:format>...</dc:format>
Extent	Optional	The size or duration of the resource.	<dct:extent>...</dct:extent>
Medium	Optional	The material or physical carrier of the resource.	<dct:medium>...</dct:medium>

Source: NSDL_DC Metadata Guidelines: http://nsdl.org/collection/metadata-guide.php.

and MODS (www.loc.gov/mods). *DC-Lib Definition* and *DC-Lib Comments* are specifically designed for this application profile, and other constraints or obligations are further defined.

Previously all DC elements had been optional; in DC-Lib however, a value for *obligation* is assigned that designates some elements as required. The values of obligations (see Figure 3-4-5) are: mandatory (M), mandatory if applicable (MA), strongly recommended (R), and optional (O). This more precise delineation facilitates the compatibility of DC-Lib with other standards (e.g., MARC 21) used by library communities.

Similarly, the DC Government (DC-Gov) Application Profile clarifies the use of DC in a governmental environment (DCMI-Government Working Group, 2001). Another example is the *Biological Data Profile* of the National

Figure 3-4-4. Element *title* defined in the DC Library Application Profile (term is from *DCMI Metadata Terms* namespace).

Name of Term	title
Term URI	http://purl.org/dc/elements/1.1/title
Label	Title
Defined By	http://dublincore.org/documents/dcmi-terms/
Source Definition	A name given to the resource
DC-Lib Definition	-
Source Comments	Typically, a title will be a name by which the resource is formally known.
DC-Lib Comments	A parallel/transliterated title is considered a main title, i.e. the Title element is repeated. Either a title or identifier is mandatory. If no title is available, best practice is to give a constructed title, derive a title from the resource or supply *[no title]*. If using qualified Dublin Core, an element refinement for titles other than the main title(s) should be included. Retain initial articles and use local sorting algorithms based on language. A language qualifier may be used to indicate language of title if appropriate. (For example, see: Initial Definite and Indefinite Articles for a list of articles in various languages).
Type of term	element
Refines	
Refined By	alternative
Has Encoding Scheme	
Obligation	M
Occurence	

Source: DC-Lib: http://dublincore.org/documents/library-application-profile/.

Biological Information Infrastructure, which is based on the *Content Standard for Digital Geospatial Metadata* (CSDGM) of the Federal Geographic Data Committee (FGDC).

3.4.3 APs Declaring Own Namespaces

According to the definitions of the DCMI Usage Board, an AP is a declaration of the metadata terms an organization, information resource, application, or user community employs in its metadata (Baker, 2003). Moreover, by definition, an AP cannot *declare* new metadata terms and definitions; it only *reuses* terms from existing element sets (Heery and Patel, 2000). An AP may also provide additional documentation on how the terms used are constrained, encoded, or interpreted for particular purposes (Baker, 2003). Heery and Patel (2000) highlight the characteristics of Application Profiles, which:

- may draw on one or more existing namespaces;
- may introduce no new data elements;
- may specify permitted schemes and values; and
- can refine standard definitions.

Figure 3-4-5. Element *DateCaptured* defined in the DC Library Application Profile (term is from *MODS* namespace).

Name of Term	dateCaptured
Term URI	http://www.loc.gov/mods/
Label	Date Captured
Defined By	
Source Definition	
DC-Lib Definition	Date that the resource was captured.
Source Comments	
DC-Lib Comments	This includes the date that a snapshot of the resource was taken (particularly for dynamic resources) if different from Date.Created. Use existing element <dateCaptured> under <publicationInfo> in the Metadata Object Description Schema. Decision by DCMI Usage Board in May 2002. Best practice is to use as a machine-processible date (ISO 8601 without hyphens or W3CDTF with hyphens).
Type of term	element refinement
Refines	Date
Refined By	
Has Encoding Scheme	ISO 8601(without hyphens) - http://purl.org/dc/terms/ISO8601 W3C-DTF (with hyphens) - http://purl.org/dc/terms/W3CDTF
Obligation	O
Occurence	

Source: DC-Lib : http://dublincore.org/documents/library-application-profile/.

The question then is: Under what conditions can new metadata terms (elements and refinements) and definitions be added to a profile? Heery and Patel further clarify:

> If an implementor wishes to create "new" elements that do not exist elsewhere then (under this model) they *must create their own namespace schema, and take responsibility for "declaring" and maintaining that schema;*. . . The application profile can refine the definitions within the namespace schema, but it may only make the definition semantically narrower or more specific. This is to take account of situations where particular implementations use domain specific, or resource specific language. (Heery and Patel 2000, www.ariadne.ac.uk/issue25/app-profiles/intro.html [emphasis in original])

Duval et al. (2002) also state that the purpose of an application profile is to adapt or combine existing schemas into a package tailored to the functional requirements of a particular application, and retain interoperability with the original base schemas. Part of such an adaptation *may include the elaboration of local metadata elements* that have importance in a given community or organization, but which are not expected to be important in a broader context.

Dublin Core Application Profile Guidelines (DCAP) also includes instructions for "Identifying terms with appropriate precision" and "Declaring new elements" (Baker et al., 2005: Section 5.7). "By definition, a DCAP identifies the source of metadata terms used—whether they have been defined in formally maintained standards such as Dublin Core, in less formally defined element sets and vocabularies, or by the creator of the DCAP itself for local use in an application" (Baker et al., 2005: Section 3). The documents from Gateway to Educational Materials (GEM), *Application Profiles for GEM 2.0* provide URIs of namespaces for each element. The following two elements have different namespaces (examples 14 and 15).

Example 14 (from GEM 2.0):

Name: coverage
Label: Coverage
Namespace: http://purl.org/dc/elements/1.1/
Registration Authority: Dublin Core Metadata Initiative (DCMI)

Example 15 (from GEM 2.0):

Name: duration
Label: Duration
Namespace: http://purl.org/gem/elements/
Registration Authority: GEM Consortium

Dublin Core Application Profile Guidelines (Baker et al., 2005) includes a further explanation for two additional situations.

1. If a term has been declared or documented somewhere but not assigned a URI, the term should be identified as precisely as possible by providing its name and pointing to a declarative document or schema in which it has been defined, cited with URI, Web address, or bibliographic reference in the field *Defined By*.

Example 16 (from Dublin Core Application Profile Guidelines):

Term URI	—
Name	AttendancePattern
Label	Attendance Pattern
Defined By	http://someones-project.org/schema.html

2. For a term that has not already been defined in any other declarative document, the field *Defined By* should simply cite the URI of the Dublin Core Application Profile (DCAP) itself (as assigned with Identifier in the DCAP Descriptive Header). For example, in a DCAP with the URI "http://my-project.org/profile.html", a new local term should be provided with its name and pointing to this URI "http://my-project.org/profile.html" (Baker et al., 2005: Section 3).

According to this statement, the standards discussed in Section 3.2, i.e., the ETD-MS and the NLM Metadata Schemas, are also application profiles.

One major problem of APs is that when a base schema changes or is modified, the APs lag behind in updating definitions and best practice guides. Changes made in DC version 1.1, for example, which were released at the end of December 2006 and passed as NISO Z39.82-2007, have not received "synchronized" changes in DC-based APs as of September 2007.

In practice then, the development of an application profile often involves the following steps: (1) selecting a "base" metadata namespace; (2) selecting elements from other metadata namespaces; (3) defining local metadata elements and declaring new elements' namespaces; and (4) enforcing application of the elements (including cardinality enforcement, value space restriction, and relationship and dependency specification) (Duval et al., 2002; Zhang, 2004).

The IMS Meta-data Best Practice Guide for IEEE 1484.12.1-2002 Standard for Learning Object Metadata (IMS, 2004) recommends the steps for successfully creating an application profile:

- Understand the requirements and clearly define the purpose(s) of the profile.
- Ensure that adequate resources are available for the process of creating and maintaining the profile.
- Review existing relevant standards, specifications, and application profiles (check metadata registries for current schemata). If an application profile is found that meets the implementer's community requirements, it should be used as is or modified to meet these requirements.
- Distinguish among profiles used for storing metadata for internal use, for exposing metadata for search and discovery, and for exchanging metadata records with other systems.
- Determine what other applications the profile needs to interoperate with.
- Follow the recommendations below regarding: Extensions; Bindings and conformance; Vocabularies; Translations; and Mapping semantics.
- Publish the application profile(s) in a metadata schema registry.

The *CORES Registry* (http://cores.dsd.sztaki.hu/; accessed February 22, 2008) contains many registered metadata element sets, application profiles, encoding schemes, as well as a large number of activity reports that describe and comment on various metadata-related activities and initiatives. Such a registry is an excellent place for "shopping" and gathering the appropriate reusable elements already defined.

3.5 Crosswalks

A crosswalk is "a mapping of the elements, semantics, and syntax from one metadata scheme to those of another" (NISO, 2004). At present, crosswalks are by far the most commonly used method to enable interoperability between and among metadata schemas. The method begins with independent metadata schemas; attempts are then made to map or create crosswalks between equivalent or comparable metadata terms, i.e., elements and refinements. (Note that sometimes other terms are used to refer to *element*, e.g., *field, label, tag*.) The mechanism used in crosswalks is usually a chart or table that represents the semantic mapping of data elements in one data standard (source) to those in another standard (target) based on the similarity of function or meaning of the elements (Baca, 2000–2008).

Crosswalks allow systems to effectively convert data from one metadata standard to another. They enable heterogeneous collections to be searched simultaneously with a single query as if contained within a single database (*semantic interoperability*). In recent years, major efforts in metadata mapping have produced a substantial number of crosswalks. Almost all schemas have created crosswalks to popular schemas such as DC, MARC, and LOM. Metadata specifications may also include crosswalks to a previous version as well as to other schemas. An example is the VRA Core 4.0, which lists mapped elements in target schemas VRA 2.0 and 3.0 (earlier versions), CDWA, and DC.

The predominant method used in crosswalking is direct mapping or establishing equivalency among elements in different schemas. Metadata "mapping" refers to a formal identification of equivalent or nearly equivalent metadata elements or groups of metadata elements from different metadata schemas, carried out to facilitate semantic interoperability (Baca, 2000–2008). Many metadata properties need to be brought into consideration for mapping. According to the NISO document *Issues in Crosswalking Content Metadata Standards* (St. Pierre and LaPlant, 1998), common properties may include:

- a semantic definition of each metadata element;
- whether a metadata element is mandatory, optional, or mandatory based on certain conditions;
- whether a metadata element may occur multiple times in the same record;
- constraints due to the organization of metadata elements relative to each other, e.g., hierarchical parent-child relationships;
- constraints imposed on the value of an element (e.g., free text, numeric range, date, or controlled vocabulary); and
- optional support for locally defined metadata elements.

Two approaches have been used in crosswalking practice. The *absolute crosswalking* approach requires exact mapping between the involved elements (for example, *vra.title* → *dc.title*) of a source schema (e.g., VRA Core) and a target schema (e.g., DC). Where no exact equivalence exists there will be no crosswalking (e.g., *vra.technique* → [empty space]) (see Figure 3-5-1). Absolute crosswalking ensures the equivalency (or closely-equivalent matches) of elements, but does not work well for data conversion. The problem is that data values in nonmapable space will then be left out, especially when a source schema has a richer structure than that of the target schema. To overcome this problem, an alternative approach, *relative crosswalking*, is used to map all elements in a source schema to at least one element of a target schema, regardless of whether the two elements are semantically equivalent (e.g., *vra.technique* → *dc.format*) (see also Figure 3-5-1). The relative crosswalking approach appears to work better when mapping from complex to simpler schema (e.g., from MARC to DC) but not vice versa.

One of the problems of crosswalking is the different degrees of equivalency (see Figure 3-5-2): one-to-one, one-to-many, many-to-one, and one-to-none (Zeng and Xiao, 2001). These situations occur in many metadata crosswalks, especially mappings between a flat structure (e.g., Dublin Core) and a

Figure 3-5-1. Absolute and relative crosswalking.

	Absolute crosswalking	Relative crosswalking
VAR Core (3.0)	Dublin Core	Dublin Core
Technique	----------	*Format*
Location.Current Repository	----------	*Contributor* *Coverage*

Figure 3-5-2. Different degrees of element equivalency in crosswalked schemas. A1 and B1 represent elements from A and B schemas.

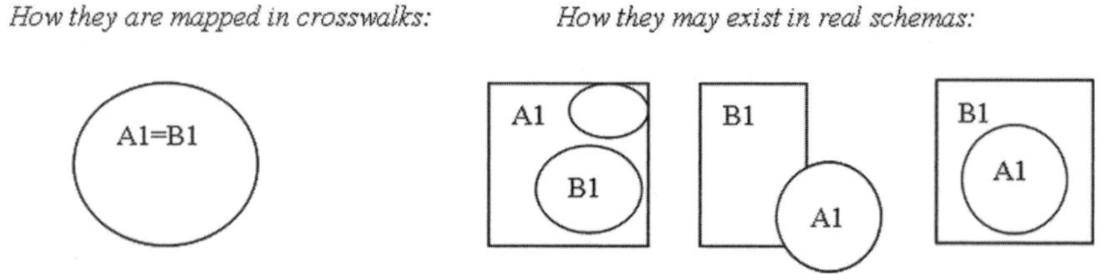

Source: Zeng, 2001.

hierarchical structure (e.g., LOM, CDWA, MODS, VRA Core 4.0); and, between two hierarchical structures that are significantly different. The level of details may extend from elements-only to elements-plus-qualifiers/refinements or subelements.

However, usually only the names of the elements and their definitions are taken into consideration in a crosswalk. This means that when mapping individual elements, often there are no exact equivalents. At the same time, many elements are found to overlap in meaning and scope. For these reasons, data conversion based on crosswalks creates quality problems.

Using a switching schema (new or existing) to channel crosswalking among multiple schemas has become a well-accepted solution. In this model, one of the schemas is used as the switching mechanism among multiple schemas. Instead of mapping between every pair in the group, each of the individual metadata schemas is mapped to the switching schema only. An example is Getty's crosswalk in which seven schemas all crosswalk to CDWA (see Figure 3-5-3).

Crosswalks have a direct impact on the quality of data conversion: any mismatched or missed pair may cause incorrect conversion or loss of thousands of values. This issue is discussed further in Chapter 7 in Section 7.4.2.

Figure 3-5-3. Crosswalk of CDWA to seven schemas.

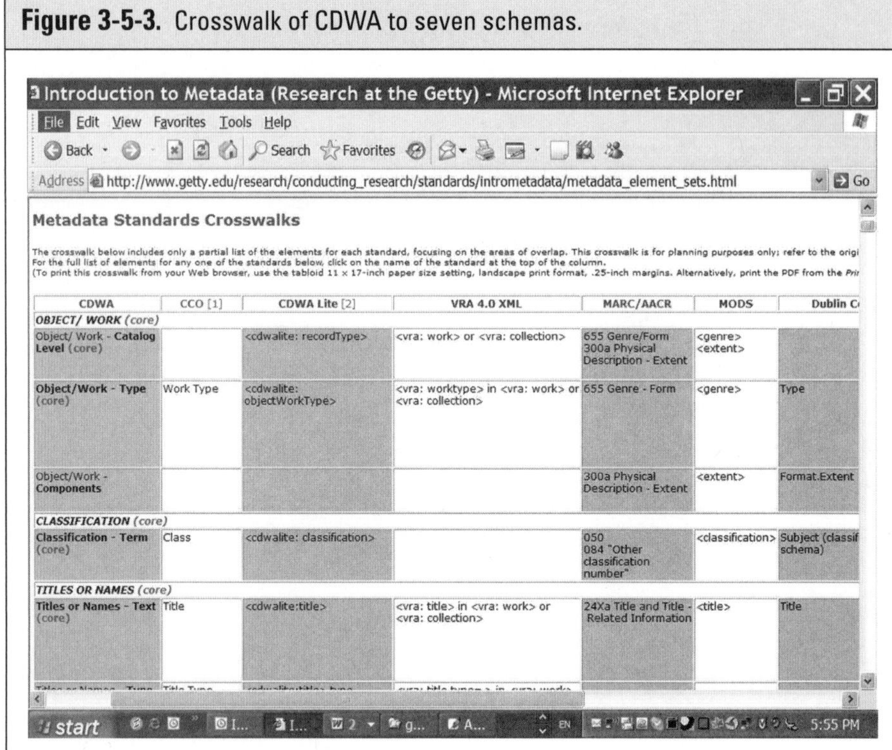

Metadata Standards Crosswalks

The crosswalk below includes only a partial list of the elements for each standard, focusing on the areas of overlap. This crosswalk is for planning purposes only; refer to the origi
For the full list of elements for any one of the standards below, click on the name of the standard at the top of the column.
(To print this crosswalk from your Web browser, use the tabloid 11 x 17-inch paper size setting, landscape print format, .25-inch margins. Alternatively, print the PDF from the *Pri*

CDWA	CCO [1]	CDWA Lite [2]	VRA 4.0 XML	MARC/AACR	MODS	Dublin C
OBJECT/ WORK *(core)*						
Object/ Work - **Catalog Level** (core)		<cdwalite: recordType>	<vra: work> or <vra: collection>	655 Genre/Form 300a Physical Description - Extent	<genre> <extent>	
Object/Work - Type (core)	Work Type	<cdwalite: objectWorkType>	<vra: worktype> in <vra: work> or <vra: collection>	655 Genre - Form	<genre>	Type
Object/Work - **Components**				300a Physical Description - Extent	<extent>	Format.Extent
CLASSIFICATION *(core)*						
Classification - Term (core)	Class	<cdwalite: classification>		050 084 "Other classification number"	<classification>	Subject (classif schema)
TITLES OR NAMES *(core)*						
Titles or Names - Text (core)	Title	<cdwalite:title>	<vra: title> in <vra: work> or <vra: collection>	24Xa Title and Title - Related Information	<title>	Title

Source: © J. Paul Getty Trust. "*Metadata Standards Crosswalk.*" Compiled by Patricia Harpring, Mary S. Woodley, Anne J. Gilliland, and Murtha Baca. www.getty.edu/research/conducting_research/standards/intrometadata/metadata_element_sets.html, accessed January 10, 2008. From *Introduction to Metadata: Pathways to Digital Information*, by Tony Gill, Anne Gilliland-Swetland, and Mary S. Woodley, edited by Murtha Baca. Reprinted with permission.

3.6 Best Practice Guides and Other Guidelines

Good design can easily be buried under the carelessness of incorrect execution. Poor use of metadata standards will impede communication of even the best concepts. Therefore it is very important to provide best practice guides for metadata standards, separately prepared guidelines, and content standards for implementations. Best practices provide guidance and information for the most efficient (least amount of effort) and effective (best results) ways of accomplishing a task, and are empirically based on repeatable procedures proven to be dependable for large numbers of people. A best practice guide is neither a standard nor regulation. In the metadata standards they can be found under headings such as comments, description, data value, explanation, value space, and examples.

In Section 3.3 we used various examples to illustrate how metadata standards provide requirements, recommendations, or instructions for the value spaces that need value encoding rules and schemes (including vocabularies and syntax encoding). They are part of the best practice guides that support processing data values associated with many elements, e.g., (as in DC) *creator, date, subject, type, format,* and *coverage,* yet for such general purpose metadata standards, best practice guides tend to be too general. A metadata creator may feel a lack of guidance in handling day-to-day problems. Application profiles designed for specialized communities more often provide detailed guides and examples. In addition, various communities have also developed content standards to assist the implementation of metadata schemes in practice. Appendix B of this book also provides a reference list of selected content standards and best practice guides.

3.6.1 Best Practice Guides

Best practice guides included in an element set give different levels of requirements, recommendations, or instructions. Examples in the following discussion will help to prepare best practice guides for metadata element sets.

Recommendations for *which* rules or vocabularies to follow are very common. These recommendations may be general or specific. Sometimes titles are listed as required or encoding schemes (such as AAT, LCSH, TGN, ULAN, etc., are recommended), and sometimes only a general direction is given to use a controlled vocabulary. Whatever recommendations or guidelines a particular institution or community uses, best practices guides are specific to the special needs that require attention. Section 3.3 provides many such examples.

When more than one vocabulary or syntax rules are optional, which should be chosen? This question might be answered in a project, but the degree of preference could be answered in more specific guides (as with an AP).

DC-LIB AP indicates a preferred encoding practice among three options, and gives instructions on a recognized practice (http://dublincore.org/documents/library-application-profile/#Date [emphasis added]).

Example 17 (from DC-LIB):

> **DC-Lib Comments:**
> Recommend use of an element refinement for type of Date. **Recommend that dates be encoded:**
>
> (1) using W3C-DTF (a profile of ISO 8601 structured with hyphens),
> (2) using ISO 8601 (structured without hyphens), or
> (3) supplied as free text that does not take the form of a string of numerals (with or without hyphens). <NL/SUB>
>
> **The second option, ISO 8601 (without hyphens), is preferred.**
> It is **acceptable** to use the widely recognized practice such as day-month-year where the day and year are represented with numerals and month with a name or standard abbreviation (e.g., "1 January 2002" or "1 Jan 2002"). Avoid the use of potentially ambiguous date representations such as DD/MM/YY or MM/DD/YY (e.g., "04/05/05").

Exhibit 3-6-1. Values assigned to *date* element in a metadata repository.	
1979	c1999, 2000
2000-03	January, 1919
2000-03-01	May, 1919
2001-01-02T21:48.00Z	B.C.E. 221
200003	128 B.C.
	1987, c2000
	?1999
	1952 (issued)
	(1982)
	1930?
	1823-1845
	Between 1680 and 1896?
	Fri April 25 1:18:19 PM, 2002

Providing encoding schemes is merely the first step to ensure consistency in metadata creation. Despite a syntax encoding scheme (ISO 8601) specified for date and time expression, additional guidelines on *how* to handle date values in various situations are still necessary. The authors, for example, have found that in a metadata repository that supports simple DC, values for *date* element include those shown in Exhibit 3-6-1 (above).

Some of these (column on the right) are clearly not consistent with the syntax defined by ISO 8601. However, guidance is lacking on how to handle these dates, e.g., copyright date, BCE dates, questionable dates, approximate dates, date ranges, and days. If we survey how different metadata standards give instructions for the *date* element, we find the following information.

Example 18 (from DC):

> **Comment:** Date may be used to express temporal information at any level of granularity. Recommended best practice is **to use an encoding scheme**, such as the W3CDTF profile of ISO 8601 [W3CDTF].

Example 19 (from ETD-MS):

> **Description:** A date associated with an event in the life cycle of the resource. **In the case of theses and dissertations**, this **should be** the date that appears on the title page or equivalent of the work. **Should be** recorded as defined in ISO 8601 and the profile recommended for implementing ISO 8601 dates in Dublin Core.

DC-Lib gives details (see Example 17) as well as expresses concerns.

Example 20 (from DC-Lib):

> **DC-Lib Comments:**
> It may be desirable to establish a DC-Lib encoding scheme or profile of ISO 8601 to cover **B.C.E. dates, questionable and approximate dates**. A date working group has been established to progress these issues.

Figure 3-6-1. Examples for the *date* element provided by VRA Core 4.0.

VRA Core Element	XML element	*XML attribute*	XML subelement	*XML attribute*	Data example (display values in bold)
DATE	date				**12th century**
		type			creation
			earliestDate		1100
			latestDate		1199
		source			Grove Dictionary of Art Online
		href			http://www.groveart.com
		dataDate			2005-06-08
	date				**destroyed mid-8th century BCE**
		type			destruction
			earliestDate		-765
			latestDate		-735
		source			Grove Dictionary of Art Online
		href			http://www.groveart.com
		dataDate			2005-06-08

Source: Reprinted from VRA Core 4.0: 7, with permission.

Detailed instructions and examples are provided for the date element in VRA Core (see Figure 3-6-1, above). Two of the accompanying examples in a table that VRA provides are displayed.

Example 21 (from VRA Core 4.0):

DATE

Subelements: **earliestDate** *circa*
latestDate *circa*

Description: Date or range of dates associated with the creation, design, production, presentation, performance, construction, or alteration, etc. of the work or image. Dates **may be expressed as** free text or numerical. The Boolean circa attribute may be added to either subelement to indicate an approximate date. For image records, the date element refers to the view date, if known. See CCO Chapter 4: "Stylistic and Chronological Information" for a more thorough discussion of dates.

Data Values: earliestDate and **latestDate** subelements **should be formulated according to** ISO 8601 standards for data content (www.cl.cam.ac.uk/~mgk25/iso-time.html), i.e., YYYY, YYYY-MM, or YYYY-MM-DD. **Dates before the Common Era** (BCE or BC) should be entered with a minus sign (-) in the form -YYYY. May contain up to 12 digits **to accommodate** ancient dates.

In addition to VRA Core 4.0, CDWA and PBCore also provide detailed guides with many examples.

3.6.2 Standard-specific Guidelines

The DCMI has systematically provided developed guidelines. A comprehensive guide for entry-level users of Dublin Core, *Using Dublin Core* (Hillmann, 2005), introduces basic concepts, syntax, storage and maintenance issues, element content, and controlled vocabularies. It also explains Dublin Core elements and qualifiers. A more specialized document is the *Guidelines for Encoding Bibliographic Citation Information in Dublin Core Metadata* (Apps, 2005). A set of encoding guidelines provided by DCMI include:

- *Expressing Simple Dublin Core in RDF/XML*
- *Guidelines for implementing Dublin Core in XML*
- *Expressing Qualified Dublin Core in RDF/XML*
- *Expressing Qualified Dublin Core in HTML/XHTML meta and link elements*
- *DCMI DCSV: A syntax for representing simple structured data in a text string*

In addition to the *DCMI Type Vocabulary,* other value standards have been developed. For example:

- *DCMI Box Encoding Scheme: specification of the spatial limits of a place, and methods for encoding this in a text string*
- *DCMI Period Encoding Scheme: specification of the limits of a time interval, and methods for encoding this in a text string*
- *DCMI Point Encoding Scheme: a point location in space, and methods for encoding this in a text string*

3.6.3 Community-oriented Best Practice Guides

The Digital Library for Earth System Education (DLESE) is a distributed community effort of teaching and learning about the Earth system at all levels. *DLESE Best Practices* provides guidelines and checklists to help generate metadata records and has provided a good model for many other digital library projects. Effective and efficient for library use, the document describes three topics: metadata quality guidelines, cataloging best practices, and individual record checks. Its cataloging best practices covers metadata field definitions, controlled vocabularies and definitions, tasks to complete each field, and mistakes to avoid in completing each field. It also provides many relevant examples.

Best Practices for OAI Data Provider Implementations and Shareable Metadata is a joint initiative between the Digital Library Federation and the NSDL. It includes two best practices guides: *Best Practices for OAI Data Provider Implementations* and *Best Practices for Shareable Metadata.* The latter is a valuable source for all metadata creators, and covers the following topics:

- Metadata should be a shareable and appropriate representation of the resource.
- Granularity of description.
- Use of metadata formats in addition to simple Dublin Core is strongly encouraged.
- Tips for crosswalking.
- Describing versions and reproductions.
- Linking from a record to a resource and other linking issues.
- Providing supplemental information to service provider.
- Expressing rights over metadata.

The document is created in a wiki and has been edited often by the contributors. This approach sets an example on developing and updating best practices by and for the community.

3.6.4 Data Content Standards

Data content standards guide the choice of terms and define the order, syntax, and form in which data values should be entered into a data structure. In the Internet arena, data content standards have been developed by the library, archival, and museum communities respectively, represented by:

- *Anglo-American Cataloguing Rules* (AACR), for the library community. It will be superseded by *Resource Description and Access* (RDA);
- *Describing Archives: A Content Standard* (DACS), for the archival community; and
- *Cataloging Cultural Objects (CCO), A Guide to Describing Cultural Works and Their Images*, for the cultural heritage community.

Content standards, such as CCO, offer guidelines for selecting, ordering, and formatting data used to populate elements in a catalog record. Their purpose is to promote high-quality shared cataloguing, contribute to improved documentation, and enhance access to information. It is noteworthy that CCO states, "In CCO, the emphasis is on principles of good cataloging and documentation, rather than on rigid rules that do not allow catalogers and system implementers to make informed judgments about the information they create and how it will be presented to their users" (Baca et al., 2006, xii). As a data content standard, CCO is complementary to both data structure standards (e.g., CDWA and VRA Core) and data value standards, e.g., Getty's *Art and Architecture Thesaurus*, the *Union List of Artist Names*, and the *Getty Thesaurus of Geographic Names*.

We have now reached a point where noticeable trends become foreseeable surrounding the development of metadata standards. The arising standards developed by the DCMI documents and CCO present an ever-improved framework that incorporates the data model, data structure, date value, data content, and data interchange standards. Another noticeable trend with far-reaching implications is the concept and practice of application profiles (with a heavy emphasis on interoperability). Although many best practices and standards have been developed, there is always a gap between the individual's practice and general best practices. Implementation issues are found at every stage of a digital library project. These issues are related to data structure, value, content, and interchange, but will be contextualized by the particular project and community.

Best practices and guidelines for all of the components discussed in this chapter must be continually updated, improved, and disseminated so that communities and individual implementers converge toward a more unified deployment of high-quality metadata. Chapter 4 will move from the general discussions of structures and semantics to the particulars of encoding, i.e., expressing them in specific computer-processable languages.

Suggested Readings

Caplan, Priscilla. 2003. Chapter 3, "Vocabularies, Classification, and Identifiers"; Chapter 4, "Approaches to Interoperability." *Metadata Fundamentals for All Librarians*. Chicago: American Library Association: pp. 25–53.

Greenberg, Jane. 2001. "A Quantitative Categorical Analysis of Metadata Elements in Image-applicable Metadata Schemes." *Journal of the American Society for Information Science and Technology* 52, no. 11: 917–924.

Heery, Rachel and Manjula Patel. 2000. "Application Profiles: Mixing and Matching Metadata Schemas." *Ariadne* [Online] no. 25. Available: www.ariadne.ac.uk/issue25/app-profiles/.

Hillmann, Diane I. and Elaine L. Westbrooks, eds. 2004. "Part I. Project-Based Implementations." *Metadata in Practice*. Chicago: American Library Association.

Hodge, Gail. 2000. *Systems of Knowledge Organization for Digital Libraries: Beyond Traditional Authority Files*. Council on Library and Information Sources. Available: www.clir.org/pubs/reports/pub91/contents.html.

Lagoze, Carl. 2001. "Keeping Dublin Core Simple: Cross-Domain Discovery or Resource Description?" *D-Lib Magazine* [Online] 7, no. 1. Available: www.dlib.org/dlib/january01/lagoze/01lagoze.html.

Sutton, Stuart A. 1999. "Conceptual Design and Deployment of a Metadata Framework for Education Resources on the Internet." *Journal of the American Society for Information Science* 50, no. 13: 1182–1192.

Weibel, Stuart. 2005. "Border Crossings: Reflections on a Decade of Metadata Consensus Building." *D-Lib Magazine* [Online] 11, no. 7/8. Available: www.dlib.org/dlib/july05/weibel/07weibel.html.

Exercises

Developing a Metadata Element Set (a Multipart Project)

General instructions: This exercise is designed for individuals to collaborate by working together in groups. All group work should be conducted after the related section in this chapter is both taught and studied. A template for each module is available on the attached CD-ROM. A "collection" of works should be identified by the instructor or students. An example would be a collection of unused postcards or bookmarks made of different materials, sizes, shapes, and published in different languages, places, and times for different purposes. Treat the items of the collection as the resource, i.e., the postcards themselves, and not the images on the postcards.

Group Work I. Identify desired metadata elements for the collection. List in a table all of the following:

1. Desired Element
2. Explanation and Description of the Element (This will be the element definition and will be included in the final schema.)

3. Example (The examples may be included in the best practice guide, either in the schema or in a separate guide.)
4. Implementation-M, O, R (Mandatory/Optional? Repeatable?)

Group Work II. Decision for value spaces: content and value specifications, vocabularies. List in the table all of the following:

1. Element Name (The element defined by the last task)
2. Value controlled? (Yes, No, and How)
3. Values (A predefined list of terms, name of an existing scheme, or rules)

Group Work III. Establish an Application Profile. Assume your own namespace (e.g., "*ksu*" of any other word). List in a table all of the following:

1. Element Name (The element defined by the last task)
2. Matched SCHEMA A Element and Qualifier (Schema A is the preliminary source schema, e.g., *vra.agent*.)
3. Matched SCHEMA B Element and Qualifier (Schema B is the secondary source schema, e.g., *dc.langauge*.)
4. Additional *ksu* qualifiers for matched SCHEMA elements (These are additional/revised qualifiers for matched SCHEMA A/B elements, e.g., *vraksu.subject.May4th*.)
5. Un-matched Element (This element will be claimed under ksu Namespace, e.g., *ksu.collectionType*.)
   - For the selection of elements from different standards, consult the AVEL METADATA ELEMENT LIST: http://avel.library.uq.edu.au/technical.html
   - For the presentation format of your application profile, consult the DC Government Application Profile: http://dublincore.org/documents/2001/09/17/gov-application-profile/
   - For the presentation of an application profile based on an existing application profile, consult the National Library of Medicine (NLM) Metadata Schema: http://www.nlm.nih.gov/tsd/cataloging/metafilenew.html

Group Work IV. Create crosswalks:

1. Create a crosswalk by mapping your element set to another group's element set.
2. Create crosswalks using the new element set just created as the source schema, mapping it to another schema, e.g., MODS, DC.

Group Work V. Write a specification for the complete element set.

Follow the examples of specifications from the original element sets; write your specification for the element set for postcards.

Examples of original element sets:

- DC: http://dublincore.org/documents/dces/
  Examples of original Application Profiles:
- NLM: http://www.nlm.nih.gov/tsd/cataloging/metafilenew.html
- DC-GOV: http://dublincore.org/documents/2001/09/17/gov-application-profile/

4

Schemas—Syntax

We have mentioned "schema" many times. What, exactly, is a schema? Why is it so important? By generally accepted definitions, a schema is "a diagrammatic representation; an outline or model." Computer science often uses schema to refer to the definition of an entire database. It defines the structure and type of contents that each data element within the structure may contain. Depending on usage, the word *schema* may mean very different things. A database administrator refers to the data fields in a table and the relationships between tables as relational schemas. Schema is used in XML standards as a language for defining XML elements and structures. In the metadata community, the word *schema* means the semantic and structural definition of metadata elements and the relationships between those elements. These representations define what an element means and how it will be encoded in a machine-processable format. Defined element sets or term declarations are often represented in XML and/or Resource Description Framework (RDF) schema languages and the results are called metadata encoding schemas. Although a metadata standard's elements may be published without an accompanying encoding schema, it has become a common practice for standards to be published with both semantic and encoding schemas at the same time. Schema authors may produce one or more specifications for different schema language bindings: EAD was developed as a Standard Generalized Markup Language (SGML) Document Type Definition (DTD) for its Beta version in 1996 and was made compliant with XML during the last stage of EAD version 1.0 just prior to release. Another example is CDWA Lite, which provides two documents on its Web site, one for a semantics definition and the other for an encoding syntax:

- *CDWA Lite Specification: A list of Elements, Tags, Description, and Examples.* (www.getty.edu/research/conducting_research/standards/cdwa/cdwalit e .pdf)
- *CDWA Lite Schema:* Version 1.1. (www.getty.edu/CDWA/CDWALite/CDWALite-xsd-public-v1-1.xsd)

In their most recent releases, CDWA Lite and VRA Core 4.0 have both included the structures and definitions of elements with XML Schemas for encoding syntax: *CDWA Lite XML Schema* and *VRA Core 4.0 XML Schema*. DCMI has also provided both XML and Resource Description Framework (RDF) schemas to support the simple DC (without refinements) and qualified DC (with element refinements and encoding schemes). LOM has published its 1484.12.1: *IEEE Standard for Learning Object Metadata* with different bindings:

- 1484.12.2: *Standard for ISO/IEC 11404 binding for Learning Object Metadata data model*
- 1484.12.3: *Standard for XML binding for Learning Object Metadata data model*
- 1484.12.4: *Standard for Resource Description Framework (RDF) binding for Learning Object Metadata data model*

Using machine-processable schemas can benefit metadata implementation in many ways. First, it provides a uniform syntax for encoding metadata elements and attributes to allow for easier implementation of standards by utilizing various tools available on the market. Second, the uniform encoding syntax also allows for more effective metadata exchange and communication among schemas residing in different registries and repositories. Encoding schemas can be used to validate both data and documents. Third (although this does not exhaust the benefits), another important application of schemas is to guide an author in developing XML documents. The *Simple DC XML Schema* (http://dublincore.org/schemas/xmls/simpledc20021212.xsd) defines terms for the Simple Dublin Core, i.e., the 15 elements from the http://purl.org/dc/elements/1.1/ namespace. A more complex example is the *VRA Core 4.0 Schema* unrestricted version (www.vraweb.org/projects/vracore4/vra-4.0.xsd).

Whereas Chapter 3 discussed how semantics in metadata elements and their structures are defined, this chapter details how the schema will be encoded and how semantics are controlled by using namespaces. The aim is to provide a basic understanding of the issues that may arise in applications regarding schema encoding. It is beyond the scope of this text to explain the basics of schema languages. Many tools are available for producing XML schemas and DTDs; the fundamentals of those tools and guidelines are the World Wide Web Consortium (W3C) recommendations regarding XML, RDF, and namespaces, available at the W3C Web site (www.w3.org).

4.1 Schema Encoding

Figure 4-1-1 shows a typical database or relational schema, which contains five data tables (also called entities). Each table has several data fields (columns). Each record (row) in a table is identified, e.g., each author in the author table has an identifier (ID), a numerical or alphanumerical code that is often assigned as the primary key (PK) for each record and can uniquely identify an author (in this example) in the entire database.

When an author is referenced in another table, for example, the *author_document* table, the only necessary information needed is the author ID code. The referenced author ID in the *author_document* table is called the foreign key (FK). Thus, the primary key for each table is underlined and designated by PK and the foreign key is designated by FK. Such matching ID codes in different tables

Figure 4-1-1. A sample relational schema for a database storing metadata.

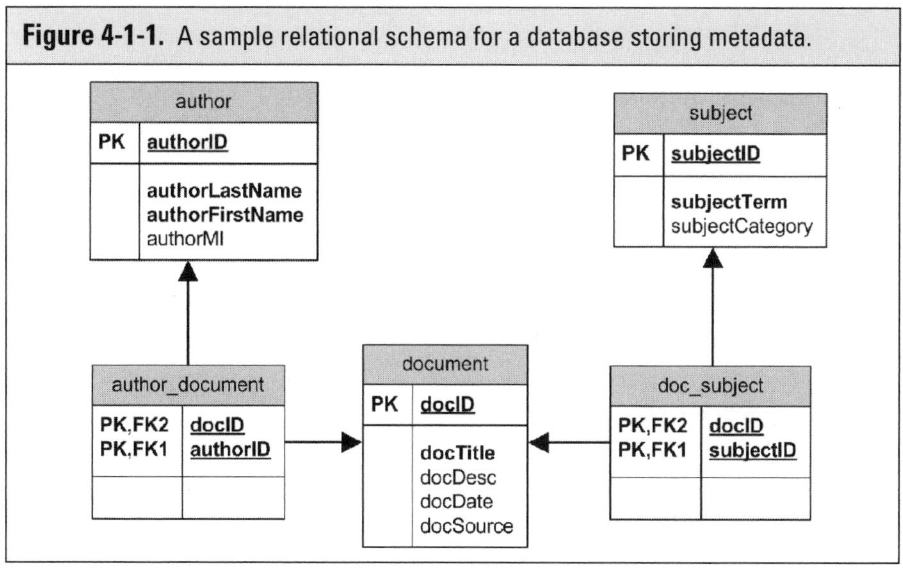

will precisely represent the relationships between two entities or tables. One author may have written one or many documents, and each document may have one or many authors; similarly, a subject term may be assigned to one or more documents and one document may be indexed by one or many subject terms. In other words, a many-to-many relationship exists between *author* and *document* tables as well as between *subject* and *document* tables. The *author_document* table maps ID codes from two tables, e.g,. author A wrote documents 1, 2, and 3, which generate three pairs of primary keys—A 1, A 2, and A 3—that will uniquely identifies author A's three documents. Since both author and document IDs together form a compound primary key for the *author_document* table while being referenced from *author* and *document* tables, respectively, these IDs are both *composite* PK and FK simultaneously, i.e., multiple field primary keys.

Database schemas represent data in the form of tables and each table contains a block of attributes describing an entity. When using XML to represent data, the same concept also applies. As Exhibit 4-1-1 shows, all data elements related to a document are grouped under the tag *document;* the components in an author's name are grouped under the *author* tag, and so on. Therefore the element *document* has a collection of subelements and some of those subelements, such as *author* and *subject,* have their own set of subelements. At each level, all subelements are nested under their parent element and continue to be defined until an element has exhausted all possible subelements. In addition to the structures of elements, there are also constraints to be considered according to what will happen when capturing metadata from a document. Is the *author* element optional or required? If it is required, should it be allowed to occur more than once, and if so how many times? A document often has multiple topics, but its topics may remain undefined until a later time. If this situation occurs, how should we set constraints for the *subject* element?

Exhibit 4-1-1. XML encoding sample of the database data from Figure 4-1-1.

```
<?xml version="1.0" encoding="UTF-8"?>
<documents xmlns:od="um:schemas-microsoft-com:officedata"
        xmlns:xsi="http://www.w3.org/2001/XMLSchema-instance"
        xsi:noNamespaceSchemaLocation="Document.xsd">
  <document>
        <URL>http://www.slis.kent.edu/~mzeng/metadatabasics/ index.htm</URL>
        <authors>
          <author>
            <authorFirstName>Marcia</authorFirstName>
            <authorMI>L.</authorMI>
            <authorLastName>Zeng</authorLastName>
          </author>
        </authors>
        <title>Metadata basics</title>
        <description>This information package is designed to provide
metadata and cataloging educators and trainers, students, and practitioners
with a common set of resources and tools.</description>
        <date>2007-05-25</date>
        <type>Tutorial</type>
        <subjects>
          <subject scheme="Keyword">Metadata concepts</subject>
<subject scheme="Keyword">Metadata standards</subject>
          <subject scheme="Keyword">Metadata value space</subject>
        </subjects>
  </document>
</documents>
```

The structure and elements in an XML document may be defined by two methods: (1) creating a Document Type Definition (DTD) or (2) using XML Schema Language (schema). DTD is simple and easy to create, but since it is not expressed in XML syntax, it is limited in terms of data types and reuse. Most metadata standards today have adopted the XML Schema Language as the encoding syntax. In this syntax, a schema is a collection of definitions of data elements, attributes, data types, and constraints of elements and attributes. Its purpose is to provide an inventory of XML markup constructs and define the application of schemas for XML documents. In a more technical sense, a schema is "to define and describe a class of XML documents by using these constructs to constrain and document the meaning, usage and relationships of their constituent parts: datatypes, elements and their content, attributes and their values, entities and their contents and notations. Thus, XML schema language can be used to define, describe and catalogue XML vocabularies for classes of XML documents" (W3C, 1999).

Exhibit 4-1-2 contains the schema for the XML instance in Exhibit 4-1-1. XML schema language distinguishes between simple and complex type elements. A simple type element has no subelements or attributes. It may have only a value of any type: Elements *URL*, *title*, *description*, *date*, and *source* are representatives because they meet the requirements for the simple type. The element *document* is a complex type because it has a sequence of subelements, as are *authors* and *subjects* as well. A sequence content model means the order of elements are fixed and the order is defined by the schema. In the example shown in Exhibit 4-1-1, *URL* will be the first element, followed by others in exactly the order defined by the schema (see Exhibit 4-1-2). As one can see, *authorFirstName* is followed by an optional *authorMI*, and then followed by *authorLastName*. This sequence for *author* element is also defined by the schema. The indication of an author's middle name initial is optional and can be found by the *minOccurs="0"* in the line that defines the *authorMI* element.

An XML element may contain one or more attributes that either add constraints or indicate the nature of the element value. An attribute is a *"name-value"* pair with *type* information. The element *subject* in Exhibit 4-1-2 uses the attribute *scheme* to indicate the source of a subject term, which means that the value of the *subject* must come from one of two sources, "LCSH" or "Keyword." Distinct values may be used for either elements or attributes in order to control the vocabulary, reduce data entry, and eliminate errors.

Exhibit 4-1-2. An example of XML schema for the XML document in Exhibit 4-1-1.

```
<?xml version="1.0" encoding="UTF-8"?>
<xs:schema xmlns:xs="http://www.w3.org/2001/XMLSchema">
  <xs:element name="documents">
  <xs:complexType>
        <xs:sequence>
          <xs:element ref="document" maxOccurs="unbounded"/>
        </xs:sequence>
      </xs:complexType>
  </xs:element>
  <xs:element name="document">
      <xs:complexType>
    <xs:sequence>
            <xs:element name="URL" type="xs:anyURI"/>
            <xs:element ref="authors"/>
            <xs:element name="title" type="xs:string"/>
            <xs:element name="description" type="xs:string" minOccurs="0"/>
            <xs:element name="date" type="xs:date"/>
            <xs:element name="type" type="xs:string" minOccurs="0"/>
            <xs:element ref="subjects" minOccurs="0"/>
            <xs:element name="source" type="xs:string" minOccurs="0"/>
      </xs:sequence>
    </xs:complexType>
  </xs:element>
  <xs:element name="author">
      <xs:complexType>
        <xs:sequence>
            <xs:element name="authorFirstName" type="xs:string"/>
            <xs:element name="authorMI" type="xs:string" minOccurs="0"/>
            <xs:element name="authorLastName" type="xs:string"/>
        </xs:sequence>
      </xs:complexType>
```

(Cont'd.)

Exhibit 4-1-2. An example of XML schema for the XML document in Exhibit 4-1-1 *(Continued).*

```
    </xs:element>
    <xs:element name="subject">
        <xs:complexType>
          <xs:simpleContent>
            <xs:extension base="xs:string">
              <xs:attribute name="scheme">
                <xs:simpleType>
                  <xs:restriction base="xs:string">
                    <xs:enumeration value="LCSH"/>
                    <xs:enumeration value="Keyword"/>
                  </xs:restriction>
                </xs:simpleType>
              </xs:attribute>
            </xs:extension>
          </xs:simpleContent>
        </xs:complexType>
    </xs:element>
    <xs:element name="authors">
        <xs:complexType>
            <xs:sequence>
              <xs:element ref="author" maxOccurs="unbounded"/>
            </xs:sequence>
        </xs:complexType>
    </xs:element>
    <xs:element name="subjects">
        <xs:complexType>
          <xs:sequence>
              <xs:element ref="subject" minOccurs="0" maxOccurs="unbounded"/>
          </xs:sequence>
        </xs:complexType>
    </xs:element>
</xs:schema>
```

When defining complex type elements, two other content models are available besides a sequence model: choice and mixed. The choice content model is used when among a limited number of elements only one may be used each time. The mixed content model is used in circumstances in which both sequence and choice models are applied at different levels of the XML structure. XML schema language allows the schema designer to define the most common data types as well as create user-defined data types for reuse purposes.

4.2 Namespaces

A namespace is a collection of names, identified by a Uniform Resource Identifier (URI) reference. The phrase "identified by a URI" may be understood as: each namespace has an Identifier (ID), and this ID is in the form of a URI. Although schemas may define XML markup constructs and help validate

XML documents, the vocabulary used in element names remains potentially problematic if not handled properly. The first problem is the inconsistency of element names for the same semantic relation found in different schemas, e.g., "PmtType" / "paymentType," "OrderQty" / "OrderQuantity" and "floorRate" / "rateFloor" from e-commerce XML applications. Conversely, another potential problem can occur when the same element name may have differing meanings in different domains. The result is ambiguity and name collision. An example is the element name *title*, a common word that can be used to refer to different things as defined in different XML Schemas in different domains (note: .xsd is the file extension for XML schemas):

title Catalog.xsd → title of a book
JournalIndex.xsd → title of a journal
ArticleIndex.xsd → title of an article
Employee.xsd → title of a position
AutoInsurance.xsd → Ownership certificate

The word *title* is usually understood as the title of a book or an article in the bibliographic universe. *Title* also means position in a human resource system. And in the insurance industry, *title* means an ownership certificate for automobiles, boats, and real estate. If the schema is noncontextual, this word becomes ambiguous or causes collisions when one system is trying to exchange data with a different system.

In addition, varying naming conventions for business documents and processes are collections of rules or norms used by designers or programmers for easy recognition and coherent order of object types in applications. Different naming conventions are often specific to individual industries and therefore difficult to control across domains. As XML is entering more and more applications, it is unavoidable that a schema often needs to incorporate elements from other schemas or several schemas need to be merged to meet representation requirements. For example, a patient's medical record consists of information on reported symptoms, physical signs, test results, diagnosis, and prescriptions. Each of these information categories is generated, and perhaps managed, by different departments and contain a set of mixed vocabularies.

Schemas are often developed at different levels—within an organization or industry, or across institutions and industries—and for different application domains such as learning objects, financial markets, archival materials, and scientific datasets. To create unambiguous and reusable schemas, vocabulary issues must be resolved first. Namespace is one such mechanism designed to solve the vocabulary problems in schemas.

A namespace defines the use of the elements as well as an *alias* that identifies which namespace the element is taken from. Suppose we have a namespace "catalog" identified by "http://www.myexample.org/cat." Although this URI appears to be a Web address, it does not point to an actual Web page on the Internet, but only serves as an ID for the namespace. The alias can be a short name for the catalog namespace, i.e., we can use "cat" as the alias for the "catalog" namespace. In another example, the namespace "http://purl.org/dc/elements/1.1/" is for the *Dublin Core Metadata Element Set* (DCMES), Version 1.1 (original 15 elements), in which "dc" is the alias. This alternative name occurs as a prefix of an XML qualified name (a.k.a. QName) when elements from DCMES appear outside of the original DCMES namespace. In an XML metadata record, the present book's title is expressed as: <dc:title>Metadata</dc:title>, or with an HTML/XHTML meta tag as <meta name="dc.title" content="Metadata"/> (see Chapter 5 on encoding in records).

As discussed earlier, the context is an important factor for determining the semantic meaning of an element label; Namespace works as a contextual referent. If we add context to element labels, it will become apparent to both humans and machines who will then clearly understand the meaning of any given element. For the *title* examples, we can use *bk:title* for book title, *jn:title* for journal title, and *hr:title* for employee position to disambiguate the element name title.

To use a namespace, one must first declare it in the schema. The declaration syntax begins with xmlns and is followed by a colon and the alias:

```
xmlns: bk="http://ns.books.com/book"
xmlns: order="http://ns.books.com/order"
```

A schema usually declares namespace in the "schema" element, which is the root element of a schema, e.g.:

```
<xsd:schema xmlns="http://adn.dlese.org"
        xmlns:xsd="http://www.w3.org/2001/XMLSchema"
        targetNamespace="http://adn.dlese.org"
        elementFormDefault="qualified"
        attributeFormDefault="unqualified"
        version="0.6.50">
```

In the first line, the schema element declares the namespace for ADN Metadata Framework: *xmlns="http://adn.dlese.org"*. ADN stands for **A**DEPT/**D**LESE/**N**ASA, and originated from the full name of the projects Alexandria Digital Earth Prototype (ADEPT), the Digital Library for Earth System Education (DLESE), and NASA's Joined Digital Library. The ADN Framework was developed by incorporating metadata elements to describe resources that are typically used in learning environments in the Earth system education. The second line indicates the namespace of the standard (www.w3.org/2001/XMLSchema) on which the schema is based. The third line states the targetNamespace, which is identical (since there is no other external namespace involved). The last two lines indicate that the elements in this schema are required to be qualified (*elementFormDefault = "qualified"*); i.e., the namespace *ADN* should be placed in front of each element as a prefix, whereas the attributes are not required to have the namespace prefix (*attributeFormDefault = "unqualified"*). The last line specifies the version of this specification (version 0.6.50; see also Section 4.3.3).

Namespace is decisive for disambiguating XML vocabulary. The XML schema language standard also allows external namespaces to be imported into a schema; different schemas may be merged into one by using the "include" element. These flexibilities in schema creation make namespace a powerful tool for maintaining explicit semantics in metadata vocabularies.

4.3 XML Schemas for Metadata Standards

Many metadata standards authorities publish XML schemas along with the element sets. Dublin Core and IEEE LOM are two good examples of this. Most application profile maintenance agencies follow the same practice as well. For every metadata schema there exist several ways to encode it and perhaps none of them may claim to be the best. Generally, an XML-based encoding schema may take any one of the three modes as shown in Figure 4-3-1.

A single encoding schema contains every data element in a metadata standard in one schema file. If a metadata standard has many elements, and structures them in many layers, using a single schema mode can result in complicated content models and deep layers of XML encoding.

In contrast, the multiple schema mode separates all data elements in a metadata standard into a number of smaller schema files based on functional clusters of elements. Each schema file usually has a relatively flat structure and is linked to a main container or overarching schema.

In the networked mode, encoding schemas may make reference to external schema files that reside remotely on an external server and are not owned by the application implementer. Such situations can become extremely complex, because the schema designers must be knowledgeable about their own data elements and structure, as well as the data elements in other related encoding schemas in order to know which ones to reference for which application units. Using three metadata standards as examples, the following sections describe

Figure 4-3-1. Schema modes: (a) single encoding schema, (b) multiple encoding schemas, and (c) networked encoding schemas.

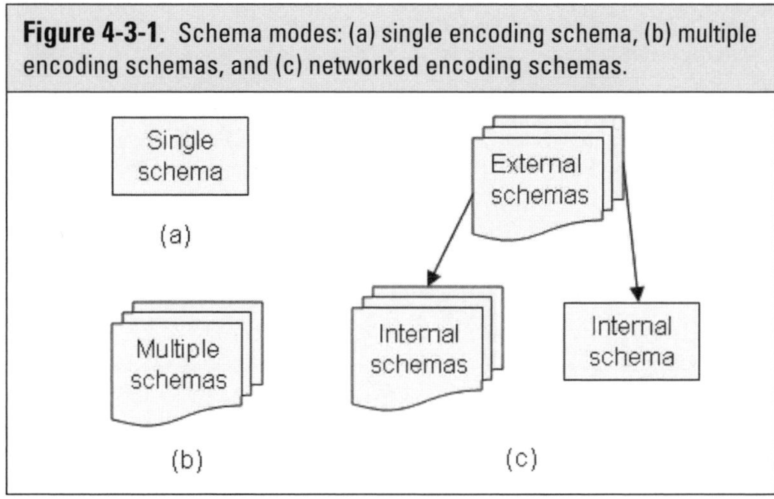

their XML schema's constructs, and demonstrate the flexibility and diversity of metadata schema encoding.

4.3.1 Dublin Core Encoding Schemas

DCMI supplies several versions of XML schemas for encoding simple and qualified DC elements. For simple DC, one can use the most recent *Simple DC XML Schema*, Version 2002-12-12, which is essentially a single schema file (http://dublincore.org/schemas/xmls/simpledc20021212.xsd) containing all 15 DC elements without qualifiers. The *Qualified DC XML Schemas*, Version 2006-01-06, consists of three schema files: one for the 15 elements (http://purl.org/dc/elements/1.1/), one for the *DCMI Type Vocabulary* (http://purl.org/dc/dcmitype/), and a third one containing all the additional DC elements and refinements (http://purl.org/dc/terms/). Since it is in a multiple schema mode, the *DC Terms* and *DCMI Type Vocabulary* schema files must be referenced in the *Simple DC XML Schema* in order to perform the validation function.

Figure 4-3-2 demonstrates how the three XML schema files work together. Using XML editing software, the dcterms.xsd and dcmitype.xsd files can be included in the dc.xsd file. The *Simple DC XML Schema* designers took into consideration reusing the schema in other metadata standards' XML schemas while maintaining the core elements as the container and allowing additional DC elements and refinements to be imported into the container schema. The title and creator elements in *Simple DC XML Schema*, for example, are encoded as:

```
<xs:element name="title" substitutionGroup="any"/>
<xs:element name="creator" substitutionGroup="any"/>
```

For the *Metadata Basics* example in Exhibit 4-1-1, the content for title and creator elements will be encoded in XML as:

```
<dc:title>Metadata basics</dc:title>
<dc:creator>Zeng, Marcia L.</dc:creator>
```

Figure 4-3-2. DC XML schemas as of December 30, 2007.

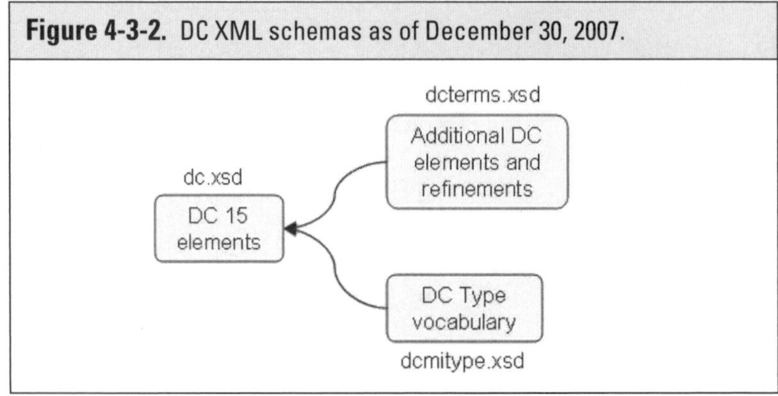

4.3.2 EAD XML Schema

The *EAD 2002 Schema* was originally developed as a DTD. As described in Chapter 2, EAD DTD is a large and complex metadata element set. Several years ago EAD DTD was converted into the XML schema format. The most recent version is *EAD 2002 Schema*, which is essentially a single schema file with deep layers of elements (Figure 4-3-3). A separate schema, *EAD XLink Schema* that must be used together with *EAD 2002 Schema*, functions as a utility schema to provide compatibility between EAD DTD and *EAD 2002 Schema*. The encoding constructs in *EAD 2002 Schema* are designed to reflect idiosyncratic features so that finding aids will be able to identify archival materials by provenance and describe them by their physical arrangement in boxes and folders. Finding aids encoders need to record not only descriptive and biographical data about archival collections as a whole but also the descriptive data for each series, box, folder, and item. The *EAD 2002 Schema* holds 12 levels of components to allow for the hierarchical relationships recorded through the nested XML structure. Although it is not impossible to create multiple XML schemas with shallower layers for EAD encoding, it would require a mechanism

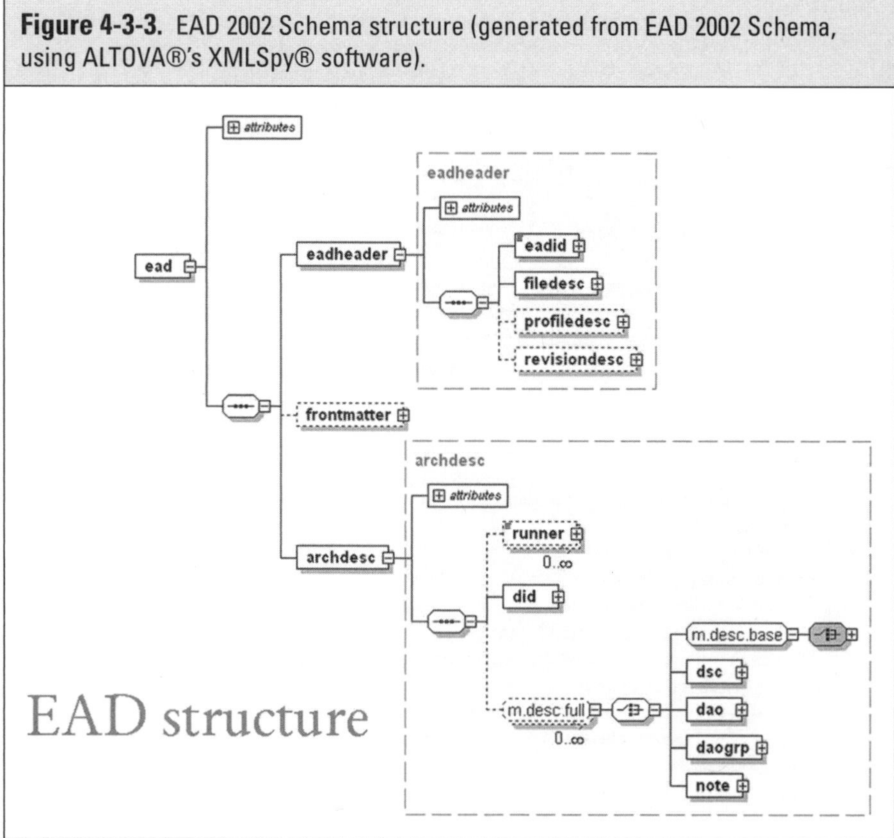

Figure 4-3-3. EAD 2002 Schema structure (generated from EAD 2002 Schema, using ALTOVA®'s XMLSpy® software).

to maintain a complete reference between different component XML schemas, which might be just as awkward and inefficient and would create a nightmare for ongoing maintenance.

Given that the length of most finding aids is almost equivalent to that of an article, the single XML schema works well for archival description needs. Exhibit 4-3-1 shows the top three layers of the EAD XML schema that describe archival components. The first element is component level *c01*, which may contain one or more second-level elements, *c02*, as the value (unbounded) of the attribute maxOccurs indicates. Element *c02* may contain one or more third-level components, *c03*, and so on. The finding aid encoding example for the schema portion is shown in Exhibit 4-3-2.

Note that although the components are at different levels, the description elements are the same at each level: *unititle* (i.e., Title of the Unit) and *unidate*

Exhibit 4-3-1. Portion of EAD XML schema.

```
<xs:complexType name="c01">
    <xs:sequence>
        <xs:element name="head" type="head" minOccurs="0"/>
        <xs:element name="did" type="did"/>
        <xs:group ref="m.desc.full" minOccurs="0" maxOccurs="unbounded"/>
        <xs:sequence minOccurs="0" maxOccurs="unbounded">
            <xs:element name="thead" type="thead" minOccurs="0"/>
            <xs:element name="c02" type="c02" maxOccurs="unbounded"/>
        </xs:sequence>
    </xs:sequence>
    <xs:attributeGroup ref="a.desc.c"/>
</xs:complexType>
<xs:complexType name="c02">
    <xs:sequence>
        <xs:element name="head" type="head" minOccurs="0"/>
        <xs:element name="did" type="did"/>
        <xs:group ref="m.desc.full" minOccurs="0" maxOccurs="unbounded"/>
        <xs:sequence minOccurs="0" maxOccurs="unbounded">
            <xs:element name="thead" type="thead" minOccurs="0"/>
            <xs:element name="c03" type="c03" maxOccurs="unbounded"/>
        </xs:sequence>
    </xs:sequence>
    <xs:attributeGroup ref="a.desc.c"/>
</xs:complexType>
<xs:complexType name="c03">
    <xs:sequence>
        <xs:element name="head" type="head" minOccurs="0"/>
        <xs:element name="did" type="did"/>
        <xs:group ref="m.desc.full" minOccurs="0" maxOccurs="unbounded"/>
    <xs:sequence minOccurs="0" maxOccurs="unbounded">
         <xs:element name="thead" type="thead" minOccurs="0"/>
         <xs:element name="c04" type="c04" maxOccurs="unbounded"/>
    </xs:sequence>
  </xs:sequence>
</xs:complexType>
```

Exhibit 4-3-2. XML encoding for a portion of a finding aid based on the schema in Exhibit 4-3-1.

```
<dsc>
    <c01 level="series">
        <did>
            <unittitle>Series I: Incorporation and Organizational Documents
</unittitle>
            <unitdate normal="1938/2002">1938-2002 </unitdate>
        </did>
        <c02 level="recordgrp">
            <did>
                <unittitle>50th Anniversary</unittitle>
                <unitdate normal="1989">1989</unitdate>
            </did>
            <c03 level="file">
                <did>
                    <unittitle>Commemorative Medals (3)</unittitle>
                    <unitdate normal="1989">1989</unitdate>
                </did>
            </c03>
        </c02>
    </c01>
</dsc>
```

(i.e., Date of the Unit) elements are enclosed in a *<did>* (i.e., Descriptive Identification) parent element and repeated for every component.

4.3.3 DLESE Metadata Framework XML Schemas

In the previous discussion about namespace (Section 4.2), the DLESE ADN Metadata Framework was used as an example. The Framework uses a main schema for the root element and subelements necessary for a metadata record (record.xsd) and two groups of schemas for metadata element categories and value spaces (ADN Metadata Framework version 0.6.50: www.dlese.org/ Metadata/adn-item/0.6.50/docs/xml-info.htm, accessed 2007). The first group has 11 *categories* schemas (*categories* are in the left circle of Figure 4-3-4), while the *vocabularies* group has over 30 schemas for each of the controlled vocabularies that are used by individual metadata fields. Figure 4-3-5 lists only a portion of the vocabularies defined in the DLESE XML schemas.

The benefit of having such a large number of schemas for vocabularies is that (with the proper help of software) not only can the metadata creator validate the record syntax against the XML schema, but that data entry can be made easier also, primarily because the capability of XML schema-encoded vocabularies can allow for values defined in the vocabulary to be displayed as a dropdown list of values ready for catalogers to choose from (Figure 4-3-5).

Figure 4-3-4. DLESE application profile XML schema structure.

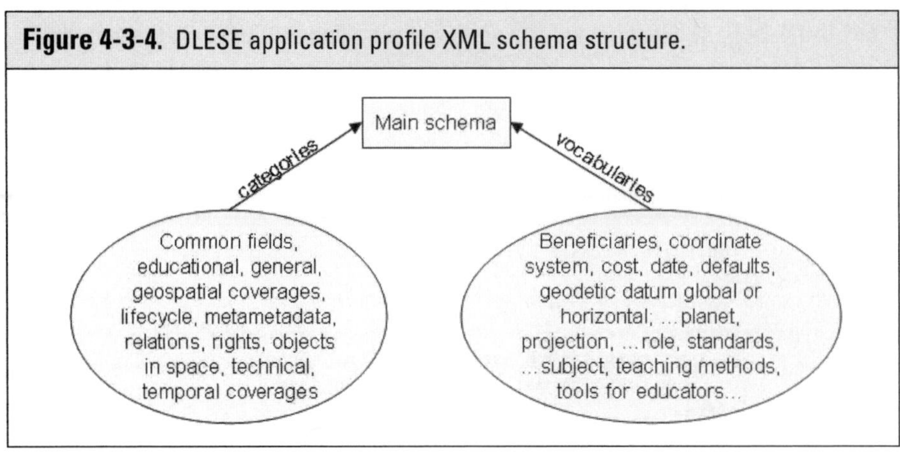

Figure 4-3-5. A pop-up box presents controlled vocabulary choices for catalogers (generated using ALTOVA®)'s XMLSpy® software).

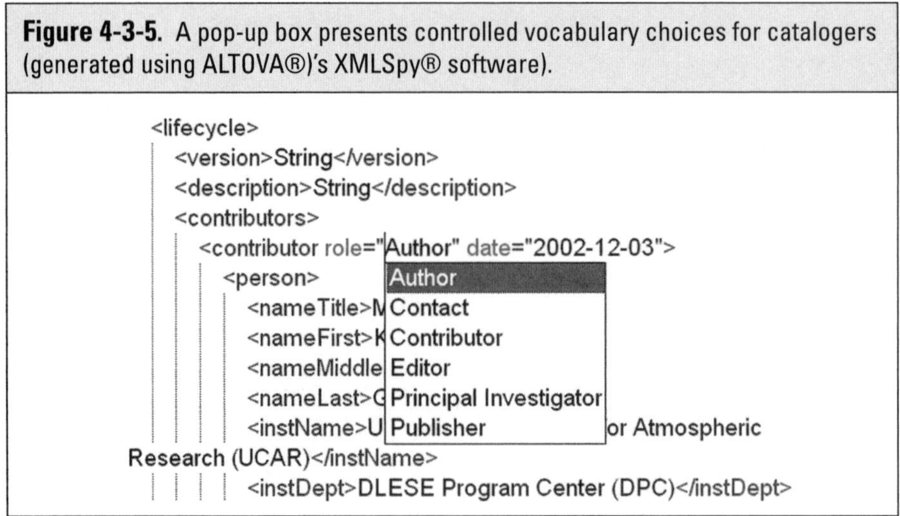

4.4 Summary

Encoding syntax is a fluid area in metadata schemas. One may choose to use a database system to retain metadata elements and data, or use XML technology to encode metadata elements and data. Present-day technology can also accommodate metadata encoded in one format so that it can be converted into another for sharing and reuse. However, the flexibilities and platform neutrality we enjoy by adopting XML technology can easily turn into a liability for the original goal behind its use. As already discussed, there is more than one way to encode a metadata element set. Even though a metadata standard authority usually recommends one or more XML schemas for encoding purposes, they are rarely applied in actual practice exactly as they are defined. This is because metadata standards are rarely applied without any modification.

Any local modification will result in changes to the standard, and so modify the XML encoding schema that is recommended by a metadata standards authority. When this occurs, the XML encoding schema for the modified metadata standard may go in any direction depending on the preference, knowledge, and skill level of the designer. Encoding syntax problems—inconsistent encoding practice, varying XML structures, and lack of encoding tools can all jeopardize the quality and effectiveness of metadata services.

Another issue in metadata schema syntax concerns which mode of XML encoding schemas is most suitable for any given format. From the examples presented in this chapter, it is clear that no one perfect mode is universally applicable in all situations. Whether to create a single XML schema encompassing all elements or to create multiple schemas for a metadata standard is determined by description needs. Generally speaking, modular encoding schemas (such as DLESE), i.e., keeping metadata elements in one schema and vocabularies in separate ones, are more flexible for reuse and expansion since adding external schemas will not affect the metadata encoding structure or other parts of the syntax. A single file schema is more limited and difficult for reuse and expansion.

Metadata schema encoding builds the constructs for computer-processable metadata content to ensure the consistency, accuracy, and completeness in metadata record creation. All are important criteria for measuring the quality of metadata records. Creating metadata records involves more than encoding syntax; it demands a well-thought-out encoding design that will play an important role in the elimination of syntax errors and the reduction of inconsistent data entry in all metadata records.

Suggested Online Readings

Costello, Roger L. 2006. "XML Schemas: Best Practices." Web page. Available: www.xfront.com/BestPracticesHomepage.html.

Refsnes Data. 2007. "XML Schema Tutorial." W3Schools. Web page. Available: www.w3schools.com/schema/default.asp.

Srivastava, Rahul. 2007. "XML Schema: Understanding Namespaces." Web page. Oracle Technology Network. Available: www.oracle.com/technology/pub/articles/srivastava_namespaces.html.

van der Vlist, Eric. 2001. "Using W3C XML Schema." O'Reilly Media. Web page. Available: www.xml.com/pub/a/2000/11/29/schemas/part1.html.

W3C. 1999. *XML Schema Requirements*. XML Schema Working Group. Available: www.w3.org/TR/NOTE-xml-schema-req.

W3C. 2004. *XML Schema Part 0: Primer Second Edition*. W3C Recommendation 28 October 2004. Available: www.w3.org/TR/xmlschema-0/.

Exercises

Note: A wide variety of XML tools are available from the W3C XML Web site: www.w3.org/XML/Schema#Tools Choose one, such as XMLSpy® or the oXygen XML Editor, both available from the tool list and install it on your computer prior to practicing the exercises for this Chapter. For XML schema and record examples, refer to the W3Schools XML Schema Tutorial (listed in the suggested readings).

Option 1. Create an XML Schema and Apply to Record Creation

1. Many online music sites offer brief descriptions for "albums" and track information contained in these albums (e.g., in CD format). The following descriptive elements are typical data presented to users:
   - Artist (or artists)
   - Album title
   - Genre
   - Date of release
   - Publisher
   - Price
   - Rating
   - Track names

   Before you start creating the schema file, analyze the eight elements to determine:

   a. whether there are any subelements, or whether an element needs a set of pre-defined values (enumerated values).
   b. whether an element is mandatory or optional.
   c. whether an element is repeatable.

   Use an XML editor (e.g. XMLSpy® or oXygen XML Editor) to start a new schema file in either the text view or graphic view interface. Define each element (including subelements, if any) with a name and annotation (for definition), and specify mandatory/optional conditions and cardinalities (number of occurrences). Upon completion, make sure to save the file in **.xsd** format.

2. Choose an album to create an XML record using the schema you created for Exercise 1. To start a new XML file, select File New in the XML software you installed in your computer. When you are prompted for a schema, select the schema file and start entering data. This time, make sure to save the file in **.xml** format.

3. When an album contains multiple tracks of songs, some songs may have different composers, arrangers, lyricists, and performers. Do you think the schema you created for Exercise 1 will be sufficient for describing the albums with multiple tracks and multiple creators, contributors, and performers? If not, how will you modify your XML schema to meet the description needs? In either case (modified or not) briefly explain your rationale for either a modification or making no changes.

4. Revise (as necessary) the XML schema you created for Exercise 1 based on your analysis in Exercise 3 to accommodate description needs for albums

with multiple tracks, multiple creators, contributors, and performers. Either way in the "revised" XML schema, you will need to incorporate at least two elements from the DC namespace and create a namespace for your home-grown elements which will include both those from Exercise 1 and (if applicable) any new elements in the revised version. Make sure to save the new version in **.xsd** format, with clearly marked version number.

5. Create an XML record for an album using the XML schema from Exercise 4. The album must have multiple tracks and multiple composers, arrangers, lyricists, and performers.

Option 2. Create an XML Schema for the Option 1 Exercise

Create an XML Schema for the element set you developed in the Chapter 3 exercise. In addition: apply the schema to create two records for two items you used in the Chapter 3 exercise.

5

Metadata Records

The metadata *record* is considered the basic unit of management and exchange and reflects the tradition of librarianship. A record uses metadata elements to describe something, e.g., Web sites, images, or technical reports. Metadata records may be characterized and defined from different perspectives:

1. their composition and relationship to other data in a digital collection;
2. the types of records such as for description, administration, and technical purposes, and physical form and/or intellectual content of materials being described;
3. physical storage of records in various databases and presentation on Web sites; and
4. requirements of minimal and full records within a particular community or domain.

Content standards and best practice guidelines provide the resources regarding record requirements. This chapter, however, addresses common concerns related to the first three issues and focuses on the *description* function of metadata records.

5.1 Basic Requirements

The DCMI Glossary (2005) defines a metadata record as "a syntactically correct representation of the descriptive information (metadata) for an information resource" (http://dublincore.org/documents/usageguide/glossary.shtml#M), and is the minimum requirement of the description function. Nevertheless, a NISO document, *A Framework of Guidance for Building Good Digital Collections*, presents a higher level set of requirements for metadata, which is seen as a unique component in a digital collection and:

1. conforms to community standards in a way that is appropriate to the materials in the collection, users of the collection, and current and future uses of the collection;
2. supports interoperability;
3. uses authority control and content standards to describe objects and collocate related objects;

4. includes a clear statement of the conditions and terms of use for the digital object;
5. supports the long-term curation and preservation of objects in collections.

The Framework also indicates that:

6. good metadata records are objects themselves and therefore should have the qualities of good objects, including authority, authenticity, achievability, persistence, and unique identification. (NISO Framework Advisory Group, 2004, 2007)

Among these basic requirements, some (1 and 3) have been implemented by the conventions of library cataloging for a long time, whereas others (4 and 5) draw new attention to the particular functions of administration, rights management, and preservation. A changed emphasis (6) is that metadata records are viewed as surrogates of objects but are *also* objects within a digital collection. All of these should be recognized as features that distinguish traditional cataloging from emergent metadata creation. Metadata creators must have knowledge that is greater than the application of rules specified by structure and content standards. They must now be involved in decisions beyond descriptive cataloging, beginning at the very outset of a digital collection project.

Augmenting this approach is the centrality that hinges upon shareable metadata (2). Today's metadata creator must think about the qualities of shareable or interoperable metadata and how this is different from creating metadata for use "in-house." Shreeves, Riley, and Milewicz (2006) provide an excellent 6C framework for shareable metadata. In a simplified synopsis, this is defined as:

- *Content:* The content of metadata records is optimized for sharing.
- *Consistent:* All records within a defined set are consistent both semantically and syntactically.
- *Coherence:* Records should be self-explanatory.
- *Context:* Information provided by records should have the appropriate context.
- *Communication:* Metadata providers and aggregators should maintain good communication.
- *Conformance:* Metadata records should conform to established standards.

Providing appropriate context is regarded as the biggest change involved in metadata records intended for local use. "Local" could mean within an institution, a system, or a union catalog that enforces certain value standards (e.g., using one controlled vocabulary). Metadata records in a local environment often omit information common to every record in the collection; this information however, is often the most important feature of the resource, and as such it is essential for inclusion in a shared environment (Shreeves, Riley, and Milewicz, 2006). Known as the "on a horse" problem, this issue was originally articulated by Wendler (2004). In this case, a photograph of Theodore Roosevelt astride a horse provides no information to identify the rider. Whereas the information "Theodore Roosevelt" should be common to every record in the Theodore Roosevelt Collection, records that omit this information will not provide any context when integrated with other collections.

Another common problem is semantic conflicts that result from a lack of indicators for encoding schemes in records from different sources. In a local collection it is normal for a particular thesaurus or subject headings list to be the only source of all subject terms assigned in records. When these records are merged with records from other sources, searching and browsing by subject may cause ambiguity and false mapping between queries and materials because no scheme information is attached to each subject term. The term *pressure* from *Medical Subject Headings* (MeSH) will have different meanings from the word *pressure* in the *INSPEC Thesaurus'* Physics section. The problem may also be encountered routinely when contending with dates encoded with different international standards and conventions. DCMI has suggested that to indicate encoding schemes in the encoded records, use of the *scheme* attribute of the XHTML <meta> element is preferable when expressing Dublin Core in HTML/XHTML, and to follow this pattern:

```
<meta name="dc.element" scheme="dcterms.scheme" content=
"value" />
```

Thus, the above examples would look like this:

```
<meta name="subject" scheme="dcterms.MeSH" content=
"pressure" />

<meta name="subject" scheme="INSPEC Thesaurus" content=
"pressure" />
```

While MeSH is a DCMI-registered DCMI *term, INSPEC Thesaurus* is not, and locally developed controlled vocabularies also exist. In the following actual example (www.ibm.com), IBM's local taxonomies are indicated in the scheme attribute. The embedded metadata statements include:

```
<meta content="ZZ999" scheme="IBM_SubjectTaxonomy" name=
"DC.Subject" />

<meta content="CT002" scheme="IBM_ContentClassTaxonomy" name=
"DC.Type" />
```

These statements explain that two locally developed taxonomies are used when assigning values of *subject* and *type*. With the detailed statements that the values "ZZ999" and "CT002" came from specific vocabularies, incorrect interpretations of the meanings of these values can be avoided when the metadata is merged with many other shared records. Issues and examples presented here show how shared metadata records (instead of in-house and local records) must be carefully considered both conceptually and in practice.

5.2 Conceptual Models

5.2.1 Metadata *Statement, Description,* and *Description Set*

To fully comprehend the components and constructs used in a metadata schema it is necessary to first understand the conceptual model behind it. A conceptual model of metadata is not tied to any specific approach to implementation: it is independent of any particular encoding syntax. DCMI Abstract Model (2007) as a DCMI Recommendation is a model that (1) defines *resources* in terms of semantic relationships among *classes, properties,* and *values,* and (2) defines a model for DCMI *descriptions, description sets,* and *records.* It serves as the foundation for future DCMI developments, and also as the conceptual model for metadata initiatives outside of DCMI (Baker, 2005; Kurth, 2006). The DCMI Abstract Model builds on the *Resource Description Framework* (RDF) and therefore it contains terminologies that RDF has developed. The following points are especially helpful for metadata creators:

- a *description set* is a set of one or more descriptions, each of which describes a single resource;
- a *description* is made up of one or more statements (about one, and only one, resource) and zero or one described resource URI (a URI that identifies the described resource); and
- each *statement* instantiates a property-value pair, and is made up of a property URI (a URI that identifies a property) and a value surrogate ("DCMI Abstract Model," 2007).

Sutton (2007) puts it more plainly, stating:

- The basic unit of metadata is a *statement.*
- A statement consists of a *property* (a.k.a. *element*) and a *value.*
- Metadata statements describe *recourses.*

He further provides an illustration, as shown in Figure 5-2-1.

Figure 5-2-1. DCMI Abstract Model in a simplified graphical example.

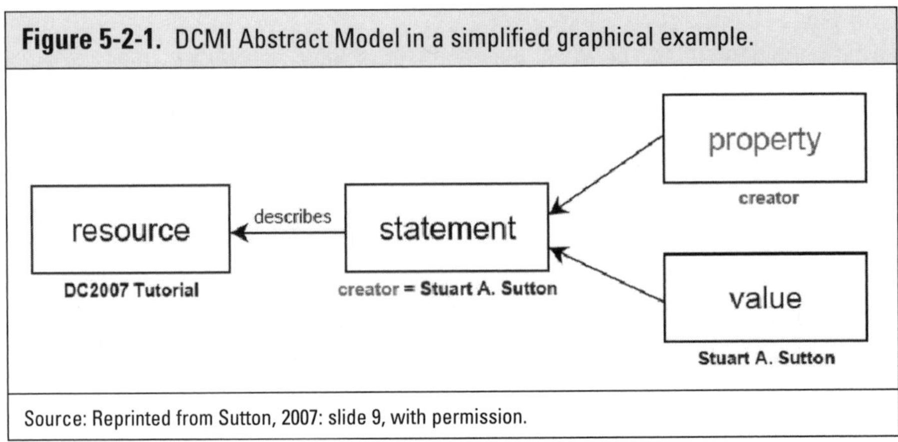

Source: Reprinted from Sutton, 2007: slide 9, with permission.

Figure 5-2-2. Basic model: Resource with properties and related to other resources.

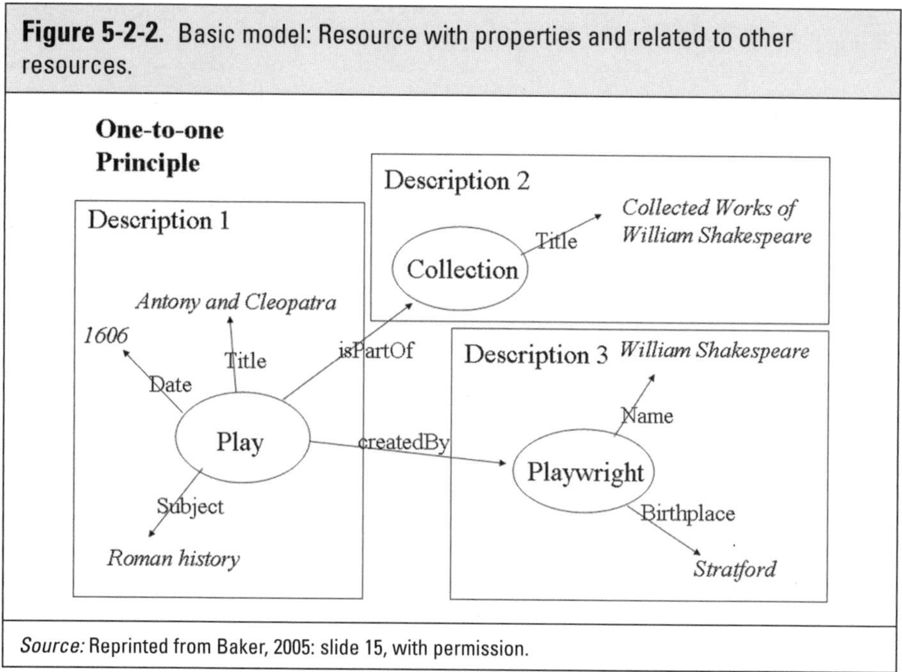

Source: Reprinted from Baker, 2005: slide 15, with permission.

Concerning the relationships between descriptions in a record, Baker also gives an excellent example to illustrate the DC Abstract Model (see Figure 5-2-2, above). Here, the play has the title *Antony and Cleopatra,* and was written in 1606 by William Shakespeare, *and* is about "Roman history." This example illustrates that a metadata record for this book contains a description set that contains three descriptions. Each description contains one or more statements. Each statement describes one property that has one value.

The DCMI Abstract Model is consistent with the DC *one-to-one principle:*

- Create one metadata description for one and only one resource—
  —Do not describe a digital image of the Mona Lisa as if it were the original painting.
  —Do not describe both a song and the song's composer in the same description, i.e., describe the composer and the work in two separate descriptions.
- Group related descriptions into a description set, i.e., record (Sutton, 2007: slide 23).

5.2.2 Relationships Between Resources

It is now obvious that metadata *statements* describe *resources*. It is also clear that a *resource* is not equivalent to a physically bound package, e.g., a book, a Web site, or an image. A resource can be a person, place, or a collectively created work containing multiple components. CDWA has also developed an abstract

Figure 5-2-3. CDWA's Entity-Relationship Diagram.

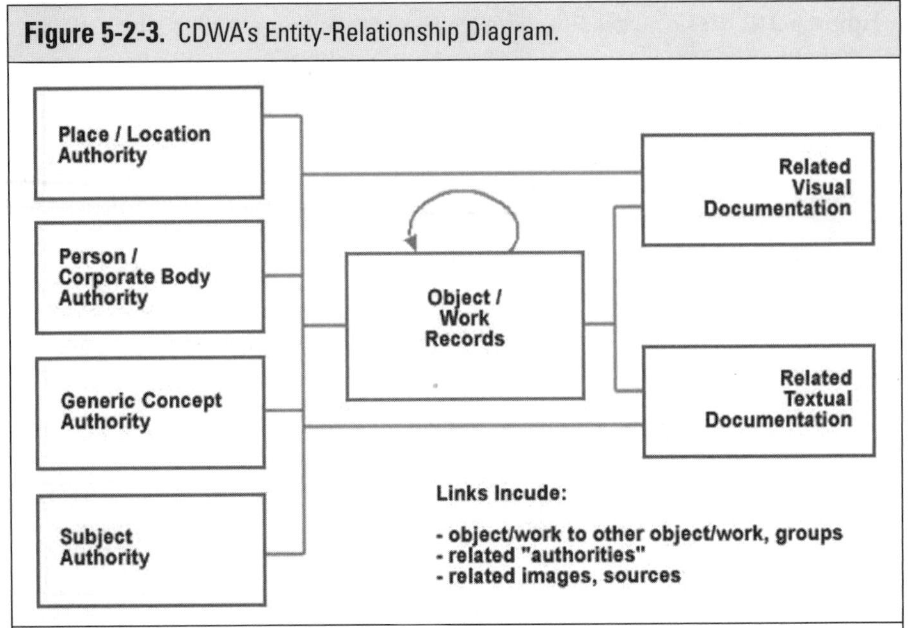

Source: www.getty.edu/research/conducting_research/standards/cdwa/entity.html. © J. Paul Getty Trust. *Categories for the Description of Works of Art.* Murtha Baca and Patricia Harpring, eds. Los Angeles: J. Paul Getty Trust and the College Art Association, 2000. www.getty.edu/research/conducting_research/standards/cdwa/, accessed January 10, 2008. Reprinted with permission.

model that designates the relationships of resources (see Figure 5-2-3, above). The model was adapted by CCO (Baca et al., 2006: 20).

Figure 5-2-3 illustrates how works may be related to other works, and how works may be related to images, sources, and authorities. A given authority file may be used to control terminology in multiple elements. Equally, a given element may use controlled terms from multiple authorities. Reflecting this model in records contained in a relational database, a record for the Eiffel Tower will have statements about the properties of this work, e.g., creator, subject, style, current location, material, and technique. The values (for example, a term or a code) for these properties are from the concept authority records that originated from value standards such as AAT, ULAN, and TGN. In a database-driven Web site, each value used for each property in each statement will also be linked to the authority records that have been established for each value. The record of an image (or images), as the surrogate(s) of the original work, will contain a statement about its relation to the original work and will link to the work record as well. Both CDWA and VRA Core have provided many examples of metadata records. At another level, CCO has provided a set of good examples of how the records for works, images, and authorities may synthetically conjoin. All examples are consistent with the DCMI one-to-one principle.

The relationships among these components are best summarized by another diagram provided by Baker (2005), and updated by Nilsson (2007a) (see Figure

Figure 5-2-4. Summary of the constructs of a record.

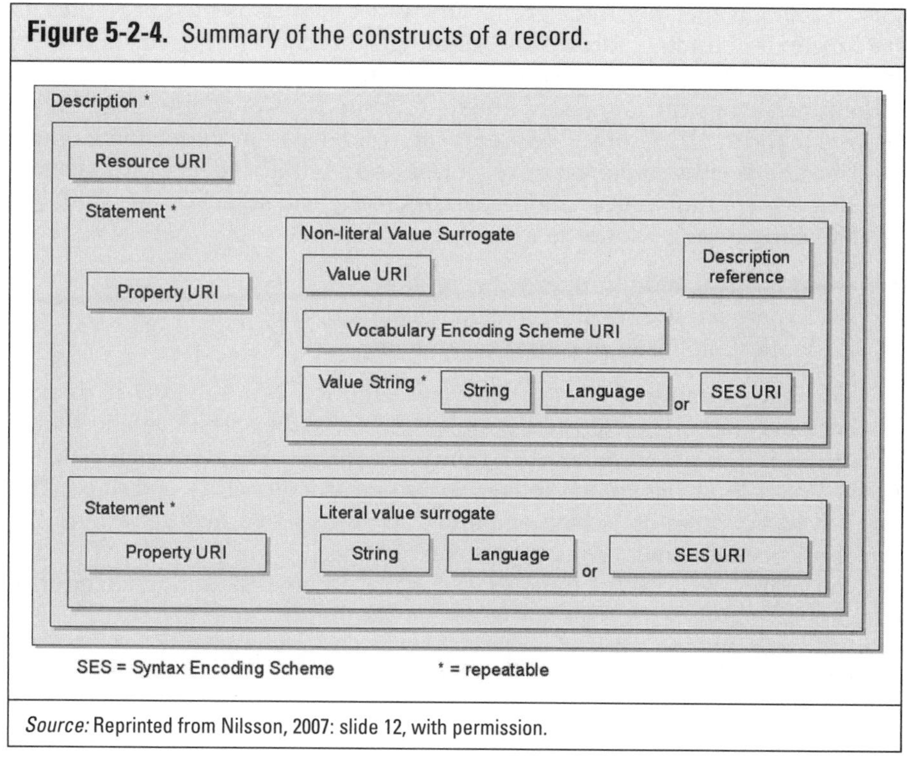

Source: Reprinted from Nilsson, 2007: slide 12, with permission.

5-2-4, above). A record consists of descriptions, using properties and values; a value can be a string or a pointer to another description.

5.2.3 Content-oriented Model for the Bibliographic Universe

The library community has a long history of creating metadata for physical media such as print books and audio/video cassettes or discs. Some noticeable effort occurred from this community to restructure their views on (and approaches to) metadata. Traditionally, the bibliographic universe has used an *object-oriented* model emphasizing the object containing a document/content. The Functional Requirements for Bibliographic Records (FRBR) is a *content-oriented* model developed by the International Federation of Library Associations and Institutions (IFLA). A final report was approved in 1997 and published in 1998 (IFLA, 1998). It was constructed based on the entity-relationship (ER) analysis that has been used for designing relational databases since the 1970s. ER modeling is a technical approach that specifies the structure of a conceptual model and defines the kinds of things that must be in it, together with the associated properties those things may have. A simplified explanation of the structure stipulated by an ER model allows the following three constructs: (1) *entities*, i.e., things, (2) *attributes*, i.e., properties or characteristics of either entities or relationships, and (3) *relationships*, i.e., interactions among entities (Carlyle and

Fusco, 2007). It specifies three groups of entities as well as their attributes for the functions of finding, identifying, selecting, and acquiring information about library materials. Group 1 consists of four entities: work, expression, manifestation, and item, which represent different perspectives of an intellectual work or artistic form. The Group 2 concerns the responsible party for the Group 1 entities, and is either a person or corporate body. Group 3 deals with the entities that serve as subjects of intellectual or artistic endeavor (IFLA, 1998). The relationships among Group 1 entities are as follows:

- A Work is realized through an Expression;
- An Expression is embodied in a manifestation; and,
- A Manifestation is exemplified by an Item.

Using the example of Harry Potter (see Figure 5-2-5), the *work* (a distinct intellectual creation) is realized through *expressions* (the specific intellectual or artistic form that a work takes each time it is realized), e.g., the English text of Harry Potter (E 1), the French spoken word performance (E 4), and so on. This English text expression is then embodied in at least two manifestations, i.e., the physical embodiment of an expression of a specific work, which in this case is two English versions (M 1 and M 2). Finally, a manifestation is exemplified

Figure 5-2-5. An interpretation of the FRBR model.

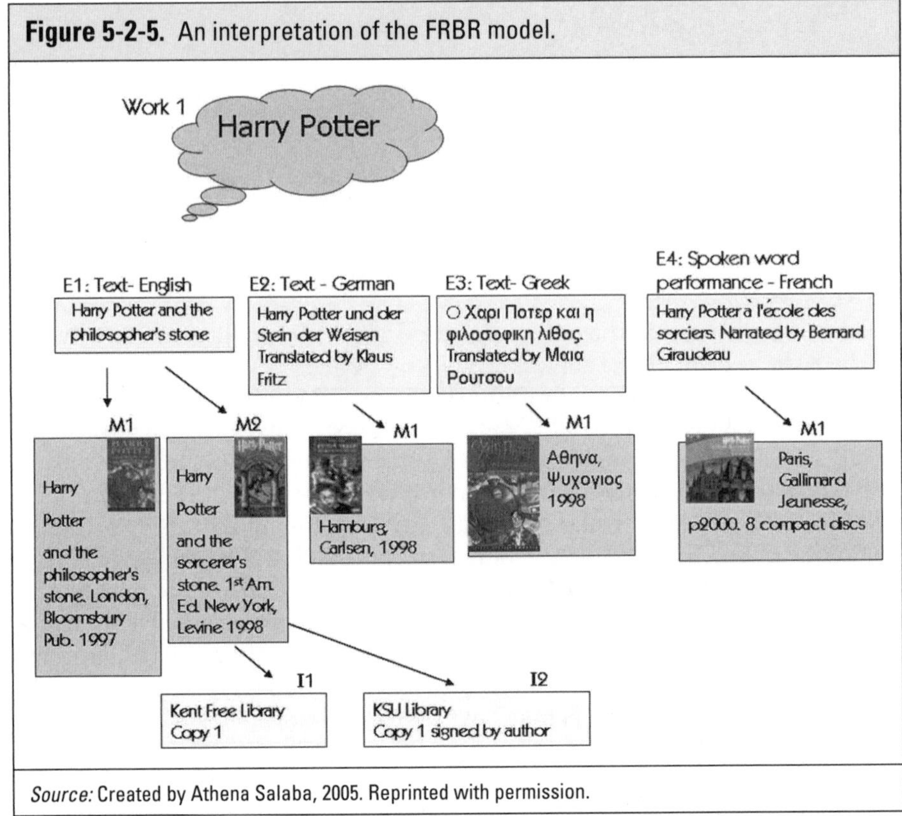

Source: Created by Athena Salaba, 2005. Reprinted with permission.

by an Item (i.e., a single example of a manifestation). Here two items are available: I 1 at the Kent Free Library and I 2 at the Kent State University (KSU) Library.

As a conceptual model, FRBR is a representation *and* a simplified description of the bibliographic universe, with its primary purpose being to improve catalog records (a product), cataloging (a process) and catalogs (a technology). The important changes that FRBR may bring are not simply changes to catalogers' routine tasks, but to their awareness as well as changes in online catalog displays (Carlyle and Fusco, 2007). To the digital world, the model's greatest potential lies in access to distributed metadata information in union catalogs, repositories, and portals. For such portals as The European Library (TEL: www.theeuropeanlibrary.org) FRBR offers meaningful clustering of search results and navigation. The same approach can then be applied to access all available cultural information (Zumer, 2007).

5.3 Levels of Granularity

5.3.1 Item and Collection Records

Levels of granularity are mainly concerned with whether a record (description set) describes the entirety of a collection or individual items in the collection. In Chapter 3 we discussed the creation level of metadata records. Section 3.1.1 explains common levels of description in different disciplines, especially in libraries, archives, and museums. In a more-or-less "either-or" situation, a project designer may decide to create metadata at the collection level for all objects in the entire collection. Specific metadata schemas (e.g., EAD) are designed for such purposes.

Different instances of the application of granularity are discussed here. First, a data provider may create a collection record (or records) in addition to all the item level records created for individual objects that constitute the whole collection. An example is the National Science Digital Library (NSDL), which consists of hundreds of digital collections, large or small, many being contributed by various NSDL projects. Each collection has a record that describes its entirety rather than specific resources or services maintained by the collection. At the NSDL Metadata Repository, the same set of elements is used for both item and collection records. Therefore a user who discovers an individual item as the result of a search will see both item and collection information returned. All collection information can be accessed at the NSDL Web site (http://crs.nsdl.org/collection/, accessed 2007). Figure 5-3-1 provides an illustration. Collection records are usually built and maintained by metadata creators and are not generally subject to the automated maintenance processes exercised on other repository records (Hillmann and Dushay, 2004–2005).

A second instance is that some of the resources in a collection may overlap. We understand that an *item* is a unit of a collection. It is usually the basic record upon which a metadata repository or database is built. However, an item is not necessarily the smallest unit represented as a resource in a project. It may be

Figure 5-3-1. A collection record of Visionlearning at NSDL.org.

Collection Information:

View "Visionlearning"

Resource Information:

Description	Visionlearning is an innovative educational resource designed for students, teachers, parents or anyone interested in learning science. Visionlearning provides peer-reviewed teaching modules in chemistry, biology, earth science and other disciplines within a fully customizable online classroom management system.
Subject Keyword(s)	Science Science--Study and teaching (Secondary) Science--Study and teaching (Higher) interdisciplinary science; national science education standards; classroom management
Grade Level	High School Undergraduate (Lower Division) Undergraduate (Upper Division)
Resource Format	image text/html
Title	Visionlearning
Rights Information	For educational use per the terms and conditions described in the Visionlearning, Inc. terms of use statement found at http://www.visionlearning.com/docs/terms.php
Resource Type	InteractiveResource Image Collection Text

Source: Courtesy of the National Science Digital Library (NSDL), reprinted from http://crs.nsdl.org/collection/index.php?collectionsPage=36 with permission.

large or small, and it may be formed by components or smaller units. So, an *item record* should be considered as describing particular resources or groups of resources within a collection (NSDL Glossary, 2005). NSDL suggests that item-level description is most appropriate for resources whose individual characteristics are of primary importance to end users, in which the differences between a resource and other similar resources are significant. E-prints, published materials, letters, photographs, and paintings are some of the categories of resources for which item-level description is most likely to be useful (NSDL, 2005). Metadata records that have been created and are available in different kinds of digital collections and libraries are predominantly item-level records.

NSDL's best practice guide also suggests that for some types of resources item-level description is *not* useful. A project with a collection made up of nearly indistinguishable items wastes time, energy, and money creating item-level descriptions; a collection-level description would be more cost-effective and functionally efficient (Hillmann and Dushay, 2004–2005). For example, a collection of coins that vary only in their accession numbers should be described as a collection, and access to the individual items should be made available within the data provider's local environment (NSDL, 2005). Within a digital library therefore, *collections* may range from an ad hoc set of objects that serve a temporary purpose, to established library collections intended to persist through time. These aggregations include those in which a creator or manager has organized or grouped component parts into a coherent whole that serves as the resource of interest to end-users. The objects in these collections vary widely, from library and data center holdings, to pointers of real-world objects, e.g., geographic places. Learning objects, Web sites, and some types of archival collections are categories of resources for which records describing groups of items might be most useful. The key to integrated use of such a variety of collections in a digital library is collection metadata that represents the inherent and contextual characteristics of a collection (Hill et al., 1999).

Collection metadata may be used for various purposes, which include the following:

- *Collection registration* with the search and retrieval and client software that will provide access;
- *Network discovery* that provides information to network search agents about what the collection contains;
- *User documentation*, that is, information provided to the user about the collection and the digital library interface;
- *Management* of the collection to provide centralized information storage (or reference) that pertains to the collection. The internal collection management includes mapping the object metadata attributes to the common search parameters of the system (Hill et al., 1999).

The Alexandria Digital Library (ADL) Project has designed and implemented collection metadata for these purposes. This brings about the third instance in which collection-level metadata may be designed for exceptional requirements. ADL is a research digital library specializing in georeferenced/geospatial information, i.e., both on the georeferenced aspects of all forms of information and on geospatial data types such as maps, aerial photographs, remote-sensing images, and data pertaining to particular geography (Smith, 1996). ADL's architecture consists of *search buckets, collection-level metadata, access metadata, standard reports,* and *browse image metadata*. The collection-level metadata provides a structure to describe the inherent and contextual attributes of the collection:

- *Contextual* information includes title, responsible party, scope and purpose, update frequency, etc. Contextual information also includes the documentation of the mapping made from selected item-level metadata elements (e.g., MARC 21 fields 100 and 110) to the ADL search buckets (e.g., Contributor).
- *Inherent* information is gathered from the collection itself, such as total number of items and subtotals by type, format, year and decade, and spatial coverage (which can be displayed on a map) (Hill and Janee, 2004).

Of the three instances of granularity application discussed here, the first approach seems certain to be applied; i.e., a collection record (or records) about the whole collection should be created in addition to all item-level records designed for individual objects that comprise the entire collection. At the same time, when contending with different subject domains and different types of resources, sometimes an item-level record is created for a group of objects, although the domain(s) concept of item may not be equal to the physically independent single object. This is a particularly important point to keep in mind. Nevertheless, what has been discussed so far considers all objects as packed or bound items. The next question however, concerns the metadata associated with information that may be contained *within* an object, i.e., any structural work that embodies the resource-rich meaning of *information container*. We now turn to the topic of decomposition.

5.3.2 Resource Decomposition

Some objects described by a metadata record may be atomic, with little or no internal structure and may not be decomposable into smaller information units. In these cases, it is sufficient to have discovered the resource—for instance, a particular image. On the other hand, many other objects are true information containers—information rich—and with a complex internal document organization. Information discovery within resources directly relates to the question of resource decomposition.

Structural decomposition of dissertations and theses (a major area that utilizes this approach) usually yields definite structural elements: Abstract, Section Headings, Chapters, Summary, and References; these are culturally bound and also reflect textual conventions in scientific and technical discourse. Other less obvious structural elements, e.g., numbered formulae and tables, are also embedded in articles. An arbitrary approach is to create a record for each important chapter of a dissertation in addition to a record for the whole dissertation. This alteration in structure may have also caused semantic decomposition because of the different topics or foci of each chapter. But in general, metadata description is for the container rather than the content inside.

Semantic decomposition such as mathematics formulae, material properties, and chemical compounds rely on markup languages designed to describe those unique semantic elements within a document. This form of decomposition is less concerned with discovering structural elements (as already outlined) than with discovering and describing useful content elements. It is possible to combine a container's structural description (e.g., using LOM) for a learning object with semantic markup (e.g., MathML) for its contents within a single metadata record. Such integration also results in new aggregated resources in a digital library (see Figure 5-3-2).

Finally, the *architectural* meaning for a collection of digital resources is that there can be a very complex structure with a significant degree of granularity. At the highest level of granularity would be a set of *parent* resource descriptions (e.g., LOM metadata records). Each of these records points to a specific

Figure 5-3-2. The decomposition of a resource.

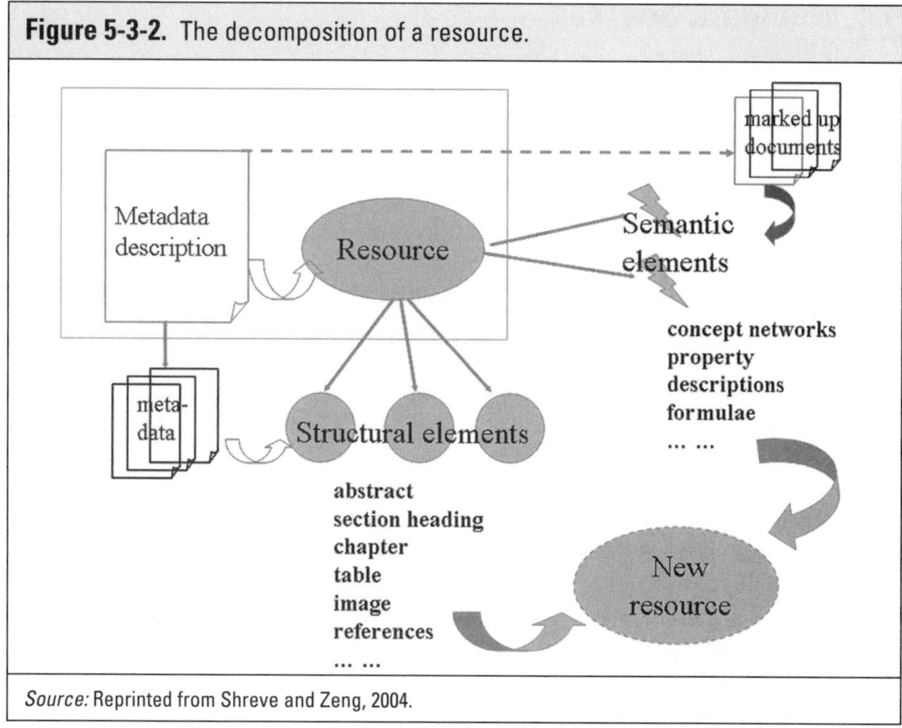

Source: Reprinted from Shreve and Zeng, 2004.

resource. Any given resource might be a composite object that is further decomposable into discrete *child* structural elements (as a book resource could be decomposed into chapters or a video resource into frames or frame sets). Or, they might be decomposable into discrete semantic objects (concept networks, property descriptions, formulae, images) that might be accessible as resources in their own right. At this point the digital collection becomes highly granular, and with the addition of new relationships that may be established between objects (either by decomposition or recombination) it also becomes highly *associative* (Shreve and Zeng, 2004).

The question of the *degree* of granularity arises here. It is possible to carry structural decomposition down to the level of very small structures. Here the purpose (and potential user community) of a digital library is of utmost importance and will determine the desired level (and focus) of decomposition and markup effort. But as NSDL's best practices indicates, it is rarely useful in the OAI environment to expose records for multiple digital items that form a complete resource when taken together. It is considered a best practice for individual page images in a digitized book that, unless each component part has significantly different descriptive information, the metadata should instead be exposed for the intellectual resource (i.e., the book). Access to the individual parts, i.e., the pages (if they have been digitized), should be supplied through navigational links in the data provider's local environment (NSDL, 2005).

5.4 Metadata Sources

Library and information professionals have been the most important contributors to the creation of metadata records for a very long time (ca. the establishment of modern librarianship and creation of the Dewey Decimal Classification). This tradition faced serious challenges when the world entered the Internet and Information era; from the early 1990s, exponential growth of distributed repositories occurred, and these were contributed to by many communities outside of the related domains of libraries, archives, and museums. To meet the new needs that describe, authenticate, and manage these resources, new metadata guidelines and architectures have been developed among different communities.

Caplan described the metadata movement as "a blooming garden, traversed by crosswalks, atop a steep and rocky road" (Caplan, 2000). This "blooming garden" has no limit for the types of professions or subject domains that can be involved in metadata standards development and applications. As a good example of the flowering brought about by the cross-pollination of many disciplines, the NSDL Metadata Repository is built upon a base of the metadata records harvested from over 100 digital collections that have been built, described, and managed with metadata by educators of K–12, undergraduate, and graduate schools in conjunction with publishers, scientists, engineers, medical doctors, professional associations, and so on. In addition, digital libraries and portals such as the NSDL also employ automatic mechanisms to generate, harvest, aggregate, and enhance metadata records. The involvement of diverse contributors (including resource creators), coupled with the advancement of automatic and automated methods, has changed the landscape of metadata sources dramatically.

From the perspective of procedures, the methods used to produce metadata records may be broadly classed into three categories: manual, automatic, and/or a combination of the two. The manual method is used when creators of digital objects or trained library and information professionals manually create metadata records through templates or a data entry interface. For example, educational digital libraries such as GEM and DLESE groomed metadata editors to perform manual data entry consistent with their metadata schemes. Involving humans in the creation of metadata can benefit metadata quality (Weinheimer, 2000); however, it can be costly and time-consuming. Automatic metadata generation includes extraction and harvesting (Greenberg, Spurgin, and Crystal, 2005). Metadata extraction is a process in which structures (e.g., title, author, corporate address, email, etc.) and semantic content in digital objects are analyzed and data values are extracted by computer algorithms designed for elements in a given metadata schema and/or a knowledge organization structure. Metadata is also harvested by using computer software, but the source of metadata comes from existing repositories.

When the conceptual framework of the DCMI Abstract Model is applied in practice, it is feasible to break down the bound metadata records into the basic unit of metadata—statements (see Section 5.2). Some statements are better completed manually but others may be more efficiently completed with automatic processes. The combination of manual with automatic mechanisms could become a solution to many projects that lack metadata creators but still place a high demand on quality.

5.4.1 Manual Generation of Metadata

The library also has been the domain primarily responsible for generating cataloging records for publications. A number of standards and tools have been used to provide a clear method for record generation operations. For the most part, library cataloging records have been created by human catalogers with professional training. Entering the digital era, this long-standing tradition is still preserved in part because of the difficulties of automatically generating satisfactory metadata records for any type of publication, and in part as a result of the belief that human intervention is requisite for producing quality metadata. Two groups of people contribute to the manual generation of metadata: librarians and information professionals, and noninformation professionals such as Web site managing staff, or creators, of the resources being described. Tools such as templates or editors are available during the process to aid in maintaining consistent format and data entry practice. An early study that examined the metadata attached in the "meta" fields of HTML documents found that metadata created by nonprofessionals varies greatly in terms of data consistency and quality (Qin and Wesley, 1998).

Using a Web-based metadata editor that allows registered members to submit records is a common practice in manual generation. Examples include those used by many digital libraries such as DLESE (www.dlese.org) and MERLOT (www.merlot.org). When a document is submitted to a digital collection, the author is often encouraged (or required) to submit metadata records, as in the cases of ePrints (Guy et al., 2004) and DSpace (Smith et al., 2003). As an assurance of quality, EPrints adopted a model of automated creation and author contribution that combines with enhancement by information specialists (Guy et al., 2004). Although there is concern about the quality of metadata, results from several studies reveal that author-generated metadata is acceptable (Barrueco and Krichel, 2000; Greenberg et al., 2001). Authors also favor collaborative metadata generation and often seek help from information specialists in selecting subject data for the resources they are creating the metadata to represent (Greenberg and Robertson, 2002).

5.4.2 Automatic Generation of Metadata

Automatically extracting metadata from digital resources or assigning values to metadata elements is a highly challenging task and often requires the use of multiple approaches for success.

Metadata extraction utilizes resource content (rather than preexisting metadata) when a given genre indicates a predictable document structure. For example, an electronic thesis or dissertation almost always has definite metadata (see Section

5.3.2). Sophisticated algorithms can be used to identify and mine relevant content and then produce structured resource discovery metadata (Wilson 2006). *Machine learning* has been experimentally tested for extracting metadata. One example is the Support Vector Machine (SVM) for classification and feature extraction (Han et al. 2003). In this case, the research team trained a classifier to recognize the different metadata types so that it could extract values for the 15 different metadata fields of DC. This method achieved an accuracy rate of 92.9 percent. Hu et al. (2005) achieved similar high-accuracy results in extracting *title* from Microsoft Office Word and Power Point documents using machine learning techniques. Another report by Paynter (2005) gives account in great detail about the extraction procedure and performance evaluation for assigning values in the title, creator, key-phrase, description, and LCSH subject heading fields.

A more challenging aspect of the extraction process is to accurately place the extracted data values with the correct metadata elements. Frequently used techniques in this research area include *natural language processing* (NLP) i.e., use of regular expressions and rule-based parsers, and machine learning strategies. The sources for the extraction of data may come from either document structure or knowledge organization systems. NLP approaches have been deployed by Liddy and her colleagues (Paik, et al., 2001; Liddy et al., 2002; Yilmazel et al., 2004) to automatically extract metadata from digital educational resources. They used shallow parsing rules and multiple levels of NLP tagging in developing an NLP system, MetaExtract, which specifically extracts terms and phrases found within single sentences. The evaluation of their NLP approach shows that the rule-based multilevel tagging achieved comparable performance to manually created metadata. Embley, Jackman, and Xu (2001) conducted an experiment using three facets of metadata: terminology relationships, data-value characteristics, and target-specific regular-expression matches in order to extract values from sources, then categorize and match them with target attributes. The results of the experiment suggest that by combining multiple-facets to extract metadata it is much more likely to be of greater advantage than using any single-facet approach alone. Greenberg, Spurgin, and Crystal (2005) provide a brief outline of automatic metadata generation research that reviews the aforementioned experimental projects.

The singular challenging issue in automatic metadata generation is *automatic indexing* or *clustering* for representing the subjects of source documents. Techniques for solving this problem fall into two categories: extracting keywords/key phrases or classifying the sources based on a knowledge organization system. The former draws out keywords from the text of the document while the latter assigns keywords or class numbers that are selected from a knowledge organization system. The extraction approaches are most appropriate for *uncontrolled fields*, e.g., title, description, creator, and keywords (Paynter, 2005).

Classification approaches, on the other hand, use algorithms to discern relationships between a document's features and labels and then assign subject terms from a controlled vocabulary. The iVia Infomine LCSH software, for instance, assigns LCSH terms to resources according to an analysis of the most frequently occurring LCSH terms in previous (and similar) resources. The system also will routinely assign INFOMINE categories and Library of Congress Classification (LCC) to the new resources added to the collection by means of automatic machine learning techniques (Paynter 2005). Statistical learning methods such as Bayes, *k*-nearest neighbor, and Support Vector Machine are appropriate for deriving rules or features for classifiers from pre-categorized data. For text categorization tasks that have less than sufficient training data, alternative methods need to be applied, which is the case of automatic assignment of educational standards to digital library content (Diekema and Chen, 2005).

Cardinaels, Meire, and Duval (2005) have developed a Web service for the automatic indexing of learning objects inside a learning management system. The automatic indexing framework includes two modules: a context-based indexer and an object-based indexer. The former derives metadata based on use of the learning object whereas the latter generates metadata based on the learning object itself. The authors have named the Web service a Simple Indexing Interface, which is "an application programmer's interface to implement the services" (Cardinaels, Meire, and Duval 2005: 552). Their evaluation of the system concludes that sometimes the manual method is preferable while at other times the automatic method is better; overall however, the results are good enough to compete with manually generated metadata. In large corporate document or content repositories, tens of thousands of pieces of documents can be stored and made accessible through restricted networks. Many of these documents, especially those created a long time ago, do not have sufficient metadata. Updating them manually on a large scale is unrealistic. Therefore, tools that assist automatic indexing and clustering can ensure both productivity and quality for ease of access to them.

5.4.3 Combination of Manual and Automatic Methods

The DCMI Abstract Model has been previously explained and elaborated upon. The model characterizes a metadata record as the sum of a group of description sets that in which each description contains statements that denote resources; each statement is expressed through describing a resource's particular properties (elements) and values. This concept revolutionizes the generation, management, and usage of metadata because we can then conceive of metadata at a basic unit level—the statement.

Combining manual and machine-generated metadata statements has improved and enhanced both productivity and accuracy. When use of a template to generate metadata is performed by humans, certain information can still be captured and filled in automatically. DC-Dot's Dublin Core metadata editor (www.ukoln.ac.uk/metadata/dcdot/) fills in the appropriate values in its element boxes after one submits a URL. As already stated, automatic methods are best applied when a given genre shows marked tendencies toward a predictable document structure. However, with a tool that opens all kinds of document structures, the values automatically generated by the software may not be accurate or the property-value pairs may be mismatched (unless the original Web page has already embedded a DC metadata record). Therefore the automatically generated metadata are usually edited using the template provided. In most cases, the software can automatically capture correct information if the title (according to the title tag embedded in the HTML file), format, date (of publishing), and identifier (the URL) are correct. Additional metadata values for all other elements must be checked and/or entered by human agents, and include identifiers such as DOI and ISBN. If the original Web page already has a minimum set of meta tags, the software can also generate more accurate data.

Metadata for digital objects (such as digital camera images) are surrogates that record not only descriptive properties, but also technical and management properties. Metadata records created for digital objects benefit most from automatic capture of technical metadata. Adobe Photoshop Creative Studio (CS), for example, provides a template to combine both automatic and human-generated metadata. The basic part of this template includes three sections: File Properties, IPTC (International Press Telecommunications Council) Core, and Camera Data. File Properties contain automatically captured data such as creation and revision dates, document type, file size, dimensions, and resolution. The Camera Data uses extensive properties defined by the Exchangeable Image File Format (Exif). The IPTC Core section allows manual editing for each element. More automated processes are also provided: the Keywords folder handles the taxonomy or list (flat or hierarchical) established by the creator along with the growth of the image collection. A screenshot showing portions of the metadata and keywords panels is found in Section 5.5.

Some automated processes can also be performed later as a project needs to add missing statements such as the values for *dc.format* to all the records that were previously created. This form of aggregation has become one metadata service for dealing with incomplete and inconsistent metadata in a repository (see Section 5.7).

As digital information rapidly increases in complexity and volume, the development of automatic metadata generation becomes a viable part of resolving the needs of resource discovery and information retrieval. Successes from lab research experiments show promising results. However, application of results to production systems requires large amounts of training data, collaborators who are leaders in their fields, well-defined strategies, and intricate algorithms. Although automatic metadata generation saves time and human labor, it does not completely eliminate human intervention and oversight from the process. In most cases, human metadata creators will continue to assign data, but the automatic programs will shadow the human-assigned data and use it to continually train the automatic classifier (Scheirer, 2006). This represents a current trend in automatic metadata generation whereby human intervention is employed as both quality control mechanism and source of training data.

5.4.4 Harvested Metadata Records

Metadata records can be harvested from remote servers where the metadata conform to formats recognized by a standard protocol (see Figure 5-4-1). A good

Figure 5-4-1. Illustration of harvesting based on a common protocol.

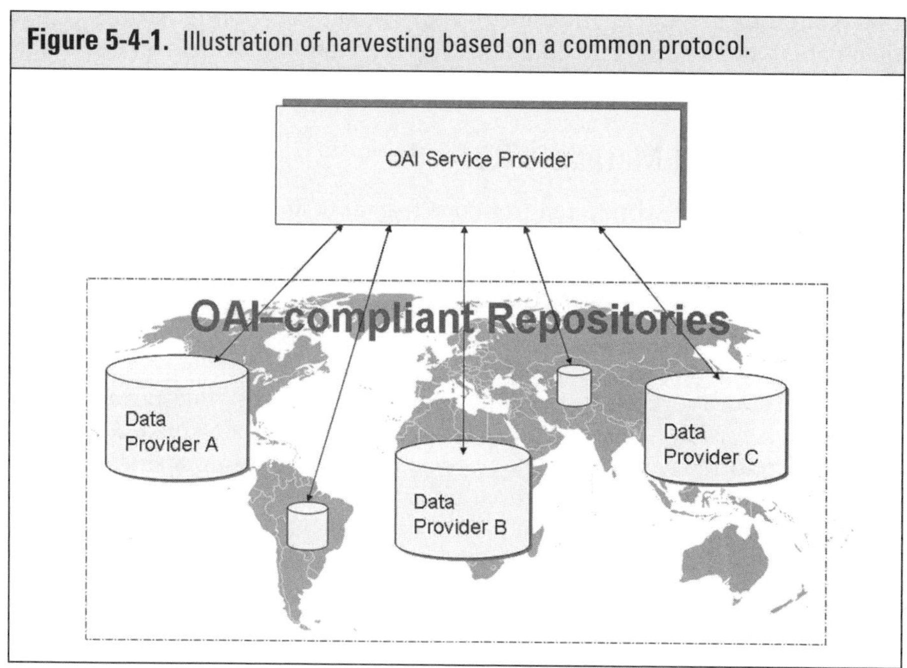

example is the National Science Digital Library (NSDL) Metadata Repository, which is a centralized database that consists of thousands of metadata records from many collections, primarily through harvesting via the Open Archives Initiative—Protocol for Metadata Harvesting (OAI-PMH). This is discussed in detail in Chapter 6, Section 6.4 on Metadata Repositories.

The harvested metadata will need to go through stages of cleaning-up, crosswalking for normalization, generation of XML encoded records, and finally loading the metadata records into the database. During these stages numerous variations may exist between the needs of service providers, the needs of data providers, and among the granularities and the types of objects characterized by harvested metadata (Arms et al., 2002). The OAI-PMH metadata approach has been tested and adopted in a wide variety of projects. In addition to text-based resources and scholarly resources, harvesting is also applied to thumbnail images (Foulonneau, Habing, and Cole, 2006) and non-scholarly environments (Chudnov et al., 2005).

Harvesting can also be employed on the documents generated by specific content creation software, such as Microsoft Word and Adobe Dreamweaver. These software may automatically insert useful metadata into file headers or allow manual input of such data during the resource creation process itself (e.g., Microsoft Word automatically records *file size*, *date created*, and *date modified*. It also assigns a title based on the first line of a document). Adobe Acrobat automatically captures all these metadata for PDF files. In addition, Adobe PDF files could have custom properties such as comments, company name, and specifically set IDs (see Section 5.5 for details). Metadata harvesting tools, such as DC-dot, can identify and collect such pre-existing tagged metadata, whether it is embedded within the resource or held in a separate database (Wilson, 2006).

5.4.5 Converted Metadata Records

Metadata records are converted from one format to another based on the need of a collection. In digital collections built by libraries, this usually involves converting very rich MARC records into other, newer formats following DC, VRA Core, LOM, and so on. These records are integrated with newly created metadata records for ease of management by digital assets software, compliance with digital library system requirements, development of systems designed for Web-based education, and to streamline and maximize the efficiency of administrative systems. In large metadata repositories, metadata contributed or harvested from different sources also need to be converted into a single format. While trying to ensure format compatibility, conversion also needs to minimize loss or distortion of the original data. Various tools have been created to facilitate such conversion. The Library of Congress provides tools (available at www.loc.gov/standards/marcxml/) to facilitate conversions between the formats of MARC 21, MARCXML, MODS, and DC.

The Picture Australia project also serves as a good example of data conversion. A digital library project encompassing a variety of institutions, it includes libraries, the National Archives, and the Australian War Memorial, all of which come with legacy metadata records prepared under different standards. Records from participants are collected in a central location (the National Library of Australia) and then translated into a common record format with fields based on the Dublin Core (Tennant, 2001).

The following figures show the result of an ADL (Alexandria Digital Library) metadata record (Figure 5-4-2) being converted into a Dublin Core record (Figure 5-4-3) when these records were harvested by the NSDL Metadata Repository. When converting an ADL record into a DC-based record for display, value strings in the ADL elements are displayed in equivalent DC-elements. For example, coordinates recorded in ADL *Bounding Coordinates* now appear in DC *Coverage*; and *Producer* becomes *Source*.

It is difficult to convert from a flat structured format (e.g., DC, VRA Core 2.0 and 3.0) to a hierarchical format (e.g., VRA Core 4.0, MARC 21). A statement in a DC record about *source* may need to be broken down into smaller units to match the subfields. Its temporal and spatial *coverage* terms as well as *subject* terms will need to be carefully put into the chunks of subfields in the MARC 6xx fields. On the other hand, values in the richer format also face the possibility of losing their context or important features. Values associated with *keywords* and *taxon* elements in a LOM record could all be lumped together in the *subject* field for a DC record. Even in the case where formats may have been correctly matched 100 percent, it does not guarantee that values can also be matched well. When terms that indicate *cultural* influence in VRA Core 3.0 are put into MARC 26x fields, two problems arise. First, the future use of these

Figure 5-4-2. A record from Alexandria Digital Library (ADL) Gazetteer: http://clients.alexandria.ucsb.edu/globetrotter/.

	Identifier for this record: doqq_bw_ca:03511664.SWS
titles:	**[FGDC] Citation—Title**
	[DOQQ, Digital orthophoto quarter quadrangle], Soda Lake South SW, California.
geographic-locations:	**[FGDC] Bounding Coordinates**
	Lat/Lon Bounding Box: North=35.0625 South=35.0 East=-116.0625 West=-116.125
dates:	**[FGDC] Time Period of Content—Date Range**
	Begin:1997-02-04 End:1997-02-04
types:	**[FGDC] Citation - Geospatial Data Presentation Form**
	aerial photographs
formats:	**[FGDC] Format Name**
	DOQQ
subject-related-text:	**[ADL] subject-related-text**
	DOQQ; quad; Band interleaved by line; BIL
assigned-terms:	**[FGDC] Theme Keyword**
	DOQ; DOQQ; digital orthophoto; digital orthophotoquad; digital image map; aerial photograph; paper map; map; Universal Transverse Mercator (UTM); digital image
	[FGDC] Place Keyword
	United States; California
	[ADL] Assigned Terms
originators:	Aerial photographs digital raster; California
	[FGDC] Citation—Originator
	U.S. Geological Survey (USGS)
	[DOQQ] PRODUCER
	Analytical Surveys, Inc.
	[DOQQ] AGENCY
identifiers:	U.S. Geological Survey Western Mapping Center
	[USGS] intelligent data set name (DSN)
	USGS:DSN: 03511664.SWS
	[USGS] Quadrangle Name
	[USGS] Quadrangle Name: Soda Lake South
	[MARC] UCSB Call Number
	UCSB Local Call Number: 3701s A4 12 .U5 CA 03511664.SWS tapes

Source: Reprinted with permission of the Alexandria Digital Library, USCB, Santa Barbara, California.

terms will be general *subject* instead of *cultural* influence as intended by the original metadata designer; second, these terms (e.g., "America") might not be selected from a controlled vocabulary as required by the target format (e.g., "United States of America").

Data conversion was, is now, and still will be a process that always accompanies and challenges digital collections. Among issues relating to metadata interoperability, quality, and maximizing, data conversion has a deep impact and should always be handled with caution because any mistakes would cause hundreds of errors in converting, or the loss of important values and identities of original data.

Figure 5-4-3. The ADL record retrieved from NSDL, after converting into DC format.

Title	[DOQQ, Digital orthophoto quarter quadrangle], Soda Lake South SW, California.
Creator	United States Geological Survey
Creator	Analytical Surveys, Inc.
Subject	Aerial photographs digital raster; California
Subject	DOQQ; quad; Band interleaved by line; BIL
Description	Digital Orthophoto Quarter Quadrangles (black & white) cover the state of California, each quarter quadrangle covering an area 3.75 degree by 3.75 degrees. Some quadrangles are still in process as of March 2002
Publisher	U.S. Geological Survey Western Mapping Center
Contributor	Alexandria Digital Library
Date	19970204
Date	19940528
Date	19971030
Type	Image
Type	remote-sensing images
Type	aerial photographs
Format	49189680 bytes
Format	BIL
Format	DOQQ
Format	Digital Orthophotographic Quarter Quadrangle
Identifier	http://middleware.alexandria.ucsb.edu/mw/wimp_metadata?view=full&id=doqq_bw_ca:03511664.SWS
Identifier	doqq_bw_ca:03511664.SWS
Identifier	Call Number:3701s A4 12 .U5 CA 03511664.SWS tapes
Source	Analytical Surveys, Inc.
coverage	northlimit=35.0625; eastlimit=-116.0625; southlimit=35.0; westlimit=-116.125; units=signed decimal degrees
coverage	Soda Lake South, California, United States
Rights	Access constraints: None.
Rights	Use constraints: Uncopyrighted.
Rights	Legal disclaimer: The Regents of the University of California disclaim any applicable implied warranties, including, but not limited to, the implied warranties of merchantability and fitness for a particular purpose. In addition, no warranty whatsoever accompanies the data available herein, and it is provided on an "as is" basis. The Regents of the University of California shall not be liable for any direct, indirect, special, incidental, or consequential damages arising out of the use of this data or from making this data available, even if it has been informed of the possibility of such damages.

Source: Data harvested from NSDL.org (http://nsdl.org/) in 2004. Reprinted with permission of the Alexandria Digital Library, USCB, Santa Barbara, California.

5.5 Encoding Metadata

Encoding denotes the process of transforming information from one format into another. In the previous chapter we discussed *metadata schema* encoding in which the semantics and structure of a metadata element set is expressed in schemas (e.g., a relational database schema or an XML schema). This section addresses how *metadata instances* (usually referred to as *records*) can be encoded. It should be considered an independent issue from schemas encoding because metadata records can be expressed in multiple formats (using multiple markup languages) regardless of how or if an element set associated with the records is encoded with a particular markup language. *Metadata encoding* is similar to *text encoding* but with some significant differences. Text encoding means using a markup language to tag the structure and other features of a text to facilitate processing by computers. The well-known Text Encoding Initiative (TEI) has developed a standard for the representation of texts in digital form. The *TEI Guidelines* define some 400 different textual components and concepts, which can be expressed using a markup language. Specifically, the *TEI Guidelines* define a set of markers (or *tags*) that may be *inserted* in the electronic representation of the text to *mark* the text structure and other textual features of interest (TEI Consortium, 2004: Section 1). Metadata encoding also uses markup languages to tag the structure and other properties of a resource according to the structures and semantics defined by a metadata standard. However, instead of being inserted in the electronic representation of objects, metadata descriptions exist as surrogates of the resources they describe. This section will provide a basic background for expressing metadata with common markup languages, which include HTML/XHTML, XML, and XML/RDF.

5.5.1 Metadata Storage

Although *record* has been viewed as the basic unit of management and exchange, it should be remembered that a record is composed of a set of metadata descriptions; each describes a resource and is composed of metadata statements. These statements may be published, aggregated, harvested, communicated, and used in multiple ways. Nevertheless, the basic components of metadata storage can be categorized according to two principal forms: *internal storage* (i.e., embedded within the resource being described) and *external storage* (i.e., stored separately from the resource being described). The following discussion provides a background for record encoding. Technologies related to data storage have been very competently discussed in numerous books and standards' specifications elsewhere.

Internal storage means that a metadata record is stored in the same file as the resource. The most common ones are metadata descriptions embedded in the source code of Web pages. Users generally are unaware of this information when they access and browse a Web site unless they choose to view the source code. The next screenshot (Figure 5-5-1) is taken from a *Metadata Basics* tutorial Portuguese version Web site (www.slis.kent.edu/~mzeng/metadatabasics/

Figure 5-5-1. The cover page and source page of *Metadata Basics* tutorial in Portuguese.

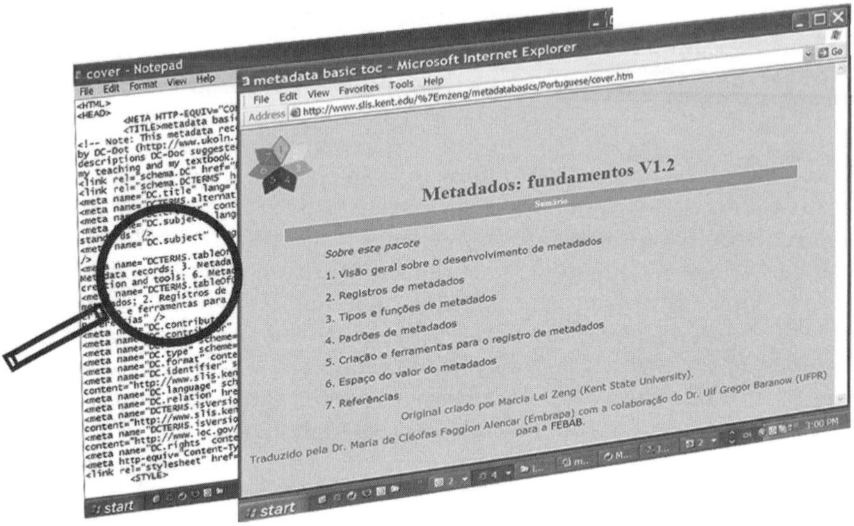

Source: www.slis.kent.edu/~mzeng/metadatabasics/Portuguese/cover.htm.

Portuguese/cover.htm). Exhibit 5-5-1 shows selected statements taken from its source code, obtained by choosing *view* → *source* of the homepage.

Many business Web sites provide accurate and detailed information with title, description, and keywords/subject elements embedded in the <head> section of their homepages. An excellent example from the business world is the IBM Web site (www.ibm.com). The homepages of IBM in various countries are all embedded with metadata statements and appropriate values. (To view different IBM sites by country and language, one would add a country code for the URL, e.g., www.ibm.com/gr for Greece.) In the "<meta content="[xyz]" name="IBM.Country" />" statement, the *content* of the element (a.k.a. tag) *IBM.Country* will have the value for that particular country, e.g., "US" for the United States, "CN" for China, "GR" for Greece, and "GB" for Great Britain. In the "<meta content="[xyz]" scheme="rfc1766" name="DC.Language" />" statement, a value for a particular language is assigned according to the international standard RFC1766 *Tags for the Identification of Languages*. Thus "en-GB" is a code for English used in Great Britain, "zh-CN" for Chinese used in mainland China, and "el" for Greek used in Greece. All IBM Web sites for each country are adjusted to reflect local language and cultural interests and therefore do not share the same appearance. Even though the homepages will change layout and images frequently, metadata embedded in all Web sites within the company are consistent and stable. The Web sites' metadata fully employ DC elements for the purposes of interoperability while also appending

Exhibit 5-5-1. Selected metadata statements from the *Metadata Basics* tutorial Portuguese version Web page shown in Figure 5-5-1.

```
<link rel="schema.DC" href="http://purl.org/dc/elements/1.1/" />
<link rel="schema.DCTERMS" href="http://purl.org/dc/terms/" />
<meta name="DC.title" lang="pt" content="Metadados: fundamentos" />
<meta name="DCTERMS.alternative" lang="en" content="Metadata basics" />
<meta name="DC.creator" content="Zeng, Marcia L." />
<meta name="DC.subject" lang="en" scheme="OCLC FAST Authority"
content="metadata; metadata-standards" />
<meta name="DC.subject" lang="en" content="metadata training; metadata value
space; metadata types" />
<meta name="DCTERMS.tableOfContents" lang="en" content="1. Metadata
development overview; 2. Metadata records; 3. Metadata types and functions;
4. Metadata standards; 5. Metadata record creation and tools; 6. Metadata
value space; 7. References;" />
<meta name="DCTERMS.tableOfContents" lang="pt" content="1. Visčo geral sobre
o desenvolvimento de metadados; 2. Registros de metadados; 3. Tipos e
funćões de metadados; 4. Padrões de metadados; 5. Criaččo e ferramentas para
o registro de metadados; 6. Espaćo do valor de metadados; 7. Referźncias" />
<meta name="DC.contributor" content="Maria de Cléofas Faggion Alencar" />
<meta name="DC.contributor" content="Ulf Gregor Baranow" />
<meta name="DC.date" scheme="DCTERMS.W3CDTF" content="2006-05-23" />
<meta name="DC.type" scheme="DCTERMS.DCMIType" content="Text" />
<meta name="DC.format" content="text/html; charset=ISO-8859-1" />
<meta name="DC.identifier" scheme="DCTERMS.URI"
content="http://www.slis.kent.edu/~mzeng/metadatabasics/Portuguese/cover.htm" />
<meta name="DC.language" scheme="DCTERMS.RFC1766" content="pt" />
<meta name="DC.relation"
href="http://www.slis.kent.edu/~mzeng/metadatabasics/index.htm" />
<meta name="DCTERMS.isVersionOf" scheme="DCTERMS.URI"
content="http://www.slis.kent.edu/~mzeng/metadatabasics/index.htm" />
<meta name="DCTERMS.isVersionOf" scheme="DCTERMS.URI"
content="http://www.loc.gov/catworkshop/readings/metadatabasics/" />
<meta name="DC.rights" content="Marcia Lei Zeng" />
```

Source: www.slis.kent.edu/~mzeng/metadatabasics/Portuguese/cover.htm (choose *view→ source* from the Web page).

a number of IBM-specific elements, e.g., *IBM.Industry, IBM.Country,* and *IBM.Effective.*

On the academic side, Caltech's (California Institute of Technology) *Collection of Open Digital Archives* (http://library.caltech.edu/digital/) sets a remarkable example: full DC records are embedded in each of the items stored in the database. In the following example, an entry found from its *Computer Science Technical Report* archive provides a detailed description about this report, with options to download the full-text files in PDF or postscript format (Figure 5-5-2). If we view the source code of this same Web page an embedded metadata record can also be seen (Figure 5-5-3). Two sets of metadata are presented in this case; one is in the browsable Web page and one is embedded within the Web page source code. The purpose is to expose

Figure 5-5-2. A screenshot of an entry of a computer science technical report.

Transistor Sizing of Energy-Delay--Efficient Circuits

Penzes, Paul and Nystroem, Mika and Martin, Alain (2002) *Transistor Sizing of Energy-Delay--Efficient Circuits.* Technical Report. California Institute of Technology. [CaltechCSTR:2002.003]

Full text available as:

PDF - Requires Adobe Acrobat Reader or other PDF viewer.

Postscript - Requires a viewer, such as GhostView

Abstract

This paper studies the problem of transistor sizing of CMOS circuits optimized for energy-delay efficiency, i.e., for optimal Et^n where E is the energy consumption and t is the delay of the circuit, while n is a fixed positive optimization index that reflects the chosen trade-off between energy and delay. We propose a set of analytical formulas that closely approximate the optimal transistor sizes. We then study an efficient iteration procedure that can further improve the original analytical solution. Based on these results, we introduce a novel transistor sizing algorithm for energy-delay efficiency.

EPrint Type:	Monograph (Technical Report)
Uncontrolled Keywords:	transistor sizing
Subjects:	All Records
ID Code:	318
Deposited By:	Paul Penzes
Deposited On:	11 April 2002
Record Number:	CaltechCSTR:2002.003
Official Persistent URL:	http://resolver.caltech.edu/CaltechCSTR:2002.003
Usage Policy:	You are granted permission for individual, educational, research and non-commercial reproduction, distribution, display and performance of this work in any format.

Source: Persistent URI: http://resolver.caltech.edu/CaltechCSTR.2002.003. Reprinted from *Caltech Collection of Open Digital Archives*: http://caltechcstr.library.caltech.edu/318/, with permission.

metadata to additional services such as OAI harvesters and other aggregators (see Chapter 6, Section 6.5).

In addition to HTML documents, vast amounts of non-HTML text documents exist, such as MS Word and PDF files. Authoring tools such as Microsoft Word for word-processing, and Adobe Acrobat for PDF files are equipped with templates to support embedding metadata within a file. In an MS Word file, the Properties section (choose from the menu File → Properties) provides forms for recording data about the documents (Figure 5-5-4). Some of the values are automatically captured (e.g., title, author, company) and others can be entered according to the default form (e.g., subject, keyword, category, comments, hyperlink base) in Properties. Custom file properties can be also be created. If a property is linked to a pre-bookmarked item in the document, the property will be updated as the item is changed. Microsoft's Properties file (or metadata file) has not been designed to follow any standardized metadata elements and so the practices may vary in different cases. For example, for the same file, one has to decide how to enter values without repetition in the fields of *subject, keyword,* and *category* in the same record.

Figure 5-5-3. Metadata statements (selected) embedded in the entry shown in Figure 5-5-2.

```
<head>
    <title >Caltech Computer Science Technical Reports—Transistor Sizing of
Energy-Delay—Efficient Circuits</title>
    <link rel="schema.DC" href="http://purl.org/DC/elements/1.0/" />
<meta content="Transistor Sizing of Energy-Delay—Efficient Circuits"
name="DC.title" />
<meta content="Penzes, Paul" name="DC.creator" />
<meta content="Nystroem, Mika" name="DC.creator" />
<meta content="Martin, Alain" name="DC.creator" />
<meta content="All Records" name="DC.subject" />
<meta content="This paper studies the problem ... ." name="DC.description" />
<meta content="California Institute of Technology" name="DC.publisher" />
<meta content="2002-01-01" name="DC.date" />
<meta content="Monograph" name="DC.type" />
<meta content="NonPeerReviewed" name="DC.type" />
<meta content="http://resolver.caltech.edu/CaltechCSTR:2002.003"
name="DC.identifier" />
<meta content="application/pdf" name="DC.format" />
<meta content="http://caltechcstr.library.caltech.edu/318/00/penzes.pdf"
name="DC.relation" />
<meta content="application/postscript" name="DC.format" />
<meta content="http://caltechcstr.library.caltech.edu/318/01/penzes.ps"
name="DC.relation" />
<meta content="http://resolver.caltech.edu/CaltechCSTR:2002.003"
name="DC.relation" />
<head>
```

Source: Persistent URI: http://resolver.caltech.edu/CaltechCSTR.2002.003. Reproduced from *Caltech Collection of Open Digital Archives*: http://caltechcstr.library.caltech.edu/318/, with permission.

Adobe Acrobat PDF files on the other hand, have benefited from the cross-products metadata framework Adobe Systems has implemented: the eXtensible Metadata Platform (XMP) framework (see www.adobe.com/products/xmp/). Each PDF file can choose from comprehensive templates to fill in metadata, as shown in Figure 5-5-5.

In addition to the description metadata (in Figure 5-5-5), other templates will help in recording technical metadata (e.g., camera data) and administrative metadata (e.g., History, IPTC Contact, and IPTC Status). Metadata statements can be reused in different formats. For example, when viewing the advanced template (Figure 5-5-6), rights information appears in both XMP Rights Management Properties (under element *Copyright*) and Dublin Core Properties (under element *rights*) (boxed highlights authors' emphasis).

These metadata records are especially important to institutional repositories and enterprise intranets that deal with these documental formats on significantly large scales. Embedded metadata, especially that which follows metadata standards such as DC and IPTC Core, can be harvested by aggregators and the information may then be stored into a centralized database. The centralized aggregation of the metadata allows better access and management, and also increases exposure for federated searching and metasearching.

Figure 5-5-4. Metadata partially captured automatically and partially entered manually are embedded in a Microsoft® Office Word file's *Properties* section.

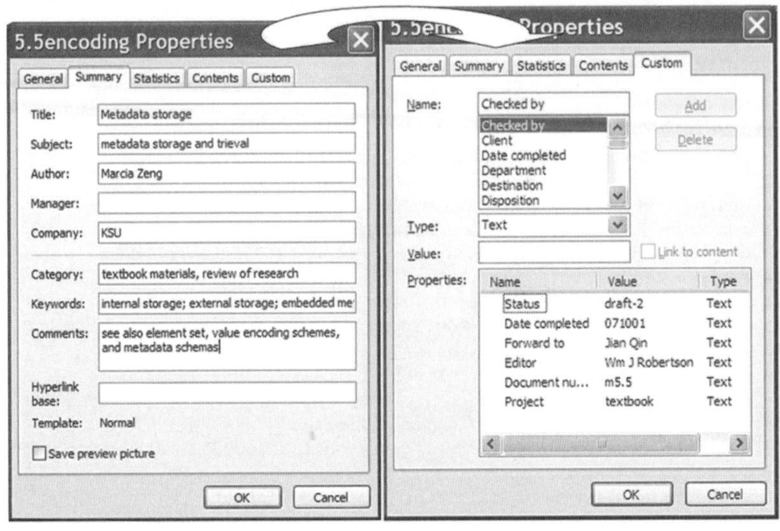

Source: Microsoft product screenshots reprinted with permission from Microsoft Corporation.

Figure 5-5-5. Description metadata partially captured automatically and partially entered manually are recorded for an Adobe® Acrobat® PDF file.

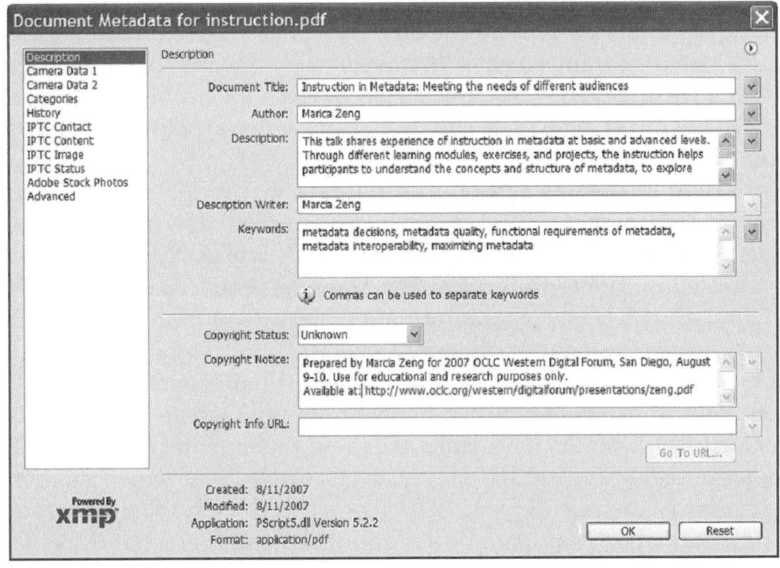

Source: Adobe product box shot reprinted with permission from Adobe Systems Incorporated.

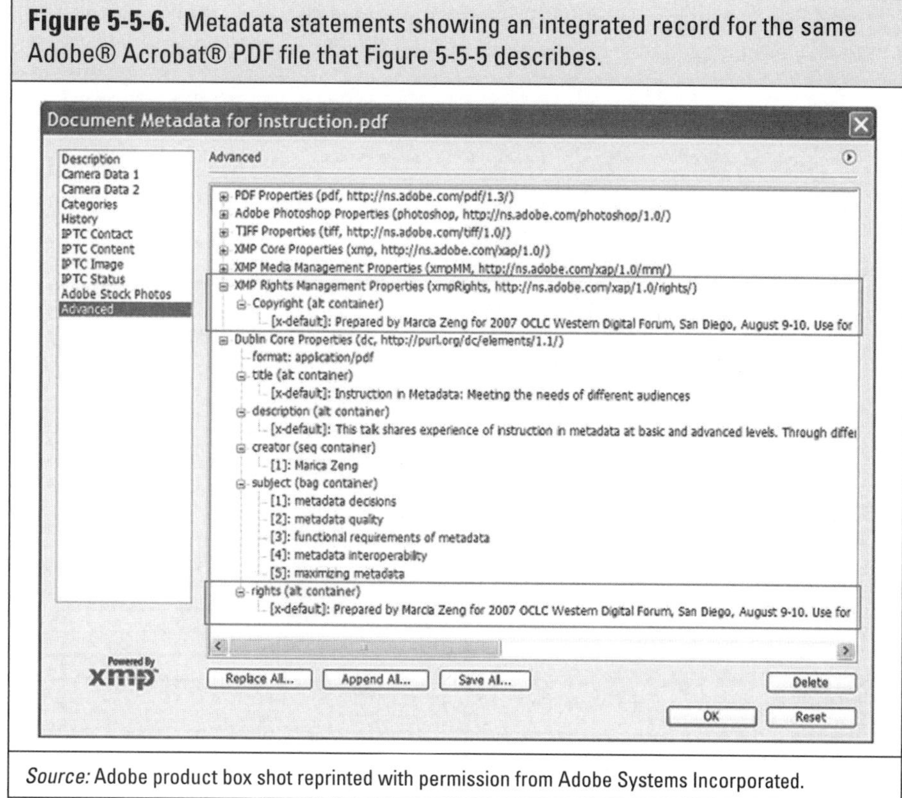

Figure 5-5-6. Metadata statements showing an integrated record for the same Adobe® Acrobat® PDF file that Figure 5-5-5 describes.

Source: Adobe product box shot reprinted with permission from Adobe Systems Incorporated.

Metadata information may also be embedded into digital image files. Image software such as Adobe Photoshop CS allows metadata statements related to an image to be recorded and integrated directly within the image. When an image is viewed from the software application, it appears as if a record is embedded in the digital image. Values in some elements are automatically generated by the software whereas others are controlled by the metadata creators. Embedded metadata can be generated at the same time that a file is created (by the creator), added later, or batch processed.

More digital file formats now provide sections in order to embed metadata. Previously the stand-alone MP3 file format did not store data about the file. Now it allows segments of the file to be designated as metadata using the ID3 standard (see Chapter 2, Section 2.7). The idea is simple: to embed ID3 tags in an audio file.

The advantages of internal storage of metadata are to ensure that the representative surrogates are bound together with the associated objects. This eliminates the problem of two separate files that are only connected by links. This more distributed approach allows creators of the resources to include their descriptions at anytime and from anywhere. Naturally, quality issues arise with such an approach, and unless a centralized process is developed

Figure 5-5-7. Metadata partially captured automatically and partially entered manually are embedded in an image file in Adobe® Photoshop Creative Suite®.

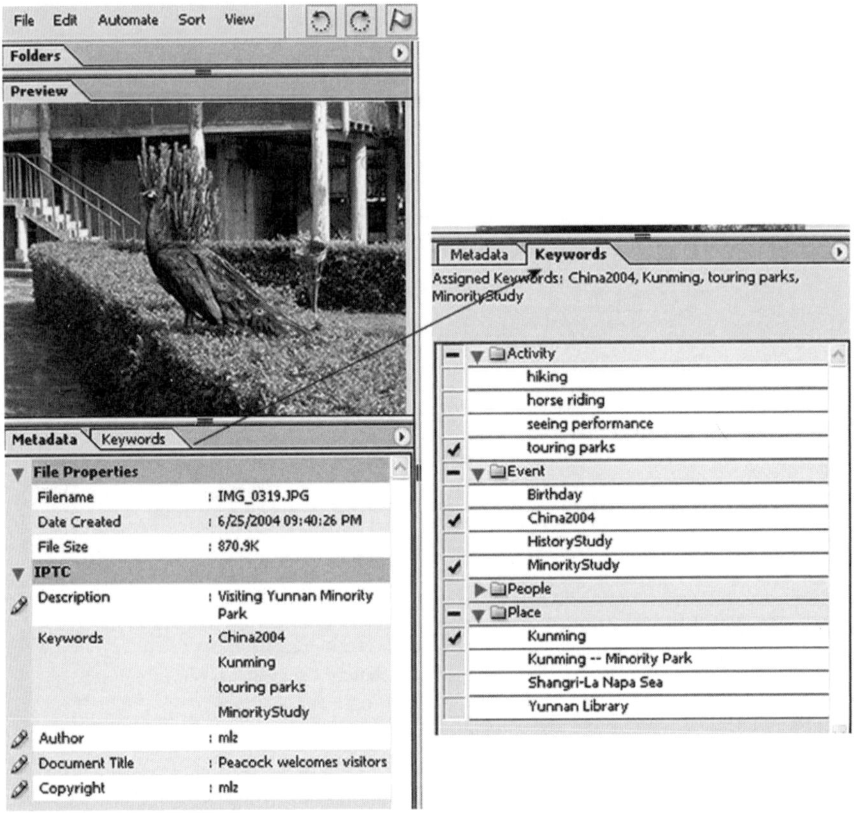

Source: Adobe product box shots reprinted with permission from Adobe Systems Incorporated.

for extracting, organizing, and reusing them, most of the information will be used only by internal management or for the Internet search engines that index it.

External storage is a common method for large collections where metadata records are usually stored separately from the resource(s) that they describe (whether these resources are available in electronic format or not). A relational database management system (or simpler file system) can be implemented to store the records. A database management system will provide many advantages for the efficient management and retrieval of data. The following examples illustrate how metadata records can be created by using a predefined or tailored format (Figure 5-5-8). After peer or administrative approval, the records are immediately integrated into the searchable database and become accessible from the Web (Figure 5-5-9 and 5-5-10). CONTENTdm

Figure 5-5-8. A screenshot of record editing using CONTENTdm software.

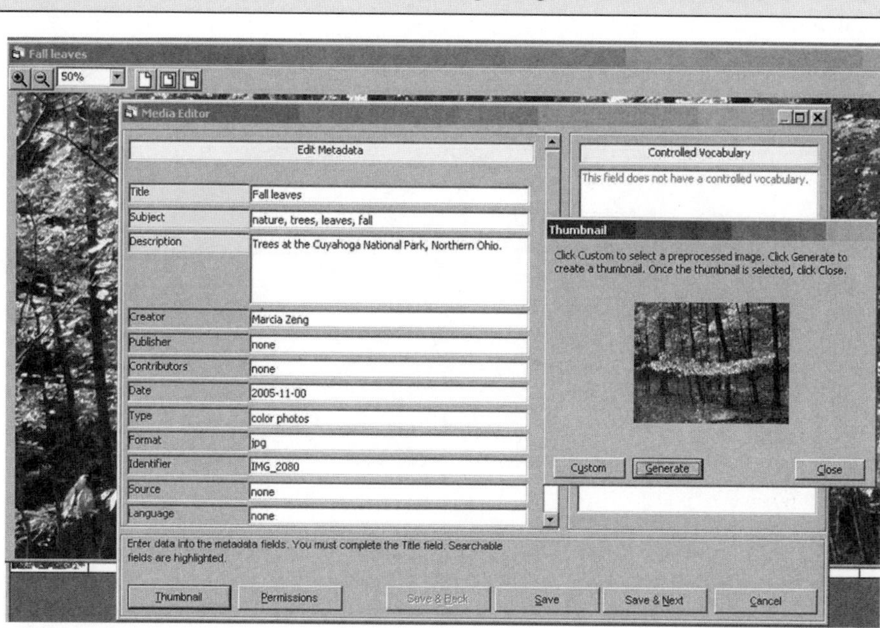

Source: Screenshot reprinted with permission from CONTENTdm software. CONTENTdm® is a registered trademark of OCLC.

Figure 5-5-9. A Web-accessible database displaying metadata records in a table.

Source: Courtesy of The Cleveland Memory Project, Cleveland State University Library: www.clevelandmemory.org/disasters/, with permission.

Figure 5-5-10. Individual metadata record in the database (on-screen blue-colored entries are searchable).

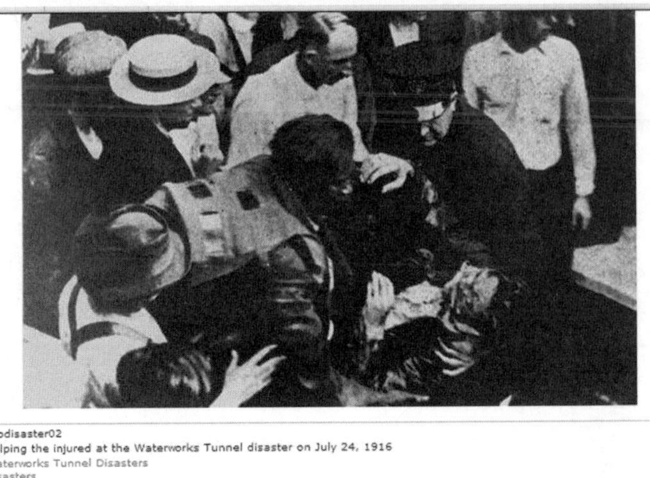

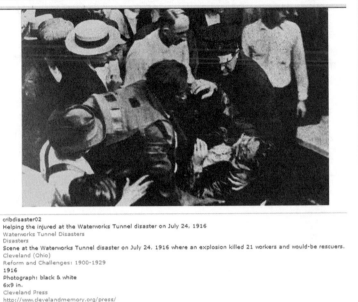

Identifier	cribdisaster02
Title	Helping the injured at the Waterworks Tunnel disaster on July 24, 1916
Subject	Waterworks Tunnel Disasters Disasters
Description	Scene at the Waterworks Tunnel disaster on July 24, 1916 where an explosion killed 21 workers and would-be rescuers.
Location Depicted	Cleveland (Ohio)
Time Period	Reform and Challenges: 1900-1929
Photograph Date	1916
Object Type	Photograph: black & white
Size of Original	6x9 in.
Collection	Cleveland Press
Collection Homepage	http://www.clevelandmemory.org/press/
Donor	Cole, Joseph E.
Copyright	http://www.clevelandmemory.org/copyright/
Format	jpeg
Digital Processing Notes	TIF File Size: 4,921 k - DPI: 300
Repository	Cleveland State University Library Special Collections
Repository Homepage	http://web.ulib.csuohio.edu/SpecColl/
Encyclopedia of Cleveland History Entry	http://ech.cwru.edu/ech-cgi/article.pl?id=WTD
Further Reading	http://scholar.csuohio.edu/search/d?disasters+.ohio

back to results :: add to favorites : reference url

Source: Courtesy of The Cleveland Memory Project, Cleveland State University Library: www.clevelandmemory.org/disasters/, with permission.

software is used here as the example. Many other tools with similar functions are available.

Due to rapidly advancing technologies, metadata records stored as XML files are easily communicated between database systems, making virtually no apparent difference to the user viewing through a well-designed interface while simultaneously performing various tasks. Using stylesheets, e.g., Cascading Style Sheets (CSS) and Extensible Stylesheet Language (XSL), retrieved metadata can be displayed in a style that the user chooses. However, because it is separate and distinct, there will be issues about associating the stored metadata with the digital resources they describe. Non-HTML documents using PDF, WORD, and other formats need to develop efficient means of associating documents so that the content is related to the necessary metadata. Sometimes a resource also may be stored on a local hard disk and therefore does not have a URI, and Web pages may be created on-the-fly using a content-management system without providing adequate metadata.

Metadata storage methods should be determined based on the requirements for resource type(s), purpose of the collection, and the technological capabilities of the organization that will maintain and manage the collection.

Metadata descriptions either stored internally or externally should have the goal and capability of as much output as possible. Full use of rich metadata is the ultimate goal for any creator and data provider (see Chapter 6 on the maximization of metadata).

5.5.2 Expressing Metadata in HTML/XHTML

It is important to gain a better understanding of the metadata statements expressed in HTML/XHML documents. Although some people still code the tags in a plain text file (i.e., *hard-coding*), most creators use an editor to more easily generate metadata statements and output with multiple formats such as DC-dot.

Before moving on to the specific tagging, it is useful to take a larger view of general markup languages (Figure 5-5-11). The figure explains relationships among markup languages. XML (Extensible Markup Language) is the universal format for structured documents and data on the Web. XML is an application profile or restricted form of SGML (Standard Generalized Markup Language, ISO 8879), the internationally accepted generic markup standard for text. By constructional definition, XML documents are in conformance with SGML documents. Both are *metalanguages*, i.e., by using the constructs of SGML or XML an infinite number of descriptive markup languages may be created. One example of an SGML-derived language is the Hypertext Markup Language

Figure 5-5-11. A taxonomy of general markup languages.

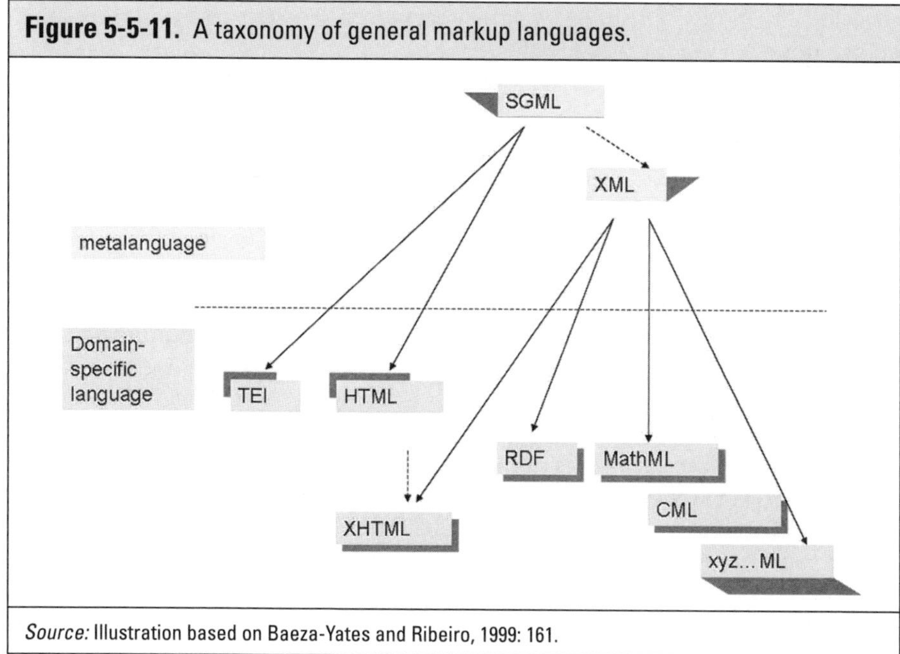

Source: Illustration based on Baeza-Yates and Ribeiro, 1999: 161.

(HTML), the standard encoding language used on the Web. As the successor to HTML, XHTML has many of the same elements as HTML but the syntax has been changed slightly to conform to the rules of XML.

A HTML document contains two main sections: <head> and <body>. The contents we see on any Web page through a Web browser are coded with HTML tags and stored in the <body> section. The <head> section is a container for information about the document, such as the title and other metadata information. The information contained in the <head> section is not displayed as part of the document. Unless one chooses to view the source code from a browser, this information is hidden. On the other hand, no matter how many times a Web page changes and new products and services (or information in the form of text and/or audio/visual media) show on the home page of the Web site, the metadata embedded in the <head> section may not change at all.

HTML documents are divided into *elements*, i.e., distinct parts of a document, which are marked by *tags* of the form *<name> . . . some text . . . </name>*, where the enclosed text is the content of the element. Some elements do not affect a block of text, hence are called *empty elements*, e.g., <img> that display an image stored elsewhere (e.g., a folder or linked page that is not accessible to the viewer). Groups of *attributes* are important constructs in HTML documents. Attributes contain additional information about an element that gives the element unique characteristics by presenting information specific to the element type in a HTML document. For example, in the <table> element attributes can define unique characteristics by presenting the width, border size, and border color of a specific table. Attributes must be tied to a specific element; an element can have only specified attributes, although some elements may share the same attributes. Attributes are always expressed as *property-value* pairs, e.g., color="blue" or color="#330099."

The examples provided in this section all conform to XHTML 1.1, and are compatible with earlier versions of HTML. Specifically, it means that all names of elements and attributes always have a lowercase first letter, given that the names consist of mixed-case. All values in attributes are enclosed with quotation marks and, as <meta> is an empty element (which does not affect a block of text and does not require a closing tag in HTML), a closing slash (/) is included in the tag <meta> as well as for the element <link>. Although not exactly the same in meaning, people used to refer to these *elements* as *tags*. The verb *tagging* then begins to make sense—it is the process of assigning values to a tag. Encoding, tagging, and expressing in HTML/XHTML are terms used interchangeably in many publications.

For the remainder of the chapter the word *tag* is used for "HTML-element" to avoid confusion with "metadata-element," which is discussed throughout the book. Four HTML-element tags are analyzed in detail in the following discussion, particularly as they pertain to XHTML.

1. The *<meta>* tag, *name* and *content* attributes. In the previous section an example of embedded metadata statements in the Metadata Basics tutorial Portuguese version Web page homepage was given (see Exhibit 5-5-1). For example:

```
<meta name="DC.title" lang="pt" content="Metadados:
fundamentos" />
```

The basic pattern for expression in XHTML format is presented in the following code. Note square brackets ([. . .]) represent a class, not an individual; therefore, text within square brackets needs to be replaced by an individual in the coding process (authors' emphasis).

```
<meta name="[prefix.metadata-element-name]" con-
tent= "[value]" />
```

Here *meta* is the tag; *name* and *content* are the two attributes. The attributes within a tag can be in any order, separated by a white space. Thus either expression is correct:

```
<meta name="[prefix.metadata-element-name]" content=
"[value]" />

<meta content="[value]" name="[prefix.metadata-element-
name]" />
```

Since HTML attributes are in property-value pairs, the pattern is also described as:

```
<meta name="[propertyName]" content="[value]" />
```

2. The *<meta>* tag and *scheme* attribute. When a value string is given according to an encoding scheme, the name of the scheme is given as the value of an attribute called *scheme*, in the XHTML <meta> tag. This *property-value* pair is then inserted into the previous statement—

```
<meta name="[prefix.metadata-element-name]" scheme=
"[scheme-name]" content="[value]" />
```

—as are the statements in the previous tutorial example—

```
<meta name="DC.date" scheme="DCTERMS.W3CDTF" content=
"2006-05-23" />

<meta name="DC.type" scheme="DCTERMS.DCMIType" content=
"Text" />
```

—and in the *Metadata Basics* Portuguese version, the metadata descriptions include statements such as:

```
<meta name="DC.subject" lang="en" scheme="OCLC FAST
Authority" content="metadata; metadata-standards" />
```

Note here that *OCLC FAST Authority* is the encoding scheme used to code the value of *subject* (authors' emphasis). This scheme is not included in the DCTERMS vocabulary encoding schemes currently. Other local controlled vocabularies can also be coded like this.

Indicating the encoding scheme is critical for ensuring semantic interoperability. Without an encoding scheme, values can be interpreted differently or meaninglessly (e.g., any subject code). Unfortunately, one can still find a great number of incomplete efforts in metadata generation. The following two statements are taken from one record embedded in a Web site of an international organization that has six official languages:

```
<meta name="dc.date.created" content="01-08-1996">
<meta name="dc.date.modified" content="2006-01-08">
```

As one can see, this presents a problem of inconsistency. When a machine processes such information, serious mapping problems will arise. Because no encoding schemes are bound to the values, a value string could be interpreted in many different ways.

3. The *<link>* tag. A link tag can be used for different purposes and always appears in a pattern as:

```
<link rel="[prefix-metadata-element-name]" href=
"[resourceURI]" />
```

OR

```
<link rel="[propertyName]" href="[resourceURI]" />
```

When the elements are from more than one metadata namespace, the <link> tags will give the URLs of the namespaces. In this example, attribute *rel* describes the relationship from the current document to the anchor specified by the *href* attribute, *href* (hypertext reference) specifies the location of a Web resource. The actual DC link relation to a persistent URI is stable and always expressed as:

```
<link rel="schema.DC" href="http://purl.org/dc/elements/
1.1/" />
```

Sometimes a local schema is not specified or some metadata elements are not defined. Mixed statements can therefore appear in one record. Another purpose for using the <link> tag is when the content actually points to a resource URL Web page. In a number of metadata standards, relations between a value and an authority record, between an original object and its digital images, or between a whole and its parts are indicated with resource URLs.

4. The language attribute family: *lang, xml:lang, hreflang.* The *lang* attribute is used to indicate the language of a value string, as with the metadata records automatically generated by DC-dot for the Portuguese version of the metadata tutorial (authors' emphasis):

```
<meta name="DC.title" lang="pt" content="Metadados:
fundamentos" />
```

The appearance of *lang* may differ slightly depending on the version of the markup language one is using. For HTML 4.01 and older versions of HTML, *lang* is used; for XHTML 1.0 Transitional (i.e. XHTML designed to be compatible with HTML) both *lang* and *xml:lang* should be used. For Version 1.1 of XHTML only xml:lang should be used. And the <link> element may have the *hreflang* attribute, e.g.:

```
<link rel="DC.relation" hreflang="el" href="http://www
.demo.com/el/" />
```

The language attribute can be used with different elements, as with the Greek language example which begins—

```
<html xmlns= "http://www.w3.org/1999/xhtml" lang="el"
xml:lang="el">
```

—where we can see both *lang* and *xml:lang* are used in the root *html* tag. The meaning is that it is coded following the XHTML 1.0 standard, and the whole *html* document is in Greek. If the *lang* or *xml:lang* attribute is not used for the root tag, the language is applied only to a particular statement. The following statement indicates that the value string of the *title* block is in Portuguese:

```
<meta name="DC.title" lang="pt" content="Metadados:
fundamentos" />
```

As an example of a complete record, a simple DC record for the *Metadata Basics* tutorial created in 2005 (Zeng) was generated by using the DC-dot metadata editor (see Exhibit 5-5-2). The URL "www.slis.kent.edu/~mzeng/metadatabasics/index.htm" was submitted and a record was first automatically generated. The tool allows for manual editing after an automatic analysis is conducted by the software. Since the original Web page has an embedded DC metadata record, the automatic process was quite accurate. The only place that needs to be modified is DC.date because the software captured the date (authors' emphasis) when the updated file was uploaded.

The limitation of the default simplified DC format prevents using refinements such as relation type (*hasVersion*), date created (*created*), and table of contents (*tableOfContent*). If the tool would allow adding these refinements (in accord with current practices) all could then be expressed as DCMI Metadata Terms (DCTERM) properties (authors' emphasis):

```
<meta name="DCTERMS.created" content="2005-05-09" />

<meta name="DCTERMS.hasVersion" scheme="DCTERMS.URI"
content="http://...Portuguese/cover.htm" />

<meta name="DCTERMS.tableOfContent" lang="en" content="1.
Metadata ..." />
```

The URL of a translated Portuguese version of this tutorial was also submitted to DC-dot ("www.slis.kent.edu/~mzeng/metadatabasics/Portuguese/cover.htm") to generate a record in XHTML (see Exhibit 5-5-3). Values that are different from the original English version (in Exhibit 5-5-2) are extracted in the following box. However, since the original embedded metadata record has used elements from DCTERMS, values from those statements (e.g.,

Exhibit 5-5-2. A complete simple Dublin Core metadata record, expressed in XHTML (generated using DC-dot for *Metadata Basics* tutorial).

```
<link rel="schema.DC" href="http://purl.org/dc/elements/1.1/" />
<link rel="schema.DCTERMS" href="http://purl.org/dc/terms/" />
<meta name="DC.title" lang="en" content="metadata basics" />
<meta name="DC.creator" content="Zeng, Marcia L." />
<meta name="DC.subject" lang="en" content="metadata standards; metadata
training; metadata value space" />
<meta name="DC.description" lang="en" content="1. Metadata development
overview; 2. Metadata records; 3. Metadata types and functions; 4. Metadata
standards; 5. Metadata record creation and tools; 6. Metadata value space;
view without frame; view with frame; 7. References;" />
<meta name="DC.publisher" content="Library of Congress: Cataloger's Learning
Workshop" />
<meta name="DC.contributor" content="ALCTS—The Association for Library
Collections & Technical Services, ALA" />
<meta name="DC.contributor" content="ALISE—Association for Library and
Information Science Education" />
<meta name="DC.date" scheme="DCTERMS.W3CDTF" content="2005-05-09" />
<meta name="DC.type" scheme="DCTERMS.DCMIType" content="Text" />
<meta name="DC.format" content="text/html; charset=ISO-8859-1" />
<meta name="DC.identifier" scheme="DCTERMS.URI"
content="http://www.slis.kent.edu/%7Emzeng/metadatabasics/index.htm" />
<meta name="DC.identifier" scheme="DCTERMS.URI"
content="http://www.loc.gov/catworkshop/readings/metadatabasics/" />
<meta name="DC.language" scheme="DCTERMS.RFC1766" content="en-US" />
<meta name="DC.relation"
content="http://www.slis.kent.edu/%7Emzeng/metadatabasics/Portuguese/cover
.htm" />
<meta name="DC.rights" content="Marcia Lei Zeng" />
```

Exhibit 5-5-3. Extracted statements from a simple Dublin Core metadata record expressed in XHTML (generated using DC-dot for the Portuguese translation of *Metadata Basics* tutorial).

```
<meta name="DC.title" lang="pt" content="Metadados: fundamentos" />
<meta name="DC.date" scheme="DCTERMS.W3CDTF" content="2006-05-23" />
<meta name="DC.identifier" scheme="DCTERMS.URI" content="http://www.slis.kent
.edu/~mzeng/metadatabasics/Portuguese/cover.htm" />
<meta name="DC.language" scheme="DCTERMS.RFC1766" content="pt" />
<link rel="DC.relation"
href="http://www.slis.kent.edu/~mzeng/metadatabasics/index.htm" />
```

DCTERMS.tableOfContent and *DCTERMS.isVersionOf*) are excluded from the record by the software.

Using an editor like DC-dot makes the process of encoding much easier. An encoded record can then be copy-pasted to be included in the <head> section of an HTML or XHTML document.

5.5.3 Expressing Metadata in XML

XML was developed by a working group formed under the auspices of the World Wide Web Consortium (W3C) beginning in 1996. W3C's XML 1.0 Recommendation was first issued in 1998. The current version is XML 1.1, published in 2006 (www.w3.org/TR/xml11/). XML is a syntax created by subsetting SGML for use on the World Wide Web. It is an application profile (or restricted form of SGML) and is classified as an *extensible language* because it allows its users to define their own tags. XML specifications have achieved major intended goals: Internet usability, general-purpose usability, SGML compatibility, a structure that facilitates the development of processing software, minimization of optional features, legibility, formality, conciseness, and ease of authoring. Having seen more and more XML documents on the Web, an incorrect impression has formed among many people that XML is a replacement for HTML. XML is *not* a replacement for HTML and the two were designed for different purposes. Stated simply, XML was designed to *describe* data and to focus on what data is; and HTML was designed to *display* data and to focus on how data looks and will appear.

XML provides a formal syntax for describing the relationships among the entities, elements, and attributes that make up an *XML document*, which can be used to allow computers to recognize the component parts of each document. A data object is an *XML document* if it is *well formed*, i.e., conforms to all of the XML syntax rules as defined by the XML 1.0 specification. In addition, the XML document is *valid* if it meets certain further constraints defined by the specification.

A fully-tagged XML document instance consists of a root element, whose element type name must match that which is assigned as the document type name in the document type declaration, within which all other elements are nested (see Figure 5-5-12). The text enclosed by the root tags may contain an arbitrary number of XML elements. The basic syntax for one element is:

```
<name attribute="[value]"> [ ... some content ... ] </name>
```

Metadata standards published during recent years tend to provide detailed encoding examples in their documents. In addition to an XML Schema, CDWA Lite provides a corporate standards document to explain the structure, semantics, as well as tagging examples for each element. When the XML Schemas or XML DTD are loaded into XML software, creators find that there is far greater convenience for creating XML records because they are able to concentrate on the content rather than syntax. For example, using general XML software such as ALTOVA®'s XMLSpy®, one can load a metadata schema in XML schema encoding into the software to automatically generate the necessary metadata elements in a blank XML document (Figure 5-5-12). The elements in the box on the right in Figure 5-5-12 can dynamically change as the record data entry proceeds. The attributes embedded in elements can also automatically display in a pop-up window to reduce typing entries and avoid checking the schema while entering data (Figure 5-5-13).

During data entry, the software can also change the shade of element names in the element window to indicate which elements are eligible for use under

Figure 5-5-12. A blank CDWA Lite record expressed in XML (automatically generated by ALTOVA®'s XMLSpy® using CDWA Lite XML schema).

```
<?xml version="1.0" encoding="UTF-8"?>
<cdwalite:cdwaliteWrap xmlns:cdwalite="
http://www.getty.edu/CDWA/CDWALite" xmlns:xsi="
http://www.w3.org/2001/XMLSchema-instance" xsi:schemaLocation
="http://www.getty.edu/CDWA/CDWALite
CDWALite-xsd-public-v1-1_noannotation.xsd">
  <cdwalite:cdwalite>
    <cdwalite:descriptiveMetadata>
      <cdwalite:objectWorkTypeWrap>
        <cdwalite:objectWorkType/>
      </cdwalite:objectWorkTypeWrap>
      <cdwalite:titleWrap>
        <cdwalite:titleSet>
          <cdwalite:title/>
        </cdwalite:titleSet>
      </cdwalite:titleWrap>
      <cdwalite:displayCreator/>
      <cdwalite:indexingCreatorWrap>
        <cdwalite:indexingCreatorSet>
          <cdwalite:nameCreatorSet>
            <cdwalite:nameCreator >
          </cdwalite:nameCreatorSet>
          <cdwalite:roleCreator/>
        </cdwalite:indexingCreatorSet>
      </cdwalite:indexingCreatorWrap>
      <cdwalite:displayMaterialsTech/>
```

```
Elements
cdwalite:objectWorkTypeWrap
cdwalite:titleWrap
cdwalite:displayCreator
cdwalite:indexingCreatorWrap
cdwalite:displayMeasurements
cdwalite:indexingMeasurementsWr
cdwalite:displayMaterialsTech
cdwalite:indexingMaterialsTechWr
cdwalite:displayStateEditionWrap
cdwalite:styleWrap
cdwalite:cultureWrap
cdwalite:displayCreationDate
cdwalite:indexingDatesWrap
cdwalite:locationWrap
cdwalite:indexingSubjectWrap
cdwalite:classWrap
cdwalite:descriptiveNoteWrap
Attributes
Entities
amp &
```

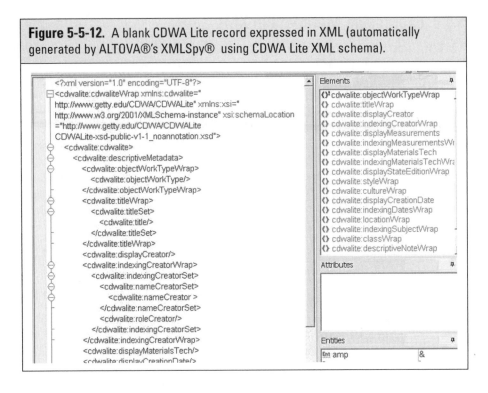

Figure 5-5-13. Attribute selection list pop-up for the *Creator Name Set* element (generated by ALTOVA®'s XMLSpy®).

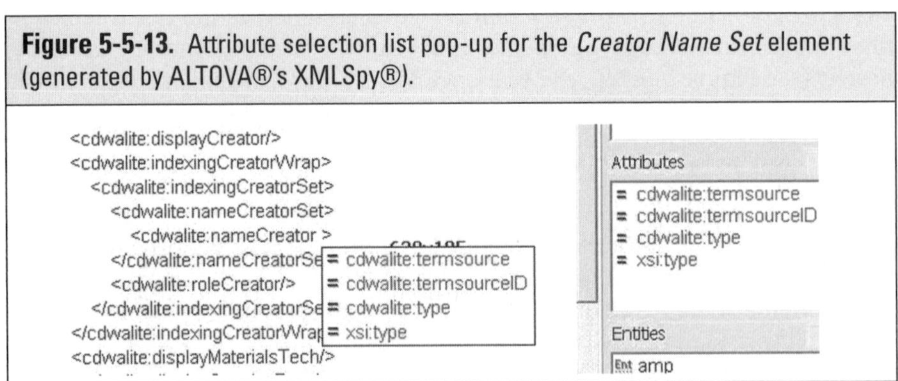

the parent element, (see box on the right in Figure 5-5-14). Noneligible elements will be displayed with a light shade of gray. Validation of data entered may be done at any time during the record creation process or after all data have been entered.

Individual XML records can be generated with tools such as DC-dot. The same record generated with DC-dot that was displayed previously (see Exhibit 5-5-2) can be output in other encoding languages including XML. Note that when expressed in XML, the DC elements are required to all be in lowercase with a colon used as a separator (rather then a period). Exhibit 5-5-4 is the

Figure 5-5-14. Sample CDWA Lite record (generated using ALTOVA®'s XMLSpy®).

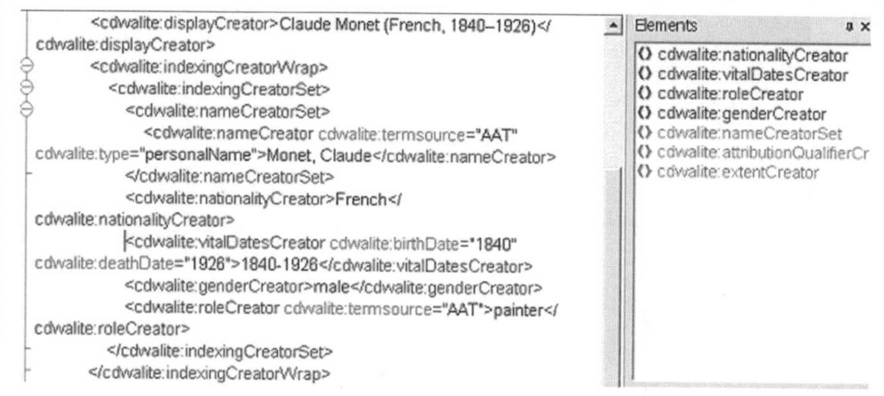

Exhibit 5-5-4. A complete simple Dublin Core metadata record, expressed in XML (generated using DC-dot for *Metadata Basics* tutorial Web page).

```
<?xml version="1.0"?>
<metadata
  xmlns="http://www.ukoln.ac.uk/metadata/dcdot/"
  xmlns:xsi="http://www.w3.org/2001/XMLSchema-instance"
  xsi:schemaLocation="http://www.ukoln.ac.uk/metadata/dcdot/
  http://www.ukoln.ac.uk/metadata/dcdot/dcdot.xsd"
  xmlns:dc="http://purl.org/dc/elements/1.1/">
    <dc:title xml:lang="en" > metadata basics</dc:title>
    <dc:creator>Zeng, Marcia L.</dc:creator>
    <dc:subject xml:lang="en" >metadata standards; metadata training;
metadata value space</dc:subject>
    <dc:description xml:lang="en" >1. Metadata development overview; ... ;
</dc:description>
    <dc:publisher>Library of Congress: Cataloger's Learning
Workshop</dc:publisher>
    <dc:contributor>ALCTS--The Association for Library Collections &
Technical Services, ALA</dc:contributor>
    <dc:contributor>ALISE -- Association for Library and Information Science
Education</dc:contributor>
    <dc:date>2005-05-09</dc:date>
    <dc:type>Text</dc:type>
    <dc:format> text/html; charset=ISO-8859-1</dc:format>
    <dc:identifier>http://www.slis.kent.edu/%7Emzeng/metadatabasics/
index.htm</dc:identifier>
    <dc:identifier>http://www.loc.gov/catworkshop/readings/
metadatabasics/</dc:identifier>
    <dc:language>en-US</dc:language>
    <dc:relation>http://www.slis.kent.edu/~mzeng/metadatabasics/Portuguese/
cover.htm</dc:relation>
    <dc:rights>Marcia Lei Zeng</dc:rights>
</metadata>
```

metadata expressed with XML. Because DC has a flat structure, all DC tags in the record are not nested.

XML-coded files are ideal for storage in databases, and because XML files are both object-oriented and hierarchical in nature they can be adapted to virtually any type of database. XML documents are commonly created with an editor. An XML processor then reads the document and verifies that the document is well formed. The processor passes the tree structure (or individual nodes of the tree) to the end application. This application may be a Web browser or another program that can interpret the data. As an extremely flexible language it may be used for many different purposes.

5.5.4 Expressing Metadata in XML/RDF

RDF (Resource Description Framework) is also a general-purpose language for representing information on the Web. It was originally created in 1999 as a standard based on XML for encoding metadata—data about data, particularly about Web resources. With the development of the Semantic Web, RDF has been playing an increasingly important role and has evolved in its own right for metadata description alone, especially since its updated specification in 2004. The greatest use of RDF is not restricted to encoding information about Web resources: RDF also provides information about, and relations between, things in the real world: people, places, concepts, etc. The RDF metadata model is based on the principle of making logical statements about resources in the form of *subject-predicate-object* expressions (called *triples* in RDF terminology. The RDF terms for the various parts of the statement are:

- The subject is the URL—http://www.slis.kent.edu/~mzeng/metadatabasics/index.htm.
- The predicate is the word *title.*
- The object is the phrase *Metadata Basics.*

RDF uses the URI as its basic mechanism for identifying subjects, predicates, and objects in statements (see Figure 5-5-16). Objects in RDF statements

Figure 5-5-15. A statement about a resource made with a *subject-predicate-object* (or *triple*) expression.

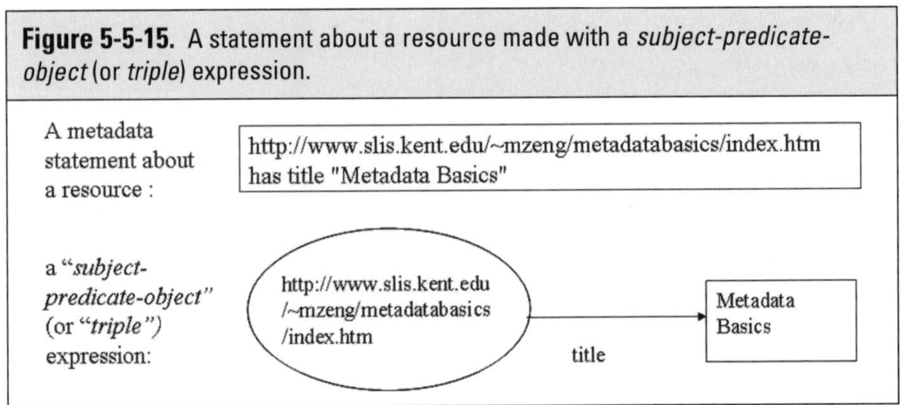
A metadata statement about a resource :
http://www.slis.kent.edu/~mzeng/metadatabasics/index.htm has title "Metadata Basics"
a "subject-predicate-object" (or "triple") expression:
http://www.slis.kent.edu /~mzeng/metadatabasics /index.htm
title
Metadata Basics

Figure 5-5-16. A group of statements in graph form.

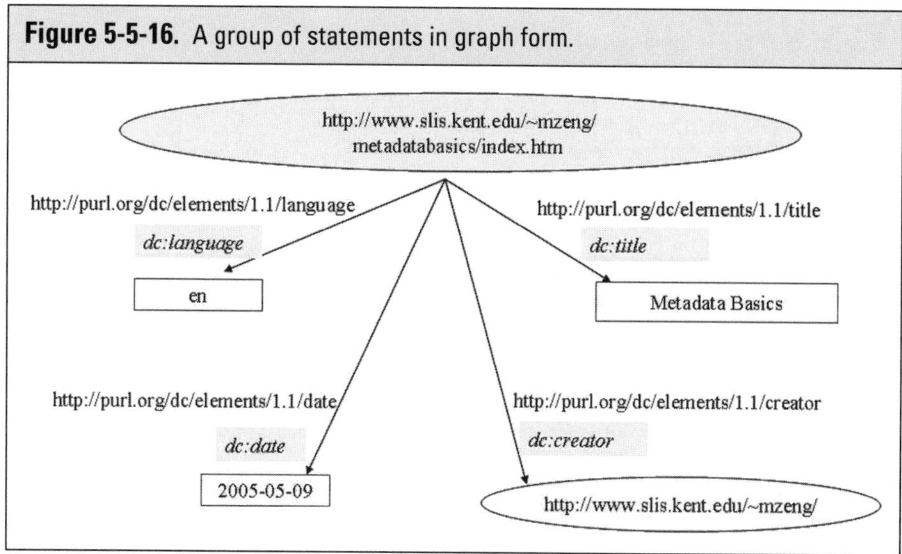

may be either *URIrefs* (e.g., the creator URI), or constant values (called *literals*) represented by character strings (e.g., the date and language), in order to represent different kinds of property values. Another term of RDF is *XML Qualified Name* (QName) which contains a prefix (e.g., dc) that has been assigned to a namespace URI, followed by a colon, and then a local name, e.g., *dc:title* is the QName of "http://purl.org/dc/elements/1.1/title". Using all of these components in an RDF graph, the tutorial can then be expressed as shown in Figure 5-5-16.

RDF/XML Syntax Specification (W3C, 2004), a W3C recommendation, allows expressing these kinds of triples in XML. This serialization syntax based on XML makes statements understandable and processable by machines. The previous graph is encoded as shown in Exhibit 5-5-5. Adding other statements, the whole record for the tutorial would be expressed with XML/RDF as in Exhibit 5-5-6 (authors' emphasis).

Exhibit 5-5-5. Encoding the triples from the RDF graph (shown in Figure 5-5-16) with XML/RDF.

```
<rdf:RDF
  xmlns:rdf="http://www.w3.org/1999/02/22-rdf-syntax-ns#"
  xmlns:dc="http://purl.org/dc/elements/1.1/">
  <rdf:Description  rdf:about=http://www.slis.kent.edu/~mzeng/
   metadatabasics/index.htm>
    <dc:title>metadata basics</dc:title>
    <dc:language>en</dc:language>
....
</rdf:Description>
</rdf:RDF>
```

Exhibit 5-5-6. A complete simple Dublin Core metadata record expressed in XML/RDF (generated using DC-dot for *Metadata Basics* tutorial).

```
1 →  <?xml version="1.0"?>
     <!DOCTYPE rdf:RDF SYSTEM
     "http://dublincore.org/documents/2002/07/31/dcmes-xml/dcmes-xml-
2 →  dtd.dtd">
3 →  <rdf:RDF
       xmlns:rdf="http://www.w3.org/1999/02/22-rdf-syntax-ns#"
       xmlns:dc="http://purl.org/dc/elements/1.1/">
       <rdf:Description
          rdf:about=http://www.slis.kent.edu/~mzeng/metadatabasics/index.htm>
4 →      <dc:title>metadata basics</dc:title>
         <dc:creator>Zeng, Marcia L.</dc:creator>
         <dc:subject>metadata standards; metadata training; metadata value space
         </dc:subject>
         <dc:description>1. Metadata development overview ... ;</dc:description>
         <dc:publisher>Library of Congress: Cataloger's Learning Workshop
         </dc:publisher>
         <dc:contributor>ALCTS--The Association for Library Collections &
          TechnicalServices, ALA</dc:contributor>
         <dc:contributor>ALISE -- Association for Library and Information
          Science Education </dc:contributor>
         <dc:date>2005-05-09</dc:date>
         <dc:type> Text</dc:type>
         <dc:format> text/html; charset=ISO-8859-1</dc:format>
         <dc:language>en-US</dc:language>
         <dc:relation>http://www.slis.kent.edu/%7Emzeng/metadatabasics/
          Portuguese/cover.htm </dc:relation>
         <dc:rights>Marcia Lei Zeng</dc:rights>
       </rdf:Description>
5 →  </rdf:RDF>
```

Using this example to explain the components of the XML/RDF file, we can identify the following important parts (as explained by the DCMI document, *Expressing Simple Dublin Core in RDF/XML*, which DC-dot software conforms to):

1. XML declaration: <?xml version="1.0"?>.
2. Referencing the XML DTD: <!DOCTYPE rdf:RDF SYSTEM "http://dublincore.org/documents/2002/07/31/dcmes-xml/dcmes-xml-dtd.dtd">.
3. Declaring the use of RDF: <rdf:RDFxmlns:rdf="http://www.w3.org/1999/02/22-rdf-syntax-ns#"xmlns:dc="http://purl.org/dc/elements/1.1/">. This declares the outer *rdf:RDF* containing tag with its XML namespace and the XML namespace for the DCMES elements.
4. Describing the resources: The required regulations follow.
   - Each resource described is enclosed in a container element, a pair of *rdf:Description* tags.
   - Resources may have no, one, or several identifiers and some of these may be URIs.

- If a resource has at least one URI, the most appropriate one should be used as the value of the *rdf:about* attribute of the rdf:Description tag. <rdf:Description rdf:about=http://www.slis.kent.edu/~mzeng/metadatabasics/index.htm> </rdf:Description>
- Inside the rdf:Description container, 12 tags are used for the statements following the DC standard. Each of the tags contains a QName, in lowercase letters, and is closed at the end of the statement, e.g., <dc:date>2005-05-09</dc:date>.

5. Closing the document: </rdf:RDF>.

This example is probably the simplest form of an XML/RDF record. Grasping this concept is the first step toward understanding more complicated records that contain description sets based on more than one metadata standard (introduced in Section 5.7).

5.6 Linkage, Wrapper, Display, and Parallel Metadata

Different types of relationships exist between and among the resources that are described by metadata. Sometimes we can see these relationships between records associated with the *same* work, e.g., one record for an original work and another record for the digital image of the work. Sometimes we can also see the relationships between different resources (e.g., the work and the creator of the work) that metadata descriptions are created for, and they usually exist in the form of a bibliographic record and authority records (which could be name, place, or subject authority records). At present there are also optional elements that can be applied to generate statements for display (rather than for indexing and retrieval) purposes. This section intends to introduce some common methods that connect metadata descriptions created for different resources. Relationships among the same type of resources (e.g., between a whole and its parts) is beyond the scope of this overview.

5.6.1 Linking Between Descriptions for Different Resources

Metadata description sets are created for different resources and usually stored separately in a database. These data are called "files" in the traditional library and museum communities. Bibliographic records files, name authority files, subject authority files, and geographical name authority files are typical units utilized by those communities. A file may physically be divided into multiple subfiles, or exist only virtually by compiling on-demand descriptions based on distributed statements. "Authority information about persons, places, concepts, and subjects may be important for retrieval of the work, but this information is more efficiently recorded in separate authority files than in records about the work itself. The advantage of storing ancillary information in an authority file is that this information needs only be recorded once, and it may then be linked to all appropriate work records" (CDWA Lite, 2006: 2).

The logical and physical design of a database should be a local implementation issue. Nevertheless conceptual models will guide in the design of information systems hosting, managing, and linking all of these files. In a previous section (see 5.2) three conceptual models were examined, all of which require understanding of the *one-to-one principle*: Each metadata description describes only one resource, and resources can be connected through metadata descriptions. In Figure 5-2-2, Description A is for the original work *Antony and Cleopatra*. This description set contains several statements about title, date, subject, and creator name. Description B is a set of statements about the relationship between this play and the collective body of work that contains this play. The third one, Description C, is a name authority biographic/geographic and categorical (i.e. playwright) description set about the creator William Shakespeare. These descriptions can be linked as necessary with one or many descriptions. The name authority, for example, can be linked with any other work this creator produced. Clearly, the linking of descriptions, especially those that exist in established authority files, is both efficient and cost-effective.

The *Cataloging Cultural Objects* (CCO) data content standards provide many instructions and examples of how and why to connect different records. Figure 5-2-3 shows a conceptual model that CCO has adopted. Although indicated by an abstract model, any work may be related to image files, resource records, or authority files. Any authority file may be used to control terminology in more than one element. At the same time, an element may use controlled terms from more than one authority. The links can then be created during the process of constructing a record.

5.6.2 Wrapping

For the standards that have built elements with a hierarchical structure, it is necessary to make sure the hierarchical relationship is correctly inherited in a description. Standards have offered a solution with very specific instructions and examples on the wrapping of tags.

In the *CDWA Lite: Specification for an XML Schema for Contributing Records via the OAI Harvesting Protocol*, wrapping elements are presented in the specification at the top level called *wrapper* and next level *set*. Thus repeatable elements and all subelements are wrapped together, as illustrated in Exhibit 5-6-1 (authors' emphasis).

MODS' top level elements too, are also wrappers in a description. Taking an example from the *name* element, five subelements are gathered under name (see Exhibit 5-6-2). Note *role* itself also has subelements therefore values are not directly entered under <role> but in its subelement <roleTerm>. In VRA Core 4.0, <elementSet></elementSet> tags are used for each element regardless of whether it has a subelement(s) (VRA Core 4.0).

Depending on system design, wrapping can be enabled with different standards. Wrapping is useful for preserving hierarchical relationships, and also for effectively controlling repeatable elements, e.g., multiple authors who

Exhibit 5-6-1. Example of wrapper, elementSet, and subelements.

[CDWA Lite elements]:	[Tagging example]:
6. **Element: Indexing Measurements Wrapper** 6.1. **Sub-element: Indexing Measurements Set** 6.1.1. Sub-element: Measurement Set 6.1.2. Sub-element: Extent Measurements 6.1.3. Sub-element: QualifierMeasurements 6.1.4. Sub-element: Format Measurements 6.1.5. Sub-element: Shape Measurements 6.1.6. Sub-element: Scale Measurements	**<cdwalite:indexingMeasurementsWrap>** **<cdwalite:indexingMeasurementsSet>** <cdwalite:extent>text area</cdwalite:extent> <cdwalite:qualifierMeasurements>sight </cdwalite:qualifierMeasurements> <cdwalite:measurementsSet value="17" unit="cm" type="height"> </cdwalite:measurementsSet> <cdwalite:measurementsSet value="13" unit="cm" type="width"> </cdwalite:measurementsSet> **</cdwalite:indexingMeasurementsSet>** ... ... </cdwalite:indexingMeasurementsWrap>

Source: Extracted and compiled based on CDWA Lite, 2006: 9–11.

Exhibit 5-6-2. Example of top level element and subelements.

[MODS elements]:	[Tagging example]:
name Subelements: namePart displayForm affiliation **role** **roleTerm** description	<**name** type="personal"> <namePart>Alterman, Eric</namePart> <displayForm>Eric Alterman </displayForm> **<role>** **<roleTerm type="text">creator** **</roleTerm>** **<roleTerm type="code">cre** **</roleTerm>** **</role>** </name>

Source: Extracted and compiled based on MODS: www.loc.gov/standards/mods/v3/mods-3-3-outline-review-new.html#name.

have different roles in a work. The example shown in Exhibit 5-6-3 also has a <display> tag, which leads us to the next part of the discussion.

5.6.3 Encoding for Display

More metadata standards now provide a method of including tags for displaying a record to allow more user-friendly descriptions to be generated for a regular user to view (i.e., *display records*) while still maintaining the efficient, required data for indexing and retrieval purposes. Display usually refers to

Exhibit 5-6-3. Example of top level element and subelements.

[VRA Core 4.0 elements]:	[Tagging example]:
DATE Subelements: earliestDate latestDate	<dateSet> <display>created 1520-1525</display> <date type="creation" source="Grove Dictionary of Art Online" href="http://www.groveart.com" dataDate="2005-06-08"> <earliestDate>1520</earliestDate> <latestDate>1525</latestDate> </date>

Source: Extracted and compiled based on VRA Core 4.0 Element Description: 7.

how the data appears to the end-user in the database, on a Web site, on a wall or slide label, or in a publication (Baca et al., 2006: 25). The previous problem with metadata was that concentration on indexing and retrieving resulted in the user reading the metadata in designed tags with technical syntax that is time-consuming to read and understand. When reading a long record, a user must piece together the information from distributed tags, for example, the physical appearance of a Chinese vase's actual dimensions and shape. The display also requires conventions such as for a personal name or a time period that the user needs to understand. In CDWA and VRA Core 4.0, a display element is often described in free-text fields, which may alternatively be concatenated from controlled fields when necessary; indexing elements are intended to be controlled. Exhibit 5-6-4 is an example using the display subelement in the date element set (authors' emphasis).

Exhibit 5-6-4. Example of statements encoded for display (based on Exhibit 5-6-3 information).

```
[In the XML record]:
<dateSet>
<display>created 1520-1525</display>
<date type="creation" source="Grove Dictionary of Art Online"
  href="http://www.groveart.com" dataDate="2005-06-08">
      <earliestDate>1520</earliestDate>
      <latestDate>1525</latestDate>
</date>
</dateSet>

[In display]:
      created 1520-1525

[Instead of displayed as:]
      Date:
            Type: Creation
            Earliest Date  1520
            Latest Date    1525
```

In VRA Core 4.0, one *display* and one *notes* subelement may be added to any element set as needed. Repeatable elements that allow multiple index values are contained, along with the display and notes subelements, within the <elementSet></elementSet> tags (VRA Core 4.0). A number of VRA Core 4.0 metadata records are used to provide three kinds of examples: (1) display records (only text taken from the display tags), (2) full records without XML tags, and (3) full records with XML tags; the last two include both display and indexing statements (see http://gort.ucsd.edu/escowles/vracore4/).

5.6.4 Encoding for Bilingual Metadata Statements

Parallel metadata is a term used for handling multilingual materials in a digital collection. Accessible via the Internet, these materials may be consulted by individuals in other cultural locales who seek information in their own languages. At the same time, they may be searched across languages by users in languages other than their own. The questions involved are twofold: the languages of the materials described by metadata and/or the languages used in metadata descriptions of the materials.

Technologically, two approaches may be taken. The first is the *inline parallel* approach that involves providing multiple local versions of, for example, a title or keyword data element in a metadata record. In the following example that uses XML, the data elements are flagged as local versions with the *lang* (i.e., language) attribute (Figure 5-6-1). This is the most common method. Note that "equivalence" is assumed via adjacency and no authority is provided.

Figure 5-6-1. An example of parallel metadata values.

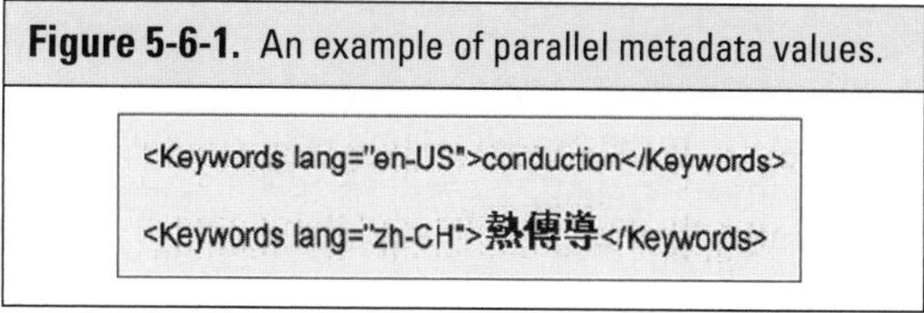

A second, and more fruitful, approach provides references to *external parallel* localized objects. The external objects can be *translation memories* employed for the translations of titles, descriptions, or other textual content (see Figure 5-6-2), or for standard glossaries including multilingual equivalents of data element names and their possible restricted vocabulary values.

Both inline parallel and external approaches can exploit the multilingual character of original sources included in the digital library collection. Through the experience of building a digital library in a small, highly specialized cross-disciplinary area involving multilingual materials, the authors have found that many non-English theses, technical reports, and specifications provide English translations, mostly for title and author (and sometimes keywords and glossaries). These equivalent pairs of terms form a basic bilingual or multilingual terminology pool. They are usually provided by authors who have done reading and research in the subject area; therefore terms are generally well-accepted

Figure 5-6-2. A localization process based on a translation memory.

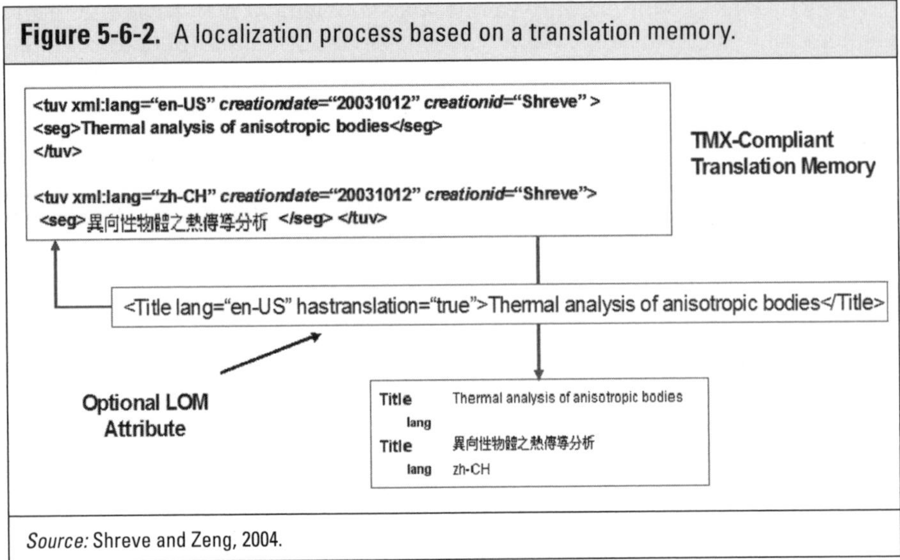

Source: Shreve and Zeng, 2004.

translations in the community and are more accurate than machine or uninformed human translation. It would be wasteful, incomplete, and culturally biased to allow such useful information to be discarded by creating English-only metadata records. The inline and external parallel approaches can preserve this important data, although the external parallel mechanism is a more robust and scalable solution to a digital collection.

At stake is a related issue that suggests some "universal" metadata elements have values that may be very culturally dependent. These could be the elements of Addresses, Calendar, Currency, Date, Numbers, Telephone, Time, and so on. International and national standards were developed to guide and control use of values for these elements. Some particular metadata elements' value spaces in certain schemas may be predefined by the schema producers. An American-based schema might control its educational context element value space with terms associated with elementary school, middle school, and upward. These choices could be extremely limited and limiting because they are derived from a single cultural context. Therefore values in one culturally dependent element may not have a real correspondence when translated into another cultural system (e.g., American and German educational systems). We firmly believe that multilingual/multicultural restricted vocabularies must be fully developed as standards by in-country domain experts and equivalence must be both standardized and authoritative. This ensures an equality of cultural sensitivity and diversity.

Creation of metadata records requires real understanding of general requirements as well as specific implementation procedures. It is at the front line that metadata records provide a means for users to be led to, or to explore, the ocean of knowledge. Metadata schemas, content standards, and value encoding schemes are created to guide and ensure the creation of high-quality metadata records which will, in turn, ensure the correct implementation of metadata standards' structures and semantics, and support information systems' functions. These building blocks need to be constructed into efficient and functional information architecture through metadata services technologies.

5.7 Combining Metadata Descriptions

With the development of shared metadata repositories and digital collections, *reusing* metadata has turned into a unique topic that draws a great deal of attention. Based on the understanding that a metadata record (as a unit) should be considered sets of descriptions, metadata recombination becomes both reasonable and feasible. The benefits of *combining* and *recombining* (the twin aspects of reuse) metadata descriptions are many. Creating basic metadata descriptions can be a combined effort of machine and human processing. Existing metadata descriptions can be reused for any appropriate projects. Quality of metadata can be enhanced through recombinant metadata, and integrated records can be generated for better access and sharing. Combining machine and human processing may be referred to in section 5.4.3 (a combination of manual and automatic methods).

5.7.1 METS

Metadata can occur in recombinant forms and originate from disparate sources. In newer projects, creators and designers have faced the tasks of how to reuse existing metadata (e.g., MARC records and EAD records) in the newly developing digital collections. Another challenge has been how to bring nondescriptive metadata into the light of exposure and discovery. By envisioning metadata in modules, different types of metadata elements (descriptive, administrative, technical, use, and preservation) from different schemas, vocabularies, applications, and other building blocks can be combined in an interoperable way. So, if we consider modularity, all components of a metadata record may be regarded as various pieces of a puzzle that find their full expression within the module. Components might be put together by combining parts of metadata sources originating from humans or machines or they might also be used and reused piece by piece when new records need to be generated. For a long time libraries have been creating rich descriptive metadata. In newer, nonlibrary catalog applications, such as digital images or assets collections, these descriptive metadata components may be reused or combined with (and when) other pieces of metadata that are generated anew.

The Metadata Encoding and Transmission Standard (METS) provides a framework for incorporating the different components from various sources within one structure and also makes it possible to "glue" the pieces together into a record. METS is a standard for packaging descriptive, administrative, and structural metadata into one XML document for interactive exchange with digital repositories. METS (created in 2001) is an XML Schema designed to create XML document *instances* (records) that express: (1) the hierarchical structure of digital library objects, (2) the names and locations of the files that constitute those objects, and (3) all associated metadata. It thus provides a framework for the combination of several internal metadata structures with external schemas. It is "a standard that provides a method to encapsulate all the information about an object—whether digital or not" (Tennant, 2001).

The seven parts that form a METS instance or record are: METS Header, Descriptive Metadata, Administrative Metadata, File Section, Structural Map, Structural Links, and Behavior, all of which are optional except for the Header and Structural Map (Guenther and McCallum 2002; McDonough, 2006) and are illustrated in Figure 5-7-1.

The descriptive, administrative and behavior sections may reside in the METS document or reside in an external location. If the metadata for these sections is external, it may be pointed to from the appropriate section of the METS document. The metadata may be of any type and format, e.g., descriptive metadata, MARC, EAD, DC records, or even an entry in a catalog if the catalog record can be adequately referenced. It is possible to extrapolate from Figure 5-7-1 that the descriptive metadata section in a METS record may point to descriptive metadata external to the METS document. Or, it may contain internally embedded descriptive metadata such as a recorded video of an interview that has been digitized, and the transcribed text has become available. METS allows reuse of the descriptive metadata (e.g., a MARC record for the video) by either including it in a new record or providing a pointer to the external record.

Figure 5-7-1. The METS architecture.

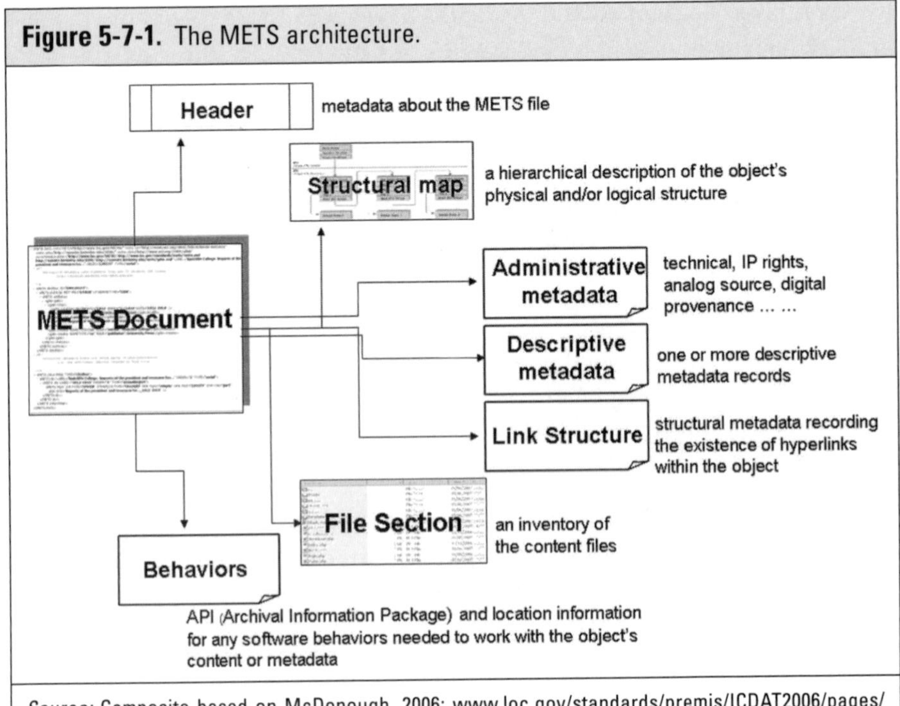
Header
metadata about the METS file
Structural map
a hierarchical description of the object's physical and/or logical structure
METS Document
Administrative metadata
technical, IP rights, analog source, digital provenance ... ...
Descriptive metadata
one or more descriptive metadata records
Link Structure
structural metadata recording the existence of hyperlinks within the object
File Section
an inventory of the content files
Behaviors
API (Archival Information Package) and location information for any software behaviors needed to work with the object's content or metadata

Source: Composite based on McDonough, 2006: www.loc.gov/standards/premis/ICDAT2006/pages/Slide15_gif.htm.

At the same time separate technical metadata of analog, digital, and text files are grouped together in the File Section to correspond to the same descriptive metadata. Sequencing of sections in a file group is managed through the Structural Map. The behavior section of the METS document contains pointers to computer programs or applications that are used to display digital objects such as page-turners or audio players. An example of a METS record is provided by the newly released *METS: Primer and Reference Manual* (METS Editorial Board, 2007). In this example (in the left partition of Exhibit 5-7-1), a MODS record is embedded in the descriptive metadata section (<mets:dmdDec>) with a wrapper (<mets:mdWrap>) (see Figure 5-7-2). An alternative to this is to store that data in a separate file and only place a

Exhibit 5-7-1. Options of including a metadata description in a METS record.

```
<mets>
  <dmdSec>
    <mdWrap>
      <xmlData>
        <!– insert data from different
         namespace here –>
      </xmlData>
    </mdWrap>
  </dmdSec>
  <fileSec></fileSec>
  <structMap></structMap>
</mets>
```

```
<mets>
  <dmdSec>
    <mdRef [file location] />
  </dmdSec>
  <fileSec></fileSec>
  <structMap></structMap>
</mets>
```

Figure 5-7-2. A METS record example with a MODS record in the description metadata section.

```
<mets:mets>
      <mets:dmdSec ID="DMD1">
            <mets:mdWrap MIMETYPE="text/xml" MDTYPE="MODS">
                  <mets:xmlData>
                        <mods:mods version="3.1">
                          <mods:titleInfo>
                                <mods:title>Epigrams</mods:title>
                          </mods:titleInfo>
                           <mods:name type="personal">
                           <mods:namePart>Martial</mods:namePart>
                                <mods:name>
                           <mods:name type="personal">
                             <mods:namePart>Ker, Walter C. A. (Walter Charles
Alan),1853-1929
                             </mods:namePart>
                           </mods:name>
                           <mods:typeOfResource>text</mods:typeOfResource>
                        </mods:mods>
                  </mets:xmlData>
            </mets:mdWrap>
      </mets:dmdSec>
      <mets:fileSec>
      </mets:fileSec>
      <mets:structMap>
      </mets:structMap>
</mets:mets>
```

Source: Reprinted from *METS: Primer and Reference Manual*, 2007: 11, with permission from the Digital Library Federation.

Figure 5-7-3. A METS record example with a reference link to a MODS record.

```
<mets:mets>
       <mets:dmdSec ID="DMD1">
              <mets:mdRef MIMETYPE="application/MODS" MDTYPE="MODS"/>
                     <mets:binData>[base 64 encoded data goes
here]</mets:binData>
       </mets:dmdSec>
</mets:mets>
```

Source: Reprinted from *METS: Primer and Reference Manual*, 2007: 11, with permission from the Digital Library Federation.

metadata reference (<mets:mdRef>) instead (in the right partition of Exhibit 5-7-1; authors' emphasis) (see Figure 5-7-3, above).

The *METS Primer* provides a full record that contains 1,943 lines of codes. More METS examples and tools are also accessible from the METS site (www.loc.gov/standards/mets/). The METS schema makes it possible to encode different types of metadata for any simple or complex digital library object (digital or not), and to express the complex links between those various types of metadata. It therefore provides a useful standard for the exchange of digital library objects between collections or repositories.

5.7.2 RDF

In Section 5.5, an example of encoding metadata descriptions in RDF is presented in Exhibit 5-5-6. In that example, one unique resource is described: the Metadata Basics tutorial. In a record, each resource described should be enclosed in a container element, i.e., a pair of <rdf:Description> tags. Therefore only one <rdfDescription> is used (see Exhibit 5-5-6 #4 area). If another resource is present, for example, a profile of the creator that is to be integrated with this record (see Figure 5-7-4), then another pair of <rdf:Description> tags is needed (see Exhibit 5-7-2; authors' emphasis).

Three namespaces (rdf, dc, and vcard) are declared at the beginning of the record where the context for a particular metadata element is defined, and can be assumed to have a unique definition within the bounds of the declared namespace. Also, each element can be identified as belonging to one or another element set. The importance of such a structure is that multiple namespaces expressed in XML may be defined to allow elements from different schemas to be combined into a single resource description. The power of such combinations is tremendous in knowledge organizations, sharing, and is especially important in the development of social computing.

5.7.3 Aggregation

A metadata repository implements aggregation for the following purposes: first, aggregation will allow incomplete and insufficient data to be enhanced through recombination (Hillmann, Dushay, and Phipps, 2004); second, aggregated data

Figure 5-7-4. Illustration of two resources to be described and integrated.

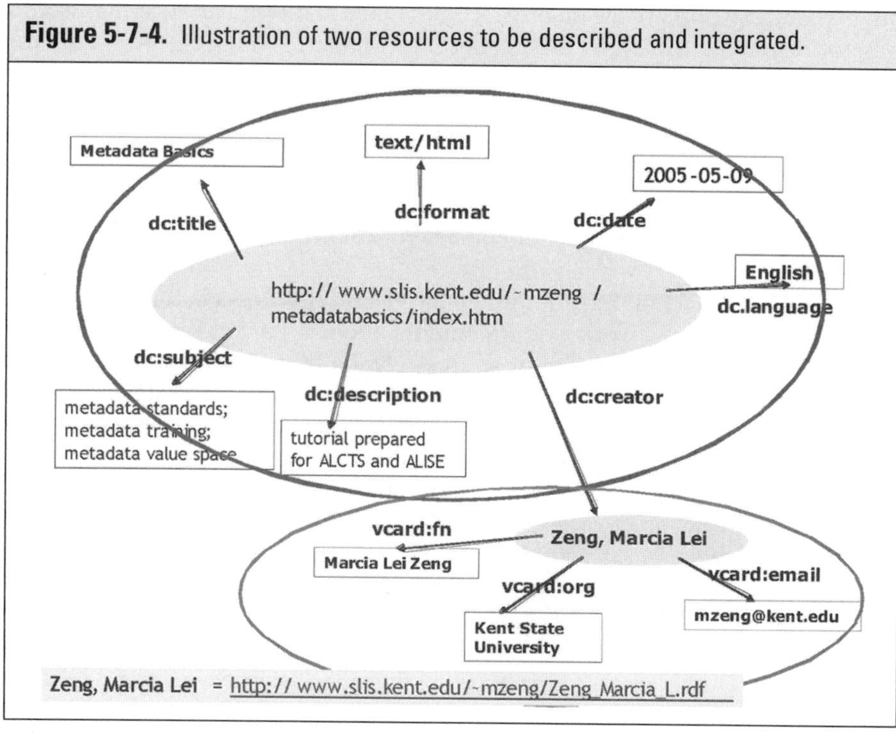

Exhibit 5-7-2. An RDF record for the visual representation in Figure 5-7-4.

```
<?xml version="1.0"?>
<rdf: RDF
      xmlns:rdf= "http://www.w3.org/1999/02/22-rdf-syntax-ns#"
      xmlns:dc= "http://purl.org/dc/elements/1.1/"
      xmlns:vcard = "http://www.w3.org/2001/vcard-rdf/3.0#">

  <rdf:Description rdf:about =
    "http://www.slis.kent.edu/~mzeng/metadatabasics/index.htm">
    <dc:creator rdf:href= "Zeng, Marcia Lei"/>
    <dc:title> Metadata Basics </dc:title>
    <dc:subject> metadata standards; metadata training; metadata value space
     </dc:subject>
    <dc:date>2005-05-09</dc:date>
    <dc:format>text/html</dc:format>
    <dc:language>en</dc:language>
    <dc:description> tutorial prepared for ALCTS and ALISE </dc:description>
  </rdf:Description>
  <rdf:Description ID= "Zeng, Marcia Lei">
      <vcard:fn>Marcia Lei Zeng </vcard:fn>
      <vcard:email>mzeng@kent.edu </vcard:email>
    <vcard:org>Kent State University </vcard:org>
  </rdf:Description>
</rdf:RDF>
```

are exploratory and create *value-added* metadata that will enhance the usefulness of resources (JISC PALS II metadata+ project, 2006). Requirements for metadata aggregation correspond to two types of interoperability services: (1) Access services provide unified machine interfaces for searching and linking metadata held in, or harvested from, different types of collections and repositories through the use of standardized access protocols. (2) Data mapping services repurpose metadata of various schemas from vastly different sources into formats that are coherent and of consistent quality for specific use contexts (Low, 2006).

The essential idea underpinning the aggregation process is that each metadata record contains a series of statements about a particular resource, and therefore metadata from different sources can be brought together to build a more complete profile of that resource. The NSDL Metadata Repository is a good example of using aggregation to handle data anomalies and schema disparity problems. The NSDL has employed an automated "ingestion" system, based on the OAI-PMH whereby metadata flows into the metadata repository with minimal human intervention or oversight. The NSDL, seen in this light, basically functions as a vast metadata aggregator (Hillmann, Dushay, and Phipps, 2004).

Figure 5-7-5 illustrates how several providers might contribute to an augmented metadata record. First, the Metadata Repository harvests a simple DC record from Provider A, which contains unqualified *title*, *identifier*, *creator*, and *type* elements. The NSDL Safe Transforms at the repository recognizes the *identifier* as a valid URI and the *type* value as a valid DCMIType; therefore, the encoding schemes "URI" and "DCMIType" are added to the statements. Second, an ENC (The Eisenhower National Clearinghouse) record for the same resource provides two additional pieces of information with the *audience* and *education level* elements. Last, the iVia Enhancement Service provides *subject* information based on three different vocabularies: *GEM (Gateway to Educational Materials) Vocabulary*, LCSH (*Library of Congress Subject Headings*), and LCC (*Library of Congress Classification*). The result is a new record that is normalized/augmented and contains information from sources Provider A, NSDL Metadata Repository, iVia, and ENC. These enhancements are then exposed via the OAI-PMH for repositories to harvest. This enables the repository to provide enhanced metadata for other services to exploit through the use of their own aggregators.

The JISC's *metadata+* project (http://baillie.lib.ed.ac.uk/metadataplus/) concentrates on technical development of the open source digital repository. With its *metadata+* test bed it demonstrates the aggregation of metadata (locally stored and remote) retrieved dynamically from cross-searchable sources. One of the outcomes of the project is metadata enrichment. Electronic book metadata, for example, can be created from a dynamic (runtime) combination of (1) publisher and library bibliographic metadata, (2) user annotations (such as ratings and reviews) retrieved from commercial book/multimedia Web sites, and (3) metadata generated within local digital library communities. The value-added annotations can be quite useful to publishers, librarians, teachers and students, especially in linking these resources to course materials and content (JISC PALS II metadata+ project, 2006). Another report describes iLumina

Figure 5-7-5. Sources, storage, and redistribution of augmented metadata in the metadata repository.

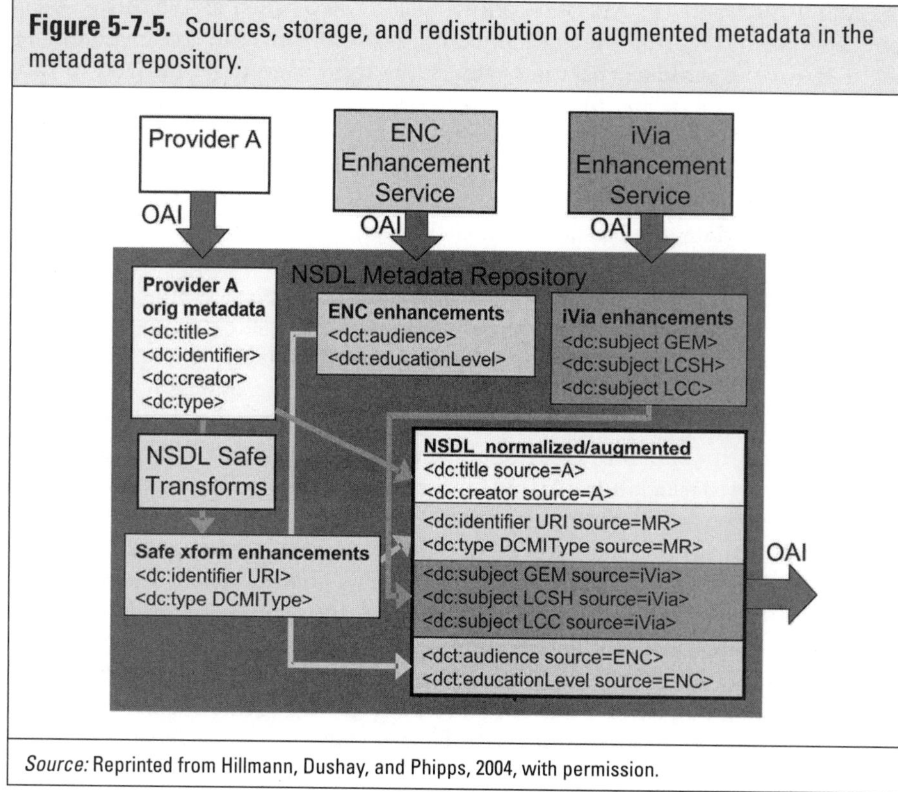

Source: Reprinted from Hillmann, Dushay, and Phipps, 2004, with permission.

(www.ilumina-dlib.org), a digital library of sharable undergraduate teaching materials for science and engineering. Like any aggregator, iLumina is both a data provider and a service provider. Previously this collection consisted of metadata that had been created by project contributors. By importing metadata from another data provider that exports IMS metadata via OAI, the project team found many opportunities to enhance and add value to local records. Nevertheless, a glaring deficiency has been identified: very little has been done to address intellectual property rights for metadata and the related protocol for services for enriched metadata.

The report also shared lessons learned. It reminds us that even though *technology* makes metadata repositories capable and functional, protocols of harvesting can not substitute (yet) for the *human* protocols and agreements about contents and values of metadata, especially regarding metadata accuracy, intellectual property, metadata specification, and specialized vocabularies (Heath et al., 2005).

5.7.4 Conclusion

Whether for greater efficiency or more user-friendly service purposes, the ultimate goal of good metadata architecture is to develop mechanisms for linking the many disparate objects of a collection into a complex associational web. Linking and navigation mechanisms and, more important, the mechanisms that express the semantic nature of those linkages, need to be utilized to connect to metadata external to the resource (that is about the resource). Equally, linkage must relate to resources within and between resources (internal and external), and then beyond to the larger superstructures created from resources at various levels of granularity. With these thoughts in mind, we explore the subject of metadata services in the next chapter.

Suggested Readings

Baca, Murtha, Ed. 2006. "VII. Database Design and Relationships." *Cataloging Cultural Objects:A Guide to Describing Cultural Works and Their Images* (pp. 20-27). Murtha Baca, Patricia Harpring, Elisa Lanzi, Linda McRae, and Ann Whiteside, on behalf of the Visual Resources Association. Chicago: American Library Association. A short version is available: http://vraweb.org/ccoweb/cco/partone.html.

Carlyle, Allyson, and Lisa Fusco. 2007. "Understanding FRBR as a Conceptual Model: FRBR and the Bibliographic Universe." *Bulletin of the American Society for Information Science and Technology*. August/September 2007. Available: www.asis.org/Bulletin/Aug-07/carlyle_fusco.html.

"DCMI Abstract Model." 2007. Andy Powell, Mikael Nilsson, Ambjörn Naeve, Pete Johnston, and Thomas Baker. Available: http://dublincore.org/documents/abstract-model/index.shtml.

Dushay, Naomi, and Diane Hillmann. 2003. "Analyzing Metadata for Effective Use and Re-use." *DC-2003: Proceedings of the International DCMI Metadata Conference and Workshop, Sept. 28-Oct. 2, 2003, Seattle, Washington*, Cornell University, National Science Digital Library, Seattle, Washington. Available: http://dc2003.ischool.washington.edu/Archive-03/03dushay.pdf.

Greenberg, Jane. 2002. "Metadata Generation: Processes, People and Tools." *Bulletin of the American Society for Information Science & Technology* 29, no. 2: 16–19. Available: www.asis.org/Bulletin/Dec-02/greenberg.html.

NISO Framework Advisory Group. 2007. *A Framework of Guidance for Building Good Digital Collections*, 3rd ed. Priscilla Caplan, Grace Agnew, Murtha Baca, Carl Fleischhauer, Tony Gill, Ingrid Hsieh-Yee, Jill Koelling, Christie Stephenson, Karen A. Wetzel. Available: www.niso.org/publications/rp/framework3.html.

Shreeves, Sarah, Jenn Riley, and Liz Milewicz. 2006. "Moving Towards Shareable Metadata." *First Monday* [Online] 11, no. 8. Available: http://firstmonday.org/issues/issue11_8/shreeves/index.html.

Exercises

1. Open any WORD document, add metadata descriptions. Instruction: Choose *File → Properties,* fill in the template provided at *Summary* and *Custom* windows. (To complete this exercise, MS WORD software is needed.)

2. Open a PDF file, add metadata descriptions. Instruction: Choose *File → Document Properties*. At the *Description* template, click *Additional Metadata* button to open a fuller template. Create metadata statements in this template. Also choose *Advanced* to view generated DC statements under *Dublin Core Properties*. (To complete this exercise, Adobe Acrobat software is needed.)
3. Open an image from Photoshop and add metadata descriptions. Instructions—Option 1: open the image from File Browser by choosing *File → Browse*. Select an image for preview and add metadata. Option 2: Choose *File → File Info* and fill in values in *Description* template. This is the same process as using an Adobe Acrobat for PDF file. Choose *Edit → Find* and set search criteria to find the image you just described. (To complete this exercise, Adobe Photoshop CS software is needed. Note: different versions of CS may perform slightly different.)
4. Use DC-dot to create a metadata record. Instructions—Go to www.ukoln.ac.uk/metadata/dcdot/, submit a URL. After the template appears, double-check each field and resubmit after all necessary values are correctly input. Choose to see output in XHTML, RDF, and XML and copy each output into a separate WORD or HTML file. Analyze records based on explanations in Section 5.5.
5. Create a set of metadata records using CONTENTdm. (To complete this exercise, a CONTENTdm client and an account are needed. Go to www.contentdm.com/ to set up a free 60-day hosted trial or a full evaluation copy.)

Part III
Metadata Services

6

Metadata Services

Case Example: An Astronomy Metadata Service

"Initially when the data, in the form of images, is collected by an instrument, such as a telescope, it is pre-processed and calibrated and stored in an archive. Metadata about the images describing the location in the sky, the calibration parameters, etc., is stored as well. Additional processing may occur to extract interesting features of particular regions of the sky or to produce images focusing on particular celestial objects. The information about the processing is captured in metadata attributes and stored as well. Once the metadata and data are prepared in this fashion, it is released to the group of scientists within the collaboration. Researchers can then pose queries on the metadata to discovery data of relevance to their work. Based on the results of the searches conducted on the metadata scientists may want to organize the metadata in a way that is most appropriate for their research. During this phase of the data publication process, the data may be further annotated by the collaborators. After a certain period of time, usually on the order of two years, the data and the metadata are released to the general public. At this time, users outside of the initial collaboration search the metadata based on attributes that are important to them." (Deelman et al., 2004: 2)

The term *metadata services* is used to describe the systems and tools supporting the creation and maintenance of metadata schemas and records. This chapter will explain what metadata services are, what standards and tools are available for metadata service operations, and how metadata services facilitate information retrieval. Chapter 5 introduced the methods and best practices used in generating metadata records. Coordination of many components is necessary when generating records to ensure the product's quality and interoperability. Metadata standards (Chapter 2) and metadata schemas (Chapter 3) aid in maintaining consistency for descriptive semantics and the encoding format (Chapter 4) for metadata records. However, record creation requires human catalogers in addition to the support of tools, procedures, and policies that ensure efficient and effective production.

Depending on the nature of the domain, metadata records can be as simple as a minimal set of data fields such as author, title, date, and URL; or, as complicated as highly technical geospatial records. In the latter, data fields may number in the hundreds and may be contained in a nested, multilayered structure. The production process is complicated because metadata generation often takes place in a distributed and collaborative environment in which metadata for a digital object or collection often needs to be updated and changed over time (see the Case Example). Today data and information silos are a common phenomenon in many organizations and are often organized according to various metadata schemas with localized elements and structures. In places where data sharing and interoperability are critical, a secure and reliable system is required to provide effective and high-quality metadata generation and management with the support of tools and procedures. This chapter describes the types of metadata services commonly used in digital libraries and repositories, and their important roles in metadata discovery.

6.1 What Are Metadata Services?

Metadata services encompass metadata registries, repositories, and development and production services. The designation of metadata services has been used to describe and refer to different things in diverse contexts. For example, computer scientists have tended to use "metadata services" to describe a relatively narrow range of functions, whereas librarians and archivists have tended to adopt a more expansive definition. At the National Aeronautics and Space Administration (NASA) Jet Propulsion Laboratory, the metadata service provides registration and retrieval of metadata elements, metadata schemata, and metadata profiles of resources (http://oodt.jpl.nasa.gov/metadata-service/index.html, accessed 2007). This application of a metadata service is central to the control and sharing of metadata schemas and application profiles; or more accurately, it is a metadata registry service within an organization. The metadata registry service is often synonymous with the term metadata services as used by computer scientists. Metadata services "maintain mappings between name attributes for data items and other descriptive metadata attributes and respond to queries about those mappings. In particular, Metadata Services support domain-independent, domain-specific, virtual organization and user metadata attributes" (Singh et al., 2003: 3). While a metadata registry is an important part of metadata services, it is not the only component. Metadata services in a rapidly evolving digital environment encompass a much larger spectrum of functions and operations.

Using the astronomy metadata service in the Case Example (on p. 211), we may deduce two primary areas of activities on the user side. The first is the discovery of data through searching or browsing a metadata service to find the information one needs. The second is sharing data by publishing it to a metadata service where others may view the information.

The discovery and publication of metadata is typical of metadata service operations in many digital collections and repositories. On the system side, metadata about data features, such as date, file size, file format, data creator and owner, is automatically extracted and stored; information about data processing is also automatically captured. Activities in publishing digital resources and data require metadata submission tools that are supported by prescribed elements and a system that authenticates users and authorizes them to publish metadata. Throughout, the system administrator and staff must maintain the metadata schemas and application profiles with either an institution-wide or domain-wide registry service as well as the metadata records submitted by users. Metadata services include the common types listed here.

- *Metadata registries:* Registries provide information for all metadata elements, schemas, and application profiles relevant to the application domain or domains; mappings of elements across standards and schemas; and a search and browse interface for discovering and locating metadata elements, value space, and schemas.
- *Metadata repositories:* In addition to metadata records, repositories store, manage, and provide access to metadata artifacts such as database schemas, XML schemas, taxonomies, and XSL Transformations.
- *Metadata development and production services:* These include a wide variety of operations ranging from metadata consulting, design, and development, to tool selection and record generation. The metadata development and production services also provide for authentication of users, distribution of notices about changes and updates, and authorization of metadata publication.

Each type of these metadata services serves different purposes and needs.

Metadata registries offer centralized maintenance for the standard description of metadata elements in terms of definition, format, semantic label, referential relationships, and encoding schemas through registration of the elements. The purpose is to standardize and reuse metadata over time, space, and applications (ISO/IEC 11179, 2004). A metadata registry needs to be compliant with the ISO/IEC (International Organization for Standardization/International Electrotechnical Commission) 11179 standard because a standard description of metadata schemas is the basis of element and vocabulary reusability and interoperability. A metadata registry may be deployed in an organization or a domain for browsing and searching available data elements and vocabularies used in different schemas.

Metadata repositories focus on metadata artifacts—the schemas and records that are critical for harvesting and ingestion. A metadata repository may belong to a digital library or may be a central storehouse of metadata harvested from various digital libraries and collections; the National Science Digital Library (NSDL, www.nsdl.org, accessed 2007) provides a good example. The records in a repository may also be submitted by resource creators or created by catalogers, which resembles in many ways the cataloging of library materials; the difference is that metadata creators may not have the training necessary for cataloging according to long-established standards such as AACR2. Repositories are required to comply with certain standards such as the Open Archive Initiative Protocol for Metadata Harvesting (OAI-PMH) standard for metadata ingestion and harvesting.

Metadata development and production services is a general category referring primarily to those activities operating within an institution to support the organization of digital collections using metadata. Some libraries have created a new institutional unit for metadata development and production (e.g., Cornell

University Library's Digital Consulting and Production Services) or restructured the traditional technical services unit to become the metadata services unit (e.g., the Metadata Services Department at the Library of University of California at San Diego). These organizational changes added functions such as metadata consultation, design, development, production, and conversion that are beyond the scope of traditional library technical services. Whereas metadata registries and repositories emphasize technical standards and enabling technologies, metadata development and production services are often the users of, and contributors to, both metadata registries and repositories and therefore entail more human involvement in the process. Development and production services may take place not only in a real-world brick- and-mortar library but also in any digital library or repository system environment.

Not every institution or digital library provides all types of metadata services. Some application domains may focus on one type of service more than others. For example, digital libraries such as the Gateway to Educational Materials (GEM) and the Digital Library for Earth Science Education (DLESE) are built mainly as Web educational resource catalogs to serve well-defined user populations. Their goal is to organize digital resources for discovery and access, which requires them to develop a metadata schema by either adopting a metadata standard or incorporating elements from several standards before creating records. Many digital collections are users of metadata registries because there is usually only one metadata schema involved for the whole collection, as in the case of GEM and DLESE. The NASA Jet Propulsion Laboratory provides another example here: in this large organization, wide variations occur among different scientific fields and description needs for datasets generated from each discipline. To share and reuse metadata schemas, a metadata registry was built within the organization for interoperability and mapping between different schemas in different disciplinary fields.

More recently, specialized Web services related to metadata processing have also been developed and put into use. "Web services are modular, web-based, machine-to-machine applications that can be combined in various ways. Web services can be accessed at various points in the metadata lifecycle, for example, when a work is authored or created, at the time an object is indexed or cataloged, or during search and retrieval" (OCLC Research, 2007, www.oclc.org/research/projects/termservices/).

Crosswalking services for exchanging and sharing metadata schemas and values have been experimented with at both OCLC and the NSDL. They are used to assist with validation of elements and values that involve using standard encoding schemes and controlled vocabularies, enhancement of metadata record quality, and multiple character encodings of the translation process. For instance, OCLC's Metadata Switch includes services such as the harvesting of metadata, "fusion" of metadata from different sources, schema transformation, and enrichment or augmentation of records (www.oclc.org/research/projects/mswitch/default.htm, accessed 2007).

Terminology services refer to Web-based, machine-to-machine applications that provide access to vocabularies concerning concepts, terms and relationships, and descriptions of the meaning of terms so as to facilitate semantic interoperability. Leading research projects include OCLC's Terminology Services. As of July 2007, mappings were made for eight knowledge organization resources (e.g., LCSH, MeSH, DDC, and ERIC Thesaurus) through direct and co-occurrence mappings (OCLC Research, 2007). These services have made authority records accessible to users via a browser and to machines through the OAI-PMH Web services mechanisms. Chapter 8 discusses both of these services in detail.

In a data grid environment, services need to distinguish between different types of metadata—application, replica, and system configuration metadata—and be able to provide a uniform means for naming, publishing, and access (Chervenak et al., 2000).

6.2 Infrastructure for Metadata Services

Metadata services support a wide variety of operations necessary for generating standardized and high-quality metadata records, and also for sharing and reuse. Functional metadata services employ a set of *soft* and *hard* enabling infrastructures. The soft infrastructural components are procedures and policies that govern how and what metadata services will be provided, and under what conditions. The hard infrastructure refers to the technology that acts as the empowering engine for the services. Besides databases, networks, and system platforms, an important part of the enabling technologies for metadata services include a series of technical standards.

The types of metadata services provided have a direct effect on service structure and functions. For a registry-only service, a Web-based submission form is necessary for users to publish and/or share their metadata elements and schemas. The ISO/IEC 11179 Information Technology—Metadata Registries (MDR) standard specifies which description fields (see Section 6.3) should be present in defining a metadata element, which most registries follow in building the backend database and front-end interface that allows users to submit data. In addition, help information is usually available on how to submit and publish a schema through a metadata registry service. If the metadata service includes a registry and also a metadata repository there will be more standards involved, more procedures required for ensuring a smooth workflow, and more technologies that enable all functions. The procedures and policies are critical to ensure the consistency and quality of metadata creation.

Metadata services have distinct needs that require different service policies. Registries function as a clearinghouse for elements and schemas that are frequently changed and updated. A versioning policy is necessary for maintaining stable identification for an element or term, and will reflect changes by assigning version numbers accordingly. Metadata repositories have other policy issues that need to be addressed, e.g., the NSDL wrote its metadata service policy for two main areas: *acceptable uses of metadata* and *trust*. The NSDL metadata repository collects metadata records from contributors (providers) via the OAI protocol for metadata harvesting. In a policy statement issued by the NSDL, "Collection holders, service providers and the Metadata Repository use metadata based solely on principles of 'fair use' and the good will of the holders of rights" (Arms and Simutis, 2002). The policy language is framed for the acceptable uses of metadata so that harvested metadata will be used for noncommercial purposes, including distribution of metadata to service providers (Arms and Simutis, 2002). Metadata policies (such as the one from NSDL) can be found at most repository Web sites.

The enabling infrastructure for metadata services includes and relies upon technical standards and technologies. Figure 6-2-1 presents the infrastructural components that underpin the services. Most organizations today have a technological infrastructure in place (see bottom blocks of Figure 6-2-1) and include networks, servers, databases, and applications that support a distributed digital environment. In Chapter 5 we illustrated the taxonomy of general markup languages (see Figure 5-5-10). XML is a simple, flexible, and universal text-based markup format for the Web, and capable of describing classes of data objects by "tagging" them with structured semantic labels. Its design goals are to support a wide variety of applications while remaining straightforwardly usable on the Internet. The documents are legible and reasonably clear when the tags are labeled correctly and accurately. Major metadata standards are encoded in XML schema (see also Chapter 4), and records are also created, stored, and communicated via XML documents (see also Chapter 5). Thus XML has become the dominant encoding format for metadata.

Metadata services facilitate metadata processing and interoperability by making elements transparent to adopters and by standardizing data communication. Although XML offers a common format for encoding data, questions remain. How should the data be encoded and what tags should be assigned to which data elements? Technical standards and conventions are being developed to regulate encoding practices and communication processes so that a common understanding of data elements across and between organizations can be established through standard description. The most widely used are the ISO/IEC

Figure 6-2-1. The infrastructure for metadata services.

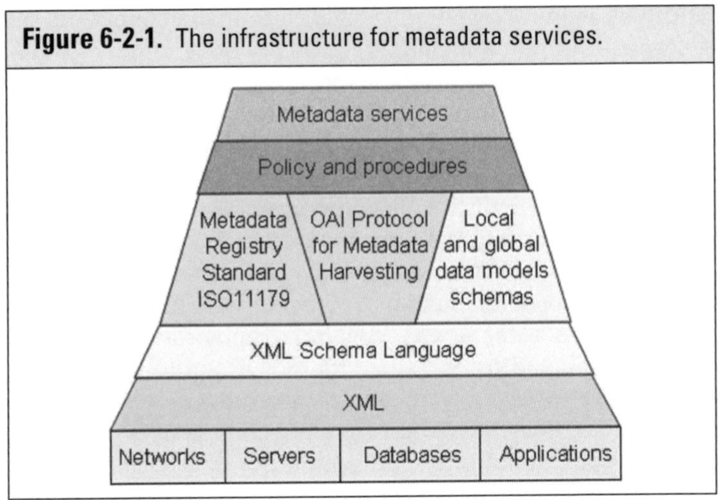

11179 Information Technology—Metadata Registries (MDR) and the OAI Protocol for Metadata Harvesting, which will be discussed in the next two sections.

6.3 Metadata Registries

6.3.1 Purposes

A metadata registry (MDR) is by definition "a database of metadata that supports the functionality of registration" (ISO/IEC 11179, 2004). As discussed previously, metadata creation involves both human intervention and software tools. It takes a combination of both to fulfill the functional requirements of metadata creation, rights management, resource discovery, and preservation (which are often referred to as descriptive metadata, rights management metadata, administrative metadata, and preservation metadata). Specialized metadata schemas were developed to serve particular populations, e.g., educational metadata for learning resources and multimedia metadata for audiovisual and 2-D or 3-D imagery resources. Practice has proven that no single standard can meet all resource description and management needs, and this point is proved by the large number of metadata standards and schemas established today. To control the semantics and quality in schemas and elements, there must be a widely agreed upon method to standardize, store, retrieve, and present information about metadata elements. It would also be highly beneficial and effective if elements from different schemas could be openly shared and reused. Users of a registry might include:

- standards creators and implementers who seek to discover and re-use existing element sets, application profiles, elements, and encoding schemas;
- metadata records creators who look for guidance on use of element sets and application profiles;
- data curators and service providers whose interests are about accessing machine-readable schemas of element sets and application profiles;
- researchers studying schema usage;
- developers and suppliers of software products and services whose interests center on schema usage and interoperability;
- commentators on deployment of element sets and application profiles; and
- other registries (Heery, 2002; JISC IE Metadata Schema Registry, 2006).

The goal of an MDR is to serve the need for "metadata design, harmonization, standardization, use, re-use, and interchange" (ISO/IEC 11179, 2004). Because the reuse of existing metadata terms is essential to achieving interoperability among metadata element sets, the identification of existing terms becomes a prerequisite in any new schema development process. Metadata registries encourage the sharing of semantics by facilitating publication of metadata schemas. A registry is intended to help implementers of information projects and services find out about metadata terms in use (both official definitions and local variations) to encourage harmonization of metadata usage within particular fields and applications (Heery, 2002).

6.3.2 Functional Requirements

Metadata registries maintain records for elements and vocabulary used for values as well as information about source schema, versions, maintenance authority, and so on. "A metadata registry provides machine-readable information about the metadata schemas in use by particular metadata-based services" (Powell, 2003: www.ukoln.ac.uk/distributed-systems/jisc-ie/arch/ssplan/, accessed 2007). The functions of the services provided by a metadata schema registry may vary, but might include:

- discovery of vocabularies and terms—the registry may provide a query interface across the aggregated data;
- verification of the status of vocabularies and terms;
- access to machine-processable descriptions of vocabularies and terms;
- location of related resources such as information on different syntactic bindings;
- navigation of the relationships between terms and vocabularies or between terms; and
- inferencing and mapping based on knowledge of the nature of the relationships between terms (Johnston, 2004).

An MDR must fulfill functional requirements for both human users and machines. For human users, the MDR needs to provide interfaces for finding and browsing reference descriptions of metadata schemas that serve as a dictionary for the design and editing of schemas. The registry, as part of a computer system, should perform functions such as searching, browsing, schema mapping, version management, multilanguage user interfaces, API (Application Programming Interface) software tools (Nagamori and Sugimoto, 2007), and links to important controlled vocabularies from which the values of metadata fields can be selected (Duval et al., 2002). The Research and Development Group of UKOLN similarly states that a registry offers authoritative definitions of schemas, change control, evolution of metadata language, declared relationships between different metadata schemas, best practices, and the promotion of existing schemas in order to avoid duplicate effort (UKOLN, 1999). UKOLN's document *Functional Requirements for CORES Schema Creation and Registration Tool* summarizes that the schema creation tool must enable a structured RDF schema to be produced that will identify and define:

- element sets;
- the elements in those element sets;
- application profiles;
- element usage which make up those application profiles;
- encoding schemes;
- values within those encoding schemes;
- the agencies who own, create, or maintain these resources;
- commentaries (contextual annotations) outlining deployment of the element sets, application profiles, and schemes; and
- links to user guidelines for the element sets, application profiles or schemes.

The CORES Registry Web site interface brings a unified path to all of this information, as illustrated in Figure 6-3-1. So, the basic functions of metadata registries include registering, publishing, and managing schemas and application profiles. A registry also facilitates searching and browsing what has been registered, and provides services for crosslinking and crosswalking among schemas and application profiles.

6.3.3 Types

A registry may be built for an individual metadata standard, for a core standard or ontology, or for extensions of a standard (Baker et al., 2002). A single-standard registry provides authoritative current and historical information on a particular metadata standard, perhaps linked to user guidelines, whereas the one for a core metadata standard often serves as a target for mappings from other diverse standards for the purpose of information integration. The registry service of application profiles focuses on "how a particular standard has been extended and localized by communities of use" (Baker et al., 2002). Other registry services such as data warehouses may be viewed as metadata registry services in a broader sense; however, they are more specialized and not necessarily used only in the context of a digital library. The following examples represent different registry ranges:

Figure 6-3-1. CORES Registry Index page.

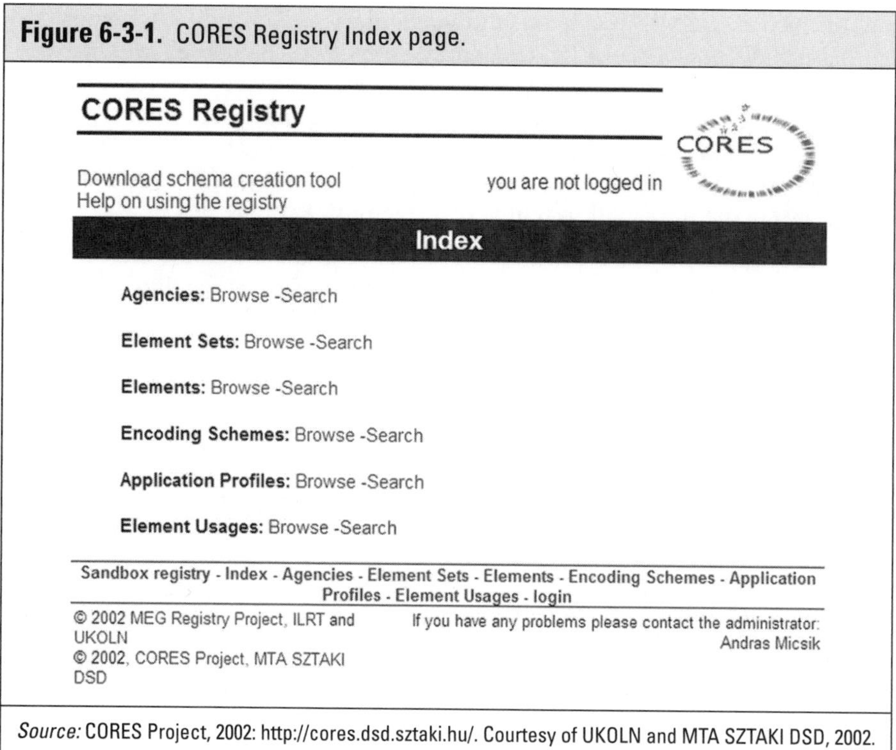

Source: CORES Project, 2002: http://cores.dsd.sztaki.hu/. Courtesy of UKOLN and MTA SZTAKI DSD, 2002.

- *Cross-domain and cross-schema registry:* UKOLN's (UK Office for Library Networking) CORES Registry contains dozens of metadata element sets, application profiles, encoding schemes, and related documents. Through a Web interface, one can search or browse according to *agencies, element sets, elements, encoding schemes, application profiles,* and *element usages* that are included in this registry (http://cores.dsd.sztaki.hu/, accessed 2007).
- *Domain-specific registry:* The Information Environment Metadata Schema Registry's (IEMSR) project (www.ukoln.ac.uk/projects/iemsr, accessed 2007), funded by the Joint Information Systems Committee (JISC) in the United Kingdom, is built upon UKOLN's MEG (Metadata for Education Group) Registry for facilitating schema registration within the educational domain. Metadata within the JISC Information Environment (JISC IE) is based largely on two key standards: DC and LOM.
- *Project-specific registry:* The European Library (TEL) metadata registry was established for recording all metadata activities associated with TEL. The registry contains translations of element names in different languages and declares whether the element is repeatable, searchable, and mandatory (Van Veen and Oldroyd, 2004).
- *Schema-specific registry:* The Dublin Core Metadata Initiative's (DCMI) Registry (http://dublincore.org/dcregistry/, accessed 2007) maintains records for valid elements within the DC schema. Currently the registry provides details about the elements, element refinements, controlled vocabulary terms (i.e., DCMI-Type Voc.), and vocabulary and encoding schemes.
- *Format-oriented registry:* The SchemaWeb (www.schemaweb.info, accessed 2007) functions as a directory of RDF schemas of metadata and ontologies expressed in W3C recommended schema languages. The registry can be browsed and searched by human agents, but also has an extensive set of Web services that may be used by software agents wishing to obtain real-time schema information whilst processing RDF data.

Registry types may also be categorized based on their architectures. In a centralized architecture, the registry acts as the repository for this data, with schemas stored at a single location and made available from that principal location through the services of the registry. Whereas responsibility for maintaining the content of the schemas may devolve to the owners of original content, responsibility for the security and continued availability of the data falls upon the central repository that hosts the content. In a distributed architecture, the schemas are created and maintained by the owners of their content, and published to the Web in standard formats either directly (by the owners) or by a third party acting on the owners' behalf. The registry may serve as one point of discovery and access to that distributed data, but the sources of that data are distributed on the Web (Johnston, 2004).

6.3.4 Essential Components

Although an MDR may fall within any of the types outlined above, it is important that its design and implementation include essential components in order to meet the functional requirements for metadata registries. The ISO 11179 Information Technology Metadata Registries (MDR) standard consists of six parts, which provide the following guidelines:

- *Framework* (Part 1) introduces fundamentals of data elements, value domains, data element concepts, conceptual domains, and classification schemes essential to the understanding of the whole set of standards.
- *Classification* (Part 2) discusses registering and administering all or part of a classification scheme, which may be used for deriving and formulating administered items, drawing upon names from a controlled vocabulary, and disambiguation of administered items (ISO/IEC 11179, 2004: Part 2).
- *Registry metamodel and basic attributes* (Part 3) specifies a conceptual model for a metadata registry.
- *Formulation of data definitions* (Part 4) provides guidance on how to develop unambiguous data definitions. This part lists a series of data definition requirements and recommendations, e.g., a concept should "be stated in the singular," the definition should "state what the concept is, not only what it is not," and "contain only commonly understood abbreviations" (ISO/IEC 11179, 2004: Part 4).
- *Naming and identification principles* (Part 5) states the formal naming and identification of metadata items.
- *Registration* (Part 6) defines identification, quality, and provenance of metadata in a metadata registry.

A record in a registry describes an *Administered Item* with administration and identification information as well as contextual information. It may be a data element, data element concept, value domain, conceptual domain, classification scheme, context (for administered item), derivation rule, object class, property, or representation class. Table 6-1 displays the administration and identification attributes for describing an administered item in an MDR. The administration and identification aspect in ISO 11179 addresses:

- Identification and registration of items submitted to the registry
- Organizations that have submitted items to the registry and/or that are responsible for items within the registry (including Registry Authorities)
- Contact information for organizations
- Supporting documentation
- Relationships among administered items (ISO/IEC 11179, 2004: Part 4)

The number of attribute occurrences represents the relationship between the administered item and its attributes. For example, an occurrence that begins with one (1) signifies a *mandatory* attribute in the administered item record, whereas one that begins with a zero *(0)* is an optional attribute. Therefore, in Table 6-3-1 five attributes that require at least one occurrence are mandatory whereas the rest are optional. The administration and identification information for an administered item provides a basis for identifying, naming, defining, classifying, and recording administrative information about the administrative item in the registry (ISO/IEC 11179-3:2004).

Table 6-3-1. Administration and identification attributes in a registry record and occurrence constraints.

Attribute	Occurrences of Attribute per Administration Record	Datatype
administered item identifier	One	*Item Identifier*
administrative note	Zero or one	String
administrative status	One	String
change description	One, conditional on presence of last change date	String
creation date	One	Date
effective date	Zero or one	Date
explanatory comment	Zero or one	String
last change date	Zero or one	Date
origin	Zero or one	String
registration status	One per	String
unresolved issue	Zero or one	String
until date	Zero or one	Date

The naming and definition region in ISO 11179 specifies the names and definitions of administered items and the contexts for those names. The attributes for this aspect address context of an administered item, terminological entry, language section, definition of administered item, and a designation (name and preferred name). In the CORES Registry (http://cores.dsd.sztaki.hu/, accessed 2007), attributes/properties are defined and presented in tables for various components: Element Set, Element, Encoding Scheme, Value, Application Profile, Element Usage, Annotation, and Commentator (see also Figure 6-3-1).

Figure 6-3-2 is a record from Dublin Core Metadata Registry. It designates that the record for the *Creator* element contains the mandatory attributes ID in URI form, name (designation), definition, description, and date of issue.

Figure 6-3-3 is another record for the same *Creator* element, but from a different registry—the CORES Metadata Registry. Although the information contained in a CORES Registry's record clearly differs from the Dublin Core Metadata Registry, essential attributes such as ID, name, definition, and description are present in both records.

ISO 11179 Part 6 recognizes that discrepancies are caused by the differing purposes and types of metadata registries, and that not all metadata registries will have the need (or the means) to support all of the attributes specified for

Figure 6-3-2. Record for the *Creator* element from the Dublin Core Metadata Registry.

http://purl.org/dc/elements/1.1/creator	
Label	Creator [en-US]
Definition	An entity primarily responsible for making the resource. [en-US]
Description	Examples of a Creator include a person, an organization, or a service. Typically, the name of a Creator should be used to indicate the entity. [en-US]
Is Defined By	http://purl.org/dc/elements/1.1/
RDF Type	Property
Type	element
Has Version	creator-005
Issued	1999-07-02
Modified	2006-12-04
Usage Example(s)	creator-001.rdf creator-001.xml

Source: DCMI, 2005: http:// dublincore.org/dcregistry.

Figure 6-3-3. Record for the *Creator* element from the CORES Registry.

ID	http://purl.org/dc/elements/1.1/creator
Name	Creator
Definition	An entity primarily responsible for making the content of the resource.
Comment	Examples of a Creator include a person, an organisation, or a service. Typically, the name of a Creator should be used to indicate the entity.
Data type	string
Obligation	optional
Maximum Occurrence	unbounded
Refines	
Element Set	The Dublin Core Element Set v1.1

Source: CORES Project, 2002: http://cores.dsd.sztaki.hu/. Courtesy of UKOLN and MTA SZTAKI DSD, 2002.

the metadata model in ISO 11179 Part 3. With these considerations in mind, the standard allows sufficient flexibility for the Registration Authority to specify the requirements in accordance with the standard and "adopt a stricter or less strict level of conformance, levying corresponding requirements on Submitting Organizations" (ISO/IEC 11179:2004: Part 3, 9).

6.4 Metadata Repositories

6.4.1 Characteristics of Metadata Repositories

Metadata repository is usually defined by its technological characteristics. Its product, i.e., metadata records that are kept and maintained, is also referred to as a repository. Plainly stated, repositories are locations where data is stored. Many digital libraries and Web portals, as well as Google Scholar, employ federated searching through local repositories that were created earlier through the accumulation of data from numerous resources. Federated searching, therefore, may be conducted on the foundational base of these repositories, which contain both metadata and raw data (although some have only the former).

Metadata repositories can be built on well-established research and academic library collections; in this respect they resemble traditional union catalogs. The Sheet Music Consortium (http://digital.library.ucla.edu/sheetmusic/, accessed 2007) consists of a group of libraries working together with the goal of building an open collection of digitized sheet music using the OAI protocol. Harvested metadata concerned with sheet music in participating collections (which, as of September 2007 included the Library of Congress, National Library of Australia, and several university libraries) is hosted by the UCLA Digital Library Program, which provides an access service via this centralized aggregate of sheet music records at the host libraries.

Nevertheless, many repositories do not always have such a highly-developed structure in the first place, but rather, the structure would emerge slowly as the result of iterative adjustments and continuous evolution. The NSDL Metadata Repository demonstrates the opportunities and challenges that a repository faces and illustrates its differences from traditional union catalogs as follows:

- The repository is composed of many metadata datasets contributed by distributed sources (e.g., the discrete NSDL collection projects), especially at the beginning stages of the NSDL project. Each of these discrete collection metadata datasets retains its independent identity and may be utilized without the support of a union catalog.
- The repository contains records created from a variety of metadata standards and practices.
- The different metadata standards used by metadata contributors enable metadata creators to provide descriptive metadata as well as administrative, technical, and usage metadata. With this support, the portal allows users to search by data elements that include technical format and educational level.
- The repository is a loosely controlled environment. It depends heavily on voluntary metadata sharing, with no central authority (or management) enforcement. It is unlike a conventional union catalog, e.g., OCLC WorldCat, which embodies strong management control over data quality, active management of files, powerful incentives for compliance with system standards, and sanctions for noncompliance.

- Metadata records are created by trained and untrained metadata authors and include professional metadata creators, content creators, and user communities or subject(s) enthusiasts (Greenberg, 2002). It is dissimilar to the practices of union catalogs that usually involve a higher level of control over metadata creation, and where expertise from the cataloging staff is mapped to different levels of authority.

At repositories where the majority of sources do not originate from data providers under one umbrella (as with the NSDL), the repository may be built completely by harvesting existing sources, and will therefore have more differing characteristics. The repository must judge whether the metadata of harvested resources point to freely available or restricted-access digital resources. OAIster (www.oaister.org, accessed 2007), which has harvested metadata from nearly 900 contributors, is just such an example. It provides access to digital resources (that most search engines will not be able to reach) by harvesting their descriptive metadata records using the OAI protocol. Its collection policy deals with different kinds and types of data sources, including those that are freely available and those with restricted-access digital resources. As a result, decisions to retain or not retain an entire harvested collection's records (based on the discovery of some restricted records), remains challenging (OAIster, 2007). These situations are discussed in the collection policy as follows:

- Freely accessible texts are easily harvested. These records contain some information about restriction policy (e.g., "This material is accessible to the public, freely and without charge."), which allows the harvester to perform filtering.
- Records often do not clearly indicate whether resources are freely available. Only by following a link (or several) to the desired digital resource does accessibility become clear.
- Regarding restricted-access records in an institution's own collections (i.e., the University of Michigan's digital collections) that *are* available via subscription (individual or institutional), a decision must be made whether to include them in the union catalog as well.

OAIster harvests records on weekly and monthly schedules. It is not a straightforward process because many incorrect UTF-8 or XML errors in those records require correction before the engine can perform a complete harvest. Consequently, when harvesting on a regular basis (weekly or monthly) has failed at least three times, and the repository is unable to discover a new OAI base URL for a repository, the collection may be dropped from the harvesting list (OAIster, 2007).

Again, the important point to recognize from the previous examples is that metadata repositories are not simply repeating the work of traditional library union catalogs and have brought about new opportunities as well as ongoing challenges. In summary, although the data still ends up aggregated in one place (a single index), the sources of the metadata records are clearly different. Data could be contributed (pushed in) by participants who are individual digital collections' data providers, delivered by vendors, or collected via harvesting. The authorship of original data is also diverse—author-contributed, metadata librarian-created, machine-generated, or any combination of these. In addition, original metadata sources usually have applied different element sets, application profiles, content standards or best practices, and encoding schemes prior to conversion that conform to a common schema supported by the repository. Metadata records in the repository generally contain a link back to the original records, and so records will exist in two (or more) places at once: the original home environment and the union repository.

6.4.2 Introduction to the Harvesting Model

Whenever a metadata repository (or by extension, metadata services) is discussed, the *Open Archives Initiative Protocol for Metadata Harvesting* (OAI-PMH) is always a name that cannot fail to come to light. Protocols such as Z39.50 may have more complete and stricter functions; for example, they delineate session management and results sets, and allow the specification of predicates that filter returned records. However, these functions are offset by an increase in difficulty of implementation with increased costs. The OAI technical framework is deliberately simple, with the intent of providing a low-barrier for participants, but not intended to replace other approaches (OAI-FAQ, 2002). Continued use of the OAI-PMH over time will prove whether such low-barrier interoperability is realistic and functional. Crucial to the understanding of harvesting, some time must be devoted to describing this important harvesting model in detail.

The word "archives" in the OAI-PMH should not be confused with conventional usage of the term archives. It refers to the e-print repositories established to communicate results of ongoing scholarly research, proceedings, peer review, and journal publication. The earliest of these was xxx (later arXiv), which began with high-energy physics (1991), and expanded to cover the entire field of physics and the related disciplines of mathematics, nonlinear sciences, and computer science (Carpenter, 2003). The development of the OAI-PMH may be considered as coalescing from three distinct stages. First, the *Santa Fe Convention* held in 1999 was the generative incarnation of the OAI-PMH, and the focus of that convention was to optimize discovery of e-prints. Secondarily, *OAI-PMH 1.0* (2001) introduced the unqualified Dublin Core element set as a baseline for metadata interoperability. The intent and focus expanded to facilitate the discovery of document-like objects. It was a low-barrier interoperability specification, based on the metadata harvesting model. *OAI-PMH 1.1* was a revision of the 1.0 specification, also published in 2001, taking into account changes of the emerging XML Schema specification. Third, and last (for the present), *OAI-PMH 2.0* was released in 2002, revised in 2004, and is a major revision of the protocol. Once again the focus of the protocol expanded to include "the recurrent exchange of metadata about resources between systems" (Carpenter, 2003).

Three important concepts are defined to distinguish between levels of metadata entities:

- *Resource:* A resource is the object that metadata is "about." The nature of a resource, be it physical or digital, and whether it is stored in the repository or is a constituent of another database is outside the scope of the OAI-PMH.
- *Item:* An item is a constituent of a repository from which metadata about a resource is disseminated. That metadata may be disseminated on-the-fly from the associated resource, cross-walked from some canonical form, or actually stored in the repository.
- *Record:* A record is metadata in a specific metadata format. A record is returned as an XML-encoded byte stream in response to a protocol request to disseminate a specific metadata format from a constituent item (Lagoze et al., 2004).

The OAI protocol defines a framework that facilitates two kinds of processes: (1) it allows *data providers* to administer systems that support the OAI-PMH as a means of exposing metadata; and (2) it allows *service providers* to use the metadata harvested from the OAI-PMH as a basis for building value-added services. By implementing this protocol, a digital library or system may *harvest* metadata from OAI-PMH-compliant repositories, or *expose* its metadata for others to harvest. In the case of OAI, harvesting refers specifically to the gathering of metadata from a number of distributed repositories into a combined data store (Lagoze et al., 2004; Carpenter, 2003). Figure 6-4-1 gives a simplified overview of the OAI-PMH structure.

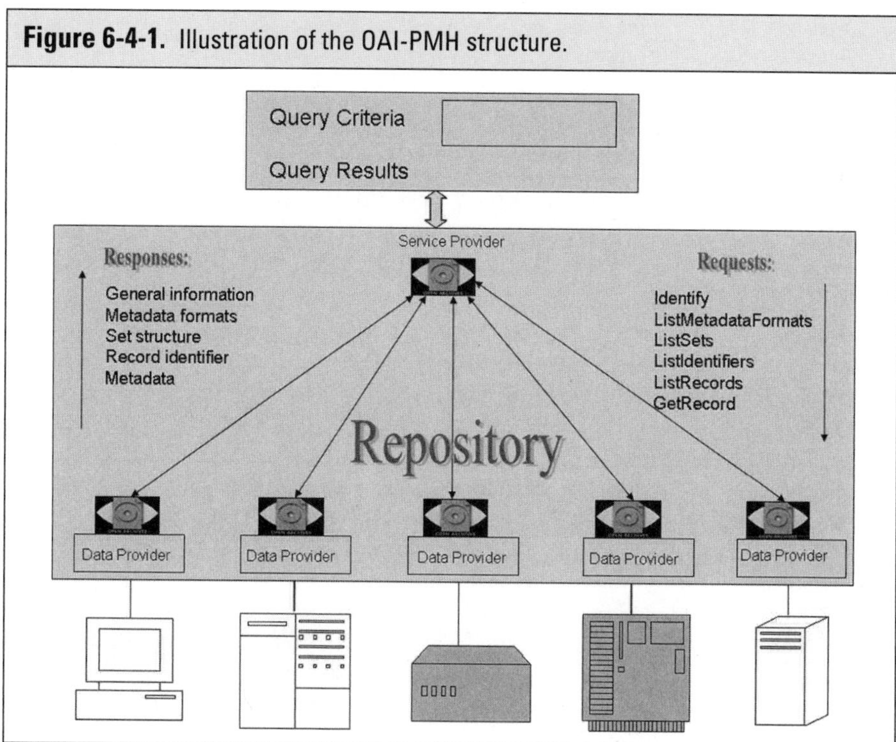

Figure 6-4-1. Illustration of the OAI-PMH structure.

6.4.3 OAI-PMH Commands

As a data communication protocol, OAI-PMH has two categories of commands: *requests* and *responses*. A repository is a network accessible server that can process the six OAI-PMH requests shown in Table 6-4-1, i.e., the six verbs used in the requests: *Identify*, *ListMetadataFormats*, *ListSets*, *ListIdentifiers*, *ListRecords*, and *GetRecord*. It is managed by a data provider to expose metadata to harvesters. Any repository can be either a data provider or harvester, or both. Each of the six verbs of the requests performs one task, as listed in Table 6-4-1.

Let us examine one record example to help understand verb actions. *getRecord* is used to retrieve an individual metadata record from a repository; this verb is required to use two arguments, *identifier* and *metadataPrefix*, which combine to request and retrieve a metadata record. For example, the resource "Paleontological Research Institution" has an identifier "oai:nsdl.org:nsdl.nsdl:00117" in the NSDL Metadata Repository (services.nsdl.org:8080/nsdloai/OAI). Entering the *identifier* and *metadataPrefix* "oai_dc" in the repository interface, the getRecord command will retrieve the record for the resource shown in Exhibit 6-4-1.

Table 6-4-1. The OAI-PMH requests and examples.

Request (Verb)	Definition	Example
GetRecord identifier metadataPrefix	Retrieve an individual metadata record from a repository	http://arXiv.org/oai2?verb=GetRecord&identifier=oai:arXiv.org:cs/0112017&metadataPrefix=oai_dc
Identify	Retrieve information about a repository	http://memory.loc.gov/cgi-bin/oai?verb=Identify
ListIdentifiers from until metadataPrefix set resumptionToken	An abbreviated form of ListRecords, retrieving only headers rather than records	http://an.oa.org/OAI-script?verb=ListIdentifiers&from=1998-01-15&metadataPrefix=oldArXiv&set=physics:hep
ListMetadataFormats identifier	Retrieve the metadata formats available from a repository	http://memory.loc.gov/cgi-bin/oai?verb=ListMetadataFormats
ListRecords from until set resumptionToken metadataPrefix	Harvest records from a repository	http://an.oa.org/OAI-script?verb=ListRecords&from=1998-01-15&set=physics:hep&metadataPrefix=oai_rfc1807
ListSets resumptionToken	Retrieve the set structure of a repository	http://an.oa.org/OAI-script?verb=ListSets

Exhibit 6-4-1. An example of OAI-PMH response to the getRecord request.

```
<?xml version="1.0" encoding="UTF-8" ?>
<OAI-PMH xmlns="http://www.openarchives.org/OAI/2.0/"
         xmlns:xsi="http://www.w3.org/2001/XMLSchema-instance"
         xsi:schemaLocation="http://www.openarchives.org/OAI/2.0/
         http://www.openarchives.org/OAI/2.0/OAI-PMH.xsd">
  <responseDate>2008-01-23T23:57:22Z</responseDate>
  <request identifier="oai:nsdl.org:nsdl.nsdl:00117" metadataPrefix="oai_dc"
   verb="GetRecord">http://services.nsdl.org:8080/nsdloai/OAI</request>
  <GetRecord>
    <record>
      <header>
        <identifier>oai:nsdl.org:nsdl.nsdl:00117</identifier>
              <datestamp>2006-05-17T13:00:25Z</datestamp>
        <setSpec>nsdl:nsdl</setSpec>
            </header>
      <metadata>
        <oai_dc:dc xmlns:oai_dc="http://www.openarchives.org/OAI/2.0/oai_dc/"
         xmlns:dc="http://purl.org/dc/elements/1.1/"
         xmlns:xsi="http://www.w3.org/2001/XMLSchema-instance"
         xsi:schemaLocation="http://www.openarchives.org/OAI/2.0/oai_dc/
         http://www.openarchives.org/OAI/2.0/oai_dc.xsd">
         <dc:title>Paleontological Research Institution</dc:title>
         <dc:subject>Balaenidae</dc:subject>
          ...
          <dc:language>en</dc:language>
          </oai_dc:dc>
      </metadata>
     <about>
       <nsdl_about xmlns="http://ns.nsdl.org/nsdl_about_v1.00"
        schemaVersion="1.00.000"
        xmlns:xsi="http://www.w3.org/2001/XMLSchema-instance"
        xsi:schemaLocation="http://ns.nsdl.org/nsdl_about_v1.00
        http://ns.nsdl.org/schemas/nsdl_about/nsdl_about_v1.00.xsd">
       ...
         <primaryIdentifier>http://www.priweb.org</primaryIdentifier>
         <link linkType="primaryCollection">oai:nsdl.org:nsdl.nsdl:00135</link>
            </nsdl_about>
      </about>
    </record>
  </GetRecord>
</OAI-PMH>
```

The request element in Exhibit 6-4-1 includes three parts: (1) the verb *GetRecord*, (2) the argument *identifier* in the form of a URI (=oai:arXiv.org:cs/0112017) as specified by OAI-PMH, and (3) the argument *metadataPrefix* (=oai_dc) that indicates the metadata format. This request generates a response from the server, which carries the record and matching ID number (identifier) to the one in the request element. The record is formatted in XML and organized into three parts: a header, a block of data based on DC metadata elements, and an optional "about" data block (Table 6-4-2).

Table 6-4-2. OAI-PMH record components and examples.		
Part	**Definition**	**Content of the Part**
header	Contains the unique identifier of the item and properties necessary for selective harvesting	unique identifier, datestamp, setSpec, status
metadata	A single manifestation of the metadata from an item	Dublin Core metadata elements without qualification
about	An **optional** and repeatable container to hold data about the metadata part of the record	rights statements, provenance statement

A *header* requires a unique identifier of the item, a datestamp, and optional setSpecs. The record in Exhibit 6-4-1 has one setSpec "nsdl," meaning that the item from which the record was disseminated belongs to the NSDL repository. A set is an optional construct for grouping items for selective harvesting and contains two required parts—*setSpec* and *setName*—and one optional part—*setDescription*. Repositories can design their own set list, which may be flat or hierarchical. A hierarchical set is presented here.

Subjects
Earth sciences
Sociology
Institutions
    Kent State University
    Syracuse University

And may be expressed as:

setName	*setSpec*
Institutions	institution
Kent State University	institution:kent
Syracuse University	institution:syracuse
Subjects	subject
Earth sciences	subject:earth
Sociology	subject:sociology

Having *setSpecs* is convenient for selective harvesting. If a harvester does not wish to harvest data from the entire repository, it can specify set membership as a criterion in order to harvest only the ones from *setSpecs*. The *metadata* section contains a complete Dublin Core metadata record (see Exhibit 6-4-1). The tag for each Dublin Core element is prefixed with its namespace, e.g., "<dc:title>."

The last section in a record is the optional *about*. When used, it provides information regarding the origins of the metadata part of the record, e.g., the example record shows that the origin of the metadata record is from NSDL by the tag <nsdl_about>, an identifier "oai:nsdl.org:nsdl.nsdl:00135," and datestamp "2002-07-04T00:32:58Z" (the last block in Exhibit 6-4-1, bold emphasis added).

OAI provides documentations for both implementation and implementers of a repository and also for the harvester. For those digital libraries who act as both harvesters and repositories, there are detailed instructions in the multipart Implementation *Guidelines for the Open Archives Initiative Protocol for Metadata Harvesting* (2005). OAI Repository Explorer (http://re.cs.uct.ac.za/, accessed 2007) is a tool provided to interactively test collections for compliance with the protocol. A variety of open source OAI tools have also been developed and used by members of the Open Archives Initiative community (www.openarchives.org/pmh/tools/tools.php, accessed 2007). All tools support the OAI-PMH v2.0 (some include legacy support for v1.0 and 1.1). Although free of charge, they are not guaranteed to be correct and free of error.

6.4.4 Support for Multiple-record Formats in OAI-PMH

Unqualified Dublin Core is the metadata format required for basic interoperability of OAI-PMH. When metadata records in a collection follow the metadata standard faithfully and without modification, it may not be difficult (ideally) for an OAI-PMH harvester to collect data. This rarely happens in the real world, however; most metadata applications will need to modify a standard (as discussed in the previous chapter). Whichever metadata format is chosen, Data Providers and Service Providers must reach agreement on its use, and the definition of an XML schema must be made publicly available for validation.

OAI-PMH uses XML Schemas to define record formats. OAI-PMH mandates the *oai_dc* schema as a minimum standard for interoperability. Technologically, *oai_dc* schema defines a container schema that is OAI-specific (namespace: www.openarchives.org/OAI/2.0/oai_dc/), and is hosted on the OAI Web site (www.openarchives.org/OAI/2.0/oai_dc.xsd). It imports a generic DC Metadata Element Set schema (namespace: http://purl.org/dc/elements/1.1/), which in turn is hosted on the DCMI site (http://dublincore.org/schemas/xmls/simpledc20021212.xsd). It also defines a container element, "dc," that lists the elements within the "dc" *container* that are allowable in oai_dc. Containers are places in OAI-PMH responses where XML that is compliant with any external schema may be supplied. Containers are utilized for extensibility and for community-specific enhancements. The OAI implementation guidelines provide a list of the existing optional containers, and links to existing schemas as well (Carpenter, 2003).

Metadata in any format can be exchanged using the OAI-PMH, but the prerequisite is that it must be encoded as XML, and an XML Schema for it must be defined. It is important to note the available XML Schema for MARC (www.openarchives.org/OAI/1.1/oai_marc.xsd) because the library communities have already hosted millions of MARC records. The XML Schema for the MARC metadata format has been successfully applied to MARC21 records. An online tutorial, *OAI for Beginners* (Carpenter, 2003), provides step-by-step instructions for adding new elements when oai_dc is not sufficient. The tasks are as follows:

- Create a name for the new schema.
- Create namespaces.
- Create the schema for the new elements.
- Create a "container schema."
- Validate the schema and records.
- Add to one's repository's "ListMetadataFormats."
- Add to one's repository's other verbs.
- Test that everything is operational and valid. (Carpenter, 2003: Chapter 5, Section 4)

This task-set can be referred to as a guide for a project developer who wants to use another metadata format. It is essential for metadata services to publish metadata schemas in these circumstances so that interested parties can obtain information about the structures and data models (for mapping purposes). As more and more metadata standards developers have developed XML schemas (and namespaces have been agreed-upon), deployment of these formats should become far smoother. To implement an existing metadata format, one must modify the "ListMetadataFormats" response to include the format one wishes to support. For example, the ADN metadata schema can be expressed as shown in Exhibit 6-4-2. Then next step requires extending the other verbs (*ListSets, ListIdentifiers, ListRecords, Identify,* and *GetRecord* requests) to accept the "metadataPrefix" set to "adn" and return records formatted appropriately.

6.5 Ensuring Optimal Metadata Discovery

For many years rich metadata resources had only been exposed to limited destinations and audiences (e.g. a library's catalog is not available for search through Internet search engines). It was only when OCLC's WorldCat opened its doors with its innovative program Open WorldCat and allowed Google (among other partners) to search and link to library catalogs (that had remained hidden behind OPACs of the world's libraries) that visibility dramatically increased. After a

Exhibit 6-4-2. Portion of the modified "ListMetadataFormats" responding to include ADN format.

```
...
<metadataFormat>
    <metadataPrefix>adn</metadataPrefix>
    <schema>http://www.dlese.org/Metadata/adn-item/0.6.50/record.xsd
</schema>
   <metadataNamespace>http://adn.dlese.org</metadataNamespace>
</metadataFormat>
...
```

pilot project in 2004, OCLC decided to allow access to the entire WorldCat collection of 53.3 million items, which linked to 928.6 million library holdings for "harvesting" by Google and Yahoo! Search (Quint, 2004). The movement to make library resources available from nonlibrary Web sites and give Web search engines the ability to guide users to library-owned materials has led to information professionals searching for methods to maximize the visibility of metadata for enhanced discovery, resource identification, and direct linkage.

Because of the relatively new and recent phenomenon of search engine hegemony, information-seekers do not immediately come to the library as a first choice. Search engines are increasingly becoming the first gate that users approach when searching for any information. The OCLC membership report *Perceptions of Libraries and Information Resources* (OCLC, 2005) indicates that 84 percent of information searches begin with a search engine, and the majority go to Google. Library Web sites were selected by just 1 percent of respondents as the source used to begin an information search, and only 2 percent start from a topic-specific Web site. Among college students, only 2 percent start their search at a library Web site (OCLC, 2005: 1–17). Thousands of well-designed portals, highly functional library OAPCs, and rich and comprehensive digital collections (many built at high cost) are facing huge competition for a fair share of users' attention. Their contents (many still have restricted access) therefore cannot be utilized as expected or desired. Furthermore, many digital collections and digital libraries started with one-term funding are stalled in development after the initial funding ceases.

Optimal usage of metadata will enable content to be found by a larger number of access aids, extending beyond portals and OPACs to the major search engines as well. With enhanced metadata exposure, materials held in digital collections will increase their visibility (and consequently user awareness), and thereby encourage uses (and appreciation) based on precision, quality, and relevance. For these reasons, we focus here on examining the role of data providers rather than harvesters or aggregators.

6.5.1 Metadata Retrieval

To understand the approaches that enhance metadata usage, this section introduces a brief overview to clarify the functions and definitions of the retrieval of data and metadata. Metadata retrieval for cross-database searching follows two models that have been used in the information world: *metasearching* and *federated searching*. To the user who does not care where the information is (or who packaged it), the search interface may provide no alert to any difference regardless of the search being processed through metasearching or federated searching, based on a distributed or centralized model. However, the search results can be decidedly different in terms of quantity, coverage, ranking, and relevance.

Metasearching is a process in which the user submits a query to numerous information resources simultaneously and receives integrated results on a single interface (Figure 6-5-1). The system sends the user's query to the search targets and brings back the retrieved results. The generalized Google search provides a typical example: sources that have been indexed by the search engine's crawler technology may be searched, retrieved, and accessed. But instead of preprocessing the data, the system processes it only when the user launches a query. Therefore, metasearch systems are based on *just-in-time* processing (Sadeh, 2006).

Metasearch systems therefore hold information about how a resource can be searched and how results can be extracted from it, but they do not contain any of the data stored in any of the resources that they can access. In other words, a metasearch system is programmed to search various databases, display results to users, but has no control of how deep (or what) it can search, how to rank relevance of results, and bring results, i.e., *hits*, to reasonable proportions. Its limits to accessing deep-Web and Internet resources are a major weakness. Deep-Web refers to Web content that is not part of the surface Web indexed by search engines, such as sites that limit access to their pages, sites that require registration and login (password-protected resources), and dynamic pages that are returned in response to a submitted query or accessed only through a form. The large volume of documents housed in databases is not usually available to Internet search engines because of the limitations of crawler technology.

Metasearching concerns revolve around the accuracy of searches and the burden that remote searches place on target resources. A countermeasure to the problem is the NISO *Metasearch Initiative* launched in 2003, with the aim of

Figure 6-5-1. A simplified illustration of metasearching.

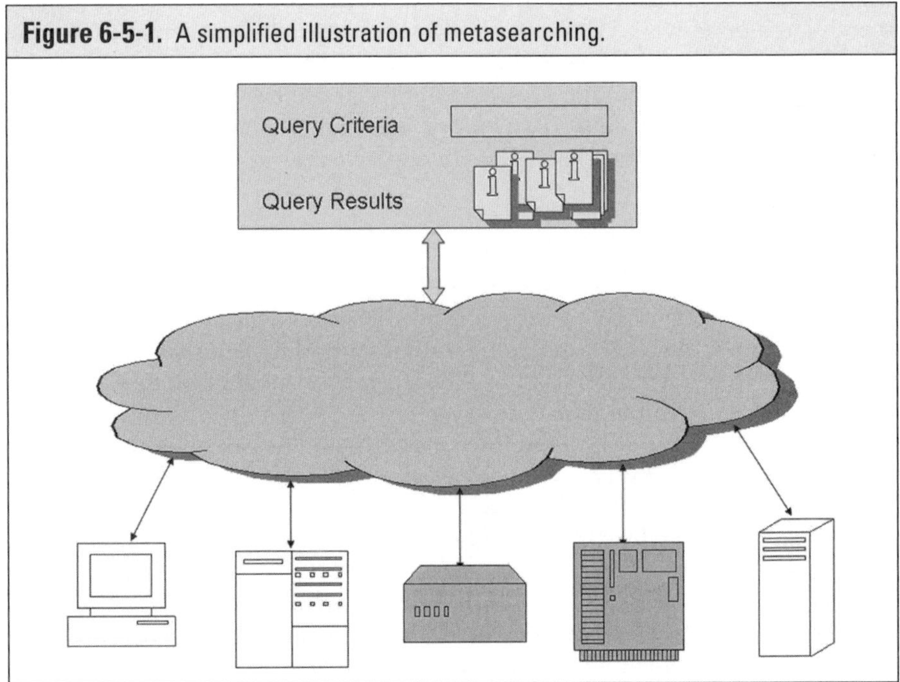

providing the industry a set of standards that will facilitate optimal metasearching. Group 2 Collection Descriptions' tasks include creating two element sets to be used by metasearch (and other) applications: collections descriptions (i.e., human-readable text to describe the contents of a database) and service descriptions (to be used by applications to access remote database services). NISO Z39.91-200x, *Collection Description Specification*, defines a method for describing collections—a collection is defined as an aggregation of items. It takes the form of a *Dublin Core Collection Description Application Profile* (DCCDAP) (Dublin Core Collection Description Working Group, 2007), to be used for simple collection-level descriptions, suitable for a broad range of collections, and providing support for collections' discovery; elements employed are associated with six namespaces (NISO, 2005a). A related standard, NISO Z39.92-200x, *Information Retrieval Service Description Specification*, is intended to allow the description of information retrieval-oriented services to enable aggregation of those descriptions into service registries. Subsequently the descriptions may be used in machine-to-machine communication to maximize automatic service discovery and interaction. The standard provides a single schema in which records may be exchanged and processed by client software, and thus allows the development of standards-based software agents that can be expected to work with other vendors' information retrieval systems (NISO, 2005b). This initiative was made possible by the collaborative efforts of numerous stakeholders—publishers, librarians, and metasearch system vendors.

Federated searching substantially resolves the problem of search engines being unable to access and process deep-Web resources. In federated searching, a wealth of information is incorporated into a single repository and is processed *prior to* the user's search. The system then searches a local repository that was created earlier from the previously accumulated data of numerous resources (Figure 6-5-2). To users, the search process itself and the interface of searching may be the same as used on major search engines: issues a query—receives search results. The results, however, are different because of the quantity, coverage, and ranking processing provided by the federated searching services. Federated searching is also referred to as *just-in-case* processing in contrast to the just-in-time metasearch systems. This preprocessing affords new opportunities for search methodologies and presentation of results. An example would be a ranking algorithm that can be applied to each data element stored in the repository. Google Scholar, many digital libraries, and Web portals are examples of entities that employ federated searching.

Federated searching has been applied to metadata databases that are built on two different yet interrelated routes: union catalogs and metadata repositories.

1. Centralized union catalogs have long been proven to be a functional model in library and information services. Usually data are contributed by members following mandated metadata standards and standards application instructions.
   - OCLC's WorldCat is the largest and most comprehensive union catalog on the planet. It had more than 88 million bibliographic records as of

Figure 6-5-2. A simplified illustration of federated searching.

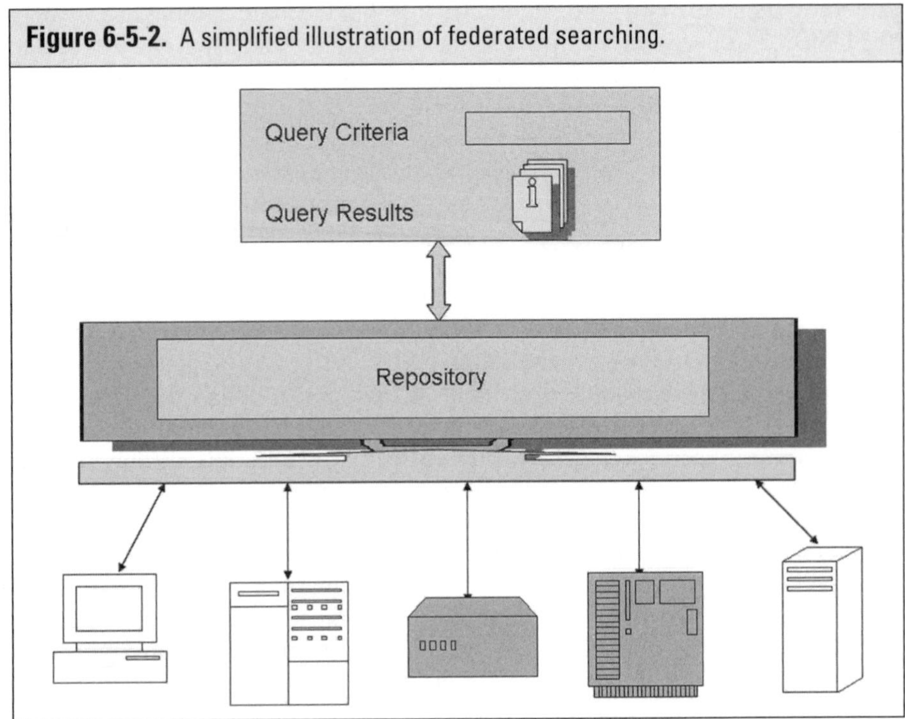

October 2007, with one record being added every ten seconds (OCLC, 2007: WorldCat facts and statistics, www.oclc.org/worldcat/statistics/default.asp). OCLC's *Bibliographic Formats and Standards* (3rd edition, 2006) is a guide to the bibliographic information necessary for records in WorldCat. It provides tagging conventions, input standards, and guidelines for entering information. Heretofore MARC and AACR2 have been the dominant standards that have been applied. For members who use Dublin Core instead, their records do not conform to AACR2.

- The Online Archive of California (OAC: www.oac.cdlib.org/, accessed 2007), a core component of the California Digital Library (CDL), is another large union catalog and brings together historical materials from a variety of California institutions which include museums, historical societies, and archives. The OAC hosts finding aids that are encoded with the EAD format and are contributed to by participating institutions. In addition, it hosts digital content described within those finding aids, including images and texts (texts are encoded in the *Text Encoding Initiative* [TEI] format). For search and delivery of EAD finding aids, full-text documents, and images, the OAC utilizes the CDL-developed eXtensible Text Framework (XTF) system. XTF consists of Java Servlets and tools that permit users to perform Web-based searching and retrieval of electronic documents (OAC, 2005: Technical Information).

2. Centralized metadata repositories bring new opportunities a well as challenges to traditional union catalogs already in place (see OAI protocol adoption, Section 6.4). The major difference between metadata repositories and traditional union catalogs is the diversity offered by the former in terms of sources, contributors, applied metadata standards, and management.

When thousands of responses are returned to a query entered by a user through either metasearching or federated searching, results showing on the first page (or within the top 50) may seize the user's attention. Thus, the strategies of discovery that appropriately respond (increase visibility) to a search engine's relevance-ranking feature become critical. Although metadata creators put great effort into adhering to accepted schemas and standards, there is still a chance that a search may not return decently relevant results to a user's query and that the relevant results may not be ranked highly enough by a search engine to ensure visibility. Maximizing metadata discovery should be a clearly defined goal and task that goes hand-in-hand with metadata creation.

6.5.2 Metadata Exposure Methods

Figure 6-5-3 compares the difference for end users before and after exposing metadata. Primary access to metadata is usually found where the metadata is hosted, e.g., the simple and advanced search interfaces of a digital collection or library. Regardless of multifaceted Boolean logic–enabled search and browse interfaces that might have been assembled, the user is restricted to a solo "front door"—the bottleneck that impedes maximal and efficient usage of content (as in the BEFORE part of Figure 6-5-3). If the same content is exposed to multiple access points, the opportunity for content discovery by users is also equally multiplied (as in the AFTER part of Figure 6-5-3).

Exposing metadata can take place in different selective contexts: becoming a data provider for a well-defined metadata repository, registering as a Static OAI Repository at a Static Repository Gateway, exposing metadata to any OAI Service Provider, exposing metadata via distributed searching, and exposing to large commercial aggregators.

1. Becoming a data provider for a well-defined metadata repository: NSDL, the Music Sheet Consortia, and the UIUC (University of Illinois Urbana-Champaign) Digital Gateway to Cultural Heritage Materials are well-established repositories that have clearly defined target audiences, collection policies, and best practice guides for contributing metadata. NSDL, for example, focuses on high-quality educational resources. In his presentation on metasearching, Tennant (2005) reported a search for "tsunami" for undergraduate students using Google Scholar, Google, and the NSDL. The first page of results are: Google Scholar—no items with general information that an undergraduate would find useful; Google—three results with useful scientific information, seven relief effort sites, and at least seven sponsored links (advertisements); and the NSDL—20 items with useful scientific information. It is not surprising to see more repositories being established, especially for educational purposes.

Figure 6-5-3. Exposing metadata to enhance the visibility of content.

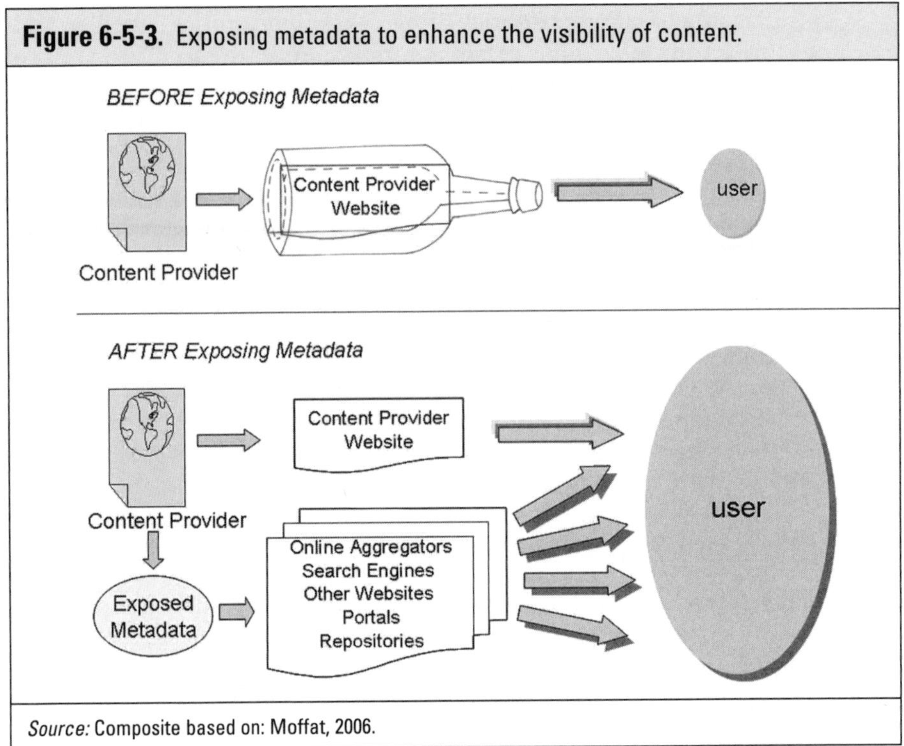

Source: Composite based on: Moffat, 2006.

2. Registering as a Static OAI Repository at a Static Repository Gateway: This approach may include overlap with the cases introduced previously, but because it is especially suited for small collections, it is presented here to draw more attention to this useful and effective method. Some collections are built on the basis of one-time funded digitization programs, or are infrequently updated after the project period has ended. For these small and relatively stable collections, static OAI repositories can be built with reasonable effort and cost. Moffat (2006) describes a static OAI repository as "a single file" containing all of the metadata records. By registering the file at a remote static repository gateway, all OAI-PMH requests for the metadata are handled by the remote static repository gateway. All metadata, identifiers, and datestamps managed in this single XML file must conform to the rules detailed in the Specification for an OAI Static Repository and an OAI Static Repository Gateway (OAI, 2004). The file may be created manually with an XML editing tool, or a text processing application. Alternatively, a Static Repository may be generated periodically by a script that extracts information from an existing database (Lagoze et al., 2005).

Moffat presents a very useful case example of such an XML file, which may be found online (hairst.cdlr.strath.ac.uk/repositories/spring.xml). It was created by the Springburn Virtual Museum for the Glasgow Digital Library project. Originally this metadata was stored in a Microsoft Access database. A simple script was created to generate the static repository file from the database. The file was then made available on the Web and registered with a static repository gateway hosted at the OAI Scotland Information Service. At a very low cost, the gateway enables access to the static repository and exposes the existing metadata for harvesting (Moffat, 2006).

A *Static Repository Gateway* provides intermediation for one or more Static Repositories. It must respond to all six OAI-PMH requests issued against the Static Repository base URL for the length of the intermediation interaction. The Gateway uses the most up-to-date version of Static Repositories with different guidelines as defined by OAI specifications. These different guidelines include the general ones for repository, harvester, and aggregator implementers, the ones for optional containers, and the community guidelines for community-specific implementers such as the e-prints community (Lagoze et al., 2005). The advantages of Static Repositories technology are twofold: it offers a simpler method of participating, and it allows a data provider to participate in multiple services. The technical requirements, at times a necessary burden to small collections, can now be handled by a third party, which relieves small collections from the technical and financial burdens. STARGATE (Static Repository Gateway and Toolkit: cdlr.strath.ac.uk/stargate/tools.htm, accessed 2007), funded by the Joint Information Systems Committee (JISC) and hosted by the Centre for Digital Library Research at the University of Strathclyde in Glasgow, has produced a number of tools to assist small journal publishers and other participants in such OAI-based services.

3. Exposing metadata to any OAI Service Provider: As discussed, OAI-PMH is a simple protocol that allows data providers to expose their metadata for harvesting and can be used for a wide range of digital materials. Its nature, contingent upon common underlying Web standards such as HTTP, XML and XML schemas, makes it very easy to implement for services, and has promoted its wide adoption on a global scale. By registering with OAI-PMH conformant repositories, data providers publicize that they have adopted the OAI-PMH. A data provider may choose to register as an independent provider or as a member of a group or community-affiliated data providers. In the latter case, the friends container in the Identify response may be used by repositories to list confederate repositories that provide an automatic mechanism allowing harvesters to discover other interesting or valuable repositories. Widespread use of this container provides a decentralized mechanism by which harvesters can discover other repositories (OAI-FAQ, 2002).

A data provider who registers with the OAI must agree to make this information public. There are no provisions for restricting access to the registry database. The protocol mandates a common metadata format: simplified Dublin Core and OAI-PMH. These allow communities to expose metadata in non-DC formats as long as the metadata records are structured as XML data, and have a corresponding XML schema for validation. Tools may need to be developed by providers who use non-DC formats. Otherwise, many free software programs (freeware or open source) can assist data providers. Some collaborators who are already data providers also may be willing to host the data of content providers. The OAI Web site has more than 900 registered data providers. The registration data base serves as a publicly accessible list of OAI-PMH conformant repositories, thus making it simple for service providers to discover sites from which metadata can be harvested.

4. *Exposing metadata via distributed searching:* Protocols such as Z39.50 have more complete functionality than OAI. For example, Z39.50 facilitates access control, accounting/resource control, and duplicate detection that OAI does not have. ("Z39.50" refers to the International Standard, ISO 23950: "Information Retrieval (Z39.50): Application Service Definition and Protocol Specification," and to ANSI/NISO Z39.50). More functionality means more requirements for implementation. Z39.50 is a client/server protocol for searching and retrieving information from remote computer databases. It specifies procedures and formats for a client to search a database provided by a server, retrieve database records, and perform a number of related information retrieval functions such as sort and browse (Z39.50-2003). Because it was developed in 1995 when most Web technology was still under development, a number of later initiatives, known collectively as ZING (**Z**39.50 **I**nternational: **N**ext **G**eneration), have attempted to bring Z39.50 up-to-date with the Web HTTP environment. SRU (Search/Retrieve via URL) protocol, developed on the basis of the fundamental aspects of Z39.50 are less complex, easier to comprehend, and simpler to implement. SRU provides a means for expressing search requests encoded in URLs, sending them to servers and retrieving results in a well-defined XML format. There is also a binding of the same protocol semantics with SOAP (Simple Object Access Protocol) so that client requests and server responses are returned as SOAP messages (HTTP is not used). This binding was previously known as SRW (Search-Retrieve Webservice) and now as "SRU over SOAP" (SRU Meeting Report, March 1–2, 2006). Similar to Z39.50, this protocol is commonly used in the library environment.

5. *Exposure to large commercial aggregators (such as Google Scholar and Yahoo!):* This is undoubtedly another good way of maximizing the use of content. However, this may need the establishment of one-to-one metadata exchange agreements between aggregators and content providers (based on aggregator-preferred proprietary means for collecting metadata). When a large number of different aggregator services exist, big or small, this mechanism does not look as efficient as the OAI-PMH, which supports the exposure of multiple forms of metadata and enables interoperability for the broadest possible audience.

6.5.3 Other Approaches

Interest in Web 2.0 technologies is growing from both the virtual community as well as technology developers. The technologies can also be used to make content discoverable through metadata. Some of these approaches merit further attention.

RSS (Really Simple Syndication) is a very flexible format now widely used to expose metadata. An RSS file (a.k.a. RSS feed or RSS channel) consists of a list of items, each of which contains a title, description, and link to a Web object—typical metadata, with the full content itself being available separately and accessed by the link in the RSS file (see Exhibit 6-5-1). Once an RSS file is made available on a Web site, interested parties can simply gather the file from the site and reuse the content in a variety of ways (RSS Advisory Board, 2007).

Included in 2.0.1—the latest stable version of this format—are channel metadata such as *link, title, description, image* (allows one to specify a thumbnail image to display with the feed), *webmaster, managingEditor,* and *lastBuildDate* (shows when the feed was last updated). *Items* have the standard *link, title,* and *description* metadata, as well as other information.

The most notable is the *RDF Site Summary 1.0 Modules: Dublin Core* (web.resource.org/rss/1.0/modules/dc/), developed in 2000. It attaches DC metadata to both feeds (in the channel metadata) and to individual items. Each of the various versions of RSS takes a different slant. In general, RSS 1.0 is extensible and targets information objects for those who are considering integration with the Semantic Web systems (see Chapter 9). RSS 2.0 is very simple and easy to author by hand. Atom is another version that has become an Internet Engineering Task Force (IETF) standard.

Wikipedia can also be used to publicize a digital collection that has been constructed with structured metadata. Librarians at the University of Washington (UW) use Wikipedia to extend digital collections for contents that are subject-specific or reflective of communities of practice (Lally and Dunford, 2007). Despite their digital collections already being harvested and heavily used by people from all over the world and having Google and its affiliates as top

Exhibit 6-5-1. An example of a minimal RSS 2.0 feed.

```
<?xml version="1.0"?>
<rss version="2.0">
  <channel>
    <title>Example Channel</title>
    <link>http://example.com/</link>
    <description>My example channel</description>
    <item>
       <title>News for September the Second</title>
       <link>http://example.com/2002/09/02</link>
       <description>other things happened today</description>
    </item>
    <item>
       <title>News for September the First</title>
       <link>http://example.com/2002/09/01</link>
    </item>
  </channel>
</rss>
```

Source: Revised based on www.mnot.net/rss/tutorial/.

referrers of users to the collections, librarians decided to add links in Wikipedia to the UW Image collections managed by the CONTENTdm Software Suite. For the entries already existing in Wikipedia, summaries were written based on the existing description of the collection and additional subject terms were added or emphasized where appropriate. For a unique topic that has no articles in Wikipedia (or the subject is not adequately covered) new articles are written, as with the J. Willis Sayre Photographs Digital Collection of 9,856 images of those who performed in Seattle between about 1900 and 1955. A one-year tracking study revealed a steady increase in usage from Wikipedia referrals. The results of an additional 10,000 plus referrals from Wikipedia were analyzed based on the articles accessed. Because of Wikipedia's heavy use, some of the articles that UW librarians contributed appear as mirrored content (with links intact) in several other online dictionaries and encyclopedias, and even non-English language Wikipedias. The librarians view this as a very low-cost way to enhance access to UW digital collections, as well as an effective way to participate in the creation of resources that are used by millions around the world. As Markey (2007) has pointed out, Google and other Web search engines give people a good start; with Wikipedia links in hand, users receive a running start for building on their basic understanding of a topic.

For individual Web pages, does the *embedded metadata* increase their visibility on search engines' results pages? The short answer is yes, but visibility is also decided by other factors. Once a page is indexed, the most important question concerns its rank among the many pages returned for a given search. Zhang and Dimitroff (2005) conducted an experiment on eight search engines, the findings from which suggest that in general:

- Web pages with metadata elements achieve better visibility performance than those without metadata elements.
- Web pages with keywords appearing in three metadata fields (*title*, *subject*, and *description*) achieve better visibility performance than other possible combinations.
- Values in the *subject* element play an extremely important role in improving Web page visibility in a search engine return list.
- The position of keywords will also determine the difference, ranking in order from the best: (1) keywords in *title* + *subject* + *description*, (2) keywords in *subject*, (3) keywords in *title* + *description*, and (4) keywords in *subject* + *description*. In any event, these keywords should be extracted from the Web page itself, particularly from title and full-text.

These experiments have at least reflected current practices of the search engines. However it is important to remember that there is no generic or single strategy that is used among the search engines. Their algorithms and criteria are also changing without notice; hence the findings summarized above may already be obsolete.

Outside of the United States, particularly in developing countries, a number of *legacy database systems* are still in use by libraries, documentation centers, and nonprofit institutions for managing bibliographic information. Among them, a widely used system is Micro CDS/ISIS, an advanced nonnumerical information storage and retrieval software program developed by UNESCO in 1985, which in turn was based on the CDS/ISIS system developed in the late 1960s for mainframe computers (www.unesco.org/isis). The popularity of the software package is attested to so that "[w]hile the official user register includes at present more than 100,000 institutions and individuals using this software, the real number of beneficiaries can probably be multiplied several times" (UNESCO, 2006a). Currently there are national distributors in some 90 countries (CDS/ISIS distributors, updated June 2006). A new utility called XML2ISIS now enables completing the "Export to XML" function of CDS/ISIS' Winisis 1.4 and is proposing XML as an alternate data exchange format to the ISO2709:1996 *Format for Information Exchange*. The official decision made after a conference of experts is to develop a new multiplatform, stable graphical user interface to manage ISIS databases (UNESCO, 2006b).

Jayakanth et al. (2005) reported *making legacy databases OAI-compliant* through both static and dynamic approaches. In the static approach for a small (less than 5,000 records) database, the database records are exported to a textual file. This file is then converted into the format that conforms to the static repository XML file and is ingested into an OAI-compliant tool developed for individual use to archive documents. Alternatively, the XML file can be made OAI-compliant through the intermediation of a static repository gateway. In a dynamic approach there is a direct interaction with the database rather than an interaction with a static file. The researchers use a freeware gateway tool called "wxis" for database connectivity to solve the problem of when no ODBC (Open Database Connectivity) or JDBC (Java Database Connectivity) drivers exist for CDS/ISIS, it is still possible to have database connectivity. This approach also requires developing an intermediary program that can accept OAI requests and translate them into a corresponding meaningful search expression for CDS/ISIS databases. The search expression is then used by the gateway tool for database interaction. The resultant records from the database interaction are encoded in XML as required for OAI-compliance. Jayakanth et al. (2005) provide demonstration of harvesting metadata from a few sample CDS/ISIS databases using the "Arc" software. Arc (http://dlib.cs.odu.edu/#arc) and OAIster (see Setion 6.4) are both OAI-based service providers.

A *search plug-in* allows a user to add collections to the search box of many Web browsers. University libraries have begun to provide instructions for students to download search plug-ins of the library's search systems and set them as search providers in the built-in Web browser search box in Internet Explorer 7, Firefox 2, or Navigator 9.0. The Open WorldCat program also provides similar plug-ins to be installed on partner sites. The search plug-in features may be available only to some browsers; however, a localized and integrated tool introduces both users and libraries to the plug-in advantages. Examples of such instructions can be found at the OAIster Web site (www.lib.umich.edu/labs/search/, accessed 2007) and various Stanford University Libraries Web sites such as the Lane Medical Library (http://lane.stanford.edu/services/tools/searchExtensions.html?template=none).

6.6 Summary

Metadata services control and manage the semantics and syntax of metadata schemas, records production, and communication processes. Registries function as a clearinghouse for metadata elements, vocabularies, and crosswalks between elements in different standards and application profiles. Metadata repositories offer mechanisms for import/export, storage, and the management of metadata records. Development and production services use registries and repositories to ensure the consistency and quality of metadata record generation, which in turn contributes new and updated information for registries and repositories.

Metadata services are a set of highly technical processes that need the support of a variety of enabling technologies, coupled with clear policies and procedures to address critical issues of copyright and workflow management. Regardless of how metadata services are to be carried out and by whom, a close collaboration between both computer science and library and information science personnel is vital to ensure compliance and precision. A new dimension that focuses on maximizing metadata discoverability requires that metadata services engage all interested parties to integrate metadata services into the larger scenario of information seeking in the digital age.

For such large-scale integration and implementation to take place, the decisive factor of quality control must be clear and coherent, and applied with a rigor that ensures the optimal conditions for metadata visibility. With this central thought in mind, we turn to the subject of the next chapter: quality control.

Suggested Readings

Baker, Thomas, Christophe Blanchi, Dan Brickley, Erik Duval, Rachel Heery, Pete Johnston, Leonid Kalinichenko, Heike Neuroth, and Shigeo Sugimoto. 2002. "Principles of Metadata Registries: A White Paper of the DELOS Workshop Group on Registries." DELOS Network of Excellence on Digital Libraries. Available: http://delos-noe.iei.pi.cnr.it/activities/standardizationforum/Registries.pdf.

ISO/IEC 11179:2004. *Information Technology—Metadata Registries (MDR)—Part 1: Framework*, 2nd ed. Geneva: International Standards Organization (ISO). Available: http://metadata-stds.org/11179/.

Lagoze, Carl, Herbert van de Sompel, Michael Nelson, and Simeon Warner, eds. 2004. *The Open Archives Initiative Protocols for Metadata Harvesting*. OAI. Available: www.openarchives.org/OAI/openarchivesprotocol.html.

van Veen, Theo, and Bill Oldroyd. 2004. "Search and Retrieval in the European Library: A New Approach." *D-Lib Magazine* [Online] 10, no. 2. Available: www.dlib.org/dlib/february04/vanveen/02vanveen.html.

Exercises

1. Give three reasons why metadata services are important for digital libraries or collections. Use a specific case or context to discuss the importance of metadata services.
2. Which types of metadata services are used for which purposes? Use a table to list the types of metadata services in the row heading and purposes in the column heading and then fill in the types and purposes in the table cells.
3. What are the required and optional description fields for a metadata registry record? Follow the examples in DCMI Metadata Registry (dublincore.org/dcregistry/navigateServlet) to create two records, each for an element or term from your metadata element set. Each record should include a table display and an RDF/XML record that is linked to the table display.
4. What methods are used in building metadata repositories and what standards are involved in this process?
5. How do metadata services facilitate information retrieval? Use a table to list the ways that metadata services facilitate information retrieval and the technical requirements involved in the process.

7

Metadata Quality Measurement and Improvement

From individual data sets to large-scale digital libraries, metadata allows enhanced description, improved classification, and more rational organization. Applying metadata, however, does not automatically improve information access or the usability of library resources. Metadata services are based on the tenet that high-quality metadata will ensure search results that are highly relevant, largely complete, and have enhanced utility.

7.1 Quality of Metadata

The usefulness and usability of a digital library's collections are dependent on the quality and quantity of the documents archived. These are equally dependent upon the quality of the metadata that structures and supports the usability and administration of those resources. Metadata, as with the resources and documents of a digital library, may have different quality levels (Duval et al., 2002). Many project developers have already spent a significant amount of time, effort, and money building high-quality collections. However, no matter how high the standards and useful the collections, metadata is at the forefront of user interaction. For instance, the National Science Digital Library (NSDL) has become a primary reference source for K–12 education. It enables the abilities of students and teachers to discover, explore, and retrieve relevant resources and assess their purpose or suitability for a particular pedagogical purpose. To achieve that goal, the resources must rely heavily on the descriptive metadata attached to them.

Metadata bears the major responsibility for presenting the contents of a collection to its users. If some portions of the metadata in the metadata database or repository are of poor or inconsistent quality, there may very well be a detrimental impact on users' continued use and adoption of the collection(s) as a primary resource. Even one item of incorrect information or one poor record has the potential to be counterproductive to the primary purpose served by otherwise excellent digital resources. Low-quality metadata will result in low recall and poor precision in retrieval; low-quality metadata will fail to direct access to relevant resources; and, low-quality metadata will be cost-inefficient (in time and money). Overall, low-quality metadata will have a negative impact on user perceptions of the collection's quality (and its usability).

Database quality emerged as an area of considerable concern only in recent decades. Errors in databases can be a minor nuisance or present major obstacles, and thereby significantly reduce recall, relevance, and precision in information retrieval. In the library and information science world, the literature on database quality has been concerned primarily with bibliographic databases, and considerable research has been devoted to data quality and methodologies for enhanced characteristics, error detection, error correction (quality control), record duplicates checking, and improved authority control. In the 1980s and early 1990s, requests for quality control for online bibliographic database services and library utilities were heard from a variety of users (O'Neill and Vizine-Goetz, 1988; O'Neill, 1992; Zeng, 1993a).

With movement toward large-scale digital libraries and the development of new metadata standards since the mid-1990s, project developers who experimented with collaborative and shared repositories have become aware of a new problem. Library growth has caused problems with quality of metadata in shared repositories and an instability that is too significant to neglect if digital libraries are to function effectively. Although quality issues had been examined for years before digital libraries began to develop, the problems described by those researchers were relatively easy to solve. Before various metadata standards were developed in the 1990s and applied to digital collections, most shared bibliographical databases used the same standards; records contributing to library union catalogs usually followed the protocols of MARC standards and *AACR2* rules. Standardized, enforced, descriptive, and measurement criteria ensured good records and good collections as defined by contributors to union catalogs.

Present-day metadata repositories have encountered more complex problems than union catalogs because current metadata records might come with very different metadata formats from a variety of practitioners. The Higher Level Skills for Industry Repository (HLSI) is an example where authors may upload their own resources and add their own metadata instances to this repository for digital learning objects. The repository is a consortium of more than ten metadata-contributing partner organizations. Not surprisingly, the HLSI project team observed that obtaining consistent metadata content is a major difficulty (Barker and Ryan, 2003). Typically, another example is provided by the NSDL, which has included 206 NSF-funded projects as of 2006 (NSDL Fact Sheet, 2006). A key component of the NSDL is the Metadata Repository, a compilation of derived metadata records from metadata providers (and copies of the native metadata records), which are maintained by the NSDL. A variety of metadata standards have been used by these providers; clearly the problem of maintaining high-quality and consistent records in an information system is magnified in an interorganizational system. In systems as just described, metadata creators have various levels of expertise about standards, and the problems are exacerbated by the absence of a central metadata authority and management oversight.

Quality management is of utmost importance for today's metadata repositories. Those issues need to be assessed and addressed as early as possible so that quality assurance systems can be developed and solutions implemented before collections reach the point where rectification of quality becomes difficult, if not impossible. As digital library creators, and as a profession, our paramount concern is to understand the unknown impact of open systems, combined with sophisticated interoperability and extensibility of technical principles, on high-quality metadata production. We ignore metadata quality issues at our own peril, and run the risk of creating large-scale collections with significant flaws. Again, those flaws may result in a wide range of deleterious effects and negative user perceptions of the library that might lead to the abandonment of these valuable resources.

7.2 Functional Requirements of Metadata Systems

The concern about metadata quality also leads to questions about what is meant by good or bad quality when measuring metadata records or metadata systems. Is a metadata record containing the most detailed description, e.g., 50 specific statements, necessary or complete? One approach is to define the functional requirements of metadata systems for different needs.

Chapter 3 discussed issues of communicating about the functional requirements in designing metadata schemas. A "wish list" for digital library system designers was presented so users could search records by Title, Author name, Keyword, Type of document, Publication, Conference name, Year, and so on. The assumption is that if a system is to satisfy the user's need, e.g., searching by *format* of document, there must be an element in the metadata records that will describe the documents' format(s). The phenomenon of missing—or missed—records then occurs: a system's indexing and searching algorithm as well as its interface might have been designed according to a "wish list" of functional requirements, but the metadata records to be indexed might not provide the required data. The initial result is that while browsing a collection, information based on document format might be missing, as shown in Figure 7-2-1.

A further search using advanced "Search by Resource Format" filter would actually be conducted through only a portion (not the whole) of all records that provide *format* information (Figure 7-2-2). Ordinarily a user would not be aware that he or she was conducting a search that would not access the entire database.

The reasons for missing information and disconnection with the interface design could be multifactorial:

1. the metadata schema might not have included such an element;
2. the metadata schema does include such an element, but no authority or sets of guidelines that enforce the use of this element; therefore, all or part of the records do not include such data;
3. the information about *format* is put under a wrong element, e.g., *type*, so that the values in this field will not be correctly indexed for *format*; or

Figure 7-2-1. A Search result display showing missing information.

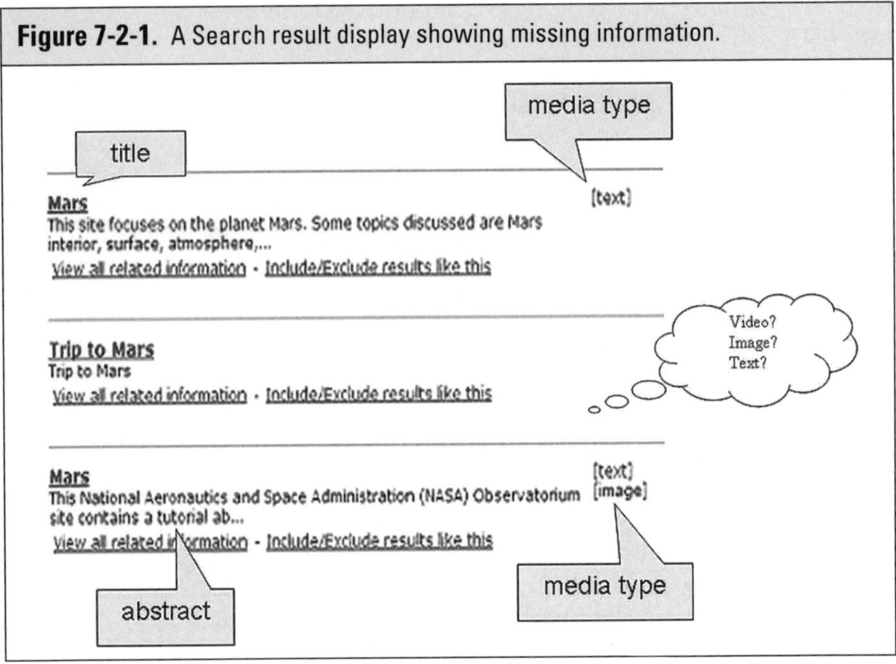

Figure 7-2-2. Advanced filters that might have been applied to just portions of database records.

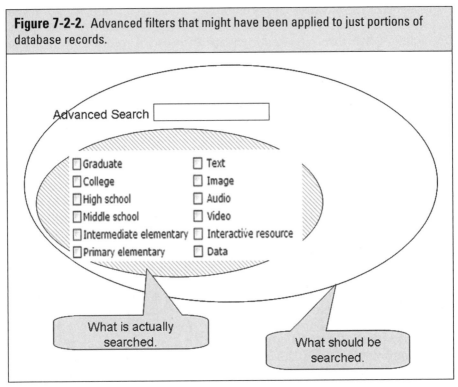

Advanced Search

Graduate
College
High school
Middle school
Intermediate elementary
Primary elementary

Text
Image
Audio
Video
Interactive resource
Data

What is actually searched.

What should be searched.

4. the values are lost when the metadata records are converted from one database to another due to incorrect mapping.

The unfortunate truth is even where there is a good metadata schema, it might easily lay buried under careless execution. Poor implementation will impede communication and usability of even the best schema. The same schema and its elements, when employed appropriately, will allow obscure data lying in the depths of an ocean to rise to the sunlit surface of comprehensible information. Functional requirements for a metadata system must be implemented and evaluated at all levels, and must include all components of a system with its attendant processes and procedures.

7.3 Quality Measurement with Different Granularities

Recognition is increasing throughout the information communities that some poor-quality data exist in most (if not all) online databases, yet there is little agreement on the magnitude or exact nature of the problem. The consensus, however, is that metadata quality is clearly a multidimensional concept. Metadata quality can be measured at different granularities (collection, record, and element), with various indicators such as completeness, correctness, and consistency. In a metadata repository, records after conversion and the duplication of records will also reveal different quality problems.

Metadata records are usually the focus of quality evaluation. Taking a whole population or a sample from an existing database, the quality of individual records can be measured according to various indicators that are discussed in the next section. When a record is submitted to a database, sometimes it has already been checked manually by a peer or automatically by a validation program. This quality control process has been well implemented in library communities for years. However, in the many projects that are building digital collections, this process is often not affordable.

To examine a metadata record, which can be regarded as a surrogate of an item, a comparison between the surrogate and the original item is absolutely necessary. For example, using the information showing on a Web page as well as the source code of that Web page, data values recorded in a metadata record can be verified. The first of the next two figures illustrates a metadata record being compared with a Web page (Figure 7-3-1). Then the source code page shows the producer-prepared *title*, *keywords*, and *description* values that are embedded in the Web page which may be used to compare against the Web page that is displayed to the user (Figure 7-3-2).

In general, a machine-generated metadata record usually takes the values embedded in the source code's <title> statement. A human-generated metadata record usually takes the "heading" of a Web page. This kind of comparison also can be used to check the appropriate *creator*, *source*, *publisher*, and *rights* information.

If metadata records reside in a repository and have been converted from another metadata format, a comparison may be made between the records of

Figure 7-3-1. A metadata record compared with the original item.

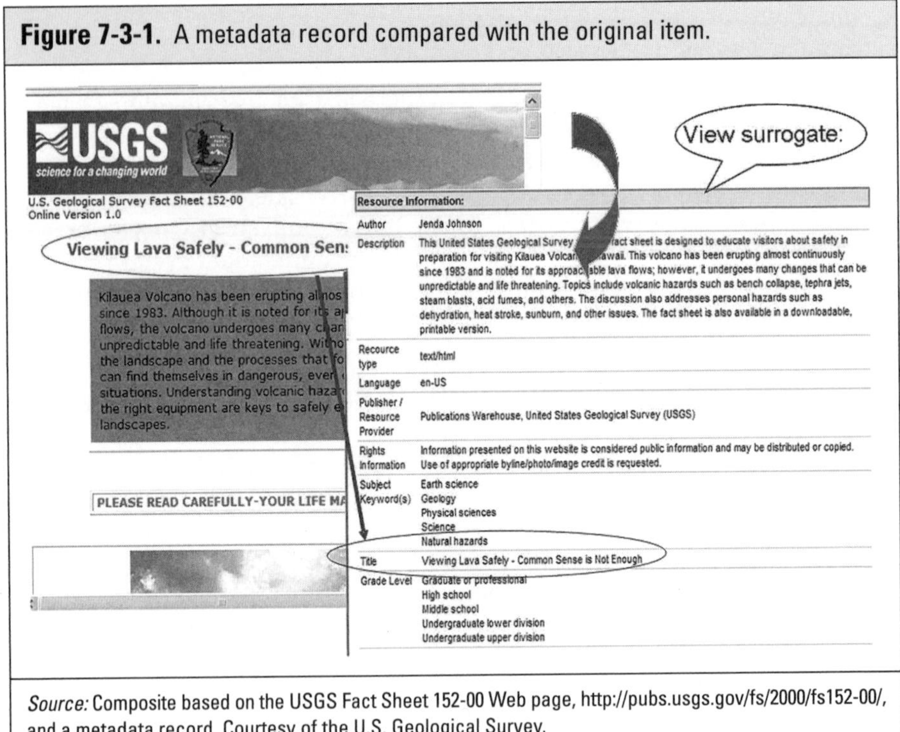

Source: Composite based on the USGS Fact Sheet 152-00 Web page, http://pubs.usgs.gov/fs/2000/fs152-00/, and a metadata record. Courtesy of the U.S. Geological Survey.

pre- and postconversion (see Figure 7-3-3). A grade for the metadata database or repository can be assigned based on the results of the analysis. Nevertheless, a stand-alone metadata database or a shared metadata repository could also be seen as a "black box" and be measured in terms of its overall quality. For example, the completeness indicator of a database shows how many, and at what level of intensity, elements from a particular schema were applied. The data can be matched to the functions of a metadata system to measure how well it performs. If 70 percent of the metadata records did not provide *rights* information, then the metadata database would be given a poor grade for its performance in fulfilling both the use and administrative function. Weakness of a whole database may be detected (and corrected) so as to enhance efficiency and improve overall quality.

A major objective of a metadata repository is to ensure interoperability; therefore, the relationships between interoperability and quality management are crucial for enhancing the infrastructure of a digital library that the metadata repository supports. A successful quality assurance and control program promotes resource sharing, knowledge sharing, and automatic metadata enhancement in the library. After harvesting, if a majority of metadata records lost significant data when compared to the original records, an investigation of the data converting tables or crosswalks would lead to the correct identification and solution of the problems.

Figure 7-3-2. An embedded metadata record compared with the Web page.

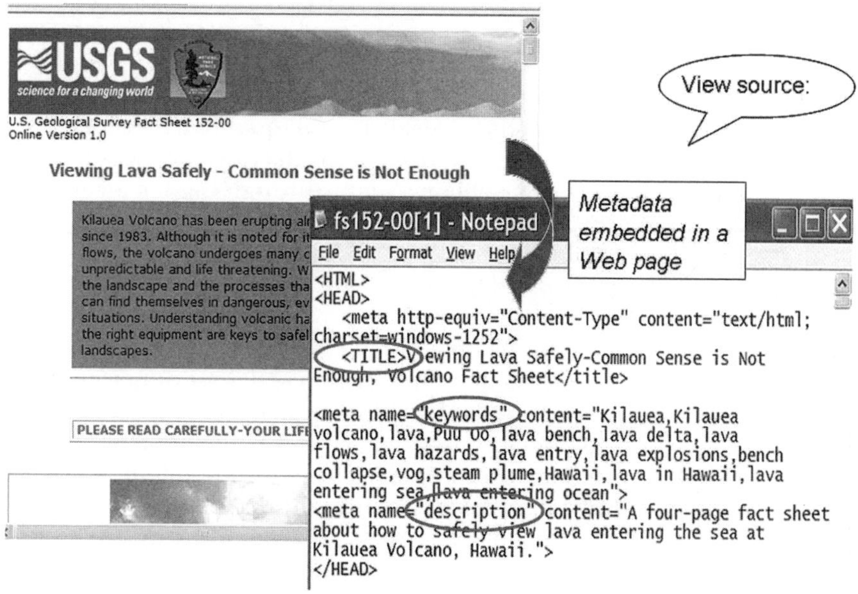

USGS
science for a changing world
U.S. Geological Survey Fact Sheet 152-00
Online Version 1.0

Viewing Lava Safely - Common Sense is Not Enough

View source:

Metadata embedded in a Web page

fs152-00[1] - Notepad
File Edit Format View Help

```
<HTML>
<HEAD>
   <meta http-equiv="Content-Type" content="text/html;
charset=windows-1252">
   <TITLE>Viewing Lava Safely-Common Sense is Not
Enough, Volcano Fact Sheet</title>

<meta name="keywords" content="Kilauea,Kilauea
volcano,lava,Puu Oo,lava bench,lava delta,lava
flows,lava hazards,lava entry,lava explosions,bench
collapse,vog,steam plume,Hawaii,lava in Hawaii,lava
entering sea,lava entering ocean">
<meta name="description" content="A four-page fact sheet
about how to safely view lava entering the sea at
Kilauea Volcano, Hawaii.">
</HEAD>
```

Source: Composite based on the USGS Fact Sheet 152-00 Web page (see Figure 7-3-1). Courtesy of the U.S. Geological Survey.

Figure 7-3-3. Comparing records between pre- and postconversion.

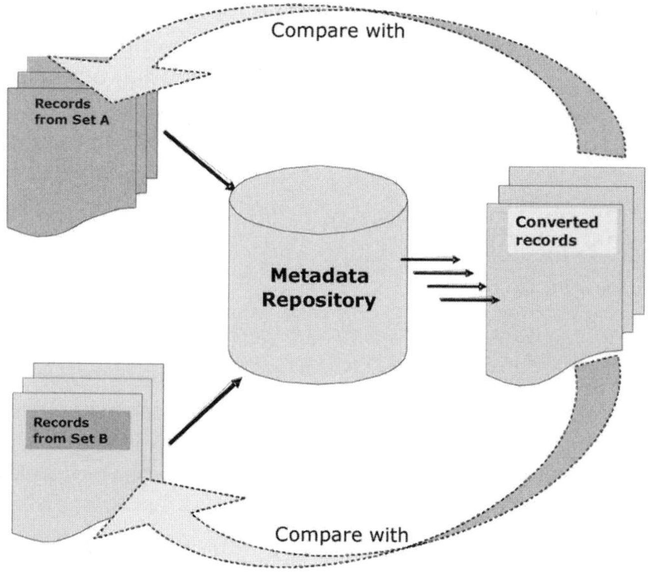

Compare with

Records from Set A

Metadata Repository

Converted records

Records from Set B

Compare with

Analysis at collection level provides macro-measurement, whereas analysis at element level provides micro-measurement. Metadata standards often provide best practices guides for the value spaces of the elements (e.g., *date*) that should follow standardized rules, and for those (i.e., *language, format,* and *type*) that should apply standard controlled vocabularies. By examining each element that was applied in a metadata database, the consistency of element usage and value selection reveals overall quality as well. Detecting errors and defects at the element level diagnoses the causes of problems, and leads to correction and further enhancement through higher-level quality control.

7.4 Measurement Indicators

Metadata assessment dimensions frequently reported in the literature include accuracy, completeness, consistency, and timeliness. Other dimensions mentioned concern redundant data, confusing data, insufficient data, and inaccessibility (Dushay and Hillmann, 2003; Bruce and Hillmann 2004; Stvilia et al., 2004) or focus on accuracy (right data in correct field), intelligibility (surrogate comprehensibility), and correctness (appropriate levels, such as specificity) (Greenberg, 2005). The choice of these dimensions is primarily based on intuitive understanding, industrial experience, or literature review, yet there is no general agreement on an exhaustive list of data quality dimensions. The following indicators are based on the two large data quality projects that one author of this text directed (Zeng, 1993a, 1993b; Zeng and Shreve, 2007).

7.4.1 Completeness

Completeness measurement concentrates on the size and distribution of elements in the records, and includes the range of descriptive detail provided by individual records as well as the overall distribution of various levels of records in a metadata database or a repository. In Section 7.2 we discussed the impact of completeness on access to a whole collection and to the functions of a metadata system. The completeness analysis specifies the degree to which the major metadata functions are fulfilled. Every project should set its own analysis criteria based on the functional requirements defined for its metadata system and the metadata application profile the system supports.

As an example, a detailed explanation based on Greenberg's framework for image collections (Greenberg, 2001) follows:

- **Discovery** metadata includes the elements that a user searches with when looking for information. Examples include *author/creator*, *title*, and *subject*.
- **Use** metadata permits the technical and intellectual exploitation of an information object:
  (1) For technical exploitation, elements may include *system requirements*, *format*, *location* (physical or virtual address), etc.;

(2) For intellectual exploitation, elements may include *property rights, policy restrictions*, or *terms and conditions.*

- **Authentication** metadata supports the evaluation of an information object's integrity, legitimacy and overall genuine quality (Bearman and Trant, 1998). Examples of the elements are: *Source, relationship, version/edition*, and *digital signature.*
- **Administration** (or **Administrative**) metadata may include the elements that assist with the management and custodial care of an object, such as *Provenance, date of acquisition, acquisition method, restrictions, ownership*, and *preservation action*. These data are usually restricted to public access. (Greenberg, 2001)

Data can be generated based on either samples or an entire population and will be used to identify the overall completeness, distribution of elements, and element types mapped to general functions. Hence a particular metadata database or repository may be given scores similar to the following:

Discovery: Good
Use: Marginal
Authentication: Very Limited
Administration: Not Available

Actions can be taken after the completeness analysis is finished, e.g., setting a benchmark of completeness according to the minimal and full level elements and requiring a set of core elements for each data set that should be included in a metadata repository. Research in this case found that in one metadata repository, five elements among the total 19 occurring elements contributed to more than 57 percent of the entries. Adding two other elements, they contributed to more than 75 percent of the entries. These elements formed a core for the entire repository (Zeng and Shreve, 2007). Analysis of data sets that reveal incomplete records helps to gain an overarching view of the dynamics of this often puzzling problem. Incompleteness may also be traced to the pre- and postconverting processes. Computer-assisted processing is an essential tool in completeness measurement and enhancement, and is discussed in the methodology section that follows.

7.4.2 Correctness

Correctness is the most challenging area in quality analysis and is largely performed by human analysis. The analysis focuses on the following areas:

- **Correct content:** Correct content analysis determines whether metadata records represent Web sites and other non-traditional resources correctly, and the metadata records should always be checked against the original sources (whenever available) they were created to describe.
- **Correct format:** Format analysis determines and characterizes the correctness of element labels and the values recorded under elements; correctness of implementation of data types, and correctness of application of element

syntax, in accordance with the best practices guide that is determined by a metadata standard.

- **Correct input:** Input analysis examines the quality of technical processes and includes problems of spelling, grammar, punctuation, word spacing, missing words or sections caused by cut-and-paste operations, handling of foreign characters, and so on.
- **Correct browser interpretation:** Browser interpretation analysis is conducted within the context of a related interface designed to display the metadata of a collection. The analysis identifies problems related to browser interpretation such as faulty rendering of HTML reserved characters, symbols, foreign characters, and so on.
- **Correct mapping/integration:** Mapping/integration analysis is usually performed in the context of an integrated metadata repository. Incorrectly mapped metadata generally show patterns of an incorrect mapping process (e.g., *author* mapped to *description*). The analysis requires a study of the native metadata formats from participating collections, the crosswalks, and the harvesting methods. Inappropriate mapping of commonly confused elements, such as mapping a *lom.taxon* to a *dc.subject* element, or mapping a *classification* to *subject* and the neglect of all *keywords*, should also be carefully investigated.

Providing correct descriptive information about a resource in a metadata record relies on the understanding of the original item at hand. When looking at correct content, original items are needed to verify the information provided by a metadata record. Content standards such as *AACR2* or *Cataloguing Cultural Objects* (CCO), best practices guides provided by metadata standards and digital libraries, and application profiles are the best sources when debating whether a value recorded in a metadata record correctly represents the original information carried by an item. The problem is that the majority of metadata records were created under conditions when no content standards, guides, and application profiles were available to the communities. At present, such content standards are still lacking or absent in many communities.

When looking at correct mapping and integration, tracing the preharvesting original records becomes necessary. This process itself is time-consuming and there is great possibility that originals cannot be obtained. Correctness of mapping and integration is closely related to completeness. Vast quantities of information are often unavailable in an integrated repository, not because they were not provided in the original records, but because they were lost or misplaced during the records' conversion. From the authors' experience, quality issues relating to data harvesting/converting has an impact on thousands of records in a metadata repository. The most serious difficulties include: (1) misrepresented data values, (2) valuable data values that are lost, (3) incorrectly mapped elements and data values, and (4) missing elements. It was discovered in research that more than 100,000 converted records did not have *rights* information because of the mismatching between element names; and six large collections' *source* values led to dead links because of missed or no longer existent static identifiers in mapping (Zeng and Shreve, 2007).

It is irrelevant to argue who is responsible for the mismatch and lost information. Collaborative approaches are needed in order to solve these problems. Re-creating the crosswalks, reharvesting records, and enriching the data are powerful correctives. A metadata repository should also supply consistent mapping tables to past, current, and future data providers when a harvesting process is to be conducted. In practice, the content crew and the information technology crew are usually separate task teams. Active collaboration, joint meetings, and open communication between groups working on crosswalking and data harvesting will help eliminate thousands of potential content errors, inconsistency, and redundant tasks.

7.4.3 Consistency

Consistency issues exist in both individual databases and shared repositories, and can therefore be examined through different lenses. Data values recorded in particular elements are the primary targets of a consistency analysis. Based on the DC metadata element set, for example, an analysis should pay attention to the following:

- **Consistent data recording:** This part of consistency analysis investigates how data is recorded for a particular element. It includes data that can be directly found in original sources (*title, date, contributor*, or *publisher*) and data that is interpreted by a metadata creator, e.g., *type* (category of the resource) or *format* (e.g., MIME type). The following values found in a sample of metadata records by Zeng and Shreve (2007) demonstrate the inconsistency in data recording (see Figure 7-4-1).
- **Consistent source links:** Here analysis targets *source* links and their references. Values associated with *source* element in some records may lead to different types of sources: a metadata record in a digital collection, an entire Web site containing the source, or particular items in a Web site.
- **Consistent identification and identifiers:** During this phase, consistency in the provision of URLs and other kinds of locators or identifiers should be assessed. Of special interest are:
  (1) identification of resources in frame-based sites (where individual pages' URLs are not displayed in a fixed frame setting);
  (2) identifiers that are search results from the database-driven Web sites that create Web pages on demand;
  (3) identification of DOI numbers that are often overlooked;
  (4) identification of images or other nontextual components embedded in a complex Web page; and
  (5) the level of granularity of location identifiers should also be scrutinized. Some records offer only a collective location. That is, if a document or site contains multiple constituent resources, all will be given the same location identification (typically the URL of the default page). Other

Figure 7-4-1. Values associated with *format* element found in a research sample

	(cont.)
text	1000149 bytes
text/html	language/java
text/plain	Application/JAVA applet
plain	Java
digital TIFF	CLASS
image/tiff	Model/VRML
other http://......../../../postscript.pdf	AVI, MOV, QTM
application/msword	1 v. (various pagings)
application/Flash (animation)	10 p., [6] p. of plates
ascii http://....../../../sample.txt	p.461-470
pdf http://....../../../sample.pdf	viii, 82 p.
ps http://....../../../sample.ps	MPEG-4
3.6 megabytes	

Source: Zeng and Shreve, 2007.

records may individually identify items, even when located within a larger collective.

- **Consistent description of source:** The *description* field usually contains a short paragraph describing the resource. It is one of the most important pieces of information that allows users to judge the value and relevance of an online resource. During consistency analysis the examination of sources of description data, description modification, editing or authoring practices, and the identification of the sources of descriptions cannot be overemphasized.
- **Consistent metadata representation:** This analysis task undertakes an in-depth examination of how metadata is represented in the search results display, especially concentrating on *title* and *description* metadata that most search engines and database-driven Web sites will display. The relationship between search result display quality and the harvesting/mapping process for collections in which records contain multiple *descriptions* should be carefully examined; sometimes only the values in the first description entry listed in a record will be displayed. If this happens to be a description of a physical item (see Figure 7-4-2) rather than a description of the content, then an adjustment of indexing should be requested (see Figure 7-4-3).
- **Consistency of data syntax:** An examination of the syntax, format, sources and number of subject terms in *subject* entries must be conducted.

Inconsistency is a major problem and most likely is caused by the absence of standards or recommended guidelines for creating metadata records. For most metadata standards, although there are guidelines regarding what standardized syntax (e.g., rules for recording *date*) and vocabularies (e.g., codes for languages) that should be followed in value spaces, there are few guides on how the data for a particular metadata element (e.g., *title, contributor, publisher,*

Figure 7-4-2. A description of physical item is displayed under in a search result.

IV. Unruh Effect, Spin Polarisation and the Derbeney-Kondratenko Formalism❐
Comment: 2 pages. No figures. Latex. Paper 4 of a set of 5. others are physics/9901038 physics/9901042 physics/9901044 **more info**

Figure 7-4-3. A description of content is displayed after adjustment and re-indexing.

IV. Unruh Effect, Spin Polarisation and the Derbeney-Kondratenko Formalism
The relationship between the level of spin polarisation caused by Unruh radiation as calculated by . . .

coverage, and so on) should be obtained or derived and how that data should be recorded.

Many inconsistency problems will be solved or prevented if best practices guides are implemented during the metadata creation process. It should not be difficult to follow an international standard when dealing with *date* or internationally accepted vocabularies for assigning values for *language* and *format*. Community-based controlled vocabularies can be developed, as with the *Learning Materials Type Vocabulary* developed through the collaboration of the NSDL community (NSDL, 2004, NSDL Metadata Working Group, 2007). Training and mentoring for starting projects are also necessary. For those value spaces where no standard vocabularies can be applied, content standards and guidelines should be developed (or shared, if some community has already created one), that define how data values should be obtained or derived from an original resource and how the values should be recorded in a metadata record. CCO, developed for the community working with cultural and heritage objects, is the best example of ensuring metadata quality for an entire community. This data content standard provides detailed guidelines and examples for preparing data contents and using authority files for each of the core elements used in describing cultural objects.

7.4.4 Duplication Analysis

Duplicate records derive from both intracollection and intercollection practices. Intracollection duplicates are clearly a local quality problem, and should be addressed within the collection. Intercollection duplicates are common when multiple collections are integrated into one source. True-duplicates are considered from two aspects: first, when a user searches a collection, the search results (usually only displayed through *title* and *description*) are identical or virtually identical (Figure 7-4-4); second, when a user searches a collection, two entries with different titles or descriptions lead to the same source (Figure 7-4-5).

Figure 7-4-4. Search results leading to the same source with virtually equivalent URLs.

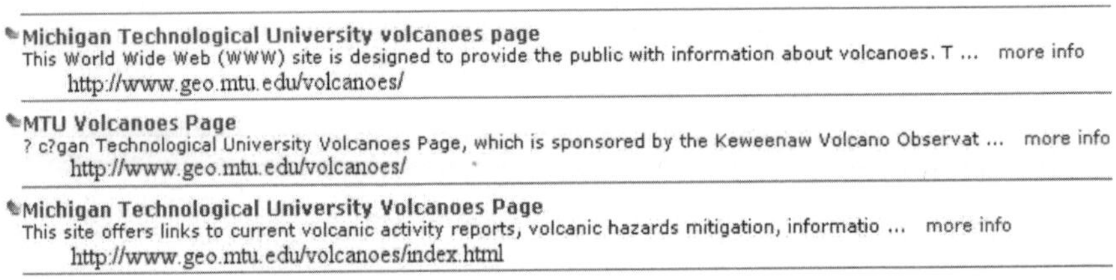

Michigan Technological University volcanoes page
This World Wide Web (WWW) site is designed to provide the public with information about volcanoes. T ... more info
http://www.geo.mtu.edu/volcanoes/

MTU Volcanoes Page
? c?gan Technological University Volcanoes Page, which is sponsored by the Keweenaw Volcano Observat ... more info
http://www.geo.mtu.edu/volcanoes/

Michigan Technological University Volcanoes Page
This site offers links to current volcanic activity reports, volcanic hazards mitigation, informatio ... more info
http://www.geo.mtu.edu/volcanoes/index.html

Figure 7-4-5. Same source and URL linked by different titles and descriptions.

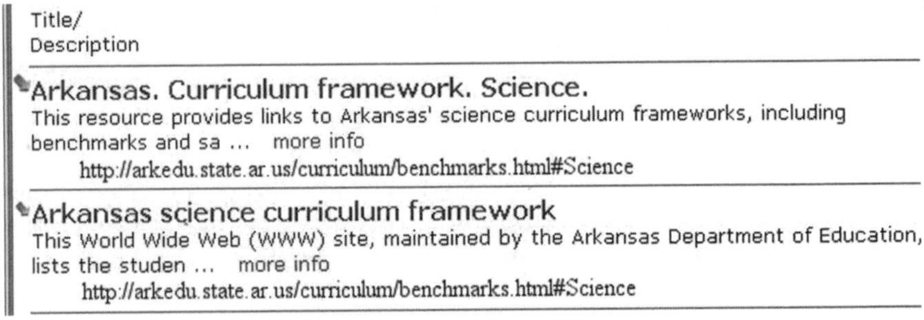

Title/
Description

Arkansas. Curriculum framework. Science.
This resource provides links to Arkansas' science curriculum frameworks, including benchmarks and sa ... more info
http://arkedu.state.ar.us/curriculum/benchmarks.html#Science

Arkansas science curriculum framework
This World Wide Web (WWW) site, maintained by the Arkansas Department of Education, lists the studen ... more info
http://arkedu.state.ar.us/curriculum/benchmarks.html#Science

The causes of intercollection duplication may be viewed from several vantage points:

1. Duplicate records point to the same source but with variant titles and descriptions. In this case the same source or document has been given a metadata record by more than one collection. Variations on this theme include titles recorded exactly (simple duplication) or titles recorded differently (masked duplication). For example, the titles "NASA homepage" and "NASA" both point to the same URL. Because there is no rule for recording title information in a record, a Web page's heading, banner, or the string coded by the <title> . . . </title> tags in the source code page can all be treated as the title of the source, which creates further duplication problems.
2. Duplicate records describe a single source but are recorded slightly differently, or have virtually equivalent locators. In this example, the same source is recorded by different collections using the same title. Whereas one record points to the homepage of the Web site, the other one points to another page on the same site, e.g., the "About" page. In other cases, the difference of the URL is determined by whether the URL carries "index.html." By default under a server's public_html directory, "index.html" is a file the server will open when the URL only points to this directory's name without

"index.html." Many Web references will provide their URLs without "index.html," but when a user types in that URL to open the site from a browser, its "/index.html" appears in the URL (see Figure 7-4-4).

3. Nondistinguishable items in searches occur when results show identical titles and descriptions many times while the identifier actually points to different pages of this resource. The problem is related to automatically extracted metadata values from source codes of a Web page. For example, an online journal may have a template for any issue and article, with the generic *title, description,* and *keyword* information in the <head> section and the template used repeatedly. Once such a problem is detected, strategies for automatically extracting metadata from this site should be reconsidered.
4. Duplicate records point to the same source that was produced in different formats. Images posted as both a gif file and a jpg file or text published in both HTML and PDF format are the cause of some duplications. In this case, the contents (especially *title* and *description*) are the same. The only difference is the format for each instance. Here, duplication is a necessity. The important distinction of the differences between formats should be indicated on the index page. A better model for the service would involve integrating different formats of the same source into one descriptive metadata.

Many titles have the same or similar appearances. However, they do not lead to the same source. These are not true duplicates. Other metadata information becomes critical to identify and understand the entry (see Figure 7-4-6).

Investigation by trained metadata creators can be conducted by searching a variety of topics and examining search results. Duplication can also be checked by validating related elements automatically. Algorithms can be applied to give scores of duplication probabilities according to the judgments rendered by similarities of strings in identifiers, dates, titles, paths, and descriptions (to name only a few of the most important).

Figure 7-4-6. Not a duplicate: Titles are same or alike but lead to different sources.

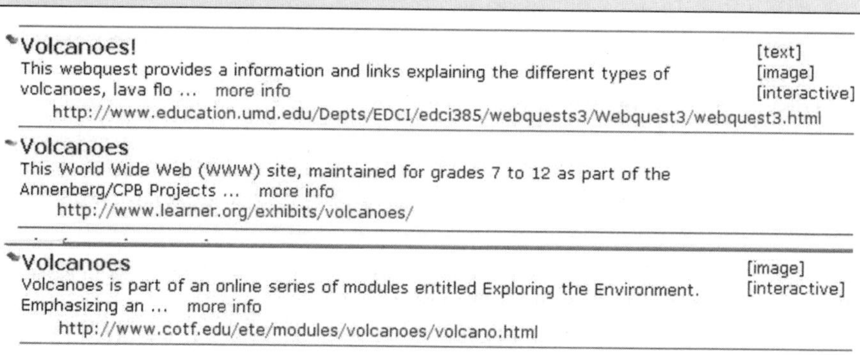

Volcanoes! [text] [image] [interactive]
This webquest provides a information and links explaining the different types of volcanoes, lava flo ... more info
http://www.education.umd.edu/Depts/EDCI/edci385/webquests3/Webquest3/webquest3.html

Volcanoes
This World Wide Web (WWW) site, maintained for grades 7 to 12 as part of the Annenberg/CPB Projects ... more info
http://www.learner.org/exhibits/volcanoes/

Volcanoes [image] [interactive]
Volcanoes is part of an online series of modules entitled Exploring the Environment. Emphasizing an ... more info
http://www.cotf.edu/ete/modules/volcanoes/volcano.html

7.5 Metadata Evaluation Methodology

Metadata evaluation is closely related to the evaluation of digital libraries' information quality and is often conducted as part of a digital library evaluation. As evaluation is not an active research area in either digital libraries or metadata, it is certainly difficult to label evaluation methodology as "metadata evaluation methodology." Fortunately, some of the methodology typologies in digital library evaluation are well suited for metadata evaluation. According to Saracevic (2004), digital libraries may be evaluated using system-centered, human-centered, usability-centered, ethnographic, anthropologic, sociologic, and economic approaches according to differing contexts. Approaches may then be divided into two broad categories: social evaluation and technical evaluation (McClure and Bertot, 2001).

Social evaluation methodologies refer to those that involve humans for collecting data of their opinions and/or behavior when using digital libraries as well as the impact of such use on their learning and work performance. This category of methodologies includes focus groups, surveys, observation, user think-aloud, experiments, and interviews. Evaluation studies involving users are viable and can provide valuable insights toward understanding users' thoughts about searching, navigation tools, and their expectations and experiences. The imbalance in these evaluation methodologies, however, suggests an urgent need for more robust and cost-effective evaluation methodologies and instruments.

Technical evaluation does not involve humans directly when collecting data; rather, it involves collection of data from query logs and/or Web server logs generated by the system that tracks users' activities: when a search is initiated, which query terms the user enters, and what filter(s) is used. In addition, it tracks which query options are employed when the query is executed, and indicates how many results are returned to the user. Analyzing the log data, usage, and patterns is then generalized to explain the extent to which the collection was searched and what the patterns are. Log data may vary in formats and fields from system to system, but they nevertheless provide valuable information about the use, and users, of a digital library on a much larger scale that is cost-efficient. A significant advantage is the potential to conduct both regular and ad hoc evaluations with the help of log-mining tools.

Programs can also be written to automatically generate data on the existence and absence of overall element-value pairs, core elements, element-element co-occurrence, corresponding values, etc. In measuring metadata quality, our experience concludes that machine-assisted processes are very useful in completeness, consistency, and duplicate checking (Zeng and Shreve, 2007). Unfortunately, correctness measurement still mainly relies on manual procedures. Automatic evaluation does not completely exclude human intervention nor should it, but it can detect errors and problems much more quickly and then bring them to a human metadata creator's attention.

Most metadata evaluations have focused on quality assessment. The hardest part of evaluation is measurement of the uses and usefulness of metadata, which has been sporadically reported in the research literature. In face of the increasing and widespread use of social semantics and free-text searching, evaluation of metadata's usefulness will be more important than ever toward understanding why metadata is or is not used, and how metadata succeeds or fails in searching processes. The quality of metadata and its usefulness in retrieval form the two most important areas in metadata evaluation. If the quality indicators measure how good the metadata representation is, then the retrieval-based evaluation judges how useful that representation is. A procedure for measuring metadata quality based on functionality analysis and functional requirements was proposed by Stvilia et al. (2004). Based on analysis of the nature of information objects, as well as the activities related to information creation and use, the functional requirements are decided accordingly. The construct of a baseline data model and components are then designed. The baseline model is used to measure the quality of related metadata objects. This model also provides guidelines for the examination of value and cost changes that would influence quality improvement (or degradation) in any given quality dimension.

Positioning a metadata aggregator (e.g., NSDL) as the mediator between metadata creators and service providers, researchers at NSDL made the point that the utility of metadata can best be evaluated in the context of services provided to users. Different services require different kinds of metadata, perhaps tailored for different purposes, or assigned different confidence ratings. "[M]etadata tailoring, recombination, and repurposing will require metadata aggregators and others to think of elements, rather than records, as the basic metadata unit." Tracking information such as source, date, and creation methodology for metadata statements is necessary in order to enable quality assessments by downstream consumers (Hillmann, Dushay, and Phipps, 2004: 7).

As more and more automated processes are employed to generate metadata records by extracting and assigning metadata values, various methods of evaluation have been reported. The degree of similarity between the automatically assigned values and the (human) expert-assigned values can be determined through user studies (Liddy et al., 2002; Yilmazel, Finneran, and Liddy, 2004). Similar evaluation goals can also be achieved by using computer programs to calculate statistics for metrics such as content-word precision and recall, exact match accuracy, and subfield precision and recall (Paynter, 2005). Another useful approach is to have metadata experts evaluate, compare, and contrast author-contributed and computer-generated metadata records (Greenberg, 2005).

7.6 Enhancing Quality of Metadata

Quality assurance establishes quality processes. Quality processes ensure that metadata records produced for a digital collection meet the quality objectives defined for the records. With quality assurance processes in place, quality control measures can be undertaken. Quality control involves testing, checking, and sampling of records to ensure adherence to quality objectives and to determine where, when, and how quality failures occur. The EPrints project has established a *Functional Requirements Specification* for the EPrints Application Profile which must support or make recommendations toward supporting 37 requirements (EPrints Application Profile: Functional Requirements, 2006).

Concern about database quality has led to calls for improvement, and for a responsive development of mechanisms to assess, ensure, and control quality. The major bibliographic utilities have undertaken a variety of approaches to quality management. O'Neill and Vizine-Goetz (1988) classified approaches to database quality control and identified several types, which include self-checking data, automated data validation, spelling and typographic error detection, authority control, and duplication detection. Spelling correction has been extensively investigated and is now an effective tool for maintaining and enhancing database quality. Automated authority control and duplicate detection has also received much attention.

As a method of error detection and correction, automated data validation has received increasing recognition as an effective and desirable technique to ensure database quality. Data validation refers to an entire spectrum of errors that can be detected automatically. It can be done in batch mode where validation is performed after the records have been released so that errors existing in the records can be trapped; or, it can occur in real-time, where validation routines are built into the metadata input and editing processes so that errors are detected before they are actually entered into a database (Zeng, 1993b). OCLC conducted a number of automated error correction projects to correct or delete obsolete codes and values, correct records against authority controls, and detect and merge duplicate records (O'Neill, 1992). With the wide applications of XML and stylesheets, structured documents can be easily validated through the validators provided by the World Wide Web Consortium (W3C), which is used primarily for structural and syntactical errors.

In the previous sections, methods for detecting errors and solving problems are discussed together with a discussion of measurement indicators. In addition, a simple but efficient way of ensuring metadata quality at input stage is to create a template to assist in metadata creation. An HTML form can be used to outline the required and optional elements, core elements, and minimal level elements; embed lists of values for certain elements; lead to best practices guides and examples; link to controlled vocabularies; and provide validation for an element-value or for a whole record before it is submitted to the database. A template needs stringent testing by experts before being widely disseminated.

Today, quality issues of metadata repositories always have an influential dimension that comes from interoperability activities. Almost all reported projects assessing metadata quality have drawn their research population from a shared repository. Metadata interoperability has become the underlying principle for networked information management. It has a direct impact on information sharing, interchange, and accessibility across the boundaries of systems, languages, and geographic locations. It also reduces the amount of time needed to create and maintain a metadata standard and maximize its utility for the widest community of users (Zeng and Xiao, 2001). Once a repository is established, quality enhancement may be done through aggregation. The reason for this procedure is that each metadata record contains a series of statements about a particular resource, and therefore metadata from different sources can be aggregated to build a more complete profile of that resource (Hillmann, Dushay, and Phipps, 2004; Phipps, Hillmann, and Paynter, 2005). Hillmann, Dushay, and Phipps (2004) report about methodology explored by the NSDL in its third year of operation: harvested metadata was augmented and then re-exposed to downstream users with detailed information on how and by whom it was created. The metadata augmentation process enables quality enhancement to automatically detect errors in source metadata, and then automatically supplies useful explanations of errors to metadata providers. Researchers at the NSDL (Phipps, Hillmann, and Paynter, 2005) have also included a crosswalking service in their sequence of metadata enhancement services. These crosswalking services are a type of metadata augmentation operation that generates new fielded metadata values that are based on crosswalking from a source (schema or vocabulary) to a target (schema or vocabulary). The improvements in the repositories offer great promise for shared databases that are built on a foundation of voluntarily-based and diverse participants-contributed records. The idea of changing the basic metadata unit from "record" to "statement" is a revolutionary direction in quality problem solving that is specifically related to these metadata databases.

Obviously, collaborative approaches are needed to solve the quality problems in large metadata repositories. A set of approaches to correct many of the errors found in a metadata repository regarding data conversion is recommended as follows (Zeng and Shreve, 2007):

1. re-create and improve crosswalks if problems are found;
2. reharvest records if quality reviews indicate the need;
3. sponsor and enforce comprehensive standards and best practice guidelines for all elements;
4. enrich data at both pre- and postharvest points by automatic means;
5. supply consistent mapping tables to past, present, and future data providers when harvesting is to be conducted; and
6. encourage and ensure active collaboration and open communication between repositories and local collection groups.

On the other hand, one essential aspect that might have been ignored for a long time is the proposition of shareable metadata, which is quite different from the metadata that is used strictly "in-house" (Shreeves, Riley, and Milewicz, 2006). A high-quality "in-house" metadata record may not be highly shareable if the intention of a metadata creator did not include sharing them in a multicollection repository. Issues regarding quality requirements for potential shareable metadata databases need to be seriously addressed.

In summary, many researchers have reported their approaches to the assessment and enhancement of metadata quality in various types of databases and domains. However, many research questions remain unanswered: How have the current design principles of a metadata repository (interoperability, extensibility, reusability, and simplicity) influenced the quality of its metadata records? What quality issues are related to harvesting? Are the quality of metadata records pre- and postharvesting different? Does a difference indicate advantages or disadvantages of current harvesting models now employed in such a diverse metadata application environment? What are the concrete steps for a metadata repository to improve, ensure, and control its quality? These questions, as well as the many questions that have been, or remain to be investigated, call for comprehensive and dedicated research.

Suggested Readings

Bruce, Thomas. R., and Diane I. Hillmann. 2004. "The Continuum of Metadata Quality: Defining, Expressing, Exploiting." In *Metadata in Practice*, edited by Diane I. Hillmann and Elaine L. Westbrooks, pp. 238–256. Chicago: American Library Association.

"EPrints Application Profile: Functional Requirements." 2006. JISC Digital Repositories Programme. Web page. Available: www.ukoln.ac.uk/repositories/digirep/index/Functional_Requirements.

Guy, Marieke, Andy Powell, and Michael Day. 2004. "Improving the Quality of Metadata in EPrint Archives." *Ariadne* [Online] no. 38. Available: http://www.ariadne.ac.uk/issue38/guy.

Hillmann, Diane I., Naomi Dushay, and Jon Phipps. 2004. "Improving Metadata Quality: Augmentation and Recombination." DC-2004 Internation Conference on Dublin Core and Metadata Applications, October 11–14, 2004, Shanghai, China. Available: http://www.cs.cornell.edu/naomi/DC2004/MetadataAugmentation—DC2004.pdf.

O'Neill, Edward T., and Diane Vizine-Goetz. 1988. "Quality Control in Online Databases." In *Annual Review of Information Science and Technology*, edited by M. Williams, Vol. 23: 125–156. Medford, NJ: Learned Information.

Exercises

1. Search a digital library (e.g., nsdl.org) using different queries (e.g., "mars," "mars exploration," "Volcano World"). If there are duplicate records, analyze and determine whether they are true duplicates. Also examine all records and compare these records describing the same resource.
2. Write a well-structured, brief report about your finding. Attach the records that you corrected or enhanced. Please mark your corrections and additions on the original records.

8

Achieving Interoperability

In this chapter we address the problem of ensuring metadata interoperability when building digital libraries or repositories. Ideally, users of a digital library or repository should be able to discover through one search which digital objects are freely available from a variety of collections, rather than having to search each collection individually (Tennant, 2001). In other words, users should not have to know or understand the methods used to describe the contents of the digital collection. In reality, however, diverse standards for describing resources, sometimes within the same digital library or repository, pose particular challenges for users as well as for those responsible for managing resources. Mechanisms to attain interoperability must be developed to facilitate the exchange and sharing of data prepared according to different metadata schemas and to enable cross-collection searching.

This chapter contains a summary of the methods previously used to achieve or improve interoperability among metadata schemas and applications for facilitating conversion and exchange of metadata as well as enabling cross-domain metadata harvesting and federated searches. The information is based on two articles published in *D-Lib Magazine* (Chan and Zeng, 2006; Zeng and Chan, 2006). A number of methods were previously discussed in detail in Chapters 3, "Schemas-Structure and Semantics," and 4, "Schemas-Syntax"; Chapter 5, "Metadata Records"; and Chapter 6, "Metadata Services."

8.1 Definitions

Interoperability is defined variously in the following excerpts:

- "Interoperability is the ability of multiple systems with different hardware and software platforms, data structures, and interfaces to exchange data with minimal loss of content and functionality" (NISO, 2004:2).
- "Interoperability is the ability of two or more systems or components to exchange information and use the exchanged information without special effort on either system" (CC: DA, 2000).
- "Interoperability: The compatibility of two or more systems such that they can exchange information and data and can use the exchanged information and data without any special manipulation" (Taylor, 2004: 369).

It is becoming generally accepted in the information community that interoperability is one of the most important principles in metadata implementation. Other basic metadata principles include simplicity, modularity, reusability, and extensibility (see Chapter 1). These principles inform metadata services' design as well as other system-dependent developments. From the very beginning of a metadata project, the principles that enable user-centered and interoperable services should be foremost in design and implementation.

8.2 Metadata Decisions at Different Stages of a Digital Library Project

At different stages of a digital library project, there are always metadata decisions to be made. If all participants of a consortium or repository were required to use the same schema, such as the MARC or the Dublin Core, a high level of consistency would be maintained from the beginning. This, of course, has been the approach in the library community for more than a century and is the ultimate solution to the interoperability problem. Examples include the MARC standards used in union catalogs of library collections and the DC-based Electronic Theses and Dissertations Metadata Standard (ETD-MS) used by members of the Networked Digital Library of Theses and Dissertations (NDLTD). However, although use of the same schema is a conceptually simple solution, it is not always feasible or practical. This nonpractical situation is found in environments that serve different user communities whose collections or components contain resources already described by various specialized schemas. The uniform standardization method is only viable at the beginning or early stages of building a digital library or repository, before different schemas have been adopted by the participants.

Figure 8-2-1 shows possible paths from creation of schemas to their applications in individual projects or in integrated repositories. The case might be:

1. A schema was created and applied to records for one or more particular projects.
2. Elements from several schemas were considered. An application profile was established based on a number of schemas; then, the element set specified by the application profile was applied to records of a particular project(s).
3. Two or more existing databases containing metadata records were exchanged or integrated based on the matching elements of the schemas involved.
4. Records from existing metadata collections were harvested or merged by a unified metadata repository. These collections had applied different schemas, or established their own application profiles before harvesting.

Each approach has definite foci, and interoperability efforts can take place at any point.

In recent years, numerous projects to achieve interoperability among different metadata schemas and their applications were undertaken by the many

Figure 8-2-1. Various levels of metadata projects.

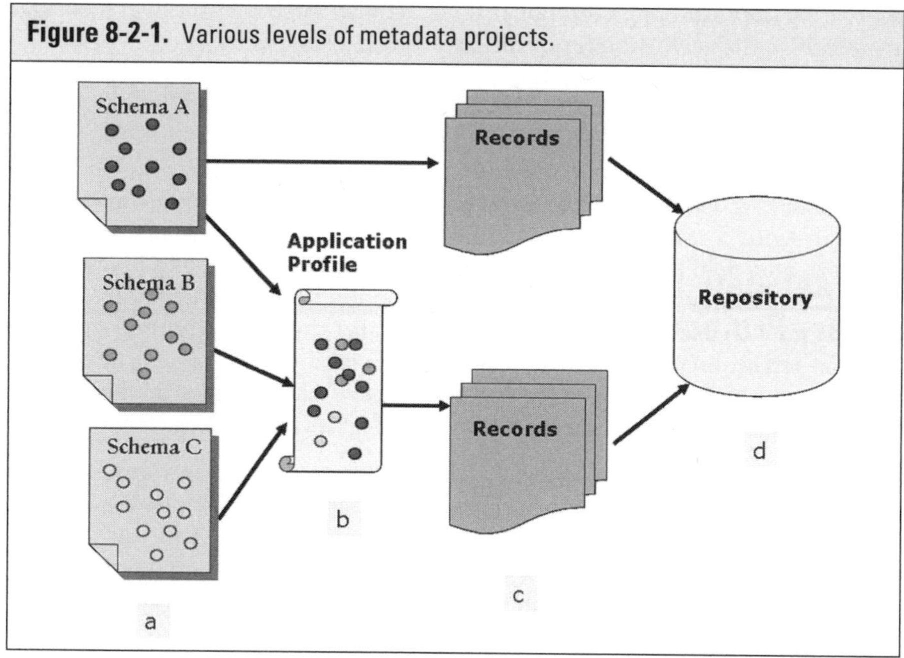

players and stakeholders in the information community. The results of these efforts may be observed at different levels and perspectives:

1. *Schema level:* Efforts focus on the elements of the schemas that are independent of any applications. The results usually appear as derived element sets, encoded schemas, crosswalks, application profiles, and element registries.
2. *Record level:* Efforts attempt to integrate the metadata records through mapping elements according to the semantic meanings of those elements. Common results include converted records, enriched records through aggregation, and new records that combine the values of existing records.
3. *Repository level:* With harvested or integrated records from varying sources, efforts at this level focus on mapping value strings associated with particular elements (e.g., terms associated with subject or format elements). This enables cross-collection searching.

Note that the models discussed in this chapter are not necessarily mutually exclusive. Sometimes, within any given project, more than one method may be used.

8.3 Achieving Interoperability at the Schema Level

Before project developers select and apply a metadata schema to a collection, an important step is to ensure that the data processed according to a given schema will result in an interoperable digital collection. At the schema level, interoperability actions usually take place before operational level metadata records are created. The actions concentrate on the elements (independent of individual applications). Methods used to achieve interoperability at this stage mainly include derivation, application profiles, crosswalks, frameworks, and registries.

8.3.1 Derivation

When a new schema is derived from an existing one, it ensures a similar basic structure with common elements while allowing different components to vary in depth and details. In a collection where different components have different needs and requirements regarding description details, an existing complex schema may be used as the "source" for new and simpler individual schemas. Specific derivation methods include adaptation, modification, expansion, partial adaptation, and translation. In each case, the new schema relies on the foundation of the source schema. Specifically, the approaches may include the following:

1. *Deriving various versions from a source or "master" schema:* Many schemas now have developed a concise or "lite" version. For example, the TEI Lite was derived from the full Text Encoding Initiative (TEI). Both MODS (Metadata Object Description Schema) and MARC Lite are derived from the full MARC 21 standard. Changes could also occur in the encoding format (e.g., MARCXML), while retaining the basic original content elements (Figure 8-3-1).
2. *Translating an existing schema into a different language:* The content of such a schema remains largely the same as the source schema. Examples include different language versions of the Dublin Core Metadata Element Set (Figure 8-3-1).
3. *Adapting an existing schema and modifying it to cater to local or specific needs:* This approach reflects the extensibility principle of metadata. Extensible metadata systems must allow for extensions and expansions so that the particular needs of a given application can be accommodated. Examples of adaptation/modification include:
   - Electronic Theses and Dissertations Metadata Standard (ETD-MS). Version 1.0 uses 13 of the 15 Dublin Core elements and an additional element: *thesis.degree* (ETD-MS).
   - Rare Materials Descriptive Metadata developed by the Peking University Library. It uses 12 DC elements, plus *edition* and *physical description*

Figure 8-3-1. Examples of schema derivation.

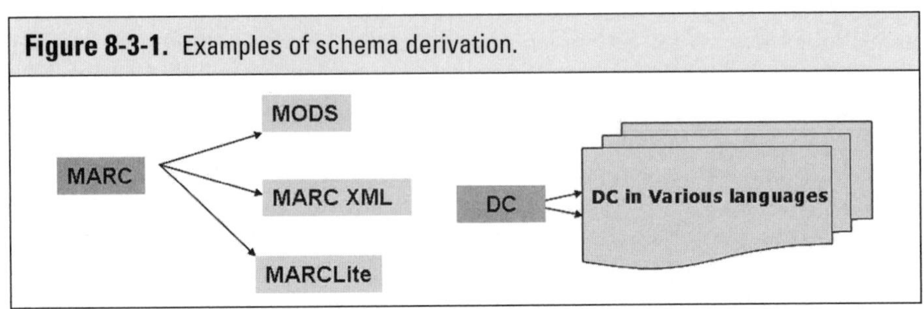

as two local core elements and a collec*tion history* element for third-level extension (Yao et al., 2004).

Note that element sets following the extension approach are sometimes regarded as application profiles as well.

8.3.2 Application Profiles (APs)

The concepts and uses of application profiles were discusses in Chapter 3 (see Section 3.4, Application Profiles). In general, three models have been developed:

1. An AP consists of metadata elements drawn from one or more metadata schemas, combined into a compound schema by implementers, and optimized for a particular local application. This model has been widely used.
2. An AP is created based on one single schema but tailored to different user communities. Examples include the DC-Library Application Profile and the DC Government Application Profile.
3. In addition to using elements from an existing schema(s), implementers who wish to create new elements may create their own namespace schema and take responsibility for declaring and maintaining that schema. An AP may also provide additional documentation on how the adapted metadata terms are constrained, encoded, or interpreted for particular purposes. The National Library of Medicine (NLM) Metadata Schema is a good example (see Chapter 3).

8.3.3 Crosswalks

Common properties and methods of crosswalking were discussed in detail in Chapter 3. A crosswalk is "a mapping of the elements, semantics, and syntax from one metadata scheme to those of another" (NISO, 2004: 11). Crosswalks allow systems to effectively convert data from one metadata standard to another, enabling heterogeneous collections to be searched simultaneously with a single query as if they were a single database. Depending on the number of schemas involved in the process, two different models may be considered:

1. *Direct crosswalking.* Figure 8-3-2 illustrates a model of direct, independent, and one-to-one mapping, which is usually applied when only two (or a limited number of) schemas are involved. In recent years, major efforts in metadata mapping produced a substantial number of crosswalks. Almost all schemas created crosswalks to widely applied schemas such as DC, MARC, and LOM. Metadata specifications may also include crosswalks to a previous version of a schema as well as to other metadata schemas (see, for example, the VRA Core).
2. *Cross-switching.* Another kind of model, this is usually applied to a situation in which multiple schemas are involved. Using the direct mapping model, a four-schema crosswalk would require twelve (or six pairs of) mapping processes that are extremely tedious and labor intensive, and also require enormous intellectual effort. Using a switching schema (new or

Figure 8-3-2. Establishing a crosswalk between two schemas.

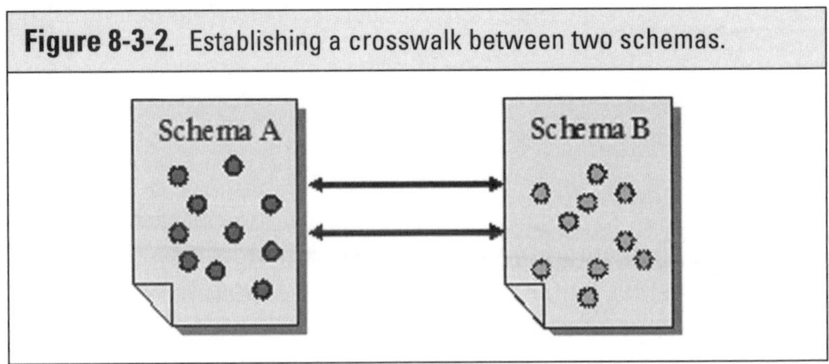

existing) to channel crosswalking among multiple schemas then becomes an alternative (see Figure 8-3-3). In this model, one of the schemas is used as a switching mechanism among multiple schemas. Instead of mapping between every pair in the group, each metadata schema is mapped directly to the switching schema. An example is Getty's crosswalk, in which multiple schemas all crosswalk to CDWA (Metadata Standards Crosswalk, accessed January 10, 2008).

Figure 8-3-3. Cross-switching when multiple schemas are involved.

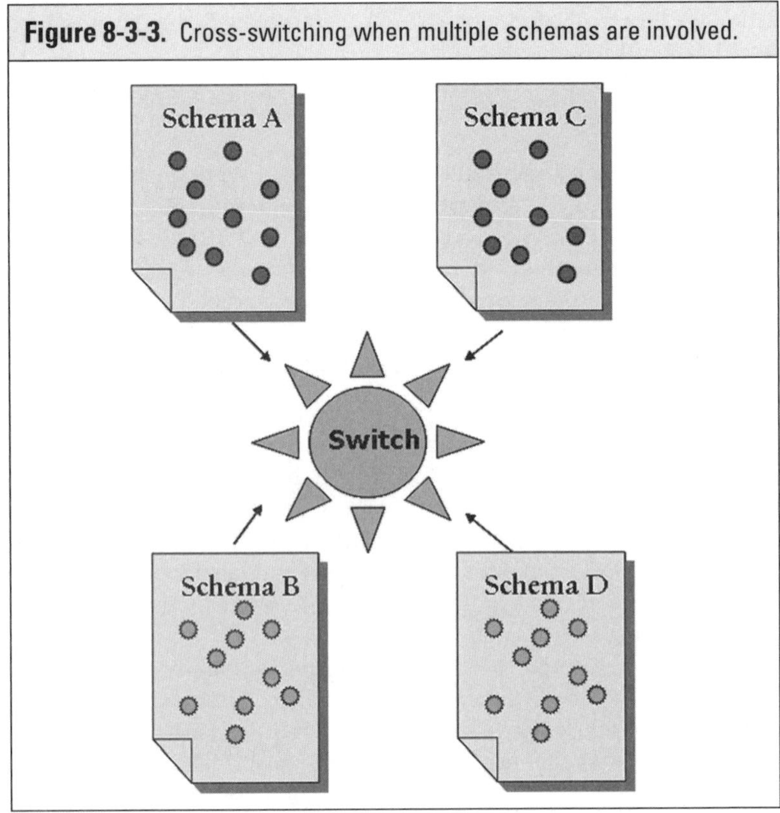

8.3.4 Frameworks

A framework can be considered a skeleton upon which various objects are integrated for any given solution (see Figure 8-3-4). The need for a metadata framework is best demonstrated by emerging digital preservation efforts. Although many organizations have developed metadata for digital preservation in support of their own activities, such efforts have been conducted largely in isolation and have lacked any substantial degree of cross-organizational coordination. It becomes obvious that a metadata framework is needed to represent a consensus of leading experts and practitioners. Such a framework could be readily applied to a broad range of such activities (OCLC/RLG Working Group on Preservation Metadata, 2002). In 2002, a conceptual framework for a generic digital archiving system emerged as the Open Archival Information System (OAIS) reference model and was issued as a recommendation by the ISO Consultative Committee for Space Data Systems (CCSDS). The committee established a common framework of terms and concepts that comprise an Open Archival Information System and so provided the basis for further standardization within an archival context.

Another example comes from the metadata framework currently used in the DLESE (Digital Library for Earth System Education) Discovery System. After a few years' exploration in establishing a framework for DLESE metadata based on the IMS Learning Resource Meta-data Specification, the ADEPT project, DLESE, and NASA's Joint Digital Library (JDL) decided in June 2001 to create an ADEPT/DLESE/NASA (ADN) metadata framework that all three organizations use.

The purpose of the ADN framework, as stated on its Web page, is to "describe resources typically used in learning environments (e.g. classroom activities, lesson plans, modules, visualizations, some datasets) for discovery

Figure 8-3-4. A framework and the schemas associated with the framework.

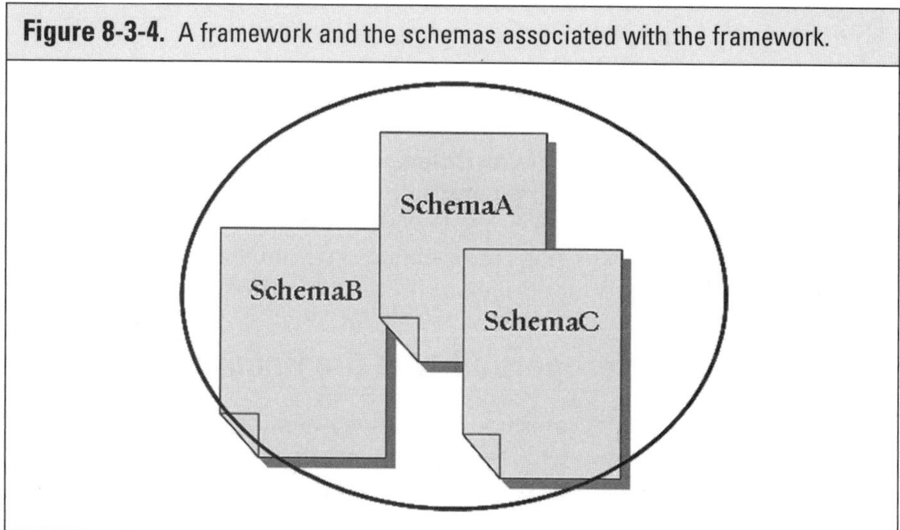

by the Earth system education community" (DLESE, 2005: ADN Framework, accessed 2007). The content information in a metadata record includes the following categories of elements, among which *educational*, *geospatial*, and *temporal* are unique (emphasis added):

- General (e.g., title, language, keywords, subjects, description)
- **Educational** (e.g., resource type, grade range)
- **Geospatial** (e.g., bounding box, geometries, elevation, place name, coordinate system)
- Relations (connecting resources to one another)
- Rights (e.g., resource, copyright, and cost)
- Technical (e.g., URL, browser, platform, plug-ins)
- **Temporal** (e.g., time, named time period)
- Administrative data (e.g., id number, metadata, copyright) (DLESE: ADN Framework Web page, www.dlese.org/Metadata/adn-item/index.htm).

The previous examples show that two approaches are possible for building a metadata framework: (1) establishing a framework before the development of individual schemas and applications and (2) building a framework based on existing schemas. Regardless of which approach is used, the function of a metadata framework is to provide a suitable bridge for the diverse audiences of involved communities.

8.3.5 Metadata Registries

As discussed in Chapter 6, a metadata registry collects data regarding metadata schemas for reuse of existing metadata terms to achieve interoperability among metadata element sets. The basic components of a metadata registry may include identification of data models, elements, element sets, encoding schemes, application profiles, element usage information, and element crosswalks. The primary functions of metadata registries include registering, publishing, and managing schemas and application profiles, as well as making the registry easily searchable within the registry. A registry also provides services for crosslinking and crosswalking among schemas and application profiles (see Figure 8-3-5).

A registry can be established with different scopes: around a single schema, (e.g., DCMI Open Data Registry); multiple schemas, (e.g., UKOLN CORES Registry); for a single project, (e.g., the European Library (TEL) Metadata Registry); in a particular domain (e.g., Information Environment Metadata Schema Registry (IEMSR)); or a format-oriented directory (e.g., the Schemaweb).

8.4. Achieving Interoperability at the Record Level

The importance of a digital collection being integrated (physically or virtually) into a collaborative environment and the influence of collaborative ventures on metadata decisions has already been emphasized (see Chapter 3, Section 3.2.2). In some cases, however, a project started within a community is not aware of

Figure 8-3-5. A metadata registry in relation to schemas.

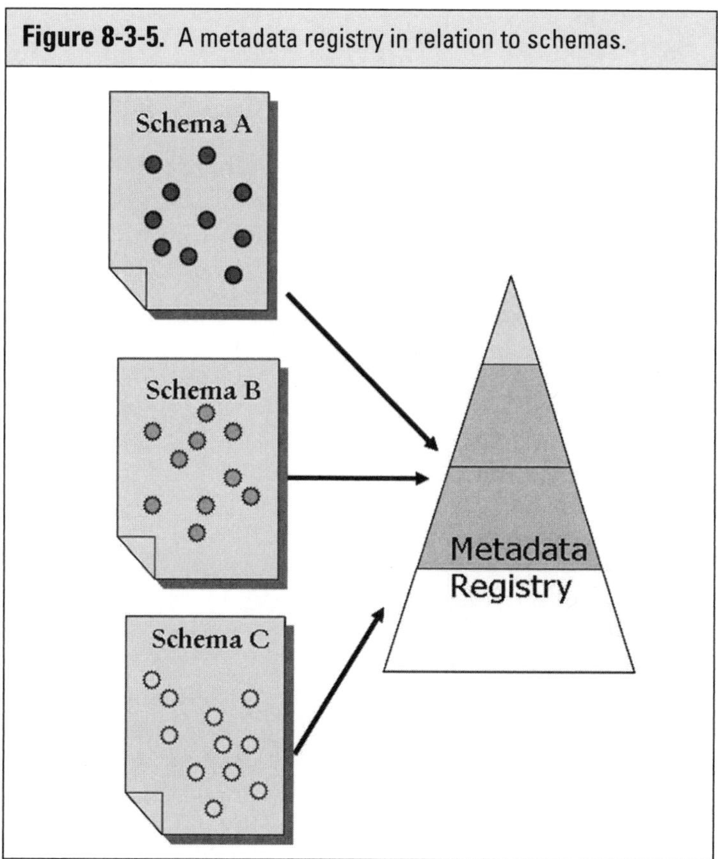

other projects that have similar material types, audiences, or subject domains. Often, a distinctive metadata schema is developed or adopted for a project when metadata records have already been created before of interoperability was carefully considered. As a result, when different projects need to be integrated or mapped, it is too late for the projects to consider any interoperability approach at the schema level (see previous discussion). Converting records becomes one of the few options for integrating established metadata databases. Recent projects have also attempted to reuse existing metadata records and combine them (or their components) with other types of metadata records (or their components) to create new records. Activities at the record level focus on integrating or converting data values associated with specific elements/fields, with or without a normalization process.

8.4.1 Conversion of Metadata Records

The biggest challenge of converting records from one scheme to another (see Figure 8-4-1) is how to minimize loss or distortion of data. Some examples and issues have been presented in Chapter 5 (Section 5.4.6). When the target format

Figure 8-4-1. Record conversion.

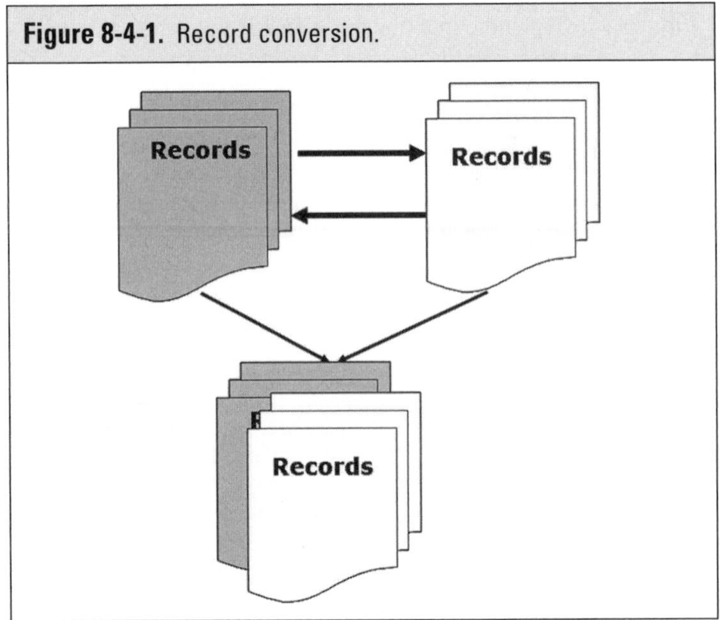

is more inclusive and contains more detailed defined elements and subelements than in the source format, the value in a source metadata record may need to be broken down into smaller units (for example, from DC elements to MARC record subfields). One result is that data values may be lost when converting from the richer to the simpler structure. Other difficult problems include converting value strings associated with certain elements that require using controlled vocabularies (Zeng and Xiao, 2001).

Crosswalks that are constructed based on real data make the conversion very different from those based on metadata specifications. Additional instructions and detailed explanations need to be provided for different needs. Unfortunately, most crosswalks focus only on mappings based on metadata specifications, not on real data conversion results. Evidence of the impact of crosswalks and incorrect mapping on the quality of large amounts of real data conversion is found in Chapter 7.

8.4.2 Data Reuse and Integration

Duval et al. consider metadata modularity to be "a key organizing principle for environments characterized by vastly diverse sources of content, styles of content management, and approaches to resource description. It allows designers of metadata schemas to create new assemblies based on established metadata schemas and benefit from observed best practice, rather than reinventing elements anew" (Duval et al., 2002: www.dlib.org/dlib/april02/weibel/04weibel.html). In a modular metadata environment, different types of metadata elements (descriptive, administrative, technical, use, and preservation) from different schemas, vocabularies, applications, and other building blocks can be combined in an interoperable way. The components of a metadata record can be regarded as various pieces of a puzzle. They might be put together by combining pieces of metadata descriptions coming from different processes (by humans or machines). They might also be used and reused piece-by-piece when new records need to be generated by humans or machines. For a long time libraries have been creating rich descriptive metadata. In newer, nonlibrary catalog applications, such as digital images or assets collections, these descriptive metadata components may be reused or combined when other pieces of metadata are generated.

The Metadata Encoding and Transmission Standard (METS) (see Chapter 5, Section 5.7.1) provides a framework for incorporating various components from various sources under one structure and also makes it possible to "glue" the pieces together into a record. METS is a standard for packaging descriptive, administrative, and structural metadata into one XML document for interactions with digital repositories. It thus provides a framework for combining several internal metadata structures with external schemas. The Resource Description Framework (RDF) of the W3C provides a mechanism for integrating multiple metadata schemes for the description of Web resources, and is discussed in detail in Chapter 5, Sections 5.5.4 and 5.7.2. RDF is a data model that provides a framework whereby independent communities can develop vocabularies that suit their specific needs and then share those vocabularies with other communities. It utilizes the XML namespace to effectively allow RDF statements to reference a particular RDF vocabulary or schema. Each metadata element set constitutes a namespace bound by the rules and conventions determined by its maintenance agency. The metadata schema designer, by declaring the namespace, will be able to define the context for a particular term, thereby assuring that the term has a unique definition within the bounds of the declared namespace. Also, by declaring various namespaces within a block of metadata, the elements within that metadata can be identified as belonging to one or another element set (Duval et al., 2002). Consequently, multiple namespaces expressed in XML may be defined to allow elements from different schemas to be combined into a single resource description.

8.5 Achieving Interoperability at the Repository Level

When multiple sources are searched using a single search engine, one of the major problems is that the retrieved results are rarely presented in a consistent, systematic, or reliable set of delineated formats. Another serious problem with distributed, independent metadata resources is that each original metadata source provider may have used different metadata schemas and/or applied them differently in the creation of metadata records. A metadata repository, which may be stored in a physical location or may consist of a virtual database in which metadata records have been drawn from separate sources, provides a viable solution to such interoperability problems by maintaining a consistent and reliable means for accessing data. This is illustrated in Figure 8-5-1 that

Figure 8-5-1. Metadata records are integrated into a repository.

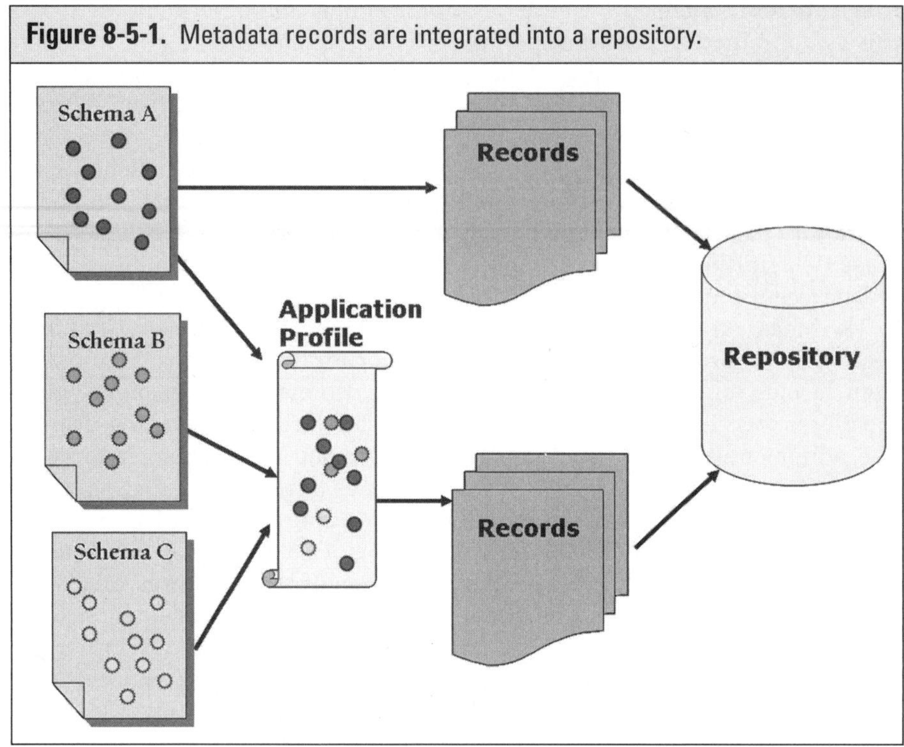

shows records from multiple sources (with differently applied metadata schemas or application profiles) being integrated into a repository.

Developmental ideas or processes related to ensuring interoperability at the repository level include metadata harvesting, supporting multiple formats, aggregation, crosswalking services, value-based mapping for cross-collection searching, and value-based co-occurrence mapping. One question a repository faces is whether to allow each original metadata source to keep its own format. If not, how will it convert or integrate all metadata records into a standardized format? If this is so, how will it support cross-collection search? A number of approaches that represent different solutions are found in the following section.

8.5.1 Metadata Repository Based on the Open Archives Initiative (OAI) Protocol

Chapter 6 introduced the primary metadata records harvesting protocol: the Open Archives Initiative—Protocol for Metadata Harvesting (OAI-PMH). A successful example of a metadata repository is the NSDL (National Science Digital Library) Metadata Repository (MR), a key component of the NSDL architecture. Its metadata repository management system is designed to collect, store, maintain, and expose metadata that are contributed by NSDL projects, which have used various metadata schemas. In addition to the thousands of item-level metadata records for individual items in the repository, it also holds collection-level metadata for each collection included in the NSDL (Arms et al., 2003). The Metadata Repository has also facilitated the construction of an automated "ingestion" system, based on the OAI-PMH. With this protocol, metadata flows into the Metadata Repository with a minimum of ongoing human intervention (Hillmann, Dushay, and Phipps, 2004).

8.5.2 Metadata Repository Supporting Multiple Formats Without Record Conversion

A different approach that circumvents the need to convert metadata records in an integrated service is utilized by DLESE. This very successful distributed community effort involves educators, students, and scientists working together to build and provide access to high-quality resources consisting of earth system imagery and data sets for teaching and learning about the Earth's systems at all levels. The mechanism that has resulted from this effort—DLESE Collection System (DCS, http://www.dlese.org/libdev/dcs_overview.html, accessed 2007)—is a tool that allows participants to build their own collections of Earth system item-level metadata records, and to develop, manage, search, and share these collections, all without converting every metadata record into a uniform format. The metadata records for each collection are structured according to an XML schema that specifies required and optional metadata (and in some cases legal values) for a particular metadata field. The DCS framework that manages metadata records has three main components: the schema, field files, and framework-settings. Each collection may have a different XML schema (DLESE, 2005).

The DLESE Collection System currently supports the DLESE metadata frameworks of ADN for resources typically used in learning environments (see Section 8.3.4). It also provides information on news and opportunities (for events or time-sensitive resources), on collections (for groups of metadata records as an entire entity), as well as annotations for additional information about resources or information not directly found in a resource. Other XML schema-based metadata frameworks can be supported by configuring the DCS to point to the XML schema file. When searching through DLESE metadata formats, both keyword and field searches are supported across and within collections. When searching through non-DLESE metadata formats, or formats for which the tool has not been configured for interpretation, only keyword searches are supported (DLESE, 2005).

8.5.3 Aggregation and Enriched Metadata Records in a Repository

Problems that limit the usefulness of metadata include incomplete data (e.g., "format" data is missing), incorrect data, confusing data, and insufficient data (e.g., no indication of encoding schemes). These problems can be partially eliminated through a process called "aggregation" in a metadata repository

Figure 8-5-2. Enriched metadata records.

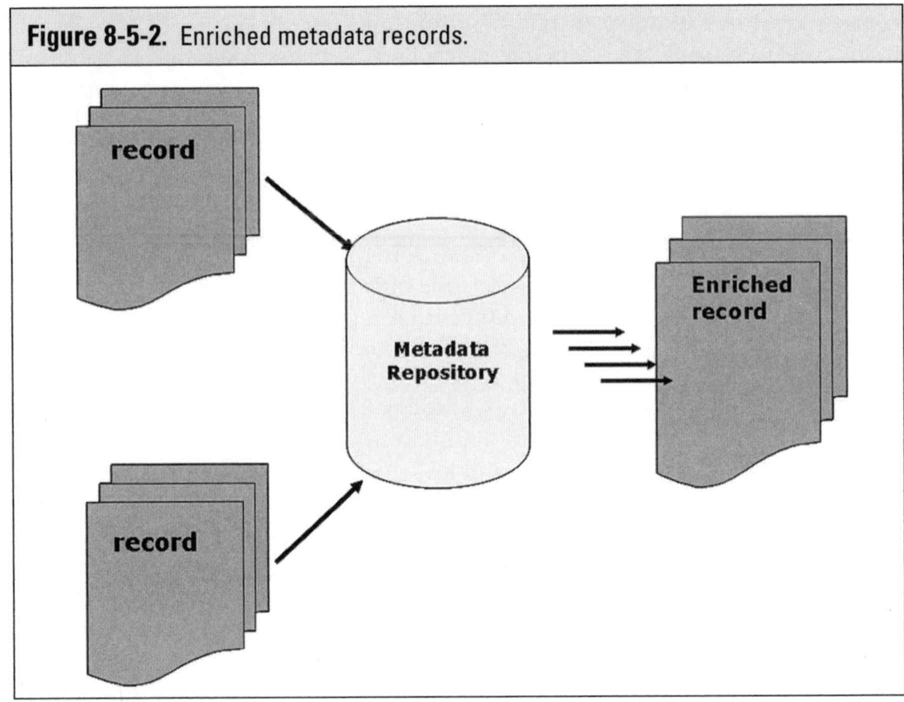

(Dushay and Hillmann, 2003; Hillmann, Dushay, and Phipps, 2004) (see Chapter 5, Section 5.7.3). The concept behind this process is that each metadata record contains a series of statements about a particular resource, and consequently metadata from different sources can be aggregated to build a more complete profile for that resource (see Figure 8-5-2, above). Thus a new role for "metadata aggregators" is to provide enhanced metadata from and for other services to reuse, and include the following tasks: integrating fragmentary metadata created by automated services, improving metadata by standardization, and exposing all relevant data in ways that will allow consumers to evaluate quality and usefulness (Hillmann, Dushay, and Phipps, 2004).

8.5.4 Element-based and Value-based Crosswalking Services

Although at present crosswalks have paved the way to relatively effective exchange and sharing of schema and data, a further need exists for effective crosswalks to solve everyday problems of ensuring consistency in large multisource databases. Efforts to establish a crosswalking service at OCLC (Godby, Young, and Childress, 2004) indicate that robust systems are needed that can handle validation, enhancement, multiple character encodings, and also allow human guidance of the translation process. The OCLC researchers have developed a model that associates three pieces of information: crosswalk, source metadata standard, and target metadata standard. The work proceeds from the hypothesis that usable crosswalks must be characterized by the following:

- A set of mappings between metadata standards that is endorsed by a stakeholder community
- A machine-processable encoding
- A well-defined relationship between source and target metadata standards, which must make reference to particular versions and syntactic encodings (Godby, Young, and Childress, 2004)

Note that various communities or applications do not usually assume the second characteristic, "a machine-processable encoding," in many of the crosswalks that have been developed. If implemented, one outcome would be "a repository that collects publicly accessible metadata into a repository that can be harvested using standard XML protocols and provides tools for creating sample services, such as customizable views of the data" (Godby, Young, and Childress, 2004).

This model of a crosswalking service could also be used for value-based crosswalking services. Researchers at the NSDL (Phipps, Hillmann, and Paynter, 2005) have also included a crosswalking service in their sequence of metadata enhancement services. These crosswalking services are a metadata augmentation operation that generates new fielded metadata values based on crosswalking from a source (schema or vocabulary) to a target (schema or vocabulary). The operation can be performed on either controlled or uncontrolled vocabulary value strings associated with specific elements.

Both element-based and value-based crosswalking services improve the reusability of metadata in various knowledge domains. They help to represent the attributes of resources in familiar terms to particular groups of users in filtering their search results (Phipps, Hillmann, and Paynter, 2005).

8.5.5 Value-based Mapping for Cross-database Searching

The Multilingual Access to Subjects (MACS) project illustrates another value-based mapping approach for achieving interoperability among existing metadata databases. MACS is a European project designed to allow users to search across library cataloging databases of partner libraries in different languages, which currently include English, French, and German. Specifically, the project aims to provide multilingual subject access to library catalogs by establishing equivalence links among three lists of subject headings: SWD/RSWK (Schlagwortnormdatei/Regeln für den Schlagwortkatalog) for German, RAMEAU (*Répertoire d'autorité-matière encyclopédique et alphabétique unifié*) for French, and LCSH (*Library of Congress Subject Headings*) for English.

Instead of integrating records or mapping data for every field, MACS only maps the values in the subject field. The method employed for mapping compares subject headings in three monolingual lists and checks the consistency of bibliographic records retrieved with these headings. The links are analyzed on three levels: terminological level, e.g., subject heading; semantic level, e.g., authority record; and, syntactic level, e.g., application (Freyre and Naudi, 2003). Using any of the three languages involved in the MACS project, a user can search and find bibliographic information of items hosted in the four national libraries of France, Germany, Switzerland, and the United Kingdom.

When a search for "all terrain cycling" is initiated, the equivalents of the English heading in SWD (German) and RAMEAU (French) will also be displayed. When no exact mapping exists, a combination of two or more headings using the AND or OR Boolean operators is provided. For example, when the searcher chooses "all terrain cycling" to search, results from all participating national library catalogs are displayed. When an item on the search result list is selected, a full record from that particular catalog is displayed. The values in the *Subjects* fields of these records include subject headings in different languages or notations. Without a mapping process among the three lists of subject headings, cross-database searches based on these strings would be impossible.

8.5.6 Value-based Co-occurrence Mapping

With regard to searching, co-occurrence mapping (Figure 8-5-3) is similar to the MACS project discussed previously. However, this approach uses values already present in the subject fields and regards as equivalent the subject terms from different vocabularies in the subject fields of the same record. When a metadata record includes terms from multiple controlled vocabularies, the co-occurrence of subject terms enables an automatic, loose mapping between vocabularies. As a group, these loosely mapped terms can answer a particular search query or group of questions.

Existing metadata standards and best practice guides have provided an opportunity to use the co-occurrence mapping method. The art- and image-related metadata standard VRA Core Categories version 3.0 requires the use of the *Art and Architecture Thesaurus* (AAT) for the *Type*, *Material*, and *Style/Period* elements and, for the *Culture* and *Subject* elements, recommends the use of AAT, LCSH, *Thesaurus of Graphic Materials* (TGM), ICONCLASS (an international classification system for iconographic research and the documentation of images), and *Sears Subject Headings* (Figure 8-5-4).

Another example of a co-occurrence mapping source is the Gazetteer Standard Report of the Alexandria Digital Library. Under *Feature Class*, terms from two controlled vocabularies are recorded (Figure 8-5-5).

Metadata records often include both controlled terms and uncontrolled keywords. Mapped subject terms can be used as access points that lead to full metadata records. With the progress of the aggregation services, more "fielded-in"

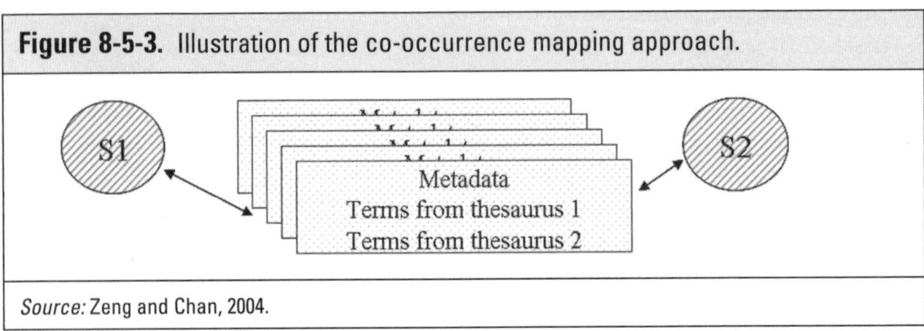

Figure 8-5-3. Illustration of the co-occurrence mapping approach.

Source: Zeng and Chan, 2004.

Figure 8-5-4. Controlled vocabularies required or recommended for use in VRA Core metadata records.

Type	Data Values (controlled):	recommend AAT
Material	Data Values (controlled):	AAT
Technique	Data Values (controlled):	AAT
Style/Period	Data Values (controlled):	recommend AAT
Culture	Data Values:	recommend AAT, LCSH
Subject	Data Values:	recommend AAT, TGM, ICONCLASS, Sears Subject Headings

Source: Compiled based on VRA Core 3.0.

Figure 8-5-5. An ADL record showing assigned values from two vocabulary sources.

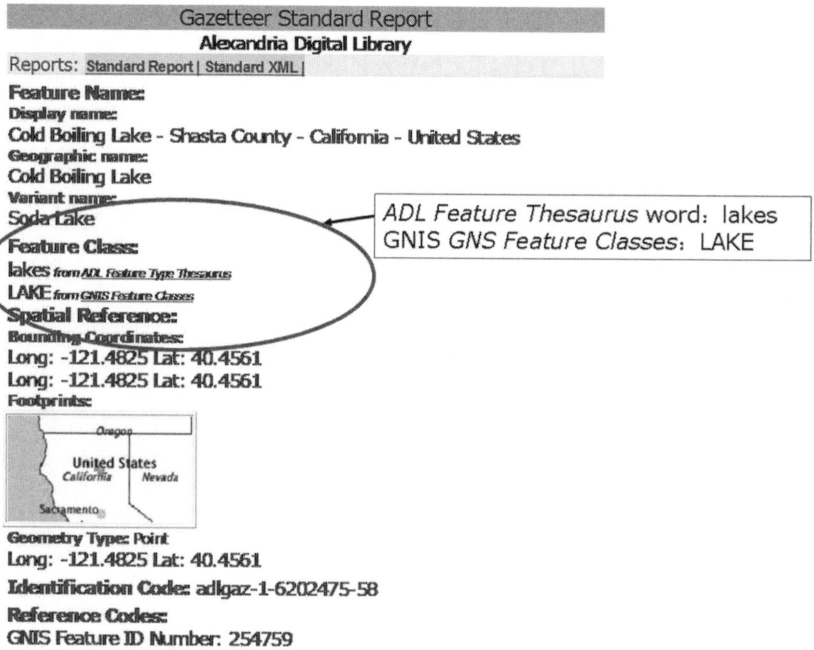

Gazetteer Standard Report
Alexandria Digital Library
Reports: Standard Report | Standard XML |
Feature Name:
Display name:
Cold Boiling Lake - Shasta County - California - United States
Geographic name:
Cold Boiling Lake
Variant name:
Soda Lake
Feature Class:
lakes *from ADL Feature Type Thesaurus*
LAKE *from GNIS Feature Classes*
Spatial Reference:
Bounding Coordinates:
Long: -121.4825 Lat: 40.4561
Long: -121.4825 Lat: 40.4561
Footprints:
Oregon
United States
California
Nevada
Sacramento
Geometry Type: Point
Long: -121.4825 Lat: 40.4561
Identification Code: adlgaz-1-6202475-58
Reference Codes:
GNIS Feature ID Number: 254759

ADL Feature Thesaurus word: lakes
GNIS *GNS Feature Classes*: LAKE

Source: Courtesy of Alexandria Digital Library, University of California Santa Barbara.

value strings associated with multiple sources may be integrated to enrich metadata records. As more co-occurrence-types of applications become widely used, loosely mapped values will become very useful in searching.

8.6. Conclusion

In present-day digital library environments, in which individual collections of massive heterogeneous objects need to be unified and linked in a single resource, we are witnessing both the growth of different metadata and the attempts to reconcile the common attributes in the existing overlapping standards (Ercegovac, 1999). Depending on the point at which interoperability efforts are initiated—at the beginning of forming a collection or repository before metadata records have been created or when participants already have existing records—different approaches and methods are being tested and employed at schema level, record level, and repository level. The results of interoperability efforts may be observed in the element-based and value-based approaches. Currently, mapping metadata schemas for the sake of interoperability still requires enormous intellectual effort even with all the assistance that computer technology provides. Nevertheless, technology has provided many more possibilities for facilitating and enhancing metadata semantic interoperability efforts. Still needed are the intellectual preparations to support the goal of interoperability and the practical tools to carry out such activities. If the information community is to provide maximal access to all the information available between and across digital libraries and repositories, information professionals must give high priority to creating and maintaining the highest feasible level of interoperability among both extant and new information services.

Suggested Readings

Arms, William Y., Diane Hillmann, Carl Lagoze, Dean Krafft, Richard Maris, John Saylor, Carol Terrizzi, and Herbert Van de Sompel. 2002. "A Spectrum of Interoperability: The Site for Science Prototype for the NSDL." *D-Lib Magazine* [Online] 8, no. 1. Available: www.dlib.org/dlib/january02/arms/01arms.html.

Heery, Rachel. 2004. "Metadata Futures: Steps Toward Semantic Interoperability." In *Metadata in Practice*, edited by Diane I. Hillmann and Elaine L. Westbrooks, pp. 257–271. Chicago: American Library Association.

Johnston, Pete. 2003. "Metadata and Interoperability in a Complex World." *Ariadne* [Online] no. 37. Available: www.ariadne.ac.uk/issue37/dc-2003-rpt/.

Phipps, Jon, Diane I. Hillmann, and Gordon Paynter. 2005. "Orchestrating Metadata Enhancement Services: Introducing Lenny." *Proceedings of the International Conference on Dublin Core and Metadata Applications*, Madrid, Spain. Available: http://arxiv.org/ftp/cs/papers/0501/0501083.pdf.

St. Pierre, Margaret, and William P. LaPlant Jr. 1998. *Issues in Crosswalking Content Metadata Standards*. Bethesda, MD: NISO Press. Available: www.niso.org/publications/white_papers/crosswalk/.

Suleman, Hussein, and Edward Fox. 2001. "The Open Archives Initiative: Realizing Simple and Effective Digital Library Interoperability." *Journal of Library Administration* 35, no. 1/2: 125–145.

Exercises

Note: This exercise is designed to have individuals collaborate by working together in groups.

Based on the discussion in this chapter, work in a group (if possible) to develop collaborative models to represent approaches that ensure interoperability. Present your model(s) in graphic form (see for example, the methods used in direct crosswalking and cross-switching models in Figures 8-3-2 and 8-3-3). Where graphic models exist, try to represent the same mechanism in a different manner that still accurately conveys the principles involved. Attempt to design a model for each approach discussed in the chapter. Be creative and highly abstract, and, where group work is possible, engage in lively discussion and brainstorming about new model designs.

Part IV
Metadata Outlook in Research

9

Metadata Research Landscape

The proliferation of metadata in more than a decade has paralleled the rapid advances in both computing technologies and Web development. Since the first Dublin Core workshop in 1995, metadata research has expanded well beyond the traditional boundaries of describing documents. The term *metadata* has become a symbol for digital information organization and management and is now widely accepted by academic and governmental institutions, industry, and other types of organizations. Metadata research embraces both conceptual and practical explorations of metadata models, schemas, tools, systems, and practices. Several reviews have been published since the mid-1990s that examine the growth of metadata research and development (Woodward, 1996; Vellucci, 1998). Specialized surveys have also been conducted to delineate technological applications in metadata (Hunter, 2003) and methodologies used in providing metadata interoperability and standardization (Chan and Zeng, 2006; Zeng and Chan, 2006).

Metadata research has gone through three phases over the past 13 years since the first DC conference in 1995. The first phase (ca. 1995–1998) was characterized by exploring and defining metadata, the roles it plays in representing and organizing Internet resources, and how metadata can adapt to domain-specific (or local) requirements for organizing networked information resources. Vellucci (1998) provides a lengthy review section documenting the debate about whether metadata is an extension of its precursor - traditional cataloging, or something in its own right. Toward the end of this period, it became clear that Dublin Core metadata elements had been accepted as the base on which many organizations and application domains developed their own metadata element sets for organizing and accessing enterprise content and/or digital collections. Various metadata creation tools also mushroomed, although many were stand-alone templates that lacked technological rigor. Only a handful of such tools have remained active today.

The rapid development of metadata soon created new issues and challenges that fell into two categories: interoperability and standardization. Metadata activities in the second phase (ca. 1998–2003) largely targeted these two areas. During this period the Dublin Core became an international standard (ISO15386:2003) and many professional and industrial associations established industrywide or domain-specific metadata standards, examples being IEEE LOM (LTSC, 2004b), the Content Standard for Digital Geospatial Metadata (FGDC, 1998), and the VRA Core (VRA, 2002). Various digital library projects also generated a large number of customized metadata schemes based on local description and retrieval needs. However, scattered and heterogeneous metadata systems created interoperability problems of differing magnitudes. Whether within the same organization or throughout a consortium, converging metadata from different collections or sources is a requirement for data sharing and federated search. Efforts began to allow metadata artifacts—application profiles, metadata repositories, metadata registries, crosswalks between metadata schemes and between traditional bibliographic standards and metadata schemes—to be interoperable.

The technological advances have intimately influenced metadata research. The third phase (ca. 2003–present) of metadata research experienced a maturing research field that continues to expand on many fronts, ranging from theoretical models and frameworks to grassroots tagging of almost any type of information object. Dilemmas about the ever- increasing volume of digital information combined with the complexities, high cost, and slow creation of metadata continue to be the main obstacles to organizing digital information. Efforts to address these challenges and dilemmas have created a highly interdisciplinary research field that blends different perspectives and orientations (as shown in Table 9-0-1).

The text thus far extensively discussed all of these perspectives, concentrating especially on schemes and schemas. Research areas covered in previous chapters are not reiterated. The following sections review major research areas in metadata architecture, modeling, and metadata semantics that have not yet been discussed.

9.1 Research in Metadata Architecture

The term *metadata architecture* first appeared in Berners-Lee's article on the axioms of Web architecture. He views metadata architecture essentially as the architecture of the Web that consists of documents, metadata, and links. "The architecture is of metadata represented as a set of independent assertions" (Berners-Lee, 1997). Berners-Lee's view on metadata architecture represents a computer science perspective in which data are encoded in machine-processable form and communicated via protocols. The paradigm of processability and executability in metadata can be found in many publications written by computer science researchers. For example, Daniel Jr. et al. propose a concept of *distributed active relationships* (DAR), which "are relations that not only may be drawn from anywhere on the network, but may also be executable" (Daniel Jr., Lagoze, and Payette, 1998). This paradigm is reflected in Duval et al. (2002), in which the authors clarify confusions about metadata and specify the principles of modularity, extensibility, refinement, and multilingualism. Early debate between metadata architecture minimalists and structuralists (Weibel and Hakala, 1998; Lagoze, 2001) reflects different views held by the library

Table 9-0-1. Topics of metadata by research perspectives.

Research perspective	Topics
Models and frameworks	Relational metadata, modeling for mobile environment, ontological models, semantic modeling, ontological conversion of metadata schemes, abstract models
Schemes and schemas	Structures, semantics, best practice guidelines, incorporation of external standards and schemes, application profiles
Metadata generation	Structured representation, conceptual linking, video metadata editing, automatic acquisition/assignment/generation, tagging, collection-level metadata
Systems and architecture	XML encoding, open source software, federated systems, multi-agent systems, personal metadata service, RDF-based annotation, bucket framework
Repository and interoperability	Harvesting, federated metadata repository, OAI protocols, low-barrier framework, federation evolution metamodel, meta-searching, mapping, maximizing metadata, metadata registry
Evaluation of quality and usefulness	Quality assessment, evaluation of automatically-generated metadata, element usage, automatic evaluation

community and the computer science community. Duval et al.'s article (2002) is a good summary on the convergence of the two schools of thought about metadata architecture.

Research in metadata architecture in the past decade was divided into two camps with differing perspectives and paradigms: the processability and executability paradigm rooted in computer science, and the description paradigm in library and information science. The processability paradigm concentrates on metadata response to system or user requests, whereas the description paradigm is more concerned with capturing the data about digital objects in the event that they are requested by user queries. An ongoing process toward unifying the two paradigms during the past decade reflects the development of XML/RDF-based languages that combine semantic structures and relationships with computational syntax, e.g., the Web Ontology Language (OWL). These XML/RDF languages provide mechanisms for expressing relationships between classes of data that can be processed by computer programs.

The convergence of the two paradigms is manifested by the rapid growth of application profiles. As localized metadata artifacts, application profiles are becoming popular because of their conformance with metadata standards (while still maintaining sufficient flexibility and extensibility for local needs). The ability of application profiles to define the implementation model in addition to element semantics opens up a promising amendment to the disconnection between conceptual metadata models and metadata schemes. Greenberg, Carrier, and Dube (2007) reported three levels of application profiles. The level-one application profile is intended for initial repository implementation, as with most existing application profiles. The second level extends level-one functionalities by capturing the complex relationships that exist among data objects and supporting expanded usage, interoperability, preservation, and administration. The third level will support "next generation" a.k.a. *NextGen*/Web 2.0 functionalities in the repository, such as personalization, social tagging, syntactic interoperability for data, data and collection visualization, and user feedback. As libraries face challenges to integrate heterogeneous metadata packets, application profiles will become a practical and effective solution for addressing interoperability problems. A main outcome of the *DC-2007 International Conference on Dublin Core and Metadata Applications* is the "Singapore Framework," a set of documents that constitutes the specification of a *Dublin Core Application Profile*. It puts a formal *Description Set Profile* into the heart of functional requirements, domain models, syntax bindings, and user guidelines (Nilsson, 2007b).

The development in metadata architecture expanded the metadata concept into new territory. Traditionally, metadata is referred to data describing information objects—documents, Web pages/sites, and audio/visual objects (rather than the content components within these objects). In the digital information world, however, conventional information objects are being constructed (sometimes assembled) from components. Each component is often marked with some tags, e.g., XML-tagged learning objects and cultural objects, which are considered forms of metadata. This trend corresponds to what some of the conceptual metadata models such as the <indecs> (see Section 2.5 and next section) have been advocating (Rust and Bide, 2000). This infrastructure project is aimed at finding practical solutions to interoperability affecting all types of rights holders in a networked, e-commerce environment. Metadata is also paralleling numerous specialized markup languages (such as MatML (Materials Markup Language), MathML (Mathematical Markup Language), or CML (Chemical Markup Language), developed for almost all industrial sectors (and in many respects overlap with the metadata conceptual approach). Resource-level description alone would be limited in generating rich, granular, associative metadata because such metadata is usually created by a third party (other than the creator) after the resource has been published or distributed. Markup languages can add semantic tags to pieces and blocks of texts or objects and organize them into structures, which equate a set of metadata elements at a greatly refined level, and thus allows automatic generation of more coherent and finely granular resource descriptions. Although merging specialized markup languages with metadata schemes has proven to be complicated and difficult to implement (Shreve & Zeng, 2003), it is a field worth watching for metadata architecture research.

9.2 Research in Metadata Modeling

Metadata models constitute just one of the many frontiers of research in recent years. In addition to the abstract models developed by the metadata community, e.g., Dublin Core Abstract Model (DCAB), the CDWA and CCO entity-relationship model, and the FRBR conceptual model (see Chapter 5), researchers have used varying approaches to analyze domains and seek effective ways to build metadata models. These approaches can be divided into two broad categories: *element-based expansion* and *ontological modeling*.

Element-based expansion involves customizing metadata standards by either expanding the standard elements or adding new local elements. Application profiles are the metadata artifacts that result from this approach (see Section 3.4). This method is common in digital library projects, where the representation of domain information requires specialized metadata elements that are absent from the standards being adopted. Examples include DLESE (www.dlese.org/Metadata/dlese-ims/index.htm), GEM (www.thegateway.org/about/documentation/metadataElements), and the GREEN project (http://appling.kent.edu/NSDLGreen/GreenDLMetadata.htm), among others. The expansion of standard elements may take domain-specific markup languages and other relevant standards as the extended structure for the domain knowledge—the GREEN project has added elements from the Mathematic Markup Language (MathML) for the mathematics formulae and expressions contained in the metadata schema to create a customized version of the LOM scheme (Shreve and Zeng, 2003). The customization of metadata schemas tailors the elements to fit local representation needs, whereas the core elements comply with an established metadata standard. The element-based expansion maintains the linear structure, i.e., hierarchical relationship among elements; horizontal associations among elements can only be established with data binding, either as database tables or XML schemas.

Ontological modeling of metadata takes an object-oriented view of all elements in a metadata scheme and treats them as concepts, concept properties, instances, and relations. One such ontological model is the <indecs> metadata framework, which "was created to address the need, in the digital environment, to put different creation identifiers and their supporting metadata into a framework where they could operate side by side, especially to support the management of intellectual property rights" (Rust and Bide, 2000: 4). Lagoze and Hunter (2001) built a conceptual model to facilitate interoperability between metadata ontologies from different domains. Their model uses *Entity* as the root class and assigns three categories—*Temporality*, Actuality, and *Abstraction*—as its subclasses. The next level of subclasses includes *Artifact, Event, Situation, Action, Agent, Work, Manifestation, Item, Time*, and *Place*. The properties of these concept classes are defined as a set of relations such as *isPartOf, inContext, contains, phaseOf*, and *hasRealization*. As stated, this model is syntax-neutral and the authors suggest using the Resource Description Framework (RDF)/XML as the data binding language (Lagoze and Hunter, 2001).

Although Logoze and Hunter are attempting to create a metadata model without the influence of traditional cataloging practices, other ontology projects have developed metadata models based on existing metadata standards and controlled vocabularies. Kamel Boulos, Roudsari, and Carson (2001) developed a Dublin Core (DC) metadata ontology for the health informatics domain, in which the *Subject* element in DC was populated with the Unified Medical

Language System (UMLS) vocabulary and clinical codes. Using a controlled vocabulary to build ontology-based metadata schemas is another approach. Qin and Paling (2001) analyzed the controlled vocabulary from the Gateway to Educational Materials (GEM) and constructed an ontology to represent the facets of subject, pedagogy, relation, audience, educational level, format, and language in learning objects. Their metadata model uses Resource as the root concept and has *Resource Type* as subclass (i.e., lesson plan is a subclass of resource) and the aforementioned facets are global properties that may be inherited by the subclasses of Resource. No matter whether ontological modeling is begun from scratch or is based on existing metadata schemas (or controlled vocabulary), a common feature shared by the projects is that they all use an object-oriented approach to analyze information objects and their content. This creates the technical conditions necessary for modularized and reusable metadata schemas.

One application in ontological modeling is building domain ontologies for content representation and categorizing digital objects. Khan et al. (2005) created a domain-dependent ontology to represent the context and meaning of audio objects' content. The most specific concepts in this ontology are considered metadata. By using automatic context extraction techniques, the more general concepts in the ontology are used to categorize audio objects. Khan, McLeod, and Hovy (2005) demonstrate how metadata may be generated and audio selection customized with the employment of this ontology model.

To summarize, the approach of element-based expansion is common to all metadata creation; it is also an easier way to adopt a metadata standard(s). The metadata artifact that results from this process is often called an "application profile." Disadvantages include limitations of offering finer-grained semantics at the conceptual level and in establishing relationships between related concepts (that can be established only at the implementation stage). The ontological modeling approach claims to compensate for the limitations of an element-based expansion approach. As a promising methodology, it is still being explored. Experiments with domain-dependent ontologies have been conducted in metadata extraction and information retrieval. However, questions remain on how to construct the metadata models that maximize the potential of born-digital information objects, and to unite semantics with syntax to minimize implementation efforts.

9.3 Research in Metadata Semantics

The perpetual issue in metadata applications is semantics—the meaning of metadata elements and the values for those elements. Semantics is considered critical for any metadata application because it is the first line of defense against inaccuracy and misunderstanding, and is *fundamental* for interoperability. Many domains have developed their metadata standards to meet the needs of their community and some of these standards comprise a large number of elements and layers (as discussed in Chapters 2 and 3). However, studies indicate that not all elements in these standards are adopted by individual application projects. Developing domain-specific application profiles has become a widespread practice (Friesen, 2004; Godby, 2004).

Metadata semantics is not simply a technical issue concerned about element definition or controlled vocabulary for value space. The new applications and tools of *social semantics* open up a new perspective for reexamining metadata semantics. Community tagging, social bookmarking, or any form of social semantics raises a great challenge to the authority and effectiveness of controlled semantics as represented by subject heading lists, thesauri, classification schemes, and taxonomies. This challenge is even greater when taking the full-text/free-text search capabilities of popular search engines into account. In this case, social semantics is comprised of the keywords or phrases employed by a community of users to represent information objects in various ways. Immediate questions arise: why does the public embrace social semantics for representing the information object content? What are the social, cultural, and technological forces behind this trend? What implications does it have on controlled semantics? Should (or could) the public be educated to become better "taggers?" What does it mean to be a better tagger anyway? These questions have been addressed by the metadata research community to some extent.

The tags added to classify or categorize digital objects—bookmarks, photos, blogs, and so on—have been given a new name, *folksonomies* (Smith, 2004). They are essentially user-assigned keywords describing personal (or any) digital information collections. The tags are often one-word or compound-word keywords, category names, or metadata (Guy and Tonkin, 2006). These tags have many flaws in the eyes of trained information professionals; they are ambiguous, have single word restriction, and lack synonym control (Mathes, 2004). Researchers have studied this new phenomenon from the perspectives of the social network (Liu, Maes, and Davenport, 2006; Mika, 2005), cooperative or social classification (Mathes, 2004), and social annotations of the Web (Wu, Xian, and Yu 2006). Clearly, the theme common to all of the folksonomy studies is socially generated semantics, or more succinctly, social semantics.

The term *social semantics* first appeared in an article by Munindar P. Singh (2000). Although the context in which Singh defines this term is *Agent Communication Languages* (ACL), social semantics describes the case (and nature) of folksonomies well. Social semantics in ACL context refers to social commitments that are the beliefs and intentions inherently present during agent communication (Singh, 2000). The social semantics approach in ACL involves a social context "in which the given agents participate and within which they communicate" and "allows metacommitments to capture a variety of social and legal relations" (Singh, 2000: 34). Metaphorically, the social semantics concept can be used to explain the semantics generated by popular online tagging activities such as:

- Agents (individual participants) communicate their explicit beliefs and intentions.
- Such beliefs and intentions are public, i.e., observable, in terms of social commitments.

- Each communication implies three aspects of meaning: objective (the communication is true); subjective, (the communication is sincere); and practical (the speaker is justified in making the communication). (Singh, 2000)

Shirky (2005) regards controlled semantics as an attempt to read users' minds, which may work for specific domains. The "mind-reading" nature of controlled semantics, however, cannot factor in online social networks. His reasoning is that many participants in online communities are uncoordinated amateur users and naïve catalogers who have no agreed-upon authority among them. The large corpus of tags (without formal categories) are unstable and unrestricted entities and display a lack of clear edges, all of which make ontological classification difficult to function effectively (Shirky, 2005). Users' choices of tags, however, represent their beliefs and intentions and they should decide the meaning of these tags rather than be forced into structured hierarchical categorization. In this, Shirky's opinion is in accord with Singh's social semantics concept.

It is not surprising that many librarians and information professionals do not adhere to Shirky's position regarding a liberal treatment of folksonomies. Several publications report efforts to derive ontologies or ontological classification. These include a case study on emergent semantics in the social bookmark site del.icio.us by Michlmayr et al. (2005); extraction of community-based ontologies (Mika, 2005); and feral hypertext in literary and creative hypertext practice (Walker, 2005). Investigation has found that some folksonomy flaws have included misspelling, incorrect coding, and personal terms or phrases that would be meaningless devoid of context. They were so ill-constructed, and contained so many errors and ambiguities, that they could easily derail the value of the emergent social semantics. This disease of social semantics naturally concerns information professionals. The term *tag literacy* was even proposed to refer to the "'etiquette' of generating tags in a way that increases their social value, and balances individual needs with the needs of the group" (Mejias, 2005). Guy and Tonkin (2006) concur with Mejias' position and argue that a need exists to educate users to add better tags, and improve the systems to allow better addition of tags.

There is no doubt that folksonomies that have spread across online social networks contain "the rich meanings bottled within social network profiles" and these latent semantics may be harvested to reveal novel ways for representing and reasoning about Web users and people in general (Liu, Maes, and Davenport, 2006: 42). This premise led to Liu and colleagues' mining of 100,000 social network profiles that are mapped into a diverse ontology of music, films, foods, etc., by using the ontology-driven natural language normalization and machine learning techniques. The mining process went through five steps:

1. acquiring the profiles from social networking sites,
2. segmentation of the natural language profiles to produce a bag of descriptors,
3. mapping of natural language fragment descriptors into formal ontology,
4. learning the correlation matrix, and
5. discovering taste neighborhoods via morphological opening, and labeling the network topology.

Although Liu and colleagues' research concentrated on mining the "taste fabric" of social networks, they also applaud the emergent and implicit semantics from the unstructured Web as a source for mining social semantics that can be further refined and "transformed into powerful (soft) semantic resources that afford the ability to mediate informal and formal entities" (Liu, Maes, and Davenport, 2006: 44). This study provides insights into the research of social semantics in that it shows how powerful social semantics may become in representing and modeling Web users, and how such representation and modeling may eventually lead to a convergence between social and formal semantics.

Although attitudes toward social semantics vary among researchers with different viewpoints, online social networks are a huge mine of source-material for studying social semantics and how such social semantics will affect (and in what form or magnitude) controlled metadata semantics and the way that metadata will be generated.

9.4 Conclusions

Metadata development has shaped a number of distinctive—yet related—research fields in just over a decade. A large and growing portion of metadata development is the result of the continuous pursuit for more effective organization, retrieval, and management of digital information. Today's digital world has changed dramatically compared to 15 years ago. The participation of digital resource creators and that of the general public in producing and organizing digital information objects has effectively ended the era of librarians' or information professionals' dominance in this field. Metadata creation has become more distributed, participatory, and diversified in methods, practices, and tools. As digital information (and environments) evolves and as methods and technologies for metadata development improve, opportunities will be created for new research in metadata.

Interoperability was and still is one of the most active research areas. Early methods used to build interoperability included crosswalking between metadata schemas, which has evolved into metadata registries (a service providing metadata element registration for sharing and reuse). As metadata application profiles become an important method for developing customized metadata schemas, metadata registries will play more important roles for application projects in selecting useful elements and assembling metadata schemas that fit their needs.

Among promising developments is automatic metadata generation using multiple techniques and combined human- and machine-processing. Automatic extraction or generation using a single approach apparently has been unable to launch from the drydocks of the research lab into the sea of effective production application. Automatic extraction of metadata from digital images or audio/visual objects is emerging as an active research area. However, the metadata generated for these objects is often a mix of social tagging from general users and automatic extraction by computer programs. The rapid growth of media objects will generate ample research topics and opportunities in this area.

Metadata semantics will continue to be a major topic of research. The diverse semantic sources—informal lists, thesauri, classification schemes, ontologies, and XML-based domain markup languages—will all contribute to building the semantic foundation needed for interoperability and automatic metadata generation.

Current developments of the cyberinfrastructure present new realms for metadata in both research and applications. The concept of cyberinfrastructure represents "the coordinated aggregate of software, hardware and other technologies, as well as human expertise, required to support current and future discoveries in science and engineering. The challenge of cyberinfrastructure is to integrate relevant and often disparate resources to provide a useful, usable, and enabling framework for research and discovery characterized by broad access and 'end-to-end' coordination" (Berman, 2005). There has been "an outpouring of lengthy reports addressing and framing" the challenges facing information professionals in becoming literate and engaging in cyberinfrastructure development and utilization (Gold, 2007a; 2007b). Metadata plays a critical role in many areas of cyberinfrastructure. As Gold points out, sufficient metadata will be needed not only for keeping digital objects usable, but also for ensuring adequate (and legal) access and retrieval over the duration. The data curation community is codifying metadata practices and standards for developing computer-understandable data descriptions, which can support discovery across heterogeneous data collections and management of metadata and data collections across all data scales (Gold, 2007a).

Overall trends in metadata and organization of digital information reflect the larger trends in computer science, library and information science, and technology research. We are witnessing an acceptance that computer science and library and information science have much to share. Studies resulting from such collaboration have appeared repeatedly in publications. Metadata evaluation, especially that of a larger scale and on use and usefulness, has yet to catch up to the pace of metadata development. For future metadata research to be more fruitful, we must draw upon the insights gained from past metadata development evaluations.

Suggested Readings

Berners-Lee, Tim. 1997. "Metadata Architecture." Web page. Available: www.w3.org/DesignIssues/Metadata.html.

Duval, Erik, Wayne Hodgins, Stuart Sutton, and Stuart L. Weibel. 2002. "Metadata Principles and Practicalities." *D-Lib Magazine* [Online] 8, no. 4. Available: www.dlib/org/dlib/april02/weibel/04weibel.html.

Gold, Anna. 2007a. "Cyberinfrastructure, Data, and Libraries, Part 1: A Cyberinfrastructure Primer for Librarians." *D-Lib Magazine* [Online] 13, no. 9/10. Available: http://dlib.org/dlib/september07/gold/09gold-pt1.html.

Gold, Anna. 2007b. "Cyberinfrastructure, Data, and Libraries, Part 2: Libraries and the Data Challenge: Roles and Actions for Libraries." *D-Lib Magazine*

[Online] 13, no. 9/10. Available: http://dlib.org/dlib/september07/gold/09gold-pt2.html.

Liu, Hugo, Pattie Maes, and Glorianna Davenport. 2006. "Unraveling the Taste Fabric of Social Networks." *International Journal on Semantic Web and Information Systems* 2, no. 1: 42–71. Available: http://mf.media.mit.edu/pubs/journal/TasteFabric.pdf.

Exercise

Select a research topic from Table 9-0-1 and write a review of the literature and/or related projects.

Appendices
Sources and References

Appendix A
Metadata Standards

The following are metadata schemas, application profiles, and registries mentioned in the book.

ADN (ADEPT/DLESE/NASA) Metadata Framework
www.dlese.org/Metadata/adn-item/

ADN stands for **A**lexandria Digital Earth Prototype (ADEPT), the **D**igital Library for Earth System Education (DLESE), and **N**ASA's Joined Digital Library. Developed by incorporating metadata elements to describe educational resources used by the Earth system education community.

Adobe Extensible Metadata Platform (XMP)
Adobe Systems
www.adobe.com/products/xmp/

A labeling technology that allows embedding metadata into the file itself. It is based on open standards and implemented as a common metadata interchange platform across Adobe products.

Australasian Virtual Engineering Library (AVEL) Metadata Set
http://avel.library.uq.edu.au/technical.html

A gateway of quality Web resources developed collaboratively by a national team through an Australian Research Council (ARC) Research Infrastructure Grant from 1998-2002. Consists of nineteen elements based on Dublin Core.

Australian Government Locator Service (AGLS) Metadata Standard
www.naa.gov.au/records-management/publications/AGLS-Element.aspx

Maintained by the National Archives of Australia and published as Australian Standard AS 5044 by Standards Australia in December 2002. A set of nineteen descriptive elements. It has been mandated for use by Commonwealth Government agencies.

Biological Data Profile of the Content Standard for Digital Geospatial Metadata
FGDC-STD-001.1-1999

www.fgdc.gov/projects/FGDC-standards-projects/metadata/biometadata/biodatap.pdf

Provides a user-defined or theme-specific profile of the FGDC Content Standard for Digital Geospatial Metadata to increase its utility for documenting biological resources data and information. This standard serves as the metadata content standard for the National Biological Information Infrastructure (NBII).

CanCore
www.cancore.ca/guidelines/drd/

The CanCore Guidelines for the Access for All Digital Resource Description are synchronized with the IEEE LOM standard, and include best practice recommendations for all LOM elements.

Categories for the Description of Works of Art (CDWA)
www.getty.edu/research/conducting_research/standards/cdwa/

A product of the Art Information Task Force (AITF) funded by the J. Paul Getty Trust; Murtha Baca and Patricia Harpring, eds, Los Angeles: J. Paul Getty Trust and the College Art Association, 2000. For describing works of art, architecture, groups of objects, and visual and textual surrogates, CDWA includes 381 categories and subcategories.

CDWA Lite
www.getty.edu/research/conducting_research/standards/cdwa/cdwalite.html

J. Paul Getty Trust and ARTstor. A subset of elements taken based on the Categories for the Description of Works of Art (CDWA) and Cataloging Cultural Objects: A Guide to Describing Cultural Works and Their Images (CCO). It is an XML schema to describe core records for works of art and material culture.

Content Standards for Digital Geospatial Metadata (CSDGM)
The Federal Geographic Data Committee (FGDC)
www.fgdc.gov/standards/projects/FGDC-standards-projects/metadata/base-metadata/index_html

A set of terminology and definitions for the documentation of digital geospatial data.

copyrightMD
California Digital Library (CDL) Rights Management Group
www.cdlib.org/inside/projects/rights/schema/

An XML schema for rights metadata. It is a part of the CDL Rights Management Framework that provides information and tools that guide project managers and participants in making and recording decisions about rights.

Core Metadata Elements: An International Metadata Standard for Geographic Information (ISO 19115)
www.iso.org/iso/en/CatalogueDetailPage.CatalogueDetail?CSNUMBER=26020&ICS1=35&ICS2=240&ICS3=70

Defines the schema required for describing geographic information and services.

CORES Registry
www.cores-eu.net/registry/

Maintained by UKOLN (UK Office for Library Networking). The CORES project provides a forum to encourage sharing of metadata semantics. The CORES Registry hosts core vocabularies and profiles enabling projects and services to declare their usage of standards in schemas based on a common model.

Darwin Core
www.nbii.gov/portal/community/Communities/Toolkit/Metadata/Darwin_Core_Metadata/

Developed by the University of Kansas Natural History Museum and Biodiversity Research Center as part of its Species Analyst research project. A standard for describing objects contained within natural history specimen collections and species observation databases.

Data Dictionary—Technical Metadata for Digital Still Images (ANSI/NISO Z39.87-2006)
www.niso.org/kfile_download?pt=RkGKiXzW643YeUaYUqZ1BFwDhIG4-24RJbcZBWg8uE4vWdpZsJDs4RjLz0t90_d5_ymGsj_IKVa86hjP37r_hM9t9qad1BrrORLqssvegis%3D

A comprehensive list of technical data elements relevant to the management of digital still images, it is designed to facilitate interoperability between systems, services, and software as well as to support the long-term management of and continuing access to digital image collections.

Digital Object Identifier (DOI)® Kernel Declaration
International DOI Foundation (IDF)
www.doi.org
DOI® Kernel Metadata Declaration specification and XML Schema
www.doi.org/handbook_2000/appendix_6.pdf

The DOI Kernel Declaration provides a basic set of interoperable, descriptive metadata exists so that DOI names can be discovered and disambiguated across multiple services and Application Profiles in a coherent way.

DCMI Government Application Profile (DC-Gov)
DCMI-Government Working Group
http://dublincore.org/groups/government/profile-200111.shtml

Clarifies the use of DC in a governmental environment.

DCMI Metadata Terms
Dublin Core Metadata Initiative (DCMI)
http://dublincore.org/documents/dcmi-terms/

An authoritative specification of all metadata terms maintained by DCMI—elements, element refinements, encoding schemes, and vocabulary terms (the DCMI Type Vocabulary).

Dublin Core—Education Application Profile (DC-ED)
DCMI-Education Working Group
http://dublincore.org/educationwiki/DC_2dEducation_20Application_20Profile

An ongoing project for clarifying the use of the Dublin Core Metadata Element Set in education and training-related applications and projects.

Dublin Core—Library Application Profile (DC-Lib)
DCMI-Libraries Application Profile Drafting Committee
http://dublincore.org/documents/library-application-profile/
Clarifies the use of the Dublin Core Metadata Element Set in libraries and library-related applications and projects.

Dublin Core Metadata Element Set (DCMES or DC)
Dublin Core Metadata Initiative (DCMI)
http://dublincore.org/documents/dces/
A standard for cross-domain information resource description. It is a U.S. national (NISO Z39.85) and international standard (ISO 15836).

Dublin Core Metadata Registry
Dublin Core Metadata Initiative (DCMI)
http://dublincore.org/dcregistry/
Provides users, and applications, with an authoritative source of information about the Dublin Core element set and related vocabularies.

Dublin Core Qualifiers
http://dublincore.org/documents/2000/07/11/dcmes-qualifiers/
Issued 2000-07-11 as a DCMI Recommendation. Defines two broad categories of qualifiers: element refinement and encoding scheme. For the latest version see DCMI Metadata Terms.

Education Network Australia (EdNA) Metadata Standard
EdNA Metadata Standard Working Group
www.edna.edu.au/metadata
Based on Dublin Core Metadata Element Set and is consistent with the Australian Government Locator Service (AGLS).

Electronic Theses and Dissertations Metadata Standard (ETD-MS)
Networked Digital Library of Theses and Dissertations (NDLTD)
www.ndltd.org/standards/metadata/current.html
A standard set of metadata elements used to describe an electronic theses or dissertations.

Encoded Archival Description (EAD)
http://lcweb.loc.gov/ead/
Maintained in the Network Development and MARC Standards Office of the Library of Congress (LC) in partnership with the Society of American Archivist. A standard for encoding archival finding aids using Extensible Markup Language (XML).

The European Library (TEL) Application Profile for Objects
TEL (The European Library) Metadata Working Group
http://www.europeanlibrary.org/tel_application_profile_v.htm (not accessible since December 2005)
A subset of terms generated from the TEL Metadata Registry.

The European Library (TEL) Metadata Registry
TEL (The European Library) Metadata Working Group
http://krait.kb.nl/coop/tel/handbook/registry.html (not accessible since December 2005)

Contains all terms and their characteristics used to generate TEL application profiles for object descriptions, collection descriptions, and name authorities.

The Friend of a Friend (FOAF)
FOAF Vocabulary Specification 0.9
http://xmlns.com/foaf/spec/20070524.html

The FOAF vocabulary provides a collection of basic terms that can be used in Web homepages for people, groups, companies, etc.

Gateway to Educational Materials (GEM) Element Set
GEM Consortium
http://64.119.44.148/about/documentation/metadataElements
GEM Element Set v2.0 schema
http://64.119.44.149/schema/2002/08/15/gem#

A set of metadata standards for GEM Consortium to organize and improve access to educational materials found on various federal, state, university, nonprofit, and commercial Internet sites.

ID3
www.id3.org/

An audio tagging format and a metadata container most often used in conjunction with the MP3 audio file format and is in active use the media industry in software and hardware.

The <indecs> metadata framework
Interoperability of Data in E-commerce Systems (indecs)
www.doi.org/topics/indecs/indecs_framework_2000.pdf

Created to address the need, in the digital environment, to put different creation identifiers and their supporting metadata into a framework, especially to support the management of intellectual property rights.

Instructional Management Systems (IMS): IMS Learning Resource Meta-data Specification
IMS Global Learning Consortium
www.imsglobal.org/metadata/index.html

A standard to promote the adoption of open technical specifications for interoperable learning technology. The IMS Learning Resource Meta-data Information Model 1.2.1 Final Specification is superseded by IEEE Std 1484.12.1-2002, IEEE Standard for Learning Object Metadata (LOM).

IPTC Core Schema for XMP
www.iptc.org/IPTC4XMP/

IPTC (International Press Telecommunications Council) is a consortium of the world's major news agencies, news publishers, and news industry vendors. A subset of the IPTC "Information Interchange Model—IIM" was adopted as the known "IPTC Headers" for Photoshop by Adobe Systems to describe digital photos since the 1990s. The IPTC Core Schema for XMP aims to transfer metadata values from the IPTC Headers to the Adobe Extensible Metadata Platform (XMP) framework.

Learning Object Metadata (LOM)
IEEE Learning Technology Standards Committee (LTSC)
http://ltsc.ieee.org/wg12/index.html
A set of attributes needed to allow learning objects to be managed, located, and evaluated. Learning Objects are defined as any entity, digital or nondigital, which can be used, re-used, or referenced during technology-supported learning.

MAchine-Readable Cataloging (MARC)
Library of Congress Network Development and MARC Standards Office
http://lcweb.loc.gov/marc/
Provides the mechanism by which computers exchange, use, and interpret bibliographic information, and its data elements make up the foundation of most library catalogs used today. MARC became USMARC in the 1980s and MARC 21 in the late 1990s.

MARC 21
MARC 21 Format for Bibliographic Data Including Guidelines for Content Designation
Library of Congress, Library and Archives Canada, British Library, and National Library of Canada. 1999. Washington: Library of Congress, Cataloging Distribution Service.

MARCXML
Library of Congress Network Development and MARC Standards Office
www.loc.gov/marcxml
A framework for working with MARC data in a XML environment.

Mathematical Markup Language (MathML)
W3C Recommendation, 2003
www.w3.org/TR/MathML2/
An XML application for describing mathematical notation and capturing both its structure and content.

Metadata Encoding and Transmission Standard (METS)
www.loc.gov/mets
Developed as an initiative of the Digital Library Federation; maintained in the Network Development and MARC Standards Office of the Library of Congress. A standard for encoding descriptive, administrative, and structural metadata regarding objects within a digital library, expressed using the XML schema language.

Metadata for Education Group (MEG) Registry
UKOLN (UK Office for Library Networking)
www.ukoln.ac.uk/metadata/education/registry/contents.html
A schema registration within the educational domain.

Metadata for Images in XML Standard (MIX)
MARC Standards Office of the Library of Congress in partnership with the NISO Technical Metadata for Digital Still Images Standards Committee and other interested experts
www.loc.gov/standards/mix/

An XML schema containing a set of technical data elements required to manage digital image collections.

Metadata Object Description Schema (MODS)
Library of Congress Network Development and MARC Standards Office
www.loc.gov/standards/mods/

Includes a subset of MARC fields and uses language-based tags rather than numeric ones, in some cases regrouping elements from the MARC 21 bibliographic format. MODS is expressed using the XML.

MPEG-4
www.chiariglione.org/mpeg/standards/mpeg-4/mpeg-4.htm (overview)

Developed by MPEG (Moving Picture Experts Group). A standard (ISO/IEC 14496) for multimedia of the fixed and mobile web.

MPEG-7
ISO/IEC 15938 Information technology—Multimedia content description interface
www.chiariglione.org/mpeg/standards/mpeg-7/mpeg-7.htm (overview)

Developed by MPEG (Moving Picture Experts Group). A standard for description and search of audio and visual content.

Multilingual Access to Subjects (MACS)
https://macs.vub.ac.be/pub/

A product of the Swiss National Library (SNL), the Bibliothèque nationale de France (BnF), The British Library (BL) and Die Deutsche Bibliothek (DDB). A multilingual search system which enables users to simultaneously search the catalogues of the project's partner libraries in the language of their choice (English, French, German) , It is based on the equivalence links created among the three indexing languages used in these libraries: SWD (for German), RAMEAU (for French) and LCSH (for English).

National Library of Medicine (NLM) Metadata Schema
www.nlm.nih.gov/tsd/cataloging/metafilenew.html

Developed based on the metadata terms maintained by the Dublin Core Metadata Initiative, incorporates some of the best practice recommendations of the DC-Library Application Profile (DC-Lib). It is designed for use with electronic resources published by the NLM and incorporates additional elements and qualifiers identified as requirements by NLM.

NetCDF Climate and Forecast (CF) Metadata Convention
http://cf-pcmdi.llnl.gov/documents/cf-conventions/1.0/cf-conventions.pdf

Developed by the NetCDF (network Common Data Form). Designed to provide a definitive description of what the data in each variable represents and of the spatial and temporal properties of the climate and forecast data.

North American Profile of ISO19115:2003—Geographic information—Metadata
North American Profile (NAP) Metadata Working Group
www.fgdc.gov/standards/projects/incits-l1-standards-projects/NAP-Metadata/napMetadataProfileV11_7-26-07.pdf

Object ID
Object ID Checklist
www.object-id.com/checklist/check_eng.html

Developed to help combat art theft by encouraging use of the standard and by bringing together organizations around the world that can encourage its implementation. It is a small subset of the CDWA categories.

ONline Information EXchange (ONIX)
www.editeur.org/onix.html

Developed and maintained by EDItEUR (http://www.editeur.org/) jointly with Book Industry Communication (UK) and the Book Industry Study Group (US), and with user groups in other countries. A standard means by which product data can be transmitted electronically by publishers to data aggregators, wholesalers, booksellers, and anyone else involved in the sale of their publications.

Open Archival Information System (OAIS) Reference Model
ISO Consultative Committee for Space Data Systems (CCSDS) Panel 2
http://public.ccsds.org/publications/archive/650x0b1.pdf

A technical recommendation for use in developing a broader consensus on what is required for an archive to provide permanent, or indefinite long-term, preservation of digital information.

Open Archives Initiative Protocol for Metadata Harvesting
www.openarchives.org/pmh/

OAI-PMH is a set of six verbs or services that are invoked within HTTP, to be used by Data Providers (repositories) to expose structured metadata and Service Providers to harvest that metadata. It enables access to Web-accessible material through interoperable repositories for metadata sharing, publishing, and archiving.

Open Digital Rights Language (ODRL)
Released as a W3C Note
www.w3.org/TR/odrl/

Available as an open source software. Intended to provide flexible and interoperable mechanisms to support transparent and innovative use of digital content in publishing, distributing, and consuming of digital media across all sectors and communities.

PREservation Metadata Implementation Strategies (PREMIS)
PREMIS Working Group at OCLC
www.oclc.org/research/projects/pmwg/
Data Dictionary and XML Schemas (maintained at the Library of Congress)
www.oclc.org/research/projects/pmwg/premis-final.pdf

PREMIS XML schemas
www.loc.gov/standards/premis/

Defines core set of preservation metadata elements, with supporting data dictionary, applicable to a broad range of digital preservation activities.

The Public Broadcasting Metadata Dictionary (PBCore)
www.utah.edu/cpbmetadata/

Created by the public broadcasting community in the United States for use by public broadcasters and related communities. The PBCore is built on the foundation of the Dublin Core.

Publishing Requirements for Industry Standard Metadata (PRISM)
IDEAlliance PRISM Working Group
www.prismstandard.org/specifications/

An XML metadata vocabulary for syndicating, aggregating, postprocessing, and multipurposing magazine, news, catalog, book, and mainstream journal content. Developed to meet the needs of publishers to receive, track, and deliver multipart content.

SCHEMAS Registry—Application Profiles
UKOLN (UK Office for Library Networking)
www.schemas-forum.org/registry/desire/appprofile.php3

Contains several metadata element sets as well as a large number of activity reports which describe and comment on various metadata related activities and initiatives.

The Sharable Content Object Reference Model (SCORM)
Advanced Distributed Learning (ADL) Initiative, Office of the Under Secretary of Defense for Personnel and Readiness (OUSD P&R)
www.adlnet.gov/scorm/index.aspx

Defines a Web-based learning "Content Aggregation Model" and "Run-Time Environment" for learning objects. The SCORM is a collection of specifications adapted from multiple sources to provide a comprehensive suite of e-learning capabilities that enable interoperability, accessibility, and reusability of Web-based learning content.

Shoreline Metadata Profile of the Content Standards for Digital Geospatial Metadata FGDC-STD-001.2-2001
www.csc.noaa.gov/metadata/sprofile.pdf

A profile developed by the Marine and Coastal Spatial Data Subcommittee, Federal Geographic Data Committee.

Standard Media Exchange Framework (SMEF)
The British Broadcasting Corporation (BBC)
www.bbc.co.uk/guidelines/smef/

A set of definitions for the information required in production, distribution and management of media assets, currently expressed as a data dictionary and set of entity relationship diagrams.

The Text Encoding Initiative (TEI) Guidelines
The Text Encoding Initiative Consortium
www.tei-c.org/

An international standard for representing all kinds of literary and linguistic texts for online research and teaching.

vCard (in RDF)
Representing vCard Objects in RDF/XML, W3C Note 22 February 2001
www.w3.org/TR/vcard-rdf

This W3C note specifies a Resource Description Framework (RDF) expression that corresponds to the vCard electronic business card profile defined by RFC 2426.

vCard—The Electronic Business Card
Internet Mail Consortium
www.imc.org/pdi/vcard-21.txt

A specification defines a format for an electronic business card, or vCard.

vCard MIME Directory Profile (RFC 2426)
http://rfc.net/rfc2426.html

A profile of the MIME Content-Type for directory information for a white-pages person object, based on a vCard electronic business card.

Visual Resources Association (VRA) Core Categories
Visual Resources Association Data Standards Committee
VRA Core 3.0
www.vraweb.org/vracore3.htm
VRA Core 4.0
www.vraweb.org/projects/vracore4/index.html

Specifies a set of core categories for creating records to describe works of visual culture as well as the images that document them.

Z39.50 Profile for Access to Digital Collection
http://lcweb.loc.gov/z3950/agency/markup/markup.html

An ANSI/NISO Z39.50 standard and the International Standard, ISO 23950: "Information Retrieval (Z39.50): Application Service Definition and Protocol Specification." The protocol addresses communication between corresponding information retrieval applications, the client and server (which may reside on different computers).

Appendix B
Value Encoding Schemes and Content Standards

Standardized Vocabularies

DCMI Type Vocabulary
http://dublincore.org/documents/dcmi-type-vocabulary/

A general, cross-domain list of Dublin Core Metadata Initiative (DCMI) approved terms that may be used as values for the resource *type* element to identify the genre of a resource.

MIME Internet Media Types
www.iana.org/assignments/media-types/

Originally called MIME (Multipurpose Internet Mail Extensions) types. Specifies identifiers for media types for file formats on the Internet.

RFC 4646 Tags for Identifying Languages
www.rfc-editor.org/rfc/rfc4646.txt

Describes the structure, content, construction, and semantics of language tags for use, as well as how to register values for use in language tags and the creation of user-defined extensions for private interchange. This document, in combination with RFC 4647, replaces RFC 3066, which replaced RFC 1766. (RFC 1766 specifies a two-letter code taken from *ISO 639 Codes for the representation of names of languages*, followed optionally by a two-letter country code taken from *ISO 3166—English country names and code elements*.)

ISO 3166—English country names and code elements

Provides a standard numeric and two-letter and three-letter alphabetic codes for countries or areas of special sovereignty. This standard family includes Part 1: Country Codes and Part 2: Country Subdivision Code.

ISO 639 Codes for the representation of names of languages

Provides two sets of language codes for the representation of names of languages:

Part 1: Alpha-2 code includes identifiers for major languages of the world for which specialized terminologies have been developed.
Part 2: Alpha-3 code (**www.loc.gov/standards/iso639-2/langcodes.html**) contains identifiers for all of the languages represented in part 1, and includes many other languages that have significant bodies of literature. It also provides identifiers for groups of languages, such as language families. When taken together, these indirectly cover most or all languages of the world.

W3C Date and Time Formats (W3C-DTF)
www.w3.org/TR/NOTE-datetime

Provide encoding rules for dates and times. As a profile based on *ISO 8601 Data elements and interchange formats—Information interchange—Representation of dates and times*, it defines a restricted range of formats. It also expresses the year as four digits in all cases.

ISO 8601:2004 Data elements and interchange formats—Information interchange—Representation of dates and times
Info: www.iso.org/iso/catalogue_detail?csnumber=40874

Subject Headings Lists and Thesauri

Art and Architecture Thesaurus (AAT)
www.getty.edu/research/conducting_research/vocabularies/aat/
Los Angeles: J. Paul Getty Trust, Vocabulary Program, 2000–.

A controlled vocabulary for fine art, architecture, decorative arts, archival materials, and material culture for the purposes of indexing, cataloging, searching, as well as research tools. The facets are conceptually organized in a scheme that proceeds from abstract concepts to concrete, physical artifacts.

ERIC Thesaurus

A thesaurus of the ERIC (Education Resources Information Center) database that provides free access to education-related literature and materials. ERIC is sponsored by the U.S. Department of Education, Institute of Education Sciences (IES). ERIC Thesaurus is available through the ERIC Web site at **www.eric.ed.gov/**.

FAST (Faceted Application of Subject Terminology) Authority File
www.oclc.org/research/projects/fast/

An adaptation of the *Library of Congress Subject Headings* (*LCSH*) with a simplified syntax. The headings have been built into FAST authority records and accessible through the OCLC FAST Test Databases Web site at http://fast.oclc.org/.

INSPEC Thesaurus

A thesaurus of the INSPEC database for scientific and technical literature in physics, electrical engineering, electronics, communications, control engineering, computers and computing, and information technology. Produced by the Institution of Engineering and Technology (IET).

Library of Congress Subject Headings (LCSH)
A comprehensive list of subject headings in print. Subject authority headings can be accessed through Library of Congress Authorities at **http://authorities.loc.gov/**.

Medical Subject Headings (MESH)
www.nlm.nih.gov/mesh/meshhome.html
A comprehensive controlled vocabulary produced by the National Library of Medicine (NLM) and used for indexing, cataloging, and searching for biomedical and health-related information and documents. MeSH descriptors are organized in 16 categories (sometimes referred to as "trees").

Thesaurus for Graphic Materials
I: Subject Terms (TGM I)
II: Genre and Physical Characteristic Terms (TGM II)
http://lcweb2.loc.gov/pp/tgmiquery.html
Accessible from: Library of Congress Thesauri Web site. Developed by the Library of Congress for indexing visual materials.

Classification Schemes

General

Dewey Decimal Classification (DDC)
Info: **www.oclc.org/dewey/default.htm**

Library of Congress Classification
Info: **http://lcweb.loc.gov/catdir/cpso/lcco/lcco.html**

Universal Decimal Classification
Info: **www.udcc.org/**

Special

The ACM Computing Classification System [1998 Version], Valid in 2007
www.acm.org/class/1998/
A subject classification system for computer science devised by the Association for Computing Machinery (ACM).

Iconclass
www.iconclass.nl/
A classification system for describing and classifying the subject of images represented in various media such as paintings, drawings, and photographs.

National Library of Medicine (NLM) Classification
http://wwwcf.nlm.nih.gov/class/
A library classification system covering the fields of medicine and preclinical basic sciences. It utilizes schedules QS-QZ and W-WZ, permanently excluded

from the *Library of Congress Classification Schedules* and is intended to be used with the LC schedules. The Index to the NLM Classification consists primarily of *Medical Subject Heading* (MeSH) concepts used in cataloging.

Name Authority Lists

Alexandria Digital Library (ADL) Gazetteer, 1999–
http://webclient.alexandria.ucsb.edu/client/gaz/adl/index.jsp
A product of the Alexandria Digital Library (ADL), a distributed digital library with collections of georeferenced materials developed at the University of California, Santa Barbara.

The Getty Thesaurus of Geographic Names (TGN)
www.getty.edu/research/conducting_research/vocabularies/tgn/
Los Angeles: J. Paul Getty Trust, Vocabulary Program, 1988–.
A structured, world-coverage vocabulary of more than 1.3 million names, including vernacular and historical names, coordinates, place types, and descriptive notes, focusing on places important for the study of art and architecture.

LC Name Authority file = Anglo-American Authority File (AAAF)
http://authorities.loc.gov/
Includes several million name authority records for personal, corporate, meeting, and geographic names.

The Union List of Artist Names (ULAN)
www.getty.edu/research/tools/vocabulary/ulan/
Los Angeles: J. Paul Getty Trust, Vocabulary Program, 2000–.
A structured vocabulary containing more than 225,000 names and biographical and bibliographic information about artists and architects, including a wealth of variant names, pseudonyms, and language variants.

Content Standards and Best Practice Guides

Anglo-American Cataloguing Rule, 1988 2nd rev. ed. *(AACR2)*
Info: **www.aacr2.org/about.html**
Rules designed for the construction of library catalogues.

Best Practices for OAI Data Provider Implementations and Shareable Metadata
http://webservices.itcs.umich.edu/mediawiki/oaibp/index.php/Main_Page
A joint initiative between the Digital Library Federation and the National Science Digital Library. Designed for generating OAI-compliant metadata.

Best Practices for Shareable Metadata
http://comm.nsdl.org/download.php/653/ShareableMetadataBestPractices.doc
Online version
http://oai-best.comm.nsdl.org/cgi-bin/wiki.pl?PublicTOC
Part of the *Best Practices for OAI Data Provider Implementations and Shareable Metadata*. Focused on generating shareable metadata.

Cataloging Cultural Objects: A Guide to Describing Cultural Works and Their Images (CCO)
Info and selections: **http://vraweb.org/ccoweb/cco/**

Authored by Baca, M., P. Harpring, E. Lanzi, L. McRae, and A. Whiteside on behalf of the Visual Resources Association. Specifies a set of core elements, comprising the most important descriptive information necessary to create a record for a work and an image. Provides guidelines for selecting, ordering, and formatting data used in cataloging to improve documentation and access to cultural heritage information.

Describing Archives: A Content Standard (DACS)
Society of American Archivists (SAA)
Info: **www.archivists.org/catalog/pubDetail.asp?objectID=1279**

A content standard of SAA. DACS outlines the elements that must be included at different levels of description and describes how those elements should be implemented for describing archives, personal papers, and manuscript collections, and other types of material.

DLESE Metadata Best Practices
The Digital Library for Earth System Education (DLESE) Collections Accessioning Taskforce
www.dlese.org/Metadata/collections/metadata-best-practices.php

Provides guidelines and checklists to help in the generation of metadata records that are effective and efficient for library use. The document describes metadata quality guidelines, cataloging best practices, and individual record checks.

RDA: Resource Description and Access
Working Documents: **www.collectionscanada.ca/jsc/rda.html**

Scheduled for release in early 2009. RDA is built on the foundations established by AACR. It will provide a comprehensive set of guidelines and instructions on resource description and access covering all types of content and media.

Glossary

Note: Terms in small capitals (singular or plural) indicate entries included in this glossary. Terms in Appendix A (for metadata schemas, application profiles, and registries) and Appendix B (for value encoding schemes and content standards) are not repeated in this glossary.

accessibility metadata: Data documenting the accessibility of a digital format resource, usually included in TECHNICAL METADATA. Accessibility is a general measurement of the degree to which a facility (physical facility or electronic resource) allows access to people with disabilities.

administrative metadata: Data used in managing and administering information resources, especially concerning acquisition, intellectual property rights and access restrictions, technical characteristics related to history of processing, PROVENANCE, and preservation.

application profile: A set of METADATA ELEMENTS, specific guidelines, or policies for application defined for and used by a particular application or community. It usually consists of METADATA ELEMENTS drawn from one or more existing metadata NAMESPACES.

attribute: (1) A characteristic of an object. (2) Used in a metadata ELEMENT SET, an attribute is a construct like ELEMENT. Attributes define properties of ELEMENTS.

authority file: A file composed of AUTHORITY RECORDS for managing established forms of names (for persons, places, meetings, and organizations), titles, and subject terms used in bibliographic records. An example is the *Getty Union List of Artist Names (ULAN)*.

authority record: A record of authority decisions, all or some of which may be used in a system display. It documents the process of reaching a consensus on the name(s) of an entity, creating cross-references from variant names, keeping track of the decisions, and displaying them in information systems.

best practices: Guidance and information for the most efficient (least amount of effort) and effective (best results) ways of accomplishing a task, and are empirically based on repeatable procedures that have proven themselves over time for a large number of people. A best practice guide is neither a standard nor a regulation.

content standard. *See* DATA CONTENT STANDARD

core elements: A set of key elements that should be used in creating metadata for particular types of resources, usually defined or recommended in DATA CONTENT STANDARDS and BEST PRACTICES.

crosswalk, metadata: A mapping of the elements, semantics, and syntax between equivalent or comparable METADATA TERMS from one metadata ELEMENT SET to another. Crosswalks can be presented in an independent chart or table, included in a metadata standard, and stored in a registry.

data content standard: Rules to guide the practices of generating metadata or cataloging, with specific instructions for the choice of terms and the order, syntax, and form in which data values should be entered into a set of METADATA STATEMENTS that collectively describes a resource. Examples of content standards include: *Anglo-American Cataloguing Rules (AACR)*, *Cataloging Cultural Objects: A Guide to Describing Cultural Works and Their Images (CCO)*, and *Describing Archives: A Content Standard (DACS)*.

data dictionary, metadata. *See* ELEMENT SET

data element: The most elementary unit of data that specifies a characteristic or property of a resource. A data element can appear as a field in a relational database, a column in a flat file, or a row or column in a spreadsheet. *See also* ELEMENT, METADATA

data exchange standard: A specification for storing, accessing, and transmitting data; referred to as different "formats" when discussed in the context of data exchange and communication. A data exchange standard may be separately designed or bound together with a metadata ELEMENT SET. An example is *ISO 2709 Format for Information Exchange*, for bibliographic description in computer-readable format.

data field. *See* DATA ELEMENT

data structure standard. *See* ELEMENT SET

data value standard: A standard designed and used for controlling or restricting values in generating METADATA STATEMENTS, indexing, and retrieval. Examples include: *Library of Congress Subject Headings (LCSH)*, *Art and Architecture Thesaurus (AAT)*, *RFC 4646, Tags for Identifying Languages*, and predefined lists provided by *IEEE Learning Object Metadata (LOM)* specifications. *See also* VALUE ENCODING SCHEME

descriptive metadata: Metadata that describes a RESOURCE for purposes of discovery and identification. (*Source:* NISO, 2004)

digital collection: A collection in which objects are selected according to prescribed criteria, stored in digital formats, organized, and made accessible to users.

digital library: An environment to bring together collections, services, and people in support of the full life cycle of creation, dissemination, use, and preservation of data, information, and knowledge. Although being served by systems that manage DIGITAL COLLECTIONS and provide services, the concept of a "digital library" is not equivalent to a DIGITIZED COLLECTION with the addition of information management tools.

Document Type Definition (DTD): A collection of markup declarations defining the structure, elements, and attributes available for use in a document that complies with the DTD. In SGML or XML, a DTD is a formal definition of the elements and the relationship among the DATA ELEMENTS (the structure) for a particular type of document. (*Source:* W3C Glossary)

educational metadata: Elements in a metadata ELEMENT SET that are designed for capturing educational attributes in resources, for example, "audience," "grade," and "typical learning time." Metadata ELEMENT SETS and application profiles are developed specifically for the purpose of describing educational resources, for example, *IEEE Learning Object Metadata (LOM)* and *CanCore*.

element, metadata: A metadata element is a formally defined term used to describe one of the properties of a resource of a particular type or for a particular purpose. For example, the "publisher" of a book, the "format" of an electronic file, or a "restoration date" of a building.

element refinement: A subdivision used to make the meaning of an ELEMENT more specific. For example, both "valid" and "modified" are used for refining the "date" element. An element refinement is also referred to as a "qualifier." It can be used independently as a metadata term or together with the element it refines in applications.

element set: An element set defines the structure and semantics of a group of ELEMENTS. A metadata element set is sometimes referred to as a metadata scheme or a data dictionary. The most well-known and widely used one is the *Dublin Core Metadata Element Set (DCMES)*.

embedded metadata: The method of embedding METADATA STATEMENTS in the specific section of a resource file, often seen in the header section of an HTML file, a digital image file, a PDF file, a dataset, or an MP3 music file.

encoding: Expressing or representing METADATA STATEMENTS in computer-processable form. For example, a METADATA STATEMENT may be encoded in the form of database tables, the <meta> fields in HTML files, or XML/RDF format. The encoding process may include using these forms to tag the structure and other properties of a resource according to the structure and semantics defined by a metadata ELEMENT SET.

encoding scheme. *See* VALUE ENCODING SCHEME

extensibility: The ability of a metadata ELEMENT SET to offer a core set of elements and to allow for extension, enabling the creation of a richer and more appropriate description of resources for particular applications and communities.

federated searching: A mechanism in which a system searches a local repository in which accumulated data of numerous resources is incorporated into a single repository and is processed prior to the user's search.

interoperability: The ability of multiple systems or components with different hardware and software platforms, data structures, and interfaces to exchange and share data with minimal loss of content and functionality.

metadata: Structured, encoded data that describes characteristics of information-bearing entities (including individual objects, collections, or systems) to aid in the identification, discovery, assessment, management, and preservation of the described entities. Metadata is often simply defined as "data about data" or "information about information."

metadata element. *See* ELEMENT, METADATA

metadata description: A metadata description is made up of one or more METADATA STATEMENTS about one RESOURCE.

metadata harvesting: Automatic gathering of metadata by collecting records from one or more METADATA REPOSITORIES through a data communication protocol, such as the *Open Archive Initiative Protocol for Metadata Harvesting (OAI-PMH).*

metadata registry. *See* REGISTRY, METADATA

metadata repository: A central place where metadata is stored and maintained according to certain protocols. An example is the Metadata Repository of the National Science Digital Library where metadata records from many digital collections are stored and maintained for supporting FEDERATED SEARCHING in the digital library.

metadata services: Systems and tools supporting the creation, maintenance, and sharing of METADATA SCHEMAS, VALUE ENCODING SCHEMES, APPLICATION PROFILES, RECORDS, CROSSWALKS, etc. Metadata services encompass metadata REGISTRIES, REPOSITORIES, and other development and production services.

metadata scheme. *See* ELEMENT SET

metadata standard: Usually refers to a named metadata ELEMENT SET and/or SCHEMA that has been approved by a national or international standard body, a community, or a professional association. Different types of metadata standards include DATA STRUCTURE STANDARDS, DATA CONTENT STANDARDS, DATA VALUE STANDARDS, and DATA EXCHANGE STANDARDS.

metadata statement: A basic unit of metadata that instantiates a property (i.e., ELEMENT) and a value. Metadata statements are components in a METADATA DESCRIPTION.

metadata terms: A general word to cover various types of metadata definitions, including ELEMENTS, classes, ELEMENT REFINEMENTS, names of VALUE ENCODING SCHEMES, and defined vocabulary terms maintained by a project or organization. Each metadata term can have an assigned unique Uniform Resource Identifier (URI) in a NAMESPACE, as well as machine- and human-readable labels. An example is the *DCMI Metadata Terms,* an authoritative specification of all metadata terms maintained by the Dublin Core Metadata Initiative (DCMI).

metasearching: A process in which the user submits a query to numerous information resources simultaneously and receives integrated results on a single interface. The system sends the user's query to the search targets and brings back the retrieved results.

modularity: The ability that different types of metadata (e.g., descriptive, rights management, preservation, or instructional management) can be combined in a compound schema as needed, which would embody the functionality of each constituent.

multilingualism: An ability of supporting linguistic and cultural diversity when designing or adopting metadata architecture.

namespace: A set of names identified by a Uniform Resource Identifier (URI) reference or a place where a schema (set of names) resides. It can be considered as a unique name that identifies a source where a schema is from. For example, "http://purl.org/dc/elements/1.1/" is the namespace for Dublin Core 1.1.

Online Public Access Catalog (OPAC): The computerized library catalog containing both descriptive and holdings data for users to search, locate, and retrieve information about library materials in a library or library system.

preservation metadata: A form of ADMINISTRATIVE METADATA documenting the preservation processes performed on resources in both conventional and digitization workflow.

provenance: Information of all known origins, custody, and ownership of a particular item or collection.

qualifier. *See* ELEMENT REFINEMENT

record, metadata: A structured representation of the descriptive, administrative, and structural information for an item or a collection. A metadata record contains one or more METADATA DESCRIPTIONS that are made up of one or more METADATA STATEMENTS about one RESOURCE. A metadata record is an instance where a set of metadata elements is applied to describing an object.

registry, metadata: A formal system for the documentation of registered ELEMENT SETS, SCHEMAS, APPLICATION PROFILES, ENCODING SCHEMES, element usage information, and element CROSSWALKS. The primary functions of metadata registries include registering, publishing, and managing these specifications, as well as facilitating easy searching within the registry.

resource: An entity that is described by one or more METADATA DESCRIPTIONS. A resource is not equivalent to a physically bound package, i.e., a book, a Web site, or an image. A resource can be a person, a place, or a collectively created work containing multiple components.

Resource Description Framework (RDF): A data model and streaming format for representing metadata about Web resources, with search engines and inference engines as potential users. A number of RDF specifications have been released as W3C (WORLD WIDE WEB CONSORTIUM) Recommendation documents.

rights management metadata: Metadata related to intellectual property, including (1) user-oriented rights information that allows users to make an informed copyright assessment of a given work or provides users with sources of further information about the copyright status; and (2) rightholder-oriented rights management information regarding the description, identification, protection, monitoring, and tracking of rights usages over the assets.

schema, metadata: A machine-processable specification that defines the structure, encoding syntax, rules, and formats for a metadata ELEMENT SET in a formal SCHEMA LANGUAGE. In literature the term "metadata schema" usually refers to an entire ELEMENT SET as well as the encoding of the elements and structure with a markup language.

schema language: A language used to define a schema. The DOCUMENT TYPE DEFINITION (DTD) language and XML SCHEMA (W3C) are the most widely used schema languages.

simplicity: In the metadata context, simplicity means the property and quality of being simple: take only those DATA ELEMENTS that are necessary and maintain a minimum set of elements for easy deployment.

Standard Generalized Markup Language (SGML): An ISO standard (ISO 8879:1986) that provides a formal mechanism for the definition of document structure via DOCUMENT TYPE DEFINITIONS (DTDS), and a notation for the markup of document instances conforming to a DTD. (*Source:* W3C Glossary)

structural metadata: Data documenting how a compound-object resource is structured or arranged, i.e., the sequence of page image files for a digitized manuscript.

syntax encoding scheme: A form of VALUE ENCODING SCHEME. It is a technical specification or set of rules for encoding data values. It is employed to ensure consistency for the values that are entered in a METADATA STATEMENT. For example, *W3C-DTF (Date and Time Formats)* is a date-and-time representation standard and is used for expressing time-related values.

technical metadata: Data concerning the physical attributes of a RESOURCE related to the creation, encoding, storage, and use of a resource, such as file format, resolution, size, software, platform required for reviewing or running an object, and accessibility information. It could be considered a form of ADMINISTRATIVE METADATA.

terminology services: Web-based, automated information services that provide integrated accesses to various vocabularies concerning concepts, terms, and relationships, usually including controlled vocabularies and common dictionaries. An example is the OCLC Terminologies Service(tm).

value encoding scheme: In the metadata community, this term is used to refer to the identified system for controlling or restricting values. It usually appears as a list of name tokens or terms from which values can be selected for the associated metadata elements. Commonly used encoding schemes recommended by metadata standards include syntax encoding schemes and vocabulary encoding schemes.

value space: In metadata standards, value spaces express the sets of values and/or rules specified for each element in an ELEMENT SET.

vocabulary encoding scheme: A form of a VALUE ENCODING SCHEME. A standard, controlled vocabulary for selecting data values associated with particular METADATA ELEMENTS. It is employed to control the values entered in a METADATA STATEMENT. A vocabulary encoding scheme may be a controlled term list, a standardized code, a classification scheme, a thesaurus, an authority file, a list of subject headings, or a predefined term list provided by a METADATA STANDARD.

W3C (World Wide Web Consortium): An international consortium that designs technologies, and develops protocols and guidelines ensuring long-term growth for the Web.

XML (Extensible Markup Language): A meta-language and a simple dialect of STANDARD GENERALIZED MARKUP LANGUAGE (SGML) developed by the W3C (WORLD WIDE WEB CONSORTIUM) for processing documents containing structured information.

XML schema: An XML schema (lowercase *s*) is a document that defines, in a formal way, the structure, content, and semantics of XML (EXTENSIBLE MARKUP LANGUAGE) documents.

XML Schema (W3C): XML Schema (uppercase *S*) is designed by W3C (WORLD WIDE WEB CONSORTIUM) as an alternative expressive schema language of DOCUMENT TYPE DEFINITION (DTD), both being developed to express XML SCHEMAS.

Bibliography and Sources of Further Information

ADEPT. 2003. "Virtual Learning Environment."Alexandria Digital Earth Prototype (ADEPT), University of California Santa Barbara. Web page. Available: www.alexandria.ucsb.edu/research/learning/index.htm.

Adobe Systems. 2007. "Runtime Wrapper Extension for Dreamweaver MX." Web page. Available: www.adobe.com/resources/elearning/extensions/dw_ud/scorm.html.

"Advanced Distributed Learning (ADL) Certification for SCORM." 2004. Wisconsin Testing Organization. Available: www.academiccolab.org/certification/scorm/process.pdf.

"Advanced Distributed Learning (ADL) Initiative." Sponsored by the Office of the Under Secretary of Defense for Personnel and Readiness (OUSD P&R). Web page. Available: www.adlnet.gov/ (accessed February 22, 2008).

Agnew, Grace. 2003. Developing a Metadata Strategy. *Cataloging & Classification Quarterly* 36, no. 3/4: 31–46.

"Alexandria Digital Library." University of California Santa Barbara. Web page. Available: www.alexandria.ucsb.edu/adl/ (accessed February 22, 2008).

"Alexandria Digital Library Gazetteer." University of California Santa Barbara. Web page. Available: http://clients.alexandria.ucsb.edu/globetrotter/ (accessed February 22, 2008).

ANSI/NISO Z39.19-2005. 2005. *Guidelines for the Construction, Format, and Management of Monolingual Controlled Vocabularies*. Bethesda, MD: NISO Press.

ANSI/NISO Z39.87-2006. 2006. *Data Dictionary—Technical Metadata for Digital Still Images*. Bethesda, MD: NISO Press.

Apps, Ann. 2005. "Guidelines for Encoding Bibliographic Citation Information in Dublin Core Metadata." Dublin Core Metadata Initiative Citation Working Group. Web page. Available: http://dublincore.org/documents/dc-citation-guidelines/.

Arms, William. Y., Naomi Dushay, Dave Fulker, and Carl Lagoze. 2003. "A Case Study in Metadata Harvesting: The NSDL." *Library HiTech*, 21, no. 2: 228–237. Available: http://www.cs.cornell.edu/lagoze/papers/Arms-et-al-LibraryHiTech.pdf.

Arms, William Y., Diane Hillmann, Carl Lagoze, Dean Krafft, Richard Maris, John Saylor, Carol Terrizzi, and Herbert Van de Sompel. 2002. "A Spectrum of Interoperability: The Site for Science Prototype for the NSDL." *D-Lib Magazine* [Online], 8, no. 1. Available: www.dlib.org/dlib/january02/arms/01arms.html.

Arms, William, and Len Simutis. 2002. *Metadata Policy: Rationale and Some Examples.* NSDL. Available: http://comm.nsdl.org/download.php/194/PC3Rationale.pdf.

AVEL. "AVEL metadata element list." Web page. Available: http://avel.library.uq.edu.au/technical.html#2 (accessed September 19, 2007).

Baca, Murtha, ed. 2000–2008. *Introduction to Metadata: Pathways to Digital Information.* Online Version 2.1 Murtha Baca, Tony Gill, Anne J. Gilliland, Mary S. Woodley. Los Angeles: J. Paul Getty Trust, Getty Research Institute. Available: www.getty.edu/research/conducting_research/standards/intrometadata/.

Baca, Murtha, Patricia Harpring, Elisa Lanzi, Linda McRae, and Ann Whiteside, eds., on behalf of the Visual Resources Association. 2006. *Cataloging Cultural Objects: A Guide to Describing Cultural Works and Their Images.* Chicago: American Library Association.

Baeza-Yates, Ricardo, and Berthier Ribeiro-Neto. 1999. *Modern Information Retrieval.* New York: ACM Press.

Baker, Thomas. 2000. "A Grammar of Dublin Core." *D-Lib Magazine* [Online], 6, no. 10. Available: www.dlib.org/dlib/october00/baker/10baker.html.

Baker, Thomas. 2003. "DCMI Usage Board Review of Application Profiles." Web page. Available: http://dublincore.org/usage/documents/profiles/index.shtml.

Baker, Thomas. 2005. "Diverse Vocabularies in a Common Model: Dublin Core at 10 Years." Presentation at *DC-2005: Vocabularies in Practice.* Available: http://dc2005.uc3m.es/program/presentations/2005-09-12.plenary.baker-keynote.ppt.

Baker, Thomas, Christophe Blanchi, Dan Brickley, Erik Duval, Rachel Heery, Pete Johnston, Leonid Kalinichenko, Heike Neuroth, and Shigeo Sugimoto. 2002. *Principles of Metadata Registries: A White Paper of the DELOS Workshop Group on Registries.* DELOS Network of Excellence on Digital Libraries. Available: http://delos-noe.iei.pi.cnr.it/activities/standardizationforum/Registries.pdf.

Baker, Thomas, Makx Dekkers, Rachel Heery, Manjula Patel, and Gauri Salokhe. 2001. "What Terms Does Your Metadata Use? Application Profiles as Machine-understandable Narratives." *Journal of Digital Information* [Online], 2, no. 2. Available: http://jodi.tamu.edu/Articles/v02/i02/Baker/.

Baker, Thomas, Makx Dekkers, Thomas Fischer, and Rachel Heery. 2005. "Dublin Core Application Profile Guidelines." Web page. Available: http://dublincore.org/usage/documents/profile-guidelines/.

Barde, Julien, Thérèse Liboure, and Pierre Maurel. 2005. "A Metadata Service for Integrated Management of Knowledge Related to Coastal Areas." *Multimedia Tools and Applications*, 25, no. 3: 419–429.

Barker, Ed, and Ben Ryan. 2003. *The Higher Level Skills for Industry Repository.* Version 1.0. http://metadata.cetis.ac.uk/usage_survey/cs_hlsi.pdf.

Barrueco Cruz, Jose Manuel, and Thomas Krichel. 2000. "Distributed Cataloging on the Internet: The RePEc Project." In *Metadata and Organizing Educational Resources on the Internet*, edited by Jane Greenberg (pp. 227–241). Binghamton, NY: The Haworth Information Press.

Bearman, David, and Jennifer Trant. 1998. "Authenticity of Digital Resources: Towards a Statement of Requirements in the Research Process." *D-Lib Magazine* [Online], June 1998. Available: www.dlib.org/dlib/june98/06bearman.html.

Berman, Fran. 2005. *SBE/CISE Workshop on Cyberinfrastructure for the Social Sciences*. Available: http://vis.sdsc.edu/sbe/SBE-CISE_Workshop_Intro.pdf.

Berners-Lee, Tim. 1997. "Metadata Architecture." Web page. Available: www.w3.org/DesignIssues/Metadata.html.

"BioMed Central Catalog of Databases." Web page. Available: http://databases.biomedcentral.com/ (accessed November 18, 2007).

Bloehdorn, Stephan, Kosmas Petridis, Carsten Saathoff, Nikos Simou, Vassilis Tzouvaras, Yannis Avrithis, Siegfried Handschuh, Yiannis Kompatsiaris, Steffen Staab, and Michael G. Strintzis. 2005. "Semantic Annotation of Images and Videos for Multimedia Analysis." In *The Semantic Web: Research and Applications*, edited by Asuncion Gomez-Perez and Jerome Euzenat (pp. 592–606). Proceedings of the Second European Semantic Web Conference, ESWC 2005, Heraklion, Crete, Greece, May 29–June 1. Berlin: Springer.

Bose, Rajendra, and James Frew. 2005. "Lineage Retrieval for Scientific Data Processing: A Survey." *ACM Computing Survey*, 37, no. 1: 1–28.

Bourne, Charles P., et al. 1976. *Analysis of Errors in the University of California Union Catalog Supplement*, ILR-7602. Berkeley, CA: Institute of Library Research.

Boutell, Matthew, and Jiebo Luo. 2005. "Beyond Pixels: Exploiting Camera Metadata for Photo Classification." *Pattern Recognition*, 38, no. 6: 935–946.

Brickley, Dan, and Libby Miller. 2007. *FOAF Vocabulary Specification 0.9*. Available: http://xmlns.com/foaf/spec/20070524.html.

Bruce, Thomas R., and Diane I. Hillmann. 2004. "The Continuum of Metadata Quality: Defining, Expressing, Exploiting." In *Metadata in Practice*, edited by Diane I. Hillmann, and Elaine L. Westbrooks (pp. 238–256). Chicago: American Library Association.

California Digital Library Rights Management Group. 2006. *copyrightMD* User Guidelines Version 0.9. Available: www.cdlib.org/inside/projects/rights/schema/copyrightMD_user_guidelines.pdf.

"Caltech Collection of Open Digital Archives." California Institute of Technology. Web page. Available: http://caltechcstr.library.caltech.edu (accessed February 22, 2008).

"Canadian Core Learning Object Metadata Application Profile (CanCore)." Web site. Available: www.cancore.ca/ (accessed November 18, 2007).

CanCore. 2004. "Frequently Asked Questions." Web page. Available: www.cancore.ca/en/faq.html#Is%20CanCore%20a%20standard.

Caplan, Priscilla. 2000. "International Metadata Initiatives: Lessons in Bibliographic Control." *Conference on Bibliographic Control in the New Millennium.* Library of Congress, November 2000. Available: www.loc.gov/catdir/bibcontrol/caplan_paper.html.

Caplan, Priscilla. 2003. *Metadata Fundamentals for All Librarians.* Chicago: American Library Association.

Cardinaels, Kris, Michael Meire, and Erik Duval. 2005. *Automating Metadata Generation: The Simple Indexing Interface.* Proceedings of the 14th International Conference on World Wide Web 2005 (pp. 548–556). New York: ACM Press. Available: www2005.org/cdrom/docs/p548.pdf.

Carlyle, Allyson, and Lisa Fusco. 2007. "Understanding FRBR as a Conceptual Model: FRBR and the Bibliographic Universe." *Bulletin of the American Society for Information Science and Technology,* August/September 2007. Available: www.asis.org/Bulletin/Aug-07/carlyle_fusco.html.

Carpenter, Leona. 2003. "OAI for Beginners—The Open Archives Forum Online Tutorial." Web page. Available: www.oaforum.org/tutorial.

CC:DA. 2000. *Task Force on Metadata: Final Report.* CCDA (ALCTS/CCS) Committee on Cataloging: Description and Access. Available: www.libraries.psu.edu/tas/jca/ccda/tf-meta6.html.

CC:DA Task Force on VRA Core Categories. 2001. *Summary Report: Task Force on VRA Core Categories.* Committee on Cataloguing: Description and Access (CC:DA).

"CCO Selections." 2006. From *Cataloguing Culture Objects, A Guide to Describing Cultural Works and Their Images.* Baca, Murtha, Patricia Harpring, Elisa Lanzi, Linda McRae, and Ann Whiteside on behalf of the Visual Resources Association. Chicago: American Library Association. Selections available: www.vraweb.org/ccoweb/cco/index.html.

CCSDS. 2002. *Reference Model for an Open Archival Information System (OAIS). CCSDS 650-0-B-1, Approved for Publication by the Management Council of the Consultative Committee for Space Data Systems (CCSDS).* Washington, DC: National Aeronautics and Space Administration (NASA) Program Integration Division. Available: www.ccsds.org/documents/pdf/CCSDS-650.0-B-1.pdf.

CDL Rights Management Group. 2005. "CDL Rights Management Framework." California Digital Library. Web page. Available: www.cdlib.org/inside/projects/rights/index.html.

CDL Right Management Group. 2006. *CopyrightMD User Guidelines.* California Digital Library. Available: www.cdlib.org/inside/projects/rights/schema/>.

CDWA (Categories for the Description of Works of Art). 2000. Murtha Baca and Patricia Harpring, eds. The J. Paul Getty Trust and College Art Association. Los Angeles: J. Paul Getty Trust, Getty Research Institute. Available: www.getty.edu/research/conducting_research/standards/cdwa/index.html.

CDWA Lite: Specification for an XML Schema for Contributing Records via the OAI Harvesting Protocol, 1.1, July 17, 2006. (Corresponds to CDWALite-xsd-public-v1-1.xsd.) ARTstor and J Paul Getty Trust. Los Angeles: J. Paul Getty Trust. Available: www.getty.edu/research/conducting_research/standards/cdwa/cdwalite.pdf.

CDWA Lite: XML Schema Content for Contributing Records via the OAI Harvesting Protocol (Version 2.0). 2006. ARTstor and J Paul Getty Trust. Los Angeles: J. Paul Getty Trust. Available: www.getty.edu/CDWA/CDWALite/CDWALite-xsd-public-v1-1.xsd.

CEN (European Committee for Standardization). 2003. *Dublin Core Application Profile Guidelines, CEN Workshop Agreement, CWA 14855*. Brussels: CEN (European Committee for Standardization). Available: ftp://ftp.cenorm.be/PUBLIC/CWAs/e-Europe/MMI-DC/cwa14855-00-2003-Nov.pdf.

Chan, Lois Mai, and Marcia Lei Zeng. 2006. "Metadata Interoperability and Standardization—A Study of Methodology Part 1: Achieving Interoperability at the Schema Level." *D-Lib Magazine* [Online], 12, no. 6. Available: www.dlib.org/dlib/june06/chan/06chan.html.

Chervenak, Ann, Ian Foster, Carl Kesselman, Charles Salisbury, and Steven Tuecke. 2000. "The Data Grid: Towards Architecture for the Distributed Management and Analysis for Large Scientific Datasets." *Journal of Network and Computer Applications*, 23, no. 3: 187–200. Available: http://loci.cs.utk.edu/dsi/netstore99/docs/papers/chervenak.pdf.

Chiariglione, Leonardo. 2005. "Riding the Media Bits, Inside MPEG-7." Web page. Available: www.chiariglione.org/ride/inside_MPEG-7/inside_MPEG-7.htm.

Chudnov, Daniel, Richard Cameron, Jeremy Frumkin, Ross Singer, and Raymond Yee. 2005. "Opening up OpenURLs with Autodiscovery." *Ariadne* [Online], no. 43. Available: www.ariadne.ac.uk/issue43/chudnov/intro.html.

"The Cleveland Memory Project." Cleveland State University Library. Web page. Available: www.clevelandmemory.org (accessed February 22, 2008).

The Cleveland Memory Project. "Disasters in Cleveland History." Special Collections at the Cleveland State University Library. Web page. Available: www.clevelandmemory.org/disasters/ (accessed February 22, 2008).

Copeland, A., M. Pelikan, and J. Attig. 2004. "Context and Meaning: The Challenges of Metadata for a Digital Image Library within the University." *College & Research Libraries*, 65, no. 3: 251–261.

CORES Project. 2002. "CORES: A Forum on Shared Metadata Vocabularies." UKOLN. Web page. Available: www.cores-eu.net/.

"CORES Registry." CORES Project, UKOLN. Web page. Available: http://cores.dsd.sztaki.hu/ (accessed February 22, 2008).

Costello, Roger L. 2006. "XML Schemas: Best Practices." Web page. Available: www.xfront.com/BestPracticesHomepage.html.

Daniel Jr., Ron, Carl Lagoze, and Sandra D. Payette. 1998. "A Metadata Architecture for Digital Libraries." Web page. Available: www.cs.cornell.edu/lagoze/papers/ADL98/dar-adl.html.

Dasiopoulou, Stamatia, Evaggelos Spyrou, Yiannis Kompatsiaris, Yannis Avrithis, and Michael G. Strintzis. 2007. "Semantic Processing of Color Images." In *Color Image Processing: Methods and Applications*, edited by Ratislav Lukac and Konstantinos N. Plataniotis (pp. 259–284). Boca Raton, FL: CRC/Taylor & Francis.

Davison, Stephen. 2003. "The Open Archives Initiative (OAI) Sheet Music Project: A Gateway to Sheet Music Collections on the Web." Sheet Music Roundtable, Music Library Association 2003, Austin, TX. Available: http://unitproj.library.ucla.edu/music/oaisheetmusic/mla.ppt.

Day, Michael W. 1998. "Metadata and Biodiversity Information: A Report from a US Symposium on 'Metadiversity'." *Ariadne* [Online], no. 18. Available: www.ariadne.ac.uk/issue18/metadiversity/.

Day, Michael W. 1999. "Image Retrieval: Combining Content-based and Metadata-based Approaches." *Ariadne* [Online], no. 19. Available: www.ariadne.ac.uk/issue19/metadata/.

Day, Michael, Andy Powell, and Marieke Guy. 2004. "Improving the Quality of Metadata in Eprint Archives." *Ariadne* [Online], no. 38. Available: www.ariadne.ac.uk/issue38/guy/.

"DC-Dot Dublin Core metadata editor." Andy Powell. UKOLN, University of Bath. Web page. Available: www.ukoln.ac.uk/metadata/dcdot/ (accessed February 22, 2008).

DCMES (Dublin Core Metadata Element Set). 2006. Version 1.1 Reference Description. Available: http://dublincore.org/documents/dces/.

DCMI. 2000. *Dublin Core Qualifiers*. DCMI Usage Committee. Web page. Available: http://dublincore.org/documents/2000/07/11/dcmes-qualifiers/.

"DCMI Abstract Model." 2007. Andy Powell, Mikael Nilsson, Ambjörn Naeve, Pete Johnston, and Thomas Baker. Web page. Available: http://dublincore.org/documents/abstract-model/index.shtml.

"DCMI Description Set Profile." 2007. Draft. Mikael Nilsson, ed. Web page. Available: http://dublincore.org/architecturewiki/DescriptionSetProfile.

"DCMI Glossary." 2005. Mary Woodley, Gail Clement, and Pete Winn. Web page. Available: http://dublincore.org/documents/usageguide/glossary.shtml.

DCMI Government Working Group. 2001. "Report on Government Working Group Breakout Sessions," Tokyo Workshop & Conference, October 22 and 23, 2001. Available: http://dublincore.org/groups/government/TokyoReport.html.

"DCMI Grammatical Principles." 2003. DCMI Usage Board. Modified 2007. Web page. Available: http://dublincore.org/usage/documents/principles/index.shtml.

"DCMI Metadata Registry." 2005. Web page. Available: http://dublincore.org/dcregistry/.

"DCMI Metadata Terms." 2006. DCMI Usage Board. Web page. Available: http://dublincore.org/documents/2006/12/18/dcmi-terms/. Replaced by 2008 version.

"DCMI Metadata Terms." 2008. DCMI Usage Board. Web page. Available: http://dublincore.org/documents/dcmi-terms/. Replaces 2006-12-18 version.

"DCMI Type Vocabulary." 2006. DCMI Usage Board. Web page. Available: http://dublincore.org/usage/terms/dcmitype/.

Dean, Rebecca J. 2004. "FAST: Development of Simplified Headings for Metadata." *Cataloging & Classification Quarterly*, 39, no. 1/2: 331–352.

Deelman, Ewa, Gurmeet Singh, Malcolm P. Atkinson, Ann Chervenak, Neil P. Chue Hong, Carl Kesselman, Sonal Patil, Laura Pearlman, and Mei-Hui Su. 2004. "Grid-Based Metadata Services." Proceedings of the 16th International Conference on Scientific and Statistical Database Management (SSDBM 2004), June 21–23, 2004, Santorini Island, Greece, 393Y402. Los Alamitos, CA: IEEE Computer Society.

Dempsey, Locan, and Stuart L. Weibel. 1996. "The Warwick Metadata Workshop: A Framework for the Development of Resource Description." *D-Lib Magazine* [Online], July/August 1996. Available: www.dlib.org/dlib/july96/07weibel.html.

Diekema, Anne R., and Jiangping Chen. 2005. "Experimenting with the Automatic Assignment of Educational Standards to Digital Library Content." *Proceedings of the Joint Conference of Digital Libraries*, June 7–11, 2005, Denver, Colorado.

"Digital Library for Earth System Education (DLESE)." Web page. Available: www.dlese.org (accessed November 19, 2007).

DLESE. 2003. "XML: ADN Version 0.6.50." Digital Library for Earth System Education (DLESE). Web page. Available: www.dlese.org/Metadata/adn-item/0.6.50/docs/xml-info.htm.

DLESE. 2004. "ADN Metadata History: Going from DLESE-IMS to AND, a Timeline of Past Developments (1999 to 2003)." Web page. Available: www.dlese.org/Metadata/adn-item/history.htm.

DLESE. 2005. "ADN Framework." Digital Library for Earth System Education (DLESE). Web page. Available: www.dlese.org/Metadata/adn-item/index.htm.

"DLESE Collection System (DCS) v2.2.0b Documentation." Digital Library for Earth System Education (DLESE). Web page. Was available: http://dlese.org/libdev/docs/v2.3/DCS.html.

"DLESE Term of Use." 2001. Digital Library for Earth System Education (DLESE). Web page. Available: http://dlese.org/documents/policy/terms_use_full.php>.

Dublin Core Collection Description Task Group. 2007. "Dublin Core Collections Application Profile." Web page. Available: http://dublincore.org/groups/collections/collection-application-profile/2007-03-09/.

Dublin Core Collection Description Working Group. 2006. "Dublin Core Collection Description Application Profile Summary." Dublin Core Metadata Initiative. Web page. Available: www.ukoln.ac.uk/metadata/dcmi/collection-ap-summary/.

Dublin Core Education Community. 2007. "Dublin Core Education Application Profile (Working draft of v0.4)." Web page. Available: http://docs.google.com/View?docid=dn8z3gs_38cgwkvv.

"Dublin Core Metadata Initiative." Web page. Available: http://dublincore.org/ (accessed November 19, 2007).

Dushay, Naomi, and Diane Hillmann. 2003. "Analyzing Metadata for Effective Use and Re-use." *DC-2003: Proceedings of the International DCMI Metadata Conference and Workshop, Sept. 28-Oct. 2, 2003, Seattle, Washington*. Cornell

University, National Science Digital Library, Seattle, Washington. Available: http://dc2003.ischool.washington.edu/Archive-03/03dushay.pdf.

Duval, Erik, Wayne Hodgins, Stuart Sutton, and Stuart L. Weibel. 2002. "Metadata Principles and Practicalities." *D-Lib Magazine* [Online], 8, no. 4. Available: www.dlib.org/dlib/april02/weibel/04weibel.html.

EAD Working Group. 2002–2007. "Encoded Archival Description Tag Library." Web page. Available: www.loc.gov/ead/tglib/index.html.

EAD Working Group. 2006. "Development of the Encoded Archival Description DTD." Web page. Available: www.loc.gov/ead/eaddev.html.

Eaton, Brian, Jonathan Gregory, Bob Drach, Karl Taylor, and Steve Hankin. 2003. *NetCDF Climate and Forecast (CF) Metadata Conventions*, Version 1.0, October 28, 2003. Available: http://cf-pcmdi.llnl.gov/documents/cf-conventions/1.0/.

EDItEUR. 2001. "ONIX product information release 2.0." Web page. Available: www.editeur.org/onixfiles2.0/ONIXProductInformationOverview2.0.pdf.

Embley, David W., David Jackman, and Li Xu. 2001. "Multifaceted Exploitation of Metadata for Attribute Match Discovery in Information Integration." *Proceedings of the International Workshop on Information Integration on the Web (WIIW'01)* (pp. 110–117).

"EPrints Application Profile: Functional Requirements." 2006. JISC Digital Repositories Programme. Web page. Available: www.ukoln.ac.uk/repositories/digirep/index/Functional_Requirements.

Ercegovac, Zorana. 1999. "Introduction. Special Topic Issue: Integrating Multiple Overlapping Metadata Standards." *Journal of the American Society for Information Science*, 50, no. 13: 1165–1168.

"The European Library (TEL)." Web page. Available: www.theeuropeanlibrary.org/portal/index.html (acessed January 27, 2008).

Father, Jenny 2004. "A Maths Dictionary for Kids." Web page. Available: www.amathsdictionaryforkids.com/maths/dictionary.html (accessed January 28, 2008).

FGDC. 1998. "Content Standard for Digital Geospatial Metadata." Version 2. FGDC Metadata Ad Hoc Working Group. Available: www.fgdc.gov/standards/projects/FGDC-standards-projects/metadata/base-metadata/v2_0698.pdf.

FGDC. 2006. "Content Standard for Digital Geospatial Metadata (CSDGM), Document Number FGDC-STD-001-1998." Web page. Available: www.fgdc.gov/standards/projects/FGDC-standards-projects/metadata/base-metadata/index.html.

FGDC. 2007. "Geospatial Metadata Standards." Web page. Available: www.fgdc.gov/metadata/geospatial-metadata-standards.

"FOAF-a-Matic." Web page. Available: www.ldodds.com/foaf/foaf-a-matic (accessed November 18, 2007).

"FOAFCorp: Corporate Friends of Friends." Web page. Available: http://rdfweb.org/foafcorp/intro.html (accessed November 18, 2007).

"FOAF Vocabulary Specification 0.9. The Friend of a Friend (FOAF)." Web page. Available: http://xmlns.com/foaf/spec/20070524.html.

Foulonneau, Muriel, Thomas G. Habing, and Timothy W. Cole. 2006. "Automated Capture of Thumbnails and Thumbshots for Use by Metadata Aggregation Services." *D-Lib Magazine* [Online], 12, no.1, Available: www.dlib.org/dlib/january06/foulonneau/01foulonneau.html.

Freyre, Elisabeth, and Max Naudi 2003. "MACS: Subject Access Across Languages and Networks." In *Subject Retrieval in a Networked Environment*, edited by I.C. McIlwaine (pp. 3–10). Proceedings of the IFLA Satellite Meeting held in Dublin, Ohio, August 14–16, 2001, and sponsored by the IFLA Classification and Indexing Section, the IFLA Information Technology Section, and OCLC. Munich: K.G. Saur.

Friesen, Norm. 2004. *International LOM Survey: Report*. Draft. Available: http://dlist.sir.arizona.edu/403.

Friesen, Norm, Jon Mason, and Nigel Ward. 2002. "Building Educational Metadata Application Profiles." *Proceedings of the International Conference on Dublin Core and Metadata for E-Commerce* (pp. 63–69). Firenze, Italy: Firenze University Press. Available: www.bncf.net/dc2002/program/ft/paper7.pdf.

Friesen, Norm, Sue Fisher, and Anthony Roberts. 2002. *CanCore Guidelines for the Implementation of Learning Object Metadata. IEEE 1484.12.1-2002*. Available: www.cancore.ca/en/guidelines.html.

Furrie, Betty 2003. *Understanding MARC Bibliographic: Machine-Readable Cataloging*, 7th ed. Washington, DC: Cataloging Distribution Service, Library of Congress. Available: www.loc.gov/marc/umb.

"Gateway to Educational Materials (GEM)." Web page. Renamed as "The Gateway to 21st Century Skills."

"The Gateway to 21st Century Skills (GEM)." Web page. Available: www.thegateway.org/ (accessed January 19, 2008).

GEM. 2004. "Listing of GEM 2.0 Top-level Elements." Web page. Available: http://64.119.44.148/about/documentation/metadataElements.

"GEM Intellectual Rights Policy." The Gateway to 21st Century Skills. Web page. Available: www.thegateway.org/about/gemingeneral/gemConsortium/policies/2004rights.

Gill, Tony. 2000. "Metadata and the World Wide Web." In *Introduction to Metadata: Pathways to Digital Information*, edited by Murtha Baca. Online Edition (Version 2.1). Los Angeles, CA: Getty Information Institute. Available: www.getty.edu/research/conducting_research/standards/intrometadata/metadata.html.

Gill, Tony, Anne Gilliland-Swetland, and Murtha Baca. 1998. *Introduction to Metadata: Pathways to Digital Information*. Version 1.0. Los Angeles, CA: J. Paul Getty Trust, Getty Research Institute.

Gilliland, Anne J. 2000. "Setting the Stage." In *Introduction to Metadata: Pathways to Digital Information*, edited by Murtha Baca. Online Edition (Version 2.1). Los Angeles, CA: Getty Information Institute. Available: www.getty.edu/research/conducting_research/standards/intrometadata/setting.html.

Global Change Master Directory. 2007. "Directory Interchange Format (DIF) Writer's Guide." National Aeronautics and Space Administration. Web page. Available: http://gcmd.nasa.gov/User/difguide/.

Godby, Carol Jean. 2004. "What Do Application Profiles Reveal About the Learning Object Metadata Standard?" *Ariadne* [Online], no. 41. Available: www.ariadne.ac.uk/issue41/godby/.

Godby, Carol Jean, Jeffrey A. Young, and Eric Childress. 2004. "A Repository of Metadata Crosswalks." *D-Lib Magazine* [Online], 10, no. 12. Available: www.dlib.org/dlib/december04/godby/12godby.html.

Gold, Anna. 2007a. "Cyberinfrastructure, Data, and Libraries, Part 1: A Cyberinfrastructure Primer for Librarians." *D-Lib Magazine* [Online], 13, no. 9/10. Available: http://dlib.org/dlib/september07/gold/09gold-pt1.html.

Gold, Anna. 2007b. "Cyberinfrastructure, Data, and Libraries, Part 2: Libraries and the Data Challenge: Roles and Actions for Libraries." *D-Lib Magazine* [Online], 13, no. 9/10. Available: http://dlib.org/dlib/september07/gold/09gold-pt2.html.

Goodchild, Michael F., and Jianyu Zhou. 2003. "Finding Geographic Information: Collection-level Metadata." *Geoinformatica* 7, no. 2: 95–112.

"Green's Functions Research and Education Enhancement Network (GREEN)." Web page. Available: http://appling.kent.edu/NSDLGreen/ (accessed November 19, 2007).

Greenberg, Jane, ed. 2000. *Metadata and Organizing Education Resources on the Internet*. Binghamton, NY: The Haworth Press, Inc.

Greenberg, Jane. 2001. "A Quantitative Categorical Analysis of Metadata Elements in Image-applicable Metadata Schemes." *Journal of the American Society for Information Science and Technology*, 52, no. 11: 917–924.

Greenberg, Jane. 2002. "Metadata Generation: Processes, People and Tools." *Bulletin of the American Society for Information Science & Technology*, 29, no. 2: 16–19. Available: www.asis.org/Bulletin/Dec-02/greenberg.html.

Greenberg, Jane. 2005. "Understanding Metadata and Metadata Schemes." *Cataloging & Classification Quarterly*, 40, no. 3/4: 17–36.

Greenberg, Jane, Sarah Carrier, and Jed Dube. 2007. "The DRIADE Project: Phased Application Profile Development in Support of Open Science." *Proceedings of the International Conference on Dublin Core and Metadata Applications 2007* (pp. 35–42). Available: www.dcmipubs.org/ojs/index.php/pubs/article/viewFile/39/19.

Greenberg, Jane, Maria Cristina Pattuelli, Bijan Parsia, and W. Davenport Robertson. 2001. "Author-Generated Dublin Core Metadata for Web Resources: A Baseline Study in an Organization." *Journal of Digital Information* [Online], 2, no. 2. Available: http://jodi.tamu.edu/Articles/v02/i02/ Greenberg/.

Greenberg, Jane, and W. Davenport Robertson. 2002. "Semantic Web Construction: An Inquiry of Authors' Views on Collaborative Metadata Generation." *Proceedings of International Conference on Dublin Core and Metadata for e-Communities* (pp. 45–52). Firenze, Italy: Firenze University Press.

Greenberg, Jane, Kristina Spurgin, and Abe Crystal. 2005. *Final Report for the AMeGA (Automatic Metadata Generation Applications) Project*. Available: www.loc.gov/catdir/bibcontrol/lc_amega_final_report.pdf.

Gregory, Jonathan. 2003. The CF Metadata Standard. Available: http://cf-pcmdi.llnl.gov/documents/other/cf_overview_article.pdf.

Guenther, Rebecca. 2004. "New and Traditional Descriptive Formats in the Library Environment." Presentation at the DC2004 Conference. Available: http://dc2004.library.sh.cn/english/prog/ppt/ifla.ppt.

Guenther, Rebecca, and Sally McCallum. 2002. "New Metadata Standards for Digital Resources: MODS and METS." *Bulletin of the American Society for Information Science & Technology*, 29, no. 2. Available: www.asis.org/Bulletin/Dec-02/guenthermccallum.html.

Guy, Marieke, Andy Powell, and Michael Day. 2004. "Improving the Quality of Metadata in EPrint Archives." *Ariadne* [Online], no. 38. Available: www.ariadne.ac.uk/issue38/guy.

Guy, Marieke, and Emma Tonkin. 2006. "Folksonomies: Tidying up Tags?" *D-Lib Magazine* [Online], 12, no. 1. Available: www.dlib.org.ar/dlib/january06/guy/01guy.html.

Han, Hui, C. Lee Giles, Eren Manavoglu, Hongyuan Zha, Zhenyue Zhang, and Edward A. Fox. 2003. "Automatic Document Metadata Extraction Using Support Vector Machines." *Proceedings of the 3rd ACM/IEEE-CS Joint Conference on Digital Libraries* (pp. 37–48). Washington, DC: IEEE Computer Society.

Handschuh, Siegfried and Steffen Staab. 2003. "CREAM: CREAting Metadata for the Semantic Web." *Computer Networks—The International Journal of Computer and Telecommunications Networking*, 42, no. 5: 579–598.

Haynes, David. 2004. *Metadata for Information Management and Retrieval*. London: Facet Publishing.

Heath, Barbara P., David J. McArthur, Marilyn K. McClelland, and Ronald J. Vetter. 2005. "Metadata Lessons from the iLumina Digital Library." *Communications of ACM* 48, no. 7: 68–74.

Heery, Rachel. 2002. "Functional Requirements for CORES Schema Creation and Registration Tool." Web site, UKOLN. Available: www.cores-eu.net/registry/d22/funcreq.html.

Heery, Rachel. 2004. "Metadata Futures: Steps Toward Semantic Interoperability." In *Metadata in Practice*, edited by Diane I. Hillmann and Elaine L. Westbrooks (pp. 257–271). Chicago: American Library Association.

Heery, Rachel, Andy Powell, and Michael Day. 1998. "Metadata: CrossROADS and Interoperability." *Ariadne* [Online], no. 14. Available: www.ariadne.ac.uk/issue14/metadata/

Heery, Rachel, and Manjula Patel. 2000. "Application Profiles: Mixing and Matching Metadata Schemas." *Ariadne* [Online], no. 25. Available: www.ariadne.ac.uk/issue25/app-profiles/.

Hill, Linda. 2006. *Georeferencing, The Geographic Associations of Information*. Cambridge, MA: MIT Press.

Hill, Linda, Scott Crosier, Terence Smith, and Michael Goodchild. 2001. "A Content Standard for Computational Models." *D-Lib Magazine* [Online], 7, no. 6. Available: www.dlib.org/dlib/june01/hill/06hill.html.

Hill, Linda, and Greg Janee. 2004. "The Alexandria Digital Library Project: Metadata Development and Use." In *Metadata in Practice*, edited by Diane I. Hillmann and Elaine L. Westbrooks (pp. 117–138). Chicago: American Library Association.

Hill, Linda, Greg Janee, Ron Dolin, James Frew, and Mary Larsgaard. 1999. "Collection Metadata Solutions for Digital Library Applications." *Journal of the American Society for Information Science*, 50, no. 13: 1169–1181.

Hillmann, Diane. 2005. *Using Dublin Core*. Available: http://dublincore.org/documents/2005/11/07/usageguide/.

Hillman, Diane, and Naomi Dushay. 2004–2005. "NSDL Metadata Primer." Web page. Was available: http://metamanagement.comm.nsdlib.org/outline.html. Replaced by "Community: Collections and Metadata" Web page. Available: http://wiki.nsdl.org/index.php/Community:Collections_and_ Metadata.

Hillmann, Diane I., Naomi Dushay, and Jon Phipps. 2004. "Improving Metadata Quality: Augmentation and Recombination." *DC-2004 International Conference on Dublin Core and Metadata Applications, October 11–14, 2004, Shanghai, China*. Available: www.cs.cornell.edu/naomi/DC2004/MetadataAugmentation—DC2004.pdf.

Hillmann, Diane, Naomi Dushay, and Jon Phipps. 2005. "Improving Metadata Quality." Available: http://metadata-wg.mannlib.cornell.edu/forum/2005-04-29/hillman.ppt.

Hillmann, Diane I., and Elaine L. Westbrooks, eds. 2004. *Metadata in Practice*. Chicago: American Library Association.

Hodge, Gail. 2000. *Systems of Knowledge Organization for Digital Libraries: Beyond Traditional Authority Files*. Council on Library and Information Sources. Available: www.clir.org/pubs/reports/pub91/contents.html.

Hodge, Gail. 2001. *Metadata Made Simpler*. Bethesda, MD: NISO Press.

Hu,Yunhua, Hang Li, Yunbo Cao, Li Teng, Dmitriy Meyerzon, and Qinghua Zheng. 2005. "Automatic Extraction of Titles from General Documents Using Machine Learning." *Proceedings of the 5th ACM/IEEE-CS Joint Conference on Digital Libraries* (pp. 145–154).

Hunter, Jane. 2001. "Adding Multimedia to the Semantic Web—Building an MPEG-7 Ontology." *Proceedings of the First Semantic Web Working Symposium (SWWS)* (pp. 261–281). New York: ACM Press.

Hunter, Jane. 2002. "An Application Profile Which Combines Dublin Core and MPEG-7 Metadata Terms for Simple Video Description." Web page. Available: www.metadata.net/harmony/video_appln_profile.html.

Hunter, Jane. 2003. "A Survey of Metadata Research for Organizing the Web." *Library Trends*, 52, no. 2: 318–344.

Iannella, Renato. 1999. "An Idiot's Guide to the Resource Description Framework." Web page. Available: http://renato.iannella.it/paper/rdf-idiot/.

Iannella, Renato. 2001. "Digital Rights Management (DRM) Architectures." *D-Lib Magazine* [Online], 7, no. 6. Available: www.dlib.org/dlib/june01/iannella/06iannella.html.

"ID3v2Easy." 2006. ID3.org. Web page. Available: www.id3.org/ID3v2Easy.

IDF. 2006a. *DOI Kernel Metadata Declaration Specification and XML Schema*. International DOI Foundation (IDF). Available: www.doi.org/handbook_2000/appendix_6.pdf.

IDF. 2006b. *DOI Handbook 2006*. Version 4.4.1 International DOI Foundation (IDF). Available: www.doi.org/hb.html, doi:10.1000/182.

IDF. 2007. "The Digital Object Identifier (DOI) System." International DOI Foundation (IDF). Web page. Available: www.doi.org/.

IEEE 1484.12.1-2002. *IEEE Standard for Learning Object Metadata*. Draft available: http://ltsc.ieee.org/wg12/files/LOM_1484_12_1_v1_Final_Draft.pdf.

IEEE 1484.4-2007. *IEEE Trial-Use Recommended Practice for Digital Rights Expression Languages (DRELs) Suitable for eLearning Technologies*. Available: http://ieeexplore.ieee.org/servlet/opac?punumber=4303009.

IEEE-LTSC WG-12. 2005. "WG12: Learning Object Metadata Homepage." IEEE Learning Technology Standard Committee. Web page. Available: http://ltsc.ieee.org/wg12/.

IFLA. 1998. *Functional Requirements for Bibliographic Records*. IFLA Study Group on the Functional Requirements for Bibliographic Records. Munich: K.G. Saur.

IMS. 2004. *IMS Meta-data Best Practice Guide for IEEE 1484.12.1-2002 Standard for Learning Object Metadata*. Version 1.3. Public Draft, edited by IMS Global Learning Consortium, Inc. Available: www.imsglobal.org/metadata/mdv1p3pd/imsmd_bestv1p3pd.html.

<indecs>. 2000. *Putting Metadata to Rights: Summary Final Report*. Rust, Godfrey, and Mark Bide. Indecs (Interoperability of Data in E-commerce Systems). Available: www.doi.org/topics/indecs/indecs_SummaryReport.pdf.

Internet Mail Consortium. 1996. "vCard—The Electronic Business Card." Available: www.imc.org/pdi/vcard-21.txt.

ISO/IEC 11404:1996. *Information Technology—Programming Languages, Their Environments and System Software Interfaces—Language-Independent Datatypes*. Geneva: International Standards Organization.

ISO/IEC 15938-5:2003. *Information Technology—Multimedia Content Description Interface—Part 5: Multimedia Description Schemes*. Geneva: International Standards Organization (ISO).

ISO/IEC 11179:2004. *Information Technology—Metadata Registries (MDR). Geneva: International Standards Organization (ISO)*. Available: http://standards.iso.org/ittf/PubliclyAvailableStandards/c035343_ISO_IEC_11179-1_2004(E).zip.

ISO/IEC 11179-3:2004. *Information Technology—Metadata Registries (MDR)—Part 3: Registry Metamodel and Basic Attributes*. Geneva: International Standards Organization (ISO). Available: http://metadata-stds.org/11179/.

ISO/IEC 21000-7:2004. *Information Technology—Multimedia Framework—Part 7: Digital Item Adaptation*. Geneva: International Standards Organization (ISO).

ISO/TS 19115:2003. *Geographic Information—Metadata*. Final draft. Available: www.ncits.org/ref-docs/FDIS_19115.pdf.

Jayakanth, Francis, Kurt Maly, M. Zubair, and Lalitha Aswath. 2005. "Static and Dynamic Approaches to Make Legacy Databases OAI-compliant." *D-Lib Magazine* [Online], 11, no. 10. Available: www.dlib.org/dlib/october05/10inbrief.html#JAYAKANTH.

JISC IE Metadata Schema Registry. 2006. "JISC Project Plan." Available: http://ukoln.ac.uk/projects/iemsr/documents/plan3/plan3.pdf.

"JISC Information Environment (IE) Metadata Schema Registry." Funded by the Joint Information Systems Committee (JISC); hosted at UKOLN. Web page. Available: www.ukoln.ac.uk/projects/iemsr/ (accessed December 27, 2007).

JISC PALS II Metadata + Project. 2006. "Metadata +: Machine Services for Metadata Discovery and Aggregation." Web page. Available: www.jisc.ac.uk/whatwedo/programmes/programme_pals2/project_metadata_plus.aspx .

Johnston, Pete. 2002. "Collaboration, Integration and 'Recombinant Potential'." *Ariadne* [Online], no. 33. Available: www.ariadne.ac.uk/issue33/oclc-scurl/.

Johnston, Pete. 2004. *Functions of the IE Metadata Schema Registry*. UKOLN. Available: www.ukoln.ac.uk/projects/iemsr/wp2/function/.

Johnston, Pete. 2003. "Metadata and Interoperability in a Complex World." *Ariadne* [Online], no. 37. Available: www.ariadne.ac.uk/issue37/dc-2003-rpt/.

Jones, Matthew B., Chad Berkley, Jivka Bojilova, and Mark Schildhauer. 2001. "Managing Scientific Metadata." *IEEE Internet Computing*, 5, no. 5: 59–68. http://knb.ecoinformatics.org/distributed-data-ic-final.pdf.

Jörgensen, Corinne. 2007. "The MPEG-7 Standard: Multimedia Description in Theory and Application." *Journal of the American Society for Information Science and Technology*, 58, no. 9: 1323–1328.

Jul, Erik. 1995. "OCLC Internet Cataloging Project." *D-Lib Magazine* [Online], December 1995. Available: www.dlib.org/dlib/december95/briefings/12oclc.html.

Kamel Boulos, M. N., A. V. Roudsari, and E. R. Carson. 2002. "A Dynamic Problem to Knowledge Linking Semantic Web Service Based on Clinical Codes." *Medical Informatics and the Internet in Medicine*, 27, no. 3: 127–137.

Khan, Latifur, Dennis McLeod, and Eduard Hovy. 2005. "Framework for Effective Annotation of Information from Closed Captions Using Ontologies." *Journal of Intelligent Information Systems*, 25, no. 2: 181–205.

Koper, Rob. 2001. "Modeling Units of Study from a Pedagogical Perspective: The Pedagogical Meta-model Behind EML." Available: http://dspace.ou.nl/bitstream/1820/36/1/Pedagogical+metamodel+behind+EMLv2.pdf.

Kurth, Martin. 2006. "Basic Dublin Core Semantics." *DC 2006: International Conference on Dublin Core and Metadata Applications*, October 3, 2006, Manzanillo, Mexico. Available: http://dublincore.org/resources/training/dc-2006/Tutorial1.pdf.

Lagoze, Carl. 1996. "The Warwick Framework: A Container Architecture for Aggregating Sets of Metadata." *D-Lib Magazine* [Online], July/August 1996. Available: www.dlib.org/dlib/july96/lagoze/07lagoze.html.

Lagoze, Carl. 2001. "Keeping Dublin Core Simple: Cross-domain Discovery or Resource Description?" *D-Lib Magazine* [Online], 7, no.1. Available: www.dlib.org/dlib/january01/lagoze/01lagoze.html.

Lagoze, Carl, and J. Hunter. 2001. "The ABC Ontology and Model." *Journal of Digital Information*, 2, no. 2. Available: http://journals.tdl.org/jodi/article/view/jodi-44/47.

Lagoze, Carl, Herbert van de Sompel, Michael Nelson, and Simeon Warner, Ed. 2004. *The Open Archives Initiative Protocols for Metadata Harvesting*. OAI. Available: www.openarchives.org/OAI/openarchivesprotocol.html.

Lagoze, Carl, Herbert van de Sompel, Michael Nelson, and Simeon Warner, 2005. *Implementation Guidelines for the Open Archives Initiative Protocol for Metadata Harvesting*. OAI. Available: www.openarchives.org//OAI/2.0/guidelines.htm.

Lally, Ann M., and Carolyn E. Dunford. 2007. "Using Wikipedia to Extend Digital Collections." *D-Lib Magazine* [Online], 13, no. 5/6. Available: www.dlib.org/dlib/may07/lally/05lally.html.

Lavoie, Brian, and Richard Gartner. 2005. *Technology Watch Report: Preservation Metadata. DPC Technology Watch Series Report 05-01*. OCLC Online Computer Library Center, Oxford University Library Services, and Digital Preservation Coalition. Available: www.dpconline.org/docs/reports/ dpctw05-01.pdf.

Library of Congress, Development and MARC Standards Office. 2005. "METS: An Overview & Tutorial." Web page. Available: www.loc.gov/standards/mets/METSOverview.v2.html.

Liddy, Elizabeth D., Eileen Allen, Sarah Harwell, Susan Corieri, and et al. 2002. "Automated Metadata Generation & Evaluation." *Proceedings of the 25th Annual International ACM SIGIR Conference on Research and Development in Information Retrieval* (pp. 401–402). New York: ACM Press.

Liu, Hugo, Pattie Maes, and Glorianna Davenport. 2006. "Unraveling the Taste Fabric of Social Networks." *International Journal on Semantic Web and Information Systems*, 2, no. 1: 42–71. Available: http://mf.media.mit.edu/pubs/journal/TasteFabric.pdf.

LOM, 2002. "Final 1484.12.1-2002 LOM Draft Standard." Web page. IEEE LTSC WG-12. Available: http://ltsc.ieee.org/wg12/20020612-Final-LOM-Draft.html.

Low, Boon. 2006. *Machine Services for Metadata Discovery and Aggregation*. metadata +. Available: www.jisc.ac.uk/media/documents/programmes/pals2/metadata_final_report.pdf.

LTSC. 2004a. "IEEE P1484.12.3/D2 Draft for Extensible Markup Language (XML) Schema Definition Language Binding for Learning Object Metadata." Web page. Available: http://ltsc.ieee.org/wg12/files/IEEE_1484_12_03_d2.pdf.

LTSC. 2004b. "IEEE WG12: Learning Object Metadata: Purpose of Proposed Project." Web page. Available: http://ltsc.ieee.org/wg12/index.html.

Malet, Gary, Felix Munoz, Richard Appleyard, and William Hersh. 1999. "A Model for Enhancing Internet Medical Document Retrieval with 'Medical Core Metadata'." *Journal of the American Medical Informatics Association*, 6: 163–172.

Manola, Frank, and Eric Miller. 2004. "RDF primer. W3C Recommendation 10." Web page. Available: www.w3.org/TR/rdf-primer/.

MARC 21 Format for Bibliographic Data Including Guidelines for Content Designation. Library of Congress, Library and Archives Canada, British Library, and National Library of Canada. 1999. Washington: Library of Congress, Cataloging Distribution Service.

"*MARC XML Design Considerations*." 2004. Library of Congress Network Development and MARC Standards Office. Web page. Available: www.loc.gov/standards/marcxml/marcxml-design.html.

Markey, Karen. 2007. "The Online Library Catalog: Paradise Lost and Paradise Regained?" *D-Lib Magazine* [Online], 13, no. 1/2. Available: www.dlib.org/dlib/january07/markey/01markey.html.

Martinez, Jose M. 2005. "MPEG-7 Overview." ISO/IEC JTC1/SC29/WG11N6828. Web page. Available: www.chiariglione.org/mpeg/technologies/mp07-mds/index.htm.

Mathes, Adam. 2004. "Folksonomies—Cooperative Classification and Communication Through Shared Metadata." Web page. Available: www.adammathes.com/academic/computer-mediated-communication/folksonomies.html.

McClelland, Marilyn, David McArthur, Sarah Giersch, and Gary Geisler. 2002. "Challenges for Service Providers When Importing Metadata in Digital Libraries." *D-Lib Magazine* [Online], 8, no. 4. Available: www.dlib.org/dlib/april02/mcclelland/04mcclelland.html.

McClure, Charles R., and John C. Bertot, eds. 2001. *Evaluating Networked Information Services: Techniques, Policy, and Issues*. Medford, NJ: Information Today.

McDonough, Jerome P. 2006. "A Daunting PREMIS: Implementing Preservation Metadata Within the METS Framework." *2006 International Conference on Digital Archive Technologies (ICDAT2006), October 19-20, 2006, Taipei, Taiwan*. Available: www.loc.gov/standards/premis/ICDAT2006/pages/Slide15_gif.htm.

Mejias, Ulises A. 2005. "Tag Literacy." Blog item. Available: http://blog.ulisesmejias.com/2005/04/26/tag-literacy/ (accessed January 26, 2008).

Meta-Data Working Group, 1993. "Meta-Data Working Group Page." Sponsored by IEEE Mass Storage Systems and Technology Committee (MSS&TC). Was available: www.llnl.gov/liv_comp/metadata/working_grp.html.

"Metadata Standards Crosswalk." Compiled by Patricia Harpring, Mary S. Woodley, Anne J. Gilliland, and Murtha Baca. In *Introduction to Metadata: Pathways to Digital Information*, edited by Murtha Baca (Version 2.1). Los Angeles: Getty Research Institute. Web page. Available: www.getty.edu/research/conducting_research/standards/intrometadata/metadata_element_sets.html (accessed January 10, 2008).

"Metadata Switch." 2007. OCLC Research. Web page. Available: www.oclc.org/research/projects/mswitch/default.htm.

METS Editorial Board. 2007. *Metadata Encoding and Transmission Standard: Primer and Reference Manual*. Available: www.loc.gov/standards/mets/METS%20Documentation%20final%20070930%20msw.pdf.

"METS Profiles that specify use of PREMIS." *Using PREMIS with METS*. Web page. Available: www.loc.gov/standards/premis/premis-mets.html.

Michlmayr, Elke, Sabine Graf, Wolf Siberski, and Wolfgang Nejdl. 2005. "A Case Study on Emergent Semantics in Communities." *Proceedings of the Workshop on Social Network Analysis, the 4th International Semantic Web Conference (ISWC 2005)*. Berlin: Springer-Verlag.

Mika, Peter. 2005. "Ontologies Are Us: A Unified Model of Social Networks and Semantics." In *Proceedings of the 4th International Semantic Web Conference (ISWC 2005)*, edited by Y. Gil et al. (pp. 522-536). Berlin: Springer-Verlag.

MODS. 2007. "Outline of Elements and Attributes in MODS Version 3.3." Library of Congress Network Developments and MARC Standards Office. Web page. Available: www.loc.gov/standards/mods/v3/mods-3-3-outline-review-new.html.

"MODS Conversions." Library of Congress Network Developments and MARC Standards Office. Web page. Available: www.loc.gov/standards/mods/mods-conversions.html (accessed January 26, 2008).

"MODS to MARC 21 Mapping." Library of Congress Network Developments and MARC Standards Office. Web page. Available: www.loc.gov/standards/mods/v3/mods2marc-mapping.html (accessed January 26, 2008).

Moffat, M. 2006. "'Marketing' with Metadata—How Metadata can Increase Exposure and Visibility of Online Content." JISC PerX Project. Web page. Available: www.icbl.hw.ac.uk/perx/advocacy/exposingmetadata.htm.

Nagamori, Mitsuharu, and Shigeo Sugimoto. 2007. "Using Metadata Schema registry As a Core Function to Enhance Usability and Reusability of Metadata Schemas." *DC-2007: International Conference on Dublin Core and Metadata Applications: Application Profiles and Their Application in Practice.* August 27–31, 2007, Singapore. Available: www.dcmipubs.org/ojs/index.php/pubs/article/viewFile/35/17.

NAP Metadata Working Group. 2007. "North American Profile of ISO19115: 2003—Geographic Information—Metadata (NAP—Metadata, Version 1.1)." Available: www.fgdc.gov/standards/projects/incits-l1-standards-projects/NAP-Metadata/napMetadataProfileV11_7-26-07.pdf.

National Library of Medicine. "Finding Aid to the Cornelius Rea Agnew Papers, 1857–1888." Archives and Modern Manuscripts Program, History of Medicine Division. Web page. Available: www.nlm.nih.gov/hmd/manuscripts/ead/agnew.html.

Nilsson, Mikael. 2007a. "DCMI Basic Syntaxes Tutorial." *DC-2007: International Conference on Dublin Core and Metadata Applications: Application Profiles and Their Application in Practice*. August 27-31, 2007, Singapore. Available: www.dc2007.sg/T2-BasicSyntaxes.pdf.

Nilsson, Mikael. 2007b. "The Singapore Framework for Application Profiles." Web page. Available: http://dublincore.org/architecturewiki/Singapore Framework.

NISO. 2004. *Understanding Metadata*. Bethesda, MD: NISO Press. Available: www.niso.org/publications/press/UnderstandingMetadata.pdf.

NISO Framework Advisory Group. 2004. *A Framework of Guidance for Building Good Digital Collections*. 2nd ed. Grace Agnew, Liz Bishoff, Priscilla Caplan, Rebecca Guenther, and Ingrid Hsieh-Yee.

NISO Framework Advisory Group. 2007. *A Framework of Guidance for Building Good Digital Collections*. 3rd ed. Priscilla Caplan, Grace Agnew, Murtha Baca, Carl Fleischhauer, Tony Gill, Ingrid Hsieh-Yee, Jill Koelling, Christie Stephenson, and Karen A. Wetzel. Available: www.niso.org/publications/rp/framework3.pdf.

NISO Z39.91-200x. *Collection Description Specification*. Draft Standard for Trial Use: Period: November 1, 2005—October 31, 2006. Bethesda, MD: NISO Press.

NISO Z39.92-200X. *Information Retrieval Service Description Specification*. Draft Standard for Trial Use: Period: November 1, 2005—October 31, 2006. Bethesda, MD: NISO Press.

NJ-BGIS. 2007. "What Are Metadata?" New Jersey Department of Environmental Protection. Available: www.state.nj.us/dep/gis/faqmeta.htm.

NSDL (The National Science Digital Library). Funded by the National Science Foundation. Web page. Available: http://nsdl.org/ (accessed January 22, 2008).

NSDL. 2001. "Recommended Metadata Elements to Support NSDL Resource Discovery." Web page. Available: http://standards.comm.nsdlib.org/ElementsTable2.html.

NSDL. 2004. "Metadata Management: Learning Resource Type Vocabulary." Web page. Was available: http://metamanagement.comm.nsdl.org/cgi-bin/wiki.pl?LRT_Wiki_Version2.

NSDL. 2005–2007. *Best Practices for Shareable Metadata*. Draft ed. Arms, Caroline, Naomi Dushay, Muriel Foulonneau, Kat Hagedorn, et al. Digital Library Federation and National Science Digital Library. Available: http://webservices.itcs.umich.edu/mediawiki/oaibp/index.php/ShareableMetadataPublic.

"NSDL Fact Sheet." Web page. Available: http://nsdl.org/about/?pager=factsheet (accessed December 19, 2006).

"NSDL Glossary." 2005. Web page. Available: http://nsdl.org/help/?pager=glossary.

NSDL Metadata Working Group. 2007. Web page. Available: www.dls.ucar.edu/people/kginger/nsdl_dc/index.html.

OAC. "OAC EAD Web Templates." Online Archive of California. Web page. Available: www.cdlib.org/inside/projects/oac/toolkit/templates/ (accessed January 23, 2007).

OAC. 2005. "OAC Technical Information." Online Archive of California. Web page. Available: www.cdlib.org/inside/projects/oac/tech.html.

OAC. "Online Archive of California Website." Web page. Available: www.oac.cdlib.org (accessed September 19, 2007).

OAI. 2004. "Specification for an OAI Static Repository and an OAI Static Repository Gateway." Available: www.openarchives.org/OAI/2.0/guidelines-static-repository.htm.

OAI. 2005. "Implementation Guidelines for the Open Archives Initiative Protocol for Metadata Harvesting." Web page. Available: www.openarchives.org/OAI/2.0/guidelines.htm.

OAI-FAQ. 2002. "Open Archives Initiative Frequently Asked Questions." Web page. Carl Lagoze, Herbert van de Sompel, Michael Nelson, and Simeon Warner, OAI. Available: www.openarchives.org/documents/FAQ.html.

"OAI Repository Explorer." Web page. Available: http://re.cs.uct.ac.za/ (accessed January 27, 2008).

OAIster. 2007. "OAIster Collection Development Policy." Web page. Carl Lagoze, Herbert van de Sompel, Michael Nelson, and Simeon Warner, eds. Available: www.oaister.org/restricted.html.

Oberle, Daniel, Steffen Staab, Rudi Studer, and Raphael Volz. 2005. "Supporting Application Development in the Semantic Web." *ACM Transactions on Internet Technology*, 5, no. 2: 328.

"Object ID." Web page. Available: www.object-id.com (accessed September 19, 2007).

OCLC. 2005. *Perceptions of Libraries and Information Resources: A Report to the OCLC Membership*. OCLC Online Computer Library Center, Inc. Available: www.oclc.org/reports/2005perceptions.htm.

OCLC. 2006. "OCLC Bibliographic Formats and Standards." Web page. Available: www.oclc.org/bibformats/.

OCLC. 2007. "WorldCat Facts and Statistics." Web page. Available: www.oclc.org/worldcat/statistics/default.asp.

OCLC Research. 2007. "Terminology Services." Web page. Available: www.oclc.org/research/projects/termservices/

OCLC/RLG. 2002. *Preservation Metadata and the OAIS Information Model: A Metadata Framework to Support the Preservation of Digital Objects*. OCLC Online Computer Library Center and the Research Libraries Group. Available: www.oclc.org/research/pmwg/.

OCLC/RLG. 2004. *Implementing Preservation Repositories for Digital Materials: Current Practice and Emerging Trends in the Cultural Heritage Community, A Report by the PREMIS Working Group*. OCLC Online Computer Library Center and the Research Libraries Group. Available: www.oclc.org/research/projects/pmwg/surveyreport.pdf.

OCLC/RLG. 2005. *Data Dictionary for Preservation Metadata*. Final Report. PREMIS Working Group. OCLC Online Computer Library Center and the Research Libraries Group. Available: www.oclc.org/research/projects/pmwg/premis-final.pdf.

OCLC/RLG Working Group on Preservation Metadata. 2002. *Preservation Metadata and the OAIS Information Model: A Metadata Framework to Support the Preservation of Digital Objects*. OCLC Online Computer Library Center and the Research Libraries Group. Available: www.oclc.org/research/projects/pmwg/pm_framework.pdf.

"OCLC Terminologies Service." OCLC Products and Services. Web page. Available: www.oclc.org/terminologies/default.htm (accessed January 27, 2008).

O'Neill, Dan. 2006. "ID3v2Easy." Web page. Available: www.id3.org/ID3v2Easy.

O'Neill, Edward T. 1992. Database Quality Control. *Annual Review of OCLC Research* July 1991–June 1992: 2-11.

O'Neill, Edward T., and Diane Vizine-Goetz. 1988. "Quality Control in Online Databases." *Annual Review of Information Science and Technology*. M. Williams, ed. Vol. 23: 125–156. Medford, NJ: Learned Information.

"Online Archive of California." Web page. Available: www.oac.cdlib.org/ (accessed January 27, 2008).

Open Archives Forum—First Workshop: Creating a European Forum on Open Archives. 2002. *Ariadne* [Online], no. 32. Available: www.ariadne.ac.uk/issue32/open-archives-forum/.

Paik, Woojin, Sibel Yilmazel, Eric Brown, Maryjane Poulin, Stephane Dubon, and Christophe Amice. 2001. "Applying Natural Language Processing (NLP) Based Metadata Extraction to Automatically Acquire User Preferences." *Proceedings of the International Conference on Knowledge Capture 2001*, edited by Y. Gil, M. Musen, and J. Shavik (pp. 116–122). New York: ACM Press.

Paskin, Norman, and Godfrey Rust. 1999. *The Digital Object Identifier Initiative: Metadata Implications*. Version 3. Available: www.doi.org/P2VER3.PDF.

Paynter, Gordon W. 2005. "Developing Practical Automatic Metadata Assignment and Evaluation Tools for Internet Resources." *Proceedings of the 5th ACM/IEEE Joint Conference on Digital Libraries (JCDL '05)* (pp. 291–300). New York: ACM Press.

Phillips, A., and M. Davis, eds. 2006. "Tags for Identifying Languages." Request for Comments: 4646. The Internet Society, Network Working Group. Web page. Available: www.ietf.org/rfc/rfc4646.txt.

Phipps, Jon, Diane I. Hillmann, and Gordon Paynter. 2005. "Orchestrating Metadata Enhancement Services: Introducing Lenny." *Proceedings of the International Conference on Dublin Core and Metadata Applications*, Madrid, Spain. Available: http://arxiv.org/ftp/cs/papers/0501/0501083.pdf.

Powell, Andy. 2003. "JISC IE Architecture: Shared Services Development Plan." Web page. Available: http://www.ukoln.ac.uk/distributed-systems/jisc-ie/arch/ssplan/.

Powell, Andy, and Phil Barker. 2004. "RDN/LTSN Partnerships: Learning Resource Discovery Based on the LOM and the OAI-PMH." *Ariadne* [Online] no. 39. Available: www.ariadne.ac.uk/issue39/powell/.

PREMIS Maintenance Activity. 2006. "Schemas for PREMIS". Web page. Available: www.loc.gov/standards/premis/schemas.html.

Qin, Jian, and Jean Godby. 2003. "Incorporating Educational Vocabulary in Learning Object Metadata Schemes." *Proceedings of the 7th European Conference on Research and Advanced Technology for Digital Libraries, ECDL 2003*, edited by T. Koch and I.T. Solvberg (pp. 52–57). Berlin: Springer-Verlag.

Qin, Jian, and Naybell Hernandez. 2006. "Building Interoperable Vocabulary and Structures for Learning Objects." *Journal of the American Society for Information Science and Technology*, 57, no. 2: 280–292.

Qin, Jian, and Stephen Paling. 2001. "Converting a Controlled Vocabulary into an Ontology: The Case of GEM." *Information Research: An International Electronic Journal* [Online], 6, no. 2. Available: http://InformationR.net/ir/6-2/paper94.html.

Qin, Jian, and Kathryn Wesley. 1998. "Web Indexing with Fields: A Survey of Web Objects in Polymer Chemistry." *Information Technology and Libraries*, 17, no 3: 149–160.

Quint, Barbara. 2004. "All of OCLC's WorldCat Heading Toward the Open Web." *Information Today, Inc. NewsBreaks* [Online], November 19, 2007. Available: http://newsbreaks.infotoday.com/nbreader.asp?ArticleID= 16592.

RDF Core Working Group. 2004. "Resource Description Framework (RDF)." Web page. Available: www.w3.org/RDF/.

Refsnes Data. 2007. "XML Schema Tutorial." W3Schools. Web page. Available: www.w3schools.com/schema/default.asp.

Rieger, Oya Y. 2007. *Preservation in the Age of Large-scale Digitization, a White Paper*. Council on Library and Information Resources. Available: www.clir.org/pubs/reports/pub141/pub141.pdf.

Rising, Hawley K., III, and Corinne Jörgensen. 2007. "Semantic Description in MPEG-7: The Rich Recursion of Ripeness." *Journal of the American Society for Information Science and Technology*, 58, no. 9: 1338–1345.

RSS Advisory Board. 2007. "RSS 2.0 Specification." Web page. Available: www.rssboard.org/rss-specification.

Rust, Godfrey. 1998. "Metadata: The Right Approach: An Integrated Model for Descriptive and Rights Metadata in E-Commerce." *D-Lib Magazine* [Online], July/August 1998. Available: www.dlib.org/dlib/july98/rust/07rust.html.

Rust, Godfrey, and Mark Bide. 2000. *The <indecs> Metadata Framework: Principles, Model and Data Dictionary*. <indecs> Framework. Available: www.doi.org/topics/indecs/indecs_framework_2000.pdf.

Sadeh, Tamar. 2006. "Google Scholar versus Metasearch Systems." *High Energy Physics Libraries Webzine* [Online], no. 12. Available: http://library.cern.ch/HEPLW/12/papers/1/.

Salembier, Philippe, and Ana B. Benitez. 2007. "Structure Description Tools." *Journal of the American Society for Information Science and Technology*, 58, no. 9: 1329–1337.

Saracevic, Tefko. 2004. "Evaluation of Digital Libraries: An Overview." *The Seventh DELOS Workshop on the Evaluation of Digital Libraries*, Padova, Italy, October 4–5, 2004. Available: http://dlib.ionio.gr/wp7/WS2004_Saracevic.pdf.

Scheirer, Jason. 2006. "Techniques for Automatic Metadata Assignment and Evaluation." *Metadata Tools for Digital Resource Repositories Workshop (JCDL 2006)*. UNC School of Information and Library Science. Available: www.ils.unc.edu/mrc/jcdl2006/abstracts/scheirer.html.

"Schemaweb." Web page. Available: www.schemaweb.info/ (accessed January 27, 2008).

"science.gov" portal. Web page. Available: http://science.gov/.

"SCORM General Common Questions, 2007." Web page. Available: www.adlnet.gov/help/CommonQuestions/SCORMGeneralQuestions.aspx#qWhatIn.

"SCORM Overview." Redbird Software Corp. 2006. Web page. Available: www.scormsoft.com/scorm/overview.

"Sheet Music Consortium." Web page. Available: http://digital.library.ucla.edu/sheetmusic/. (accessed January 27, 2008).

Shirky, Clay. 2005. "Ontology Is Overrated: Categories, Links, and Tags." *Clay Shirky's Writings About the Internet: Economics & Culture, Media & Community*. Web page. Available: www.shirky.com/writings/ontology_overrated.html.

Shreeves, Sarah L., Thomas G. Habing, Kat Hagedorn, and Jeffrey A. Young. 2005. "Current Developments and Future Trends for the OAI Protocol for Metadata Harvesting." *Library Trends*, 53, no. 4: 576–589.

Shreeves, Sarah, Jenn Riley, and Liz Milewicz. 2006. "Moving Towards Shareable Metadata." *First Monday* [Online], 11, no. 8. Available: http://firstmonday.org/issues/issue11_8/shreeves/index.html.

Shreve, Gregory M., and Marcia L. Zeng. 2003. "Integrating Resource Metadata and Domain Markup in an NSDL Collection." *DC-2003: Proceedings of the International DCMI Metadata Conference and Workshop* (pp. 223–229). Available: www.siderean.com/dc2003/604_paper62.pdf.

Shreve, Gregory M., and Marcia L. Zeng. 2004. "Providing Parallel Metadata for Digital Libraries with Linguistically Heterogeneous Documents." *7th International Conference on Asian Digital Libraries* (pp. 341–344). Digital Libraries: International Collaboration and Cross-Fertilization, ICADL.

Simou, N., V. Tzouvaras, Y. Avrithis, G. Stamou, et al. 2005. "A Visual Descriptor Ontology for Multimedia Reasoning." *Proceedings of Workshop on Image Analysis for Multimedia Interactive Services (WIAMIS '05).*

Simple DC XML Schema. 2002. Eds. Johnston, Pete, Carl Lagoze, Andy Powell, and Herbert van de Sompel. Available: http://dublincore.org/schemas/xmls/simpledc20021212.xsd.

Singh, Gurmeet, Shishir Bharathi, Ann Chervenak, Ewa Deelman, et al. 2003. "A Metadata Catalog Service for Data Intensive Applications." *Proceedings of Supercomputing 2003 (SC2003)ACM.* Available: www.globus.org/alliance/publications/papers/mcs_sc2003.pdf.

Singh, Munindar P. 2000. "A Social Semantics for Agent Communication Languages." In *Issues in Agent Communication (Lecture Notes in Computer Science),* edited by F. Dignum and M. Greaves (pp. 31–45). Vol. 1916. London: Springer.

Smith, Gene. 2004. "Folksonomy: Social Classification." Web page. Available: http://atomiq.org/archives/2004/08/folksonomy_social_classification.html.

Smith, Mackenzie, Mary Barton, Mick Bass, Margret Branschofsky, and et al. 2003. "DSpace: An Open Source Dynamic Digital Repository." *D-Lib Magazine* [Online], 9, no. 1. Available: www.dlib.org/dlib/january03/smith/01smith.html.

Smith, Terence R. 1996. "A Brief Update on the Alexandria Digital Library Project: Constructing a Digital Library for Geographically-referenced Materials (Briefing)." *D-Lib Magazine* [Online], March 1996. Available: www.dlib.org/dlib/march96/briefings/smith/03smith.html.

Smith, Terence R., Marcia Lei Zeng, and ADEPT (The Alexandria Digital Earth Prototype) Project Team. 2004. "Building Semantic Tools for Concept-based Learning Spaces—Knowledge Bases of Strongly Structured Models for Concepts in Advanced DL." *Journal of Digital Information* [Online], 4, no. 4: Article No. 263. Available: http://journals.tdl.org/jodi/article/view/jodi-123/110.

Society of American Archivists. 2004. "The EAD Cookbook 2002." Web page. Available: www.archivists.org/saagroups/ead/ead2002cookbookhelp.html.

Society of American Archivists. 2007. *Describing Archives: A Content Standard (DACS).* Chicago: Society of American Archivists.

Srivastava, Rahul. 2007. "XML Schema: Understanding Namespaces." Web page. Oracle Technology Network. Available: www.oracle.com/technology/pub/articles/srivastava_namespaces.html.

SRU. 2006. "SRU Implementors Group Meeting/Integration Workshop: Meeting Report March 1–2, 2006." Web page. Available: www.loc.gov/standards/sru/march06-meeting/report.html.

St. Pierre, Margaret, and William P. LaPlant Jr. 1998. *Issues in Crosswalking Content Metadata Standards*. Bethesda, MD: NISO Press. Available: www.niso.org/publications/white_papers/crosswalk/.

Stvilia, Besiki, Les Gasser, Michael B. Twidale, Sarah L. Shreeves, and Tim W. Cole. 2004. "'Metadata Quality for Federated Collections' (research-in-progress), IQ Concepts, Models, Case Studies." *The 9th International Conference on Information Quality, MIT*. Available: www.isrl.uiuc.edu/~gasser/papers/metadataqualitymit_v4-10lg.pdf.

Sufi, Shoaib, and Brian Mathews. 2004. *CCLRC Scientific Metadata Model: Version 2*. CCLRC Technical Report: DL-TR-2004-001. Available: http://epubs.cclrc.ac.uk/bitstream/485/csmdm.version-2.pdf.

Suleman, Hussein, and Edward Fox. 2001. "The Open Archives Initiative: Realizing Simple and Effective Digital Library Interoperability." *Journal of Library Administration*, 35, no. 1/2: 125–145.

Sutton, Stuart A. 1999. "Conceptual Design and Deployment of a Metadata Framework for Education Resources on the Internet." *Journal of the American Society for Information Science*, 50, no. 13: 1182–1192.

Sutton, Stuart. 2007. "Basic Semantics (tutorial)." *DC-2007: International Conference on Dublin Core and Metadata Applications*. August 27–31, 2007, Singapore. Presentation materials available: www.dc2007.sg/T1-BasicSemantics.pdf.

Taylor, Arlene. 2004. *The Organization of Information*. 2nd ed. Westport, CN: Libraries Unlimited.

TEI Consortium. 2004. "The Text Encoding Initiative (TEI) Guidelines." Web page. Available: www.tei-c.org/.

Tennant, Roy. 2001. "Different Paths to Interoperability." *Library Journal*, 126, no. 3: 118–119.

Tennant, Roy. 2005. "Google Scholar Beta: Is Metasearch Dead?" *SFX-MetaLib User Group (SMUG) Meeting*. Presentation materials available: http://escholarship.cdlib.org/rtennant/presentations/2005niso/.

Thornes, Robin, Peter Dorrell, and Henry Lie. 1999. *Introduction to Object ID, Guidelines for Making Records That Describe Art, Antiques, and Antiquities*. Anita Keys, ed. The J. Paul Getty Trust. Available: www.object-id.com/guide/guide_index.html.

"Translations of DCMI Documents." Web page. Available: http://dublincore.org/resources/translations/ (accessed January 27, 2008).

Tsinaraki, Chrisa, Eleni Fatourou, and Stavros Christodoulakis. 2003. "An Ontology-driven Framework for the Management of Semantic Metadata Describing Audiovisual Information." *Advanced Information Systems Engineering: 15th International Conference, CAiSE 2003* (pp. 340–356). Berlin: Springer.

Turner, James M., Veronique Moal, and Julie Desnoyers. 2003. "MetaMap." Web page. Available: www.mapageweb.umontreal.ca/turner/meta/english/index.html.

UKOLN. 1999. "DESIRE Metadata Registry." Web page. Available: http://desire.ukoln.ac.uk/registry/index.html (accessed September 19, 2007).

Underwood, William E., David R. Chesnutt, and Elizabeth H. Dow. 2001. "Burlington Agenda: Research Issues in Intellectual Access to Electronically Published Historical Documents—Summary of the Research Agenda Produced by a Conference in Burlington, Vermont, April 2000." *American Archivist*, 64, no. 2: 292–307.

UNESCO. 2006a. "Expert Group Makes Proposals for Future of UNESCO's CDS/ISIS Software." Web page. Available: http://portal.unesco.org/ci/en/ev.php-URL_ID=22423&URL_DO=DO_TOPIC&URL_SECTION=201.html.

UNESCO. 2006b. "Report of the Two-Day Consultation of the Potential DSX/ISIS Funding Partners to Elaborate a Project Proposal for the Development of a New Open Source CDS/ISIS and to Set Up the Funding Mechanisms." Web page. Available: http://portal.unesco.org/ci/en/ev.php-URL_ID=22427&URL_DO=DO_TOPIC&URL_SECTION=201.html.

"UNESCO CDS/ISIS Distributors." Web page [updated 2006]. Available: http://portal.unesco.org/ci/en/ev.php-URL_ID=8587&URL_DO=DO_TOPIC&URL_SECTION=201.html.

U.S. Geological Survey. 2006. "Frequently Asked Questions on FGDC Metadata." Web page. Available: http://geology.usgs.gov/tools/metadata/tools/doc/faq.html.

U.S. Geological Survey. 2007. "Formal Metadata: Information and Software." Web page. Available: http://geology.usgs.gov/tools/metadata/.

van de Sompel, Herbert, Michael L. Nelson, Carl Lagoze, and Simeon Warner. 2004. "Resource Harvesting Within the OAI-PMH Framework." *D-Lib Magazine* [Online], 12, no. 10. Available: www.dlib.org/dlib/december04/vandesompel/12vandesompel.html.

van der Vlist, Eric. 2001. "Using W3C XML Schema." O'Reilly Media. Web page. Available: www.xml.com/pub/a/2000/11/29/schemas/part1.html.

van Veen, Theo, and Bill Oldroyd. 2004. "Search and Retrieval in the European Library, A New Approach." *D-Lib Magazine* [Online], 10, no. 2. Available: www.dlib.org/dlib/february04/vanveen/02vanveen.html.

vCard MIME Directory Profile. 1998. Internet RFC 2426. Dawson, F., and T. Howes. The Internet Society. Available: ftp://ftp.isi.edu/in-notes/rfc2426.txt.

Vellucci, Sherry L. 1998. "Metadata." In *Annual Review of Information Science and Technology*, Vol. 33, edited by M. Williams (pp. 187–222). Medford, NJ: Information Today.

Vellucci, Sherry L. 2004. "Music Metadata." In *Metadata Applications and Management*, edited by G.E. Gorman, and D.G. Dorner (pp.37-65). Lanham, Maryland: The Scarecrow Press.

Visual Resources Association. 2002. "VRA Core." Web page. Available: www.vraweb.org/projects/vracore4/index.html (accessed November 19, 2007).

VRA Data Standards Committee, Visual Resources Association. "VRA Core Categories. Version 2.0." Web page. Available: www.vraweb.org/ resources/datastandards/core2.html (accessed November 19, 2007).

VRA Data Standards Committee, Visual Resources Association. "VRA Core Categories. Version 3.0." Web page. Available: www.vraweb.org/resources/datastandards/vracore3/categories.html (accessed November 19, 2007).

VRA Data Standards Committee, Visual Resources Association. 2007. "VRA Core Categories. Version 4.0." Web page. Available: www.vraweb.org/projects/vracore4/index.html (accessed November 19, 2007).

W3C Web site. Available: www.w3.org/ (accessed January 26, 2008).

W3C. 1999. *XML Schema Requirements*. XML Schema Working Group. Available: www.w3.org/TR/NOTE-xml-schema-req.

W3C. 2002. *Open Digital Rights Language (ODRL)*, Version 1.1. W3C Note September 19, 2002. Available: www.w3.org/TR/odrl/.

W3C. 2004. *XML Schema Part 0: Primer Second Edition*. W3C Recommendation October 28, 2004. Available: www.w3.org/TR/xmlschema-0/.

W3C Incubator Group. 2007. "Image Annotation on the Semantic Web. W3C Incubator Group Report 14 August 2007." Rafael Troncy, Jacco van Ossenbruggen, Jeff Z. Pan, and Giorgos Stamou. Web page. Available: www.w3.org/2005/Incubator/mmsem/XGR-image-annotation/.

W3C Multimedia Semantics Incubator Group. 2005. "Image Annotation on the Semantic Web: Vocabularies Overview." Web page. Available: www.w3.org/2001/sw/BestPractices/MM/resources/Vocabularies.html.

Wagner, Harry, and Stuart Weibel. 2005. "The Dublin Core Metadata Registry: Requirements, Implementation, and Experience." *Journal of Digital Information* [Online], 6, no. 2. Available: http://jodi.tamu.edu/Articles/v06/i02/Wagner/DCMI-Registry-final.pdf.

Walker, Jill. 2005. "Feral Hypertext: When Hypertext Literature Escapes Control." *Proceedings of the Sixteenth ACM Conference on Hypertext and Hypermedia* (pp. 46–53). New York: ACM Press.

Waugh, Andrew. 1998. "Specifying Metadata Standards for Metadata Tool Configuration." *Computer Networks and ISDN Systems*, 30, no. 1–7: 23–32.

Weibel, Stuart. 1999. "State of the Dublin Core Metadata Initiative: April 1999—Report from the Sixth Dublin Core Metadata Workshop, November 1998, Washington, D.C." *Bulletin of the American Society for Information Science*, 25, no. 5: 18–22.

Weibel, Stuart. 2005. "Border Crossings: Reflections on a Decade of Metadata Consensus Building." *D-Lib Magazine* [Online], 11, no. 7/8. Available: www.dlib.org/dlib/july05/weibel/07weibel.html.

Weibel, Stuart, Jean Godby, Eric Miller, and Ron Daniel. 1995. *OCLC/NCSA Metadata Workshop Report*. Available: http://dublincore.org/workshops/dc1/report.shtml.

Weibel, Stuart, and Juha Hakala. 1998. "DC-5: The Helsinki Metadata Workshop: A Report on the Workshop and Subsequent Developments." *D-Lib Magazine* [Online], February 1998. Available: www.dlib.org/dlib/february98/02weibel.html.

Weibel, Stuart, and Eric Miller. 1997. "Image Description on the Internet: A Summary of the CNI/OCLC Image Metadata Workshop." *D-Lib Magazine*

[Online], September 24–25, 1996. Available: www.dlib.org/dlib/january97/oclc/01weibel.html.

Weinheimer, James. 2000. "How to Keep the Practice of Librarianship Relevant in the Age of the Internet." *Vine (Special Issue on Metadata, Part 1)*, 116: 14–27.

Wendler, Robin. 2004. "The Eye of the Beholder: Challenges of Image Description and Access at Harvard." In *Metadata in Practice*, edited by Diane Hillmann (pp. 51–69). Chicago: American Library Association.

Whalen, Maureen. 2008. "Rights Metadata Made Simple." In *Introduction to Metadata: Pathways to Digital Information*, edited by Murtha Baca. Online Edition (revised ed.). Los Angeles: Getty Publications. Forthcoming.

Wiley, David A. 2000. "Connecting Learning Objects to Instructional Design Theory: A Definition, a Metaphor, and a Taxonomy." *The Instructional Use of Learning Objects*. Online Version. Available: http://reusability.org/read/chapters/wiley.doc.

Will, Leonard D. 1997. "Data Structures and Indexing for Museum Collections Management." *Knowledge Organization for Information Retrieval* (pp. 36–41). Proceedings of the Sixth International Study Conference on Classification Research, London, June 16–18, 1997. The Hague, Netherlands: International Federation for Information and Documentation.

Wilson, Andrew. 2006. *Metadata Generation for Resource Discovery Project Plan*. JISC. Available: http://ahds.ac.uk/about/projects/metadata-generation/index.htm.

Wiser, S. K., P. J. Bellingham, and L. E. Burrows. 2001. "Managing Biodiversity Information: Development of New Zealand's National Vegetation Survey Databank." *New Zealand Journal of Ecology*, 25, no. 2: 1–17.

Woodward, Jeannette. 1996. "Cataloging and Classifying Information Resources on the Internet." In *Annual Review of Information Science and Technology*, edited by M. Williams (pp. 189–220), Vol. 31.

Wu, Xian, Lei Zhang, and Yong Yu. 2006. "Exploring Social Annotations for the Semantic Web." *Proceedings of the 15th International Conference on World Wide Web 2006* (pp. 417–426). New York: ACM Press.

Yao, Boyue, Zhang Lijuan, Yu Yifang, and Miao Sansan. 2004. "Rare Materials Descriptive Metadata Standard: Its Design and Implementation." (Text in Chinese). Available: www.idl.pku.edu.cn/pdf/rarebook_metadata.pdf.

Yilmazel, Ozgur, Christina M. Finneran, and Elizabeth D. Liddy. 2004. "MetaExtract: An NLP System to Automatically Assign Metadata." *Proceedings of the 2004 Joint ACM/IEEE Conference on Digital Libraries (JCDL '04)* (pp. 241–242). New York: ACM Press.

Zeng, Lei. 1993a. "Quality Control of Chinese-Language Records Using a Rule-Based Data Validation System: Part 1, An Evaluation of the Quality of Chinese-Language Records in the OCLC OLUC Database." *Cataloging & Classification Quarterly*, 16, no. 4: 26–66.

Zeng, Lei. 1993b. "Quality Control of Chinese-Language Records Using a Rule-Based Data Validation System: Part 2, A Study of a Rule-Based Data Validation System for Online Chinese Cataloging." *Cataloging & Classification Quarterly*, 18, no. 1: 3–26.

Zeng, Marcia Lei. 1999. "Metadata Elements for Object Description and Representation: A Case Report from a Digitized Historical Fashion Collection Project—at Kent State University Museum." *Journal of the American Society for Information Science*, 50, no. 13: 1193–1208.

Zeng, Marcia Lei. 2001. "Supporting Metadata Interoperability: Trends and Issues." In *Global Digital Library Development in the New Millennium*, edited by Chin Chih Chen (pp. 405–412). Beijing: Tsinghua University Press.

Zeng, Marcia Lei. 2005. "Metadata Basics." Web page. Available: www.slis.kent.edu/%7Emzeng/metadatabasics/index.htm.

Zeng, Marcia Lei, and Lois Mai Chan. 2004. "Trends and Issues in Establishing Interoperability Among Knowledge Organization Systems." *Journal of American Society for Information Science and Technology*, 55, no. 5: 377–395.

Zeng, Marcia Lei, and Lois Mai Chan. 2006. "Metadata Interoperability and Standardization—A Study of Methodology. Part II: Achieving Interoperability at the Record and Repository Levels." *D-Lib Magazine* [Online], 12, no. 6. Available: www.dlib.org/dlib/june06/zeng/06zeng.html.

Zeng, Marcia Lei, and Gregory Shreve. 2007. *Quality Analysis of Metadata Records in the NSDL Metadata Repository*. A report submitted to the National Science Foundation—National Science Digital Library (NSDL) Program.

Zeng, Marcia Lei, and Long Xiao. 2001. "Mapping Metadata Elements of Different Format." *E-Libraries 2001, Proceedings, May 15–17, 2001, New York* (pp. 91–99). Medford, NJ: Information Today.

Zhang, Jin, and Alexandra Dimitroff. 2005. "The Impact of Metadata Implementation on Webpage Visibility in Search Engine Results (Part II)." *Information Processing and Management*, 41, no. 3: 691–715.

Zhang, Xiaolin. 2004. "Tutorial on Metadata." *Tutorials, 7th International Conference of Asian Digital Libraries (ICADL)*. December 13-17, 2004, Shanghai China (pp. 107–136). Shanghai: Jiaotong University Library.

Zumer, Maja. 2007. FRBR: "The End of the Road or a New Beginning?" *Bulletin of the American Society for Information Science and Technology*, August/September 2007. Available: www.asis.org/Bulletin/Aug-07/zumer.html.

Index

***Boldface** locators indicate terms included in Appendix A, Appendix B, and the Glossary. Locators followed by "f" indicate figures and exhibits; locators followed by "t" indicate tables.*

D

N

O

P

About the Authors

Marcia Lei Zeng is Professor of Library and Information Science at Kent State University. She holds a PhD from the School of Information Sciences at the University of Pittsburgh and an MA from Wuhan University in China. Her major research interests include knowledge organization systems (taxonomy, thesaurus, ontology, etc.), metadata and markup languages, database quality control, multilingual and multiculture information processing, and digital libraries for cultural objects and learning objects. Her scholarly publications include more than 60 papers and three books, as well as many national and international conference presentations. She was invited to give lectures and workshops in various countries. She was the Principal Investigator (PI) and Co-PI of two National Science Foundation (NSF) National Science Digital Library (NSDL) projects. She has chaired and served on standards committees and working groups for the International Federation of Library Associations and Institutions (IFLA), Special Libraries Association (SLA), American Society for Information Science and Technology (ASIST), U.S. National Information Standards Organization (NISO), and International Organization for Standardization (ISO). Her profile can be found at *Journal of Internet Cataloging*, 7, no. 2 (2006).

Jian Qin is Associate Professor at the School of Information Studies, Syracuse University. Her research interest areas include knowledge modeling and organization, ontologies, learning object vocabulary, metadata, Web content management, and scientific communication. She has published more than 50 papers and has given presentations at numerous national and international conferences. Her research has been funded by the National Science Foundation, OCLC Online Library Computer Center, and Institute for Scientific Information (ISI). She teaches information organization, knowledge organization systems, Web content management, and metadata. She was a visiting scholar at OCLC in 2002 and is a member of the editorial board for two international journals. Dr. Qin holds a PhD degree from the University of Illinois at Urbana-Champaign and an MLIS from the University of Western Ontario.